I0891891

Critical Approaches to Joseph Conrad

CRITICAL APPROACHES TO JOSEPH CONRAD

EDITED BY

Agata Szczeszak-Brewer

THE UNIVERSITY OF SOUTH CAROLINA PRESS

© 2015 University of South Carolina

Published by the University of South Carolina Press
Columbia, South Carolina 29208

www.sc.edu/uscpress

Manufactured in the United States of America

24 23 22 21 20 19 18 17 16 15
10 9 8 7 6 5 4 3 2 1

Library of Congress Cataloging-in-Publication Data
can be found at http://catalog.loc.gov/.

ISBN: 978-1-61117-529-5 (cloth)
ISBN: 978-1-61117-530-1

This book was printed on recycled paper with
30 percent postconsumer waste content.

Contents

PART III
Critical Approaches to Other Major Texts

Acknowledgments

My special thanks go to John G. Peters and Gregory Britton for providing invaluable feedback on this project in its early stages and to Emiliano Aguilar and Ryan Horner for helping out with editing and indexing. I also appreciate the hospitality of the National Library of Ireland and the University of Gdańsk during my sabbatical leave in Europe. All the contributors to this volume deserve applause for tireless work despite Hurricane Sandy's widespread destruction and several other life-changing events. Finally, I am deeply grateful to Josh and Kuba for their patience, love, and an occasional comic relief.

Chronological List of Works by Joseph Conrad

Fiction

Almayer's Folly, 1895
An Outcast of the Islands, 1896
The Nigger of the "Narcissus," 1897
Tales of Unrest, 1898
Lord Jim, 1900
Youth, a Narrative; and Two Other Stories, 1902
Typhoon and Other Stories, 1903
Nostromo, 1904
The Secret Agent, 1907
A Set of Six, 1908
Under Western Eyes, 1911
'Twixt Land and Sea, 1912
Chance, 1914
Within the Tides, 1915
Victory, 1915
The Shadow-Line, 1917
The Arrow of Gold, 1919
The Rescue, 1920
The Rover, 1923
Tales of Hearsay, 1925

Collaborations

The Inheritors, 1901
Romance, 1903
The Nature of a Crime, 1909

Nonfiction

The Mirror of the Sea, 1906
Some Reminiscences (A Personal Record), 1912
Notes on Life and Letters, 1921
Last Essays, 1926

Introduction

Agata Szczeszak-Brewer

I

Joseph Conrad does not go out of style. Despite the controversy surrounding *Heart of Darkness* and the debate about racism in Conrad's depiction of Africa, or maybe because of that dispute, Conrad occupies a prominent spot in literature curricula and scholarly conversations. Could his guardians, concerned about young Joseph's less-than-stellar school performance and his cigar habit, predict that this defiant son of a Polish revolutionary would become one of the most prominent authors in the British canon? That almost ninety years after his death, his fiction would still be debated, not only at professional conferences and in classrooms, but on the public radio? In 2009, National Public Radio aired Robert Siegel's interview with Chinua Achebe, one of Conrad's fiercest critics. Listening to Siegel's "All Things Considered," I was struck by how contemporary and relevant Conrad's fiction, including the famous (or infamous?) novella, still is. Achebe insists in the interview that "the language of description of the [African] people in *Heart of Darkness* is inappropriate."[1] At that time, I was pondering whether to include *Heart of Darkness* in my undergraduate course's reading list. I thought of other critics who still disagree with Achebe's claim. I thought of intense and engaged debates in my classroom on this very topic whenever I taught the novella. And I decided to include the book in my syllabus.

Aware that most of my undergraduate students would be reading Conrad for the first time, I wanted to give them resources outlining his life, the cultural and historical context of his fiction, and sample critical essays written in a comprehensible language and inviting first-time readers of Conrad to a conversation. It would be helpful, I thought, if those essays came from a diverse group of scholars, emphasizing not only Conrad's global reach, but also representing a wide range of responses to his texts. I managed to create a patchwork of critical materials in a makeshift course-work file. It was stunning, though, that among many high-quality companions to Conrad there was no single book that would give my students a collection of international voices speaking directly to them in clear prose. That is how this book was born. It contains an overview of the development of Conrad scholarship and a good number of case studies offering a wide and up-to-date range of approaches to his most popular fiction.

Conrad's texts inspire fascinating conversations about racism, political violence, terrorism, ecology, loyalty, honor, and many other topics. His books brilliantly merge adventure with thoughtful investigation of human motives and desires, but the writer's own life was so adventurous and complex that it would provide great material for an action-packed movie. And though I personally dislike voiceovers in movies, I can imagine the opening scene: young Conrad sitting over a sepia-colored map, his adult voice narrating: "It was in 1868, when nine years old or thereabouts, that while looking at a map of Africa of the time and putting my finger on the blank space then representing the unsolved mystery of that continent, I said to myself, with absolute assurance and an amazing audacity which are no longer in my character: 'When I grow up I shall go there.' And of course I thought no more about it until, after a quarter of a century or so, an opportunity offered to go there, as if the sin of childish audacity was to be visited on my mature head."[2] "There" was, of course, the Congo. Conrad's journey there inspired one of the most beautiful and debated texts in the English language.

Conrad was a man of contradictions. He was socially conservative, and he cherished tradition and honor; yet he rejected the Catholic faith, the religion of his ancestors and compatriots. He adored and respected several women in his life, including his mother and a Belgian-born novelist, Marguerite Poradowska (the wife of Conrad's distant cousin), and yet his texts sometimes reveal a condescending attitude toward his female characters. He was thoughtful and yet spontaneous and even rash; begging family and friends for money, though often generous to others. He was a Polish expatriate whose writing entered the English canon—yet his spoken English was marked by a strong Polish accent. In fact, during his visit to the United States late in his career—already as a widely published and popular Anglophone author—when he addressed workers at Doubleday's printing works, his listeners "found his accent impenetrable, and the secretaries assigned to take down his every word in shorthand abandoned the task in despair."[3] Nevertheless, his foreign sounds and appearance didn't prevent him from entertaining some of the most prominent literary and cultural figures in his Capel House and in other locations, where he discussed literature, ethics, and politics with H. G. Wells, Henry James, R. B. Cunninghame Graham, John Galsworthy, Stephen Crane, Ford Madox Ford, and others. George Gissing summed up many of Conrad's contemporaries' amazement: "That a foreigner should write like this, is one of the miracles of literature."[4]

II

Joseph Conrad is a pen name of Józef Teodor Konrad Nałęcz Korzeniowski, born in 1857 in Berdyczów—on a land once under the Polish rule, though at the time of Conrad's birth it had already been taken by Russia in what is known as the Great Partition of Poland. (It now belongs to Ukraine.) The son of a revolutionary, he recalls "the oppressive shadow of the great Russian empire" as a strong, formative presence in his childhood.[5] At that time, Poland existed only as a concept, not a political entity. "Poland" was synonymous with "a culture, a history, a language and a geographical region, but not as an independent nation."[6] The name "Konrad" testifies to these political tensions, as a tribute to two Konrads in Polish Romantic literature, two patriots—one in Adam Mickiewicz's *Konrad Wallenrod* and one in Mickiewicz's *Dziady.*

Apollo Korzeniowski, Conrad's father, was a member of *szlachta,* or Polish landed gentry, a poet, playwright, and translator of Shakespeare, Dickens, and Victor Hugo. For his anti-Russian revolutionary activities he was exiled to Vologda in 1862, together with his wife and five-year-old son. Conrad's mother, Ewa Bobrowska, came from a more wealthy family than Apollo. Throughout their exile, Ewa Korzeniowska was ill, and she died in 1865, when Conrad was seven. Conrad's father died soon after, in 1869, after which young Józef's maternal uncle, Tadeusz Bobrowski, became his guardian. They moved to Kraków, which was then under Austrian rule. To make up for some gaps in Conrad's education, Bobrowski hired a private tutor, Adam Marek Pullman—a person Conrad describes with warmth and affection in his memoir *A Personal Record.* He also spoke affectionately about his uncle, who loved his nephew dearly and worried about his safety and well-being. Some biographers of Conrad, including John Batchelor and Zdzisław Najder, say that Bobrowski misrepresented Apollo's political activities as impulsive and destructive, contrasting them with his own cautious nature.[7] Although Conrad's letters to his uncle were destroyed in the 1917 fire that broke out in Kazimierzówka, we can still peruse letters from Bobrowski to Conrad, writings testifying to a strong bond between the two men, despite Conrad's challenging behavior. His biographers mention Conrad's "talent for cigars," his nervous breakdowns, and his disobedience.[8] Later, Conrad suffered from severe depression, debilitating attacks of gout, and—needless to say—irritability. When Bobrowski died in 1894, Conrad looked for a father figure in his literary agent, James Brand Pinker, who fulfilled this role to some extent, lending him money and warning against irresponsible behavior.

But before Conrad began his literary career, his passion was the sea. Having read adventure stories and fiction about distant lands, steeped in the Romantic tradition of quest and exile, he decided at the age of sixteen to go to the coast of France and start a new life on a ship. He remembers this decision in *A Personal*

Record, talking about himself in the third person: "After reading so many romances he desired naively to escape with his very body from the intolerable reality of things. He wished to meet, eye to eye, the valorous giant Brandabarbaran, Lord of Arabia, whose armour is made of the skin of a dragon, and whose shield, strapped to his arm, is the gate of a fortified city. Oh, amiable and natural weakness! Oh, blessed simplicity of a gentle heart without guile! Who would not succumb to such a consoling temptation?"[9] Battling numerous setbacks and constantly in debt, he did spend twenty years at sea, first as a tourist, then as a shipmate, and finally as a captain, though he was rather unlucky in securing commands. He credits these years with shaping his sensibilities and values, when he speaks of "the English and Scots seamen (a much-caricatured folk) who had the last say in the formation of my character."[10]

It seems that Conrad's determination, talent, and luck made it possible for him to defy other people's doubts about his future. When as a boy he boasted to his classmates that he was going to become a famous writer, they laughed at him. Similarly, his plan to go to sea was actively discouraged in his family. When in 1873 he went on a twelve-week trip around Europe, Adam Pulman, his tutor, called him "an incorrigible, hopeless Don Quixote."[11] Yet—despite all these doubts—his family, especially his uncle, helped him realize his dreams and supported him through uncertain times. Conrad occasionally lied to his uncle in his letters to get money from him for what Batchelor calls his "extravagant habits" and failed financial speculation.[12] Bobrowski patiently sent more and more money to his nephew, admonishing him for irresponsible spending. Apart from sea life, Conrad may have engaged in gun-running as a young man, smuggling on behalf of the Spanish Royalists (a claim disputed by Najder), and may have fought in a duel, although Conrad's biographers almost universally doubt the existence of that duel, claiming that Conrad invented the story to cover a failed suicide prompted by gambling debts.[13]

After his 1874 journey to Marseille to join the French merchant marine service and his first voyage on a French ship, he eventually started gaining experience at sea and earned more posts and promotions. During his four years in the French merchant marine service, he traveled to the West Indies and Central and South America. Later, while in the British merchant marine service, he sailed to South Africa, India (where he bought a pet monkey), Australia, Thailand, and other remote places.[14] His extensive travel experience gives way to vivid settings in his fiction: the Malay Archipelago, the Congo, the imaginary Latin American republic of Costaguana, a sleepy Kentish village, a teeming metropolis in the heart of the British empire, and Geneva appear in *Almayer's Folly, An Outcast of the Islands, Heart of Darkness, Nostromo,* "Amy Foster," *The Secret Agent, Under Western Eyes,* and other novels and short stories.[15]

In 1878, Conrad went to Constantinopole (present-day Istanbul) on an English steamer, and upon his return he came to England for the first time. Although he didn't speak English upon arrival, two years later, he passed his exam for third mate and his subsequent exams for higher positions in the English merchant marine service. A little over a decade after arriving in England and enlisting on an English steamer, he began working on his first novel—in English—*Almayer's Folly.* He continued for several more years, writing chapters during his employment at sea and between trips, while waiting for another opportunity to go to sea. "Unknown to my respectable landlady," says Conrad of his stay in an apartment in London, "it was my practice directly after my breakfast to hold animated receptions of Malays, Arabs, and half-castes."[16]

One of the most formative voyages in Conrad's career was his trip to the Congo in 1890, one he describes in his diary and then, in a fictionalized form, in *Heart of Darkness.* The cruelty and futility of the Belgian imperial endeavors in the Congo affected his life, as did the life-threatening fever he contracted in Africa. To his first biographer and a friend, Gérard Jean-Aubry, Conrad reportedly said: "Before the Congo I was just a mere animal." Peter Edgerly Firchow understands this statement not only through the prism of Africa itself but also of the terrible illness that forced Conrad to be bedridden for months and, therefore, encouraged "self-conscious contemplation" and revealed his artistic sensibilities.[17] Although Conrad had refused to collect human skulls and send them in batches to the Museum of Craniology in Kraków,[18] the voyage to and through the Congo was still filled with nightmares and proved to be traumatizing.[19]

Conrad always stood out among rugged sailors, with his suit and bowler hat, a foreign accent, and impeccable manners. His colleagues ironically called him "the Russian Count."[20] He finally earned his master's certificate in 1886 and became a naturalized English subject, which released him from the Russian authority. He seemed, however, to harbor guilt over leaving Poland, which many critics, including Gustav Morf and John Batchelor, see reflected in *Lord Jim* and other texts. But some scholars—Zdzisław Najder, Ian Watt, and others—contest this "guilt theory" and suggest that shame may be a more faithful explanation of Conrad's complex relationship with his homeland, considering the dominance of a widely understood concept of honor in Polish culture and history. On the whole, Conrad rarely made public statements about politics, but he did pen several political essays, including "Autocracy and War" and "The Crime of Partition"; his fiction, too, is steeped in the political climate of nineteenth- and early twentieth-century Europe and European imperial conquests around the world.[21]

Conrad also abandoned the Catholic faith, a cornerstone of Polish identity at the time of political obliteration of the nation. When in 1896 he married Jessie George, a lower-middle-class woman from London, he decided against a church wedding. They married in a registry office. Jessie, intellectually inferior to her husband, was nevertheless a faithful, down-to-earth companion not only running the household and taking care of their children, Borys and John (born eight years apart), but also occasionally typing for Conrad. Lady Ottoline Morrell famously said of Conrad's wife that she "seemed a nice and good-looking fat creature, an excellent cook, as Henry James said, and was indeed a good and reposeful mattress for this hypersensitive, nerve-wracked man, who did not ask from his wife high intelligence, only an assuagement of life's vibrations."[22] Lady Ottoline Morrell's words, though condescending, do emphasize Jessie's comforting presence in Conrad's life.[23] Even the way Conrad proposed to her foreshadowed his future reliance on her care, despite her own health problems. On the steps of the National Gallery, he urged Jessie to marry him quickly, as he anticipated a decline in his health.

Conrad did fall gravely ill, but not until 1910, when he suffered from a series of gout attacks and nervous breakdowns. Some critics ascribe this illness to his work on *Under Western Eyes* and to his occupation with topics close to his heart—patriotism, loyalty, and betrayal. Others look back to his break with Ford Madox Ford (his collaborator and friend) and his quarrel with J. B. Pinker as warning signs that his emotional and financial trouble would come to a head. Although he recovered and continued writing until his death in 1924, the frequent attacks of neuralgia and gout made him increasingly irritable with age.

Conrad died in 1924, probably of a heart attack, alone in his room. He was buried in Canterbury, with the epitaph from Spenser's *Faerie Queene* carved out in stone: "Sleep after Toyle, Port after stormie seas, / Ease after Warre, Death after Life, doth greatly please." That originally these words are spoken by Despayre who is trying to talk the Red Cross Night into suicide is quite significant here. The maritime allusion of "Port after stormie seas" and the theme of perseverance despite life's obstacles, indeed despite despair, are touching and apt in the context of Conrad's adventurous and difficult life.

III

Conrad embarked on his career as a writer when he was already thirty-eight. His first novel, *Almayer's Folly*, was published in 1895. Many of his novels, short stories, and essays first appeared in literary magazines such as *The Fortnightly Review*, *The English Review*, and *Harper's Magazine*. His goal as a writer was, in his own words, "by the power of the written word to make you hear, to make you feel—it is, before all, to make you see."[24] His creative process was intense, distressing, and often filled with self-doubt. His biographers report that he conversed with his characters from *Under Western Eyes* when he was suffering from a post-novel breakdown and battling high fever.[25] But even in good health, he agonized over each sentence, living the life of his characters, inhabiting their worlds, thinking their thoughts. In *A Personal Record,* he describes a complete immersion in the lives of his characters in *Nostromo.* Writing the novel, he engaged his whole being in the landscape of Costaguana and in its complex plot when, all of a sudden, he was interrupted by a visitor. With exasperation, he exclaims: "what are twenty lives in a mere novel that one should be rude to a lady on their account?"[26]

In his letter to H. Sanderson, Conrad confesses his doubts about the creative process and his skills: "I am like a tight-rope dancer who, in the midst of his performance, should suddenly discover that he knows nothing about tight-rope dancing. He may appear ridiculous to the spectators, but a broken neck is the result of such untimely wisdom."[27] He wrote in fits and starts, moving between bursts of creative energy and long periods of writer's block that often overlapped with depression. Significantly, he called his study, where he wrote his fiction, a "torture chamber."[28] Even his collaboration with Ford Madox Ford, which seemed to lift his spirit on occasion, turned into what he called "The Fatal Partnership."[29]

A nearly disastrous trip to Kraków on the eve of the First World War and his narrow escape via Italy back to England only exacerbated Conrad's depression and self-doubt. Suffering from another case of writer's block, Conrad asked in one of his letters to Richard Curle: "And who can be articulate in a nightmare?"[30] But Conrad was articulate throughout his writing career; some claim he was, in fact, too eloquent. F. R. Leavis has criticized Conrad's "adjectival insistence," and some of Conrad's contemporaries claimed his writing was too foreign and too wordy. Yet, his fiction opens up a vast panorama of human behavior, with all its passions, allegiances, guilt, and contradictions. To read Conrad is to enter a vibrant world of nature's whims, political and personal betrayal, and personal miscommunications.

Conrad straddled at least two literary modes, the late-Victorian realist and the Modernist. "As a novelist, he sat astride two traditions, the nineteenth-century tradition of the thickly plotted novel anchored in action and adventure and the twentieth-century tradition of the novel with its emphasis on irony, on analysis, and on psychological depth."[31] His Chinese-box narrative style, his impressionism, his narrators' mocking wit, their frequent confession that it is impossible to describe human beings with veracity and certainty made his novels much more than just sea adventures, as some mistakenly thought. Yes, the sea is a godlike force in many of his novels, but some have very little to do with marine fiction. Conrad's subject matter includes honor, self-knowledge, loyalty, manliness, political violence, loss of innocence, and testing the limits of loyalty and morality. As Marlow narrates "Youth," *Heart of Darkness, Lord Jim,* and *Chance,* the readers are often left with more questions than answers about what drives human behavior. Conrad's narrators do not pretend to know the answer.

In his 1896 letter to Garnett, he despairs that "one's own personality is only a ridiculous and aimless masquerade of something hopelessly unknown."[32] Conrad remains an elusive writer and, despite the abundance of biographical material available to his readers, a man whose inner life remains a matter of speculation. But this is what makes his fiction so compelling—the constant "becoming" of his characters, the active, wandering mind of his narrators, the conflicts, the paradoxes, and the unresolved questions in his fiction.

Though Conrad was recognized later in life as one of the most talented and important Anglophone writers, generally the texts he himself considered second-rate brought him the most money and popularity. *Chance,* for example, which appeared in 1914, often considered inferior by literary critics, was his first major financial success. All of his novels, though, are challenging. Conrad's prose "requires, among other things, that we both fight with and parse out his imagery; that we reconstruct the sequence of a novel's action and grapple with the significance, at once proleptic and delayed, that his very violation of chronology has produced. And if we can do that, his fiction will yield a most peculiar reward. For no matter how dark his world and how miserable the fates of his characters, his books are almost never depressing. Instead we read them with an exhilarating sense of difficulties faced and met, held by the drama of the writing itself, as if we have submitted ourselves to the destructive element, and kept our heads up."[33] J. M. Barrie, the author of *Peter Pan,* described Conrad as "nervous and intent on the subject at hand. I used to imagine that he was really a pirate, who at any moment was likely to leap from his chair and stick a knife into me!"[34] Barrie's wild imagination notwithstanding, reading Conrad's fiction is a risky and rewarding experience, one prone to rob us of our illusions and certainties about the world, but also one that makes us wander and wonder, question and analyze.

IV

All the contributors to this volume engage Conrad in different ways, from postcolonial and ecocritical perspectives, through explorations of gender, to psychoanalysis, narrative theory, and political analysis. The book opens with Barry Morton's essay presenting the cultural and historical canvas of Conrad's life and fiction. It is conveniently divided into three sections: one on Poland, one on the Malay Archipelago, and one on the Congo. Morton's approach is quite different from the traditionally presented historical background in Conrad companions, often based on inflated historical accounts bordering on Polish nationalist martyrology. His objective presentation of important historical facts will aid readers in their understanding of the historical background of Conrad's fiction and nonfiction. This chapter is followed by John Peters's overview of Conrad's critical reception, indispensable for a beginning reader of Conrad's fiction. Peters's suggestions for further reading can be found in the Appendix. Both can serve as excellent reference assignments for undergraduate and graduate students.

Readers who want to explore *Heart of Darkness* will find the following section illuminating. "Critical Approaches to *Heart of Darkness*" opens with two essays merging ecocritical and postcolonial approaches in their investigation of the natural resources and power struggle in the Congo. Greg Winston's essay looks at the reception of Conrad in a specialized circle of ecocritical tradition. He explains the history of ecocritical readings of Conrad, and he enters the conversation among Conrad scholars linking the rise of imperial capitalism with Conrad's descriptions of nature's depletion in the Congo. William Atkinson next discusses the meaningful absence of the word "elephant" in the novella, an absence particularly troubling because its metonym—ivory—seems so prevalent in the narrative. He links the history of elephant hunting to the history of colonialism and the capitalist unwillingness to consider conserving the earth's limited resources. The following two essays engage *Heart of Darkness* in comparative conversations with other texts. Jonathan Elmore considers Conrad's novella vis-à-vis Coppola's movie *Apocalypse Now* in light of modernist aesthetics, Hardt and Negri's concept of empire, and the sovereignty of the modern nation state. He calls for a reorientation of scholarship on Conrad with an eye toward the distinction between imperialism and empire, or its biopolitical capital. Finally, Mawuli Adjei's essay considers Conrad's *Heart of Darkness* and Michaela Wrong's *In the Footsteps of Mr Kurtz* as texts steeped in the same historical, political, and narrative tradition rooted in the Eurocentric imperial discourse.

Nisha Manocha's "The Imitable Joseph Conrad" opens the last section of the book. Manocha begins her essay about the author's reception with Conrad's letter to Pinker, in which he claims that "I don't resemble anybody; and yet I am not specialised enough to call up imitators as to matter or style." Moving between Conrad's contemporaries' response to his early fiction and the more recent imitations of and allusions to Conrad's style and subject matter, Manocha draws a picture of Conrad as a generative writer who echoes in numerous fictional accounts of non-European settings and people.

In "Maternal Return: *Lord Jim*'s Spectral Narrative," Carola Kaplan investigates the silences and gaps in *Lord Jim,* more specifically the omission of the stories of Jewel's mother and grandmother—untellable and spectral, and yet drawing our attention to the limitations of language and the suppression of signs of social injustice. The text cannot speak directly about the mother, who is a victim and witness of historical trauma, because the text itself is supported by that white, male, colonial history. Narrative gaps are also the subject of Tom Rice's essay on *Typhoon,* which explores the novella's narrative complexity, the epistolary elements in its narration, and the intentional silences seemingly teasing the reader but, in the end, demonstrating Conrad's "awareness that indifferent and inattentive readers routinely fail to reciprocate the writer's attention." Conrad, on the one hand, panders to his readers by appealing to their religious sensibilities in his indirect references to the Christmas story and, on the other, foretells a shift in his attitude toward his audience, as he is unwilling to cater to inattentive readers.

This volume also includes case studies of other canonical texts by Conrad. Ruth Nadelhaft discusses the strong presence of women in *Nostromo* and looks at the novel through the angle of feminist theory and class analysis. Nadelhaft claims that Conrad's inclusion of strong women has long been underappreciated and misunderstood. While her main focus is on Linda and Giselle Viola, Antonia Avellanos, Emilia Gould, and Decoud's sister, she discusses Conrad's depiction of the natural world, represented in his text by women, plundered and destroyed by profit-driven men. In "History in Ruins: Reading *Nostromo,*" Camelia Raghinaru explores *Nostromo*'s panorama of history, sovereignty, state of emergency, and catastrophe. Her interpretation is supported by Walter Benjamin's view on the nature of sovereignty in his *Trauerspiel.*

Andrew Glazzard discusses the composition and publication of *The Secret Agent,* from its beginning as a short story to its serial publication and, finally, its volume publication in 1907. Glazzard's essay shows that our knowledge of the history of the composition and publication of *The Secret Agent* enhances our understanding the novel's themes and techniques. Anna Krauthammer's "*The Secret Sharer*: When the Other Is the Self" demonstrates that Conrad uses the trope of the double in his story to describe Leggatt as the captain's hidden self. By presenting the hidden recesses in the human mind and infusing his images of the sea with symbolic connotations, the narrator illustrates "the interdependence of relationships aboard the ship" and the consequences of the captain's suppression of Leggatt as other.

Jennifer Malia's and Robert McParland's essays focus on *Under Western Eyes.* Malia talks about Conrad as a critic of sensationalism in the media, especially the Western press's feeding the audience with "spectacles of violence." McParland's "Chance and Betrayal in *Under Western Eyes*" focuses on free choice, coincidence, morality, and their relation to Conrad's technique of narrative disruption. McParland interprets Razumov's choices and thoughts "within the epistemological crisis that has arisen from the implications of Darwinian evolution."

This variety of critical responses is geared mostly toward the students of Conrad—undergraduate and graduate—as well as their professors, who will find a wealth of resources designed to illuminate Conrad's most popular texts and the breadth of literary criticism generated by his fiction. Reading Conrad, especially reading his fiction for the first time, can be challenging, but the rewards are plenty. Conrad's fiction prompts us to explore thoughtfully the value and challenges of loyalty, integrity, and the ethical code. It teases us with difficult form only to open up vast possibilities of interpreting the formal challenges that mirror the inner turmoil of fictional characters—their choices, regrets, betrayals, and acts of courage. A recently published book about Conrad's relevance to the contemporary world, *Conrad in the Twenty-First Century,* edited by Carola Kaplan, Peter Mallios, and Andrea White, proves that Conrad's fiction is still relevant today, in the wake of September 11 attacks.[35] We now read his novels with new questions about terrorism, colonialism, anarchism, ecology, and sexuality.

Part I

Conrad's Contexts

Joseph Conrad

Historical and Cultural Contexts

Barry Morton

Three different geographical zones bear considerably on Conrad's social and political outlook: first, his native Poland and its troubled history as a partitioned country. Conrad was in a sense exiled from his homeland—which did not even exist as an independent nation for most of his life—yet he thought of himself as a Pole. Second, Conrad worked as a merchant sailor and almost all of his early fiction was set in the Congo area of Central Africa and the Malaysian Archipelago in southern Asia. After some two decades of sailing, Conrad would settle in England and would remain a professional writer for the rest of his life. As an extremely well-traveled person, Conrad was also very cosmopolitan in outlook and eventually branched out greatly both in theme and geographical range. Even so, his upbringing and his pre-novelist years as a sailor are vital to understanding his *oeuvre.*

Poland: The Partitioned Homeland

Joseph Conrad was born to Polish parents in 1857, although the country that they aspired to belong to had been extinct for over six decades. During the so-called "Partition Period" from 1795 to 1918, the formerly independent Poles were divided up and ruled by Prussia, Russia, and Austria. Not until after World War I, when Conrad was over fifty years old, would Poland reemerge as an actual political unit—once again sandwiched precariously between its traditional enemies Germany, to its west, and Russia, to its east. So although Poland had existed as a country for some eight hundred years prior to being carved up in 1795, during the nineteenth century it existed as a mere idea. Poland was, in the words of one intellectual, "a nation that refused to die."[1] During this "long century" a small but vocal Polish-speaking intelligentsia kept the idea of an independent Poland alive.[2] Nationalism was probably the major ideology circulating amongst the Poles, just as it was elsewhere in Europe. In Italy or Germany, for instance, nationalist politicians sought to merge (both by force and by persuasion) small states, principalities, and kingdoms and eventually produced the unitary states that we recognize today.

Polish nationalism, though, faced far greater obstacles than Italian nationalism, for instance. Following the demise of the Polish-Lithuanian Commonwealth in 1795, the Poles found themselves as small, minority populations divided between three major powers. In all three cases the Poles were subject populations who did not enjoy anything resembling modern notions of democratic civil rights. They lived instead in absolutist monarchies, and hence they lacked the freedom of speech to oppose their governments. Additionally, as newly introduced minorities to the countries they lived in, the Poles were far from centers of power and rarely had any influence or lobbying privileges. Almost all formerly influential and important Poles were, in other words, marginalized. Any incipient leaders who spoke out too forcefully in favor of Polish rights and autonomy could expect to be prosecuted, leading to either punishment or exile.

It would be hard to make the objective case that the Poles were an especially oppressed group. As far as subject groups in Eastern Europe went, they did not suffer from the extensive restrictions or persecutions that the Jews, for instance, faced. In fact, the tsars initially allowed the Russian Poles to retain their own vernacular school system.[3] Access to education was thus straightforward, and many Polish nationalists emerged from Russia as a result. In Austria, many Polish nobles were admitted to the aristocracy and retained their former influence. While Poles in Prussia had to be educated in German, they nevertheless were free to organize countless voluntary organizations to look after their religious, cultural, farming, and business interests. In all three states the Poles were free to own land and had access to courts to defend their property. Even in Prussia, where the state eventually set aside funds to buy up Polish farmland in order to promote German migration to the east, the Polish farmers sold at high prices and ultimately rebought at lower ones so that they actually increased their holdings. The peasants, who represented the majority of the Polish population, were generally better off during Partition than before as many old impositions and restrictions placed on them were phased out. Serfdom gradually ended, and many peasants became small landowners.[4] Increasing industrialization, trade, and urbanization also raised the standard of living of the Poles as the decades went by. The landless and poor, meanwhile, emigrated in large numbers to America and elsewhere.[5]

Notwithstanding this relatively benign picture, the evolving language of Polish nationalism remained fervent throughout the nineteenth century. At the forefront of the movement were the marginalized members of the *szlachta,* the former aristocracy who had enjoyed prestige and privilege in the Polish-

Lithuanian commonwealth. Now, often shorn of their wealth and position, the *szlachta* remained a vocal and educated class with strong international ties. With many of the defeated former Polish elite exiled in France following the Partition, the emerging nationalists were highly influenced by the rhetoric of the French Revolution. These strong ties with France were cemented as Napoleon's armies (which included several exile battalions) took control of Poland and established a client state, the Duchy of Warsaw, in 1807. If the Poles showed greater fervor for French overrule, they nevertheless paid for that allegiance quickly. As many as 100,000 Poles served in Napoleon's army that invaded Russia in 1812, and in the aftermath of this disastrous invasion Russia not only routed Napoleon but regained Poland in 1813. For the remainder of the nineteenth century many Polish exiles would reside in France, and many Polish nationalists wrote in French. Polish nationalists thereafter would direct their appeals at an international audience using Romantic, idealistic, and revolutionary sentiments rather than write specifically for local audiences. Using their opportunity to publish abroad without fear of retribution, many of these exiles became the leading nationalist spokesmen.

While the Russians soon repartitioned the Poles with the Prussians and Austrians, they nevertheless retained most of the Duchy of Warsaw as a separate, quasi-independent state known as the "Congress Kingdom." This kingdom, established and controlled by the modernizing autocrat Alexander the Great, featured a constitution that allowed for a Polish national assembly and considerable autonomy. Although Alexander in practice was far less accommodating to Polish freedoms than the constitution promised, nevertheless the "Congress Kingdom" era from 1815 to 1831 was one in which Polish nationalism developed coherence.

During the Congress Kingdom period, Adam Mickiewicz (1795–1855), now revered as Poland's greatest poet, became the leading Polish nationalist and Romantic writer. A member of the *szlachta,* the young Mickiewicz emerged as an intellectual while still a university student with his strident poem "Ode to Youth," and soon became a leader in nationalist secret society circles.[6] After being imprisoned, Mickiewicz was eventually exiled to Russia in 1824, where he moved in polite society and was able to write many of his most famous works. These included his famous *Konrad Wallenrod,* a nationalist epic poem describing the military exploits of Teutonic knights under the Polish-Lithuanian Commonwealth. Russian censors seemed oblivious to its thinly veiled central theme: the need for Poles to oppose their traditional Russian enemies. The book was published and almost immediately established Mickiewicz as the greatest poet and writer ever to use the Polish language.[7] After the publication of *Konrad Wallenrod,* Mickiewicz was allowed to leave Russia. He thereafter lived in permanent exile, chiefly in Rome and Paris, where the rest of his works were composed, most notably *Pan Tadeusz* (1832), another epic poem set during the fall of the Duchy of Warsaw to the Russians.

Just as Mickiewicz was achieving such influence as a nationalist writer, the Poles unsuccessfully tried to overthrow their Russian shackles during the "November Uprising" of 1830. During the 1820s the Polish parliament, the Sejm, had rarely been allowed to assemble, and many outspoken intellectuals and nationalists such as Mickiewicz had been exiled or imprisoned. Meanwhile, several official policies also led to a dramatic increase in the population of landless peasants. Hence, by 1830 a large coalition of disaffected Poles ended up joining an ambitious revolt led by lower-ranking Polish officers in the Russian army. Once the poorly planned revolt broke out, the Sejm endorsed it "as an act of the nation"[8] and before long could muster a sizable army consisting primarily of defecting Russian army troops led by a former Napoleonic general from the Duchy of Warsaw era. Despite valiant efforts, the Polish government failed to win international support, and its overmatched forces eventually succumbed to a Russian invasion in mid-1831.

In the face of the inevitable Russian advance and brutal crackdown, most of the Polish leadership and intelligentsia went into exile in France. Famous Poles such as Mickiewicz and the composer Frederic Chopin were well known in Paris. These two were at the center of a burgeoning Romantic movement amongst the Poles. Mickiewicz's famous declaration, "And finally Poland said: Whosoever will come to me shall be free and equal, for I am freedom," indicated the idealistic, revolutionary, and international outlook of this group. Another young exile, the prolific dramatist and poet Juliusz Słowacki (1809–1849), was less influential in Paris than Mickiewicz but developed a large following in several parts of Polish Russia that would only grow larger in the late nineteenth century. A third Romantic nationalist writer to emerge in Paris was Count Zygmunt Krasiński (1812–1859). Another dramatist and poet, the nobleman would eventually be heralded with Słowacki and Mickiewicz as one of the "Three Bards" seen as the unofficial Polish national poets—men who could lay bare "the national feeling."[9] Although all three died young in exile, their reputations among Poles only grew as the partition continued.

The Three Bards were by no means the only Polish writers of their time, and they competed with many others for critical attention. By the 1880s large compendia of Polish verse were being translated into English and featured more than fifty other poets beside the acclaimed Three Bards.[10] One such minor writer was Apollo Korzeniowski (1820–1869), the father of Joseph Conrad. The elder Korzeniowski, although never in Paris, followed a fairly standard trajectory for Polish intellectuals of his time. A highly educated member of the traditional *szlachta* living in Russian Poland, Korzeniowski was involved both in nationalist secret societies and in radical publishing (including his dramas and translations).

His engagement in plotting various failed uprisings and in organizing secret societies ultimately led him to be imprisoned, tried, and exiled in 1861.[11] Ultimately, he spent his last years in Austrian Poland engaged in similar political and literary work. Conrad himself did not set much of his fiction in Russia, although his novel *Under Western Eyes* (1911) is an exception.

During the later nineteenth century Polish nationalism increased in intensity across its partitioned regions. Failed insurrections in Russia came and went. In Austria and Germany, Poles preferred to join voluntary associations to promote their cultural and business interests. Writers and intellectuals were always at the forefront of these groups, although in the early twentieth century Romantic and idealistic values were shed in favor of a more ruthless, ethnically driven movement—"a strongly organized, disciplined army" that made anti-Semitism a key feature of its ideology.[12] By this time, though, Joseph Conrad was no longer a Pole—but during his youth he had read and been influenced by many of the Romantic nationalists, most notably Mickiewicz and Słowacki.[13] During and after World War I, Conrad actively propagandized on behalf of an independent Poland in such texts as *The Polish Question* (1919). In doing so he used Woodrow Wilson's concept of "self-determination" as a rationale for Poland to be finally freed from German, Austrian, and Russian overrule. After the Versailles Conference, Poland was indeed reborn.

The Malaysian Archipelago

After Conrad's iconoclastic act (for a member of the *szlachta*) of opting to become a seaman in the late 1870s, many of his early voyages took him to the East Indies—where many of his early stories and books were to be set. This area was an ancient and lucrative destination for sailors, with the Straits of Malacca being a particularly important trade route and entrepôt located between Asia and the Middle East. The entire archipelago, which would include modern-day Indonesia, the Philippines, Papua New Guinea, and Malaysia, consisted of thirteen thousand islands (of which a thousand were inhabited) spread out in the ocean over an area roughly twice the size of Australia.[14] These tropical islands feature consistently hot, humid weather, which, combined with volcanic soils, can support year-round cultivation. Located on these densely populated islands is a bewildering array of different ethnic and language groups. By the time of Conrad's voyages, the vast majority of the population was Muslim, but large groups of Hindus, Christians, and Chinese could also be found. While most of the population consisted of peasants, there were also many seafaring communities engaged in fishing, trading, and piracy. Novels such as *Almayer's Folly* (1895), *Lord Jim* (1900), and *Victory* (1915) are set in this milieu.

Europeans had sought to control the region's commerce as soon as they entered the Indian Ocean. Not only was the area the world's sole producer of clove and nutmeg, but the seizure of the Straits of Malacca would eliminate Arab middlemen from East-West commerce and deliver massive profits to those who would ship Asian merchandise directly to Europe. The Portuguese were the first to do this, around 1500, and they controlled the Malay Archipelago's key trade routes for a century.[15] Around 1600, though, they were eclipsed by the Dutch—who would go on to dominate the area for more than three centuries. At the time of Conrad's visit, then, the East Indies were primarily controlled by the Dutch, although the British by this time would also have large outposts in what is now Malaysia and Singapore.

Dutch colonialism in the East Indies was marked by one chief attribute—a focus on profit making. The Dutch were masters of achieving higher returns from seafaring trade than any other nation of their era.[16] In Asia they focused on profits far more than empire-building for its own sake. As a result, the Dutch language barely affected the East Indies, which had its own Malay-based lingua franca. Nor did Dutch culture have much impact, either, although their capital Batavia (modern-day Jakarta) was a large enclave with a distinct creole population and a plantation system. Emblematic of this commercial emphasis was the fact that the Dutch East India Company (VOC), the world's first listed stock market company, controlled the Indies for the first two hundred years of Dutch colonialism.[17] While the VOC did have to engage in initial conquests and maintained an armed seafaring force of some ten thousand men, it was almost always in its interest to use diplomacy and treaties with the kingdoms and states of the East Indies rather than taking the expensive option of ensuring their compliance by force. Furthermore, the VOC almost always chose to minimize production of its most lucrative commodities such as cloves, nutmeg, and pepper, in order to keep their prices high.[18] This meant that their Asian subjects were not pushed into producing for the international market and retained their traditional agriculture.

After the VOC fell apart and the British seized Malaysia in the early 1800s, the Dutch state took control of the region and would not relinquish it until ejected by the Japanese during World War II. While the Dutch state made full use of its commercial monopolies, ultimately it had a far greater impact on the people of the islands. Whereas the company had been content to maintain nominal power through alliances with local leaders, the Dutch state sought much tighter control over its territory—particularly the forested interiors. A better-financed and more efficient military, consisting largely of native-born troops, gradually began to conquer more of the archipelago. The populations now brought under control were systematically taxed, and surplus revenues were repatriated to Holland to reduce the government's massive debts. As a part of this effort to increase revenues, the Dutch colonialists became increasingly insistent on increasing peasant production of cash crops that the VOC had neglected. During this regime of "Compulsory Planting" (or "Culture System") between 1830 and 1870, the government mandated production of coffee, sugar, and indigo, among other crops, on a certain percentage of all agricultural landholdings. Additionally, peasants were forced to provide free labor for public works projects that would facilitate trade and export.[19]

The effects of this harsh new colonialism were striking. From the Dutch perspective, it was highly effective since trading profits and tax revenues from the colony grew rapidly and enabled the government to pay off its crushing debts without having to tax its own citizens at home. For the peasants under Dutch control, the program was a nightmare. Large amounts of land formerly devoted to rice and subsistence cultivation were now forcibly devoted to growing crops for export. Food production declined, and mass starvation occurred in many areas. Nor was growing cash crops an effective substitute for the average producer, since the Dutch state was the only buyer—and it paid well below the market rate at fixed prices.[20] Only after some decades, following considerable migration by the peasants, as well as liberalization of crop prices by the Dutch, was the system discontinued. By the end of the nineteenth century the Indonesian population began to grow rapidly and generate large surpluses in both foodstuffs and cash crops.

Although the worst effects of the Compulsory Planting regime were being mitigated, the last two decades of the nineteenth century saw policies that encouraged a massive influx of Dutch investment into the region. With their external debts paid off, the Dutch began exporting capital and invested heavily across the archipelago. Rubber, tobacco, and tea plantations were built and linked to the ports by railway lines. Newly built steamships carried huge cargoes back cheaply and quickly to Europe via the new Suez Canal. Several of the world's largest modern-day multinational companies also had their origins at this time, with Royal Dutch Shell controlling Indonesia's oil production and the Billiton mining company opening large tin and bauxite mines.[21] All this investment required large-scale Dutch immigration, and the Dutch population had grown dramatically by 1900. By this time the use of quinine was able to keep the European population safe from malaria, beriberi, and other tropical diseases that had kept their numbers to a minimum in the past.

Conrad's visits to the Malay Archipelago on various British merchant ships were thus a direct by-product of this intensified trade, production, and exploitation of the region. During the 1880s, when Conrad voyaged to the region, cash-crop exports doubled, while new industries such as rubber and mining also boomed. These trades were largely in the hands of Dutch and European trading houses. Additionally, there were sizable ethnic minorities such as Chinese, Arabs, and Indians who also took advantage of niche export opportunities with Asia and the Middle East.[22] At the various ports in the archipelago, Conrad would have set foot in a fast-growing, cosmopolitan setting that did not owe a great deal to traditional Indonesian culture. As the major ports expanded, they became the East Indies' first urban centers, and eventually large new populations of male contract workers abandoned peasant life to live in them. Unlike the situation in China or Japan, for instance, these growing city ports did not yet feature established populations, but were home to large groups of new or itinerant workers—the displaced who would eventually form the Indonesian and Malaysian working and middle classes. The systematic education of this group's children, which would be undertaken by the Dutch early in the twentieth century, had barely begun. So the displaced peasant encountered by travelers was most likely Indonesian. Given that these peasants typically spoke a Malay lingua franca, were Muslims, and lacked formal education or experience in international trade, they typically did not interact much with travelers.

The Congo Free State

When Joseph Conrad arrived (after a decade or so in the Indies) in the inaptly named Congo Free State in 1890 to work as a steamer operator for a Belgian company, he could hardly have chosen a more brutalized location in which to ply his profession or in which to set his chilling *Heart of Darkness* (1899). On the one hand the Congo had suffered the debilitating effects of four centuries of sustained involvement in the Atlantic and Indian Ocean slave trades. Just after this trade reached its pitiless climax during the mid-nineteenth century, the vast Congo region was claimed by the ruthless and Machievellian king of Belgium, Leopold II, as his personal domain during the chaotic "Scramble For Africa." This vast new country, cynically named the Congo Free State by Leopold, encompassed almost the entire Congo River and the territories that lay between it and the Atlantic Ocean—an enormous region of tropical forests inhabited by pygmy hunter-gatherers and by numerous other societies who typically combined slash-and-burn farming with hunting and fishing to eke out a precarious surplus.

Prior to the growth of the Atlantic slave trade in the late 1400s, the massive forests of the Congo were in the process of being populated by settlers from West Africa. Using iron tools and slash-and-burn agriculture, they brought virgin soils under cultivation.[23] Since the presence of the tsetse fly made the raising of livestock impossible, farmers typically obtained proteins from fishing and hunting. Fish were fairly plentiful, and the largest amounts were caught by specialists who employed a host of strategies to take advantage of the varying river levels that resulted from the alternating two rainy and dry seasons.[24] Hunting and the collection of forest products were also often undertaken by specialists, and the hunters and fishermen routinely traded with those who primarily cultivated. Where the surplus was biggest, ambitious politicians were often able to form large chiefdoms and kingdoms. Where it was smallest, autonomous clans organized their own affairs at the village level.[25]

The arrival of the slave trade cast a vicious new dynamic to the situation, although it took some time before all of Central Africa was affected. Very often the catalyst for the trade was not demand for slaves per se, but rather the extension of credit by coastal merchants to ambitious young men seeking to build up political followings. This credit, often initially used to purchase stylish textiles, alcohol, and guns, trapped the ingénue politicians in the long run. Once they had exhausted the supply of locally available goods such as ivory that could be used to pay off their creditors, they had to turn to the supply of humans to keep them happy. Inevitably, justice would be perverted so that new categories of "criminals" could be sold into slavery, while raiding expeditions would be launched against neighboring societies to obtain captives. Attacks of this kind were seldom successful for long, since the remaining populations would retreat into easily defensible and highly fortified locations. Indeed, they often proved capable of conducting their own retaliatory attacks and kidnappings in order to obtain funding for armaments that helped guarantee their safety. Once a region degenerated into a hostile armed camp and obtaining further slaves proved impossible, the coastal merchants moved further inland to sell their goods there, and the whole cycle was repeated over the course of the eighteenth and nineteenth centuries.[26] Adding to the general mayhem was the creation of new nihilistic, peripatetic, predatory societies that arose amongst vulnerable refugee populations. These groups, such as the notorious Imbangala, spread fear far and wide.[27]

One of the new societies that emerged was the Bobangi, who dominated the Upper Congo River—the long-winding seventeen-hundred-kilometer stretch between the two impassable waterfalls near the ocean at Pool Malebo, and at Kisangani in the interior. This was to be the stretch of water that Conrad traversed on steamers in 1890. Once a small group of fishermen, the Bobangi managed to control the lower Congo by transforming themselves into competing commercial canoe "houses" in the eighteenth century. Initially these commercial transport groups specialized in taking captives down the Congo in canoes to Pool Malebo—where they could be marched to the coast. During the nineteenth century, rising ivory prices made the slave trade less lucrative, and the Bobangi increasingly purchased slaves for their own use. Bobangi traders soon found it easier and cheaper to abandon the traditional family as a basis of the society. Instead of marrying and raising children, Bobangi men simply purchased people as they needed them. Since their slave "wives" were notoriously barren, young captives were bought and molded into oarsmen, armed retainers, or elephant hunters. By the late 1800s practically all Bobangi were slaves. Meanwhile, free Bobangi competed fiercely amongst each other—both for control of their own canoe house and against other canoe houses. They viewed life and prosperity entirely as a zero-sum game. One man's prosperity always came at another's expense, and success was attributed as much to witchcraft as to business acumen. Traders routinely sacrificed their retainers and junior kinsmen to achieve commercial success. The weak and vulnerable, meanwhile, could always use accusations of witchcraft against the powerful if they felt in peril.[28] If the Bobangi exemplified a highly efficient commercial reaction to international capitalism, their experience also exemplified the perversion the slave trade wrought on traditional structures and values.

The arrival of Belgian colonialism in the 1880s only intensified the violence and exploitation which the many peoples of the Congo were exposed to. Leopold's private "Congo Free State" was almost certainly the most vicious colony any European ever established in Africa—no mean feat given the competition for that honor. While exact demographic details are shaky, reputable scholars have made the case that between 1885 and 1907 the Congo's population declined by 50 percent or more.[29] Even if this figure is too high, there is no doubt that a substantial population decline took place. The cause of this catastrophe is simple: Leopold sought to extract the maximum amount of wealth out of the Congo as quickly as possible. In doing so, he diverted the population away from subsistence activities and had executed those who refused to follow official directives. Starvation and population relocations followed, productive areas went fallow, disease spread quickly, and mortality increased rapidly while life expectancy and birth rates plunged.

When Conrad arrived in the Congo Free State in 1890, the colony was only five years old. At this stage it still had a strong international reputation due in no small measure to the efforts of famed journalist and adventure seeker Henry Morton Stanley. Stanley had famously tracked down the crusading antislavery missionary David Livingstone in Central Africa in 1871, and then found the source of the Congo River in 1879.[30] Soon afterwards in the same year, Stanley entered the employ of Leopold II's "International African Society." Ostensibly sent to explore commercial, humanitarian, and missionary opportunities in Central Africa, Stanley's five-year expedition actually was seeking to claim Central Africa for the Belgian king. This effort succeeded, and Leopold's claims to the Congo were recognized when the European powers met in Berlin to carve up the African continent in 1885. Stanley remained in Leopold's employ until 1889, embarking on several highly publicized expeditions to the eastern borders of the Congo.[31] His famous "rescue" of the deposed Egyptian leader, Emin Pasha, in particular maintained the popular profile of the new colony.

Leopold was working hard in the meantime to get the maximum return for his considerable outlays in colonizing the Congo. His new country was carefully divided up into different concession zones. In some of these areas government employees directly taxed the citizenry and exploited all resources.[32] In other concessions, private companies obtained these rights and paid dividends and taxes to the monarch. Ivory and red rubber would soon prove the most lucrative products, and both these resources were ruthlessly stripped from the country in twenty years. Government and military officials could try to obtain these resources with their own employees, but usually they imposed large quotas on the local populations.[33] At the time of Conrad's sojourn in 1890 the worst excesses of this system had still to materialize. Even so, from the beginning it was very obvious that Leopold and his acolytes were going to condone the most brutal excesses that their men on the ground were perpetrating to keep the quotas met.

During the mid-1890s, conditions deteriorated rapidly as "red rubber" was collected. In particular, the widespread practice of severing hands for failure to meet quotas led to an international outcry.[34] This barbaric punishment, brought to light after 1903 by a coalition of moral reformers in Europe and America that included such notables as Mark Twain and Sir Arthur Conan Doyle,[35] eventually led the Belgian government to strip Leopold of his private colony. Hand severing was far from the only crime that was committed, though, and the Congo Reform movement highlighted numerous other atrocities and policies that eventually would halve the population.[36] Following its takeover of the Congo, Belgium governed the area until 1960 with a lighter, if not particularly enlightened, hand.

The landscape that Conrad witnessed in the Congo was not its natural one. In the early 1880s Leopold's mercenary and commercial forces seized control of the lower Congo River from the Bobangi. Steamers were brought in trawl the lucrative trade route, and the Bobangi were summarily crushed. Within a few years smallpox and other epidemics wiped out most of the Bobangi, and their slaves left them en masse.[37] The river villages that had been used to supply the old canoe trade were abandoned, and the once-bustling lower Congo appeared to Conrad to be empty—governed by a small cohort of Europeans with unlimited license to extract wealth from the local environment and population (such as those depicted in his early short story "An Outpost of Progress," 1896).

Conrad's Critical Reception

JOHN G. PETERS

Early Commentary

Throughout most of the first two decades of Conrad's literary career, his works were favorably reviewed. Reviewers frequently commented upon Conrad's descriptions and settings, particularly the sea and the exotic East. They also noted his literary style and ability to draw characters and his dark view of the world. Along with reviews in these early years, occasional articles appeared discussing Conrad's work as a whole. Two important early commentaries were Edward Garnett's "Academy Portraits: Mr. Joseph Conrad" (1898)[1] and Hugh Clifford's "The Trail of the Book-Worm: Mr. Joseph Conrad at Home and Abroad" (1898).[2] Both were ostensibly book reviews, but they took the opportunity to comment more broadly on Conrad's career. Garnett argued that Conrad presented humanity in relation to its place in the universe, while Clifford praised Conrad's works but famously suggested that Conrad knew nothing of Malays.

The dominant schools of literary criticism of this period were biographical/historical criticism and *belles lettres* (commentary that simply praised the beauty of a literary work rather than providing significant analysis). John Albert Macy's "Joseph Conrad" (1906)[3] and John Galsworthy's "Joseph Conrad: A Disquisition" (1908)[4] were two notable examples of this latter approach. Macy praised Conrad's genius, arguing that Conrad possessed two crucial elements that made a novelist great: stylistic prowess and significant experience (although he was critical of Conrad's achronological narratives). Galsworthy's article was similar, praising Conrad's work to date and echoing Garnett in suggesting that Conrad focus on the relationship between humanity and the universe.

Along with these early essays, two others stood out as especially insightful: Ford Madox Hueffer's (Ford's) "Joseph Conrad" (1911)[5] and Stephen Reynolds's "Joseph Conrad and Sea Fiction" (1912).[6] Both sought to push against the biographical/historical tendency to focus on Conrad's Polish heritage and instead emphasized the literature itself. Ford presented Conrad's work in light of

Elizabethan tragedy and insisted on the importance of honor to Conrad's conception of the world. Somewhat similarly, Reynolds argued for the Englishness of Conrad's works and his emphasis on morality, which Reynolds contended come from his experience at sea. Frederic Taber Cooper's "Representative English Story Tellers: Joseph Conrad" (1912)[7] approached other aspects of Conrad's fiction and argued against two common criticisms of Conrad's work: his narrative methodology and the uneven length of his works. Cooper suggested that Conrad's narratives were akin to a spider's web whose final form is admirable but whose method appears haphazard. Cooper likewise rejected complaints about length and contended that subject determines length, not the other way around. Like Cooper, Henry James's "The Younger Generation" (1914)[8] considered Conrad's narrative methodology, but he approached the topic differently, limiting his discussion to Conrad's *Chance* (1914) and arguing that the novel's subject matter does not justify its narrative complexity. Somewhat differently, Grace Isabel Colbron's "Joseph Conrad's Women" (1914)[9] was notable as the first extended look at Conrad's female characters. Colbron felt they are similar to his settings: their value comes in how they develop the male characters.

The first book-length commentary appeared in 1914. Richard Curle's *Joseph Conrad: A Study*[10] lacked an overarching perspective on Conrad's works and instead considered a number of individual issues. For instance, Curle noted Conrad's ability to evoke atmosphere and his emphasis on fixed ideas among his characters. He was also perhaps the first of a long line of commentators to remark on Conrad's fusion of realism and romance. Curle's was the first book on Conrad, but Wilson Follett's *Joseph Conrad* (1915)[11] was the first good book on Conrad. Follett's commentary was particularly insightful for the time, as he argued that Conrad's universe is indifferent and that Conrad lauds human struggle in the face of such circumstances. Follett also commented on Conrad's radical skepticism and need for solidarity. He praised Conrad's narrative methodology, suggesting a necessary link between methodology and meaning, between form and content. Contrary to most commentators of the time, William Lyon Phelps's "The Advance of the English Novel: VIII" (1916)[12] rejected the idea that Conrad's works are romantic and emphasized his psychological analyses, exotic settings, and moral law. Like Phelps, H. L. Mencken in *A Book of Prefaces* (1917)[13] noted the psychological struggles Conrad investigates, but he saw Conrad instead as an ethical agnostic, rejecting conventional social values. Like Follett, Mencken considered Conrad's universe as indifferent and argued that his narrative methodology comes out of his view of the world.

While Conrad's works were well received by the reviewers and literary world, popularity among the reading public eluded him until the 1914 publication of *Chance.* Afterwards, he was feted by critics and readers alike. Two notable exceptions were authors E. M. Forster and Virginia Woolf, who both expressed words of caution. Forster's "The Pride of Mr. Conrad' (1921),[14] a review of *Notes on Life and Letters,* took the opportunity to comment at large on his works and famously suggested that only a vapor rather than a jewel lay at the center of Conrad's fiction. Similarly, Woolf, in a review of *The Rescue,* "A Disillusioned Romantic" (1920),[15] and a later article, "Mr. Conrad: A Conversation" (1923),[16] questioned the quality of Conrad's later work, particularly *The Arrow of Gold* and *The Rescue,* arguing that Conrad had lost faith in the romance that infused his early works.

Several important commentaries appeared shortly after Conrad's death. Perhaps the most significant was Ford's *Joseph Conrad: A Personal Remembrance.*[17] Although criticized by Garnett and Conrad's wife Jesse for factual inaccuracies, Ford nevertheless provided useful information about Conrad's theory of literature, particularly his impressionist narrative methods. That same year, Ramón Fernández's "L'art de Conrad"[18] (translated into English in 1927), argued that Conrad relies on sensory perception to provide for a subjective experience. Similarly, Donald Davidson's "Joseph Conrad's Directed Indirections" (1925)[19] took up Conrad's impressionist narration and contended that his achronological narrative methodology allows him to emphasize issues rather than being constrained by the movement of plot. Along with these critical works, G. Jean-Aubry's *Joseph Conrad: Life and Letters* (1927),[20] was a collection of letters integrated with the first biography of Conrad.

Conrad's Decline

At the time of Conrad's death, he was considered one of the most prominent figures in English letters, but by 1930 the literary landscape had shifted significantly, and Conrad's reputation fell into decline. It would take some twenty years for it to recover. During this time, critical approaches to literature would begin to shift away from biographical/historical criticism and *belles lettres* toward psychological investigations (heavily influenced by Freud) and New Criticism (commentary that focused on literature itself, essentially ignoring historical and biographical context).

Despite the decline in Conrad's reputation, a handful of significant studies were published during this time. The first was Gustav Morf's *The Polish Heritage of Joseph Conrad* (1930).[21] Still working in the biographical/historical tradition (but also strongly influenced by Freud's psychology), Morf emphasized the importance of Conrad's Polish past on his literary works, especially focusing on what he viewed as Conrad's guilt at leaving Poland and living abroad as it played itself out in his works. Two other studies focused on Conrad's literary method. The first, V. Walpole's *Conrad's Method* (1930),[22] compared Conrad's first-person and omniscient narratives and their associated achronological aspects, contending that omniscient narratives avoid the necessity of justifying how information is acquired. Similarly, Joseph Warren Beach's *The Twentieth Century Novel* (1931)[23] investigated Conrad's narrative methodology and suggested that his use of first-person narrative, particularly his creation of Marlow, marks a significant step forward in his literary development. Beach viewed Conrad's method as impressionist and argued that the multiple points of view and achronology are necessary to render the complexity of human existence. Edward Crankshaw's *Joseph Conrad: Some Aspects of the Art of the Novel* (1936)[24] was one of the two most important early books of commentary (the other being Follett's *Joseph Conrad*). Unlike some, Crankshaw argued that Conrad was not a natural psychologist because he could not enter his characters' minds. Instead, he worked best through what Crankshaw termed objective methodology, which takes observation and experience and transforms it into fiction. He considered the development of Marlow as an example of this objective methodology. Crankshaw also emphasized the contrapuntal aspect of Conrad's narratives (his irregular use of chronology), which allows the parts to be lit by the whole. This early period of commentary ended with David Daiches's chapter on Conrad in *The Novel and the Modern World* (1939).[25] Daiches argued that Conrad is more concerned with humanity in the context of nature than in society. He echoed Crankshaw in asserting Marlow's value, contending that he let Conrad render phenomena objectively while simultaneously sympathizing such renderings. Daiches argued as well that Conrad follows no systematic philosophy, which allows him to present conflicting ideas side by side, such as his pessimistic world view juxtaposed against his value in human existence.

Recovering Conrad's Reputation

Conrad commentary came into maturity in the 1940s, beginning with John Dozier Gordan's *Joseph Conrad: The Making of a Novelist* (1940),[26] as Conrad's literary reputation slowly began to recover. Gordan's was the first extended textual study of Conrad's works. He focused on Conrad's composition process in his early works and concluded that the author worked instinctively rather than through outlines and was a tireless reviser. Like Crankshaw, Gordan argued that Conrad rarely wrote solely from imagination but instead from experience filtered through imagination. In contrast, M. C. Bradbrook's *Joseph Conrad: Poland's English Genius* (1941)[27] emphasized the importance of morality and fidelity in Conrad's works. She was also the first to present an extended argument positing a decline in the literary quality of Conrad's later works. Morton Dauwen Zabel's lengthy introduction to *The Portable Conrad* (1947)[28] continued the recovery of Conrad's literary reputation. Along with the morality and fidelity that Bradbrook noted, Zabel comments on the importance of honor in Conrad's works. Furthermore, Zabel sees Conrad infusing life into a literary milieu that had become moribund. Albert Guerard's *Joseph Conrad* (1947) was the most important commentary to date. Guerard insightfully analyzed Conrad's skepticism and emphasis on isolation. He argued that Conrad considers the plight of humanity in an indifferent universe, positing that moral action in the face of the absurd creates meaning for human existence. Guerard also expanded on Bradbrook's argument concerning the decline in Conrad's later works. F. R. Leavis's *The Great Tradition* (1948)[29] also aided in recovering Conrad's reputation. Leavis saw Conrad as part of the great tradition that worked from a position of moral realism. Although Leavis viewed Conrad's works highly, he was particularly critical of *Heart of Darkness,* arguing that Conrad relied on adjective-heavy language to insist upon the novella's profundity rather than actually demonstrating it.

Re-establishing Conrad Place in the Canon

The criticism of the 1950s would complete the recovery of Conrad's reputation. The first significant commentary of this period was Robert Penn Warren's essay "Nostromo" (1951).[30] (This essay would later serve as the introduction to the Modern Library edition of the novel.) In the essay, Warren argued that Conrad looks to the inner life of individuals to arrive at truth, and although he believes that the truth of all values is illusory, he nevertheless posits the necessity of such values for human beings to make life livable. Warren was followed by several other commentaries. For example, Douglas Hewitt's *Conrad: A Reassessment* (1952)[31] argued for the significance of Conrad's structure and settings in reinforcing the struggles of his characters. He also pointed to the importance of fidelity, courage, and codes of conduct in Conrad's fiction. Finally, although Bradbrook and Guerard had previously posited an artistic decline in Conrad's later fiction, Hewitt continued this trend and came to be closely associated with this view. Paul L. Wiley's *Conrad's Measure of Man* (1954)[32] was the first extended response to the theory of decline in Conrad's later works. Wiley contended instead that Conrad investigates different aspects of human experience, considering first individuals in isolation, next individuals struggling with society, and finally individuals acting as rescuers. Unlike other commentators, Irving Howe's two-part essay "Order and Anarchy: The Political Novels" (1953–54)[33] focused for the first time on Conrad's politics. Howe argued for Conrad as a political conservative because he could not accept liberalist values. He also accused Conrad of bias in his portrayal of revolutionaries.

Thomas Moser's *Joseph Conrad: Achievement and Decline* (1957)[34] continued the trend established by Bradbrook, Guerard, and Hewitt and was also a major step forward in Conrad commentary. Moser also investigated the decline in Conrad's later career, but he associated it with Conrad's shift toward romantic love (which he saw as an uncongenial subject for Conrad) and a universe governed by chance. Moser contends that this trend contrasts with Conrad's earlier works, which emphasized testing human beings, as well as the values of fidelity and solidarity. Albert Guerard's *Conrad the Novelist* (1958)[35] was a major work of commentary that remains valuable today. Guerard worked less from an overarching theory than from strong readings of Conrad's individual works. Nevertheless, he did identify what he considered key elements in Conrad's writings. For instance, he found a focus on moral challenges and an effort to know one's self, as well as an inquiry into the inexplicable nature of human existence. Finally, Guerard discussed Conrad's impressionism, detachment, and evasiveness, arguing that these elements lead to Conrad's unique effect. As in his earlier book, Guerard emphasized an achievement and decline in Conrad's career. This period ended with Jocelyn Baines's *Joseph Conrad: A Critical Biography* (1959),[36] the first excellent biography of Conrad. This was a literary biography and, unlike most previous biographers, Baines refused to take Conrad at his word about his life and instead relied on documented sources, which often run counter to what Conrad wished people to believe about himself. Consequently, this biography was much more accurate than those that preceded it.

Constructing Essential Critical Debates

With Conrad's literary reputation no longer in doubt, commentators began to turn in new directions, establishing debates and pursuing new avenues of inquiry. The first debate picked up where Howe left off—with Eloise Knapp Hay's *The Political Novels of Joseph Conrad* (1963).[37] Like Howe, Hay considered Conrad a political conservative, but with reservations; she also saw elements of Polish liberalism in his political views. In general, Hay found Conrad suspicious of democracy and revolutionary activities, siding with the political establishment while remaining skeptical of all political systems. Avrom Fleishman also took up this thread in *Conrad's Politics* (1967),[38] but contrary to Howe and Hay he did not consider Conrad a political conservative and instead suggested that he follows an Organicist tradition that endorses communal, cultural, and family ties. Fleishman also sees Conrad advocating community and rejecting anarchy in his political writings.

J. Hillis Miller's *Poets of Reality* (1965)[39] influenced a number of later commentators. Miller contended that Conrad's works exhibit a nihilism resulting from his positing consciousness as the origin of all reality. Consequently, all values are constructs erected above an abyss that consists of what Miller called the darkness. Miller argued that Conrad paved the way for modern writers as he led his readers into the darkness and then brought them out the other side. Unlike Miller, Edward W. Said's *Joseph Conrad and the Fiction of Autobiography* (1966)[40] focused on Conrad's correspondence and shorter fiction, suggesting that Conrad rewrote his life in his fiction in order to try to come to a knowledge of himself. Said saw Conrad employing mind to confront the chaos of existence and, contrary to the achievement and decline theory, Said sees something of a progression in Conrad's career, culminating in *The Shadow-Line.* A different look at the relationship between Conrad's life and works was Andrzej Busza's "Conrad's Polish Literary Background and Some Illustrations of the Influence of Polish Literature on His Work" (1966).[41] As the title suggests, Busza traced the relationship between Conrad's works and his Polish literary background. Similarly, Norman Sherry's *Conrad's Eastern World* (1966)[42] also considered Conrad's background, but Sherry looked more broadly at the sources that served as raw material for Conrad's works set in the East.

James Guetti's *The Limits of Metaphor* (1967)[43] introduced the major topic of language, arguing that Conrad's works reveal a linguistic indeterminacy that results in his inability to represent the meaninglessness his works encounter. Donald C. Yelton's *Mimesis and Metaphor* (1967)[44] considered a different aspect of language, specifically symbol and metaphor. Yelton argued that Conrad negotiates between French symbolism and Flaubert's realism, two primary influences, through his use of the visual and evocative. In this way, Conrad interiorizes imagery and thus makes it indicative of moral states. John A. Palmer's *Joseph Conrad's Fiction: A Study in Literary Growth* (1968)[45] is primarily of value as another extended response to the dominant achievement and decline theory of Conrad's career. Palmer posited a career of growth rather than decline. He saw three periods that focus on moral issues, culminating in a theory for moral action and moral affirmation.

New and Continuing Directions

The 1970s would continue some of the previous debates as well as initiating new ones. For example, Bruce Johnson's *Conrad's Models of Mind* (1971)[46] was an early commentary focusing on the relationship between Conrad and philosophy. Johnson posited that Conrad begins with a will-passion model and then moves to an ego-sympathy model that then leads to the importance of self-knowledge. Johnson contended that in this way self-knowledge becomes the only means for freedom in Conrad's works. H. M. Daleski's *Joseph Conrad: The Way of Dispossession* (1977)[47] also emphasized the self in Conrad's works, but Daleski focused on self-possession. He contended that possession of the self is crucial to Conrad, so that his characters exhibit for instance fidelity, courage, solidarity, and duty. On the other hand, for Daleski, loss of self leads to destruction, although he also argued that by letting go of self Conrad's characters can come to a better awareness of self.

With his essay "An Image of Africa" (1977),[48] Chinua Achebe ushered in one of the most longstanding debates in Conrad commentary. Achebe insists that Conrad is racist in his portrayal of Africans in *Heart of Darkness,* and therefore the story should not be considered a great work of literature. Both Achebe's argument concerning *Heart of Darkness* and the subject of Conrad's relationship to colonialism have been major topics of discussion ever since. Moving in a different direction, Jeremy Hawthorn's *Joseph Conrad: Language and Fictional Self-Consciousness* (1979)[49] picked up the debate concerning language in Conrad's works, as he posited that Conrad uses language to transform subjectivity into objectivity. Hawthorn further contended that language for Conrad provides a means toward self-consciousness. Jacques Berthoud, in *Joseph Conrad: The Major Phase* (1978),[50] looked at Conrad's works less through an overarching perspective than by considering works individually. Nevertheless, he did focus on particular issues such as vision and insight. Berthoud also argued that many of Conrad's characters only find values through defeat. Like Guerard's *Conrad the Novelist,* Ian Watt's *Conrad in the Nineteenth Century* (1979)[51] was a landmark in Conrad commentary. Taking a pluralist approach to Conrad's works by employing formalism, historicism, and intellectual history, Watt presented strong readings of Conrad's early career, especially his discussion of Conrad's impressionism and symbolism.

Closing out this period, Frederick R. Karl's major biography, *Joseph Conrad: The Three Lives* (1979),[52] divided Conrad's life into youth, maritime career, and literary career. Like Baines's biography, Karl's was a literary biography that focused on Conrad's life and his works, and on the relationship between them. Also like Baines, Karl benefits from newly discovered sources. Along with Karl's biography, another significant biographical work was Norman Sherry's *Conrad's Western World* (1971).[53] As with his earlier book, Sherry traced the sources for Conrad's works. In this case, though, he concentrated on Conrad's works set in the Western world.

Poststructuralism, Postcolonialism, and Beyond

The commentary of the 1980s took a leap forward, as an emphasis on postcolonialism (criticism that considers literature in light of issues surrounding the former colonial world) and poststructuralism (criticism that rejects metaphysics and stable meaning and insists on plurality of meaning) and other contemporary literary theories began to infuse the scholarship. The first of these studies was William W. Bonney's *Thorns & Arabesques* (1980),[54] which, like Miller, argued for a nihilism at the core of Conrad's works. More particularly, as others have noted, romance appears in Conrad's works, but Bonney contended that this romance contains elements that ultimately undermine it. He argued as well that Conrad's shifting narrative perspectives emphasize subjectivity and indeterminacy. Fredric Jameson's *The Political Unconscious* (1981)[55] combined Marxism with poststructuralist theory to interrogate Conrad's impressionist narrative methodology in *Lord Jim* and *Nostromo.* In particular, Jameson looked at romance and reification in these works to argue that Conrad's impressionism is both utopian (providing a compensation for the dislocation of individuals) and ideological (obscuring reality), this ideological component serving to suppress history. Aaron Fogel also employed contemporary literary theory in *Coercion to Speak* (1985).[56] Drawing upon Mikhail Bakhtin's ideas, Fogel argued that Conrad represents characters forcing one another to speak, such that both the character forcing speech and the character forced to speak are not free in their dialogue. Moving in a somewhat different direction, Jakob Lothe's *Conrad's Narrative Method* (1989)[57] used contemporary literary theory, especially contemporary narrative theory, to comment on Conrad's narrative methodology. Lothe looked at the relationship between theme and narrative, rejecting the idea that content precedes form and arguing that interpretation ought to consider both content and narrative. Unlike these other commentaries, Benita Parry's *Conrad and Imperialism* (1983)[58] presented a postcolonial and poststructural approach to Conrad's fiction. Parry argued that Conrad both subverts and affirms colonialism. Although often critical of colonial practice, he often presents the East as exotic and affirms traditional Western values and stereotypes.

Along with contemporary literary theory, more traditional approaches to Conrad continued to flourish. For example, Cedric Watts's *The Deceptive Text* (1984)[59] argued that both overt and covert plots exist in many of Conrad's works. The covert plots move in a different direction from the overt plot and typically come to different conclusions. Focusing on another area of study and in contrast to many commentaries, Daniel R. Schwarz's *Conrad: The Later Fiction* (1982)[60] defended the later fiction (although Schwarz also recognizes its limitations). Schwarz considered these works individually rather than through an overarching perspective and argued that they tend to exhibit the same skepticism, humanistic interest, and search for value and self-definition that mark Conrad's earlier works. In another direction, Paul B. Armstrong's *The Challenge of Bewilderment* (1987)[61] asserted that the reader's bewilderment causes a reassessment of realism and interpretation. For Armstrong, Conrad longs for stability but finds only contingency. Nevertheless, he rejects nihilism and affirms values, knowing that those values can only be contingent.

Along with critical works, two important biographical works appeared during this time. The first was Zdzislaw Najder's *Joseph Conrad: A Chronicle* (1983),[62] still the most important biography of Conrad (only superseded by Najder's 2007 updated edition, *Joseph Conrad: A Life*).[63] Najder had the advantage of an intimate knowledge of Polish culture and language, as well as access to many sources previously unavailable. Najder's is not a literary biography and seeks to limit speculation to a minimum. In contrast, Cedric Watts's *Joseph Conrad: A Literary Life* (1989)[64] focuses specifically on Conrad's publishing career, discussing the literary climate in which he wrote as well as the pressures and conventions affecting his writing.

Further Developments

The 1990s furthered trends begun in the 1980s as postcolonial, poststructuralist, and other contemporary literary theories continued to influence Conrad commentary. At the same time, more traditional critical theory continued to play a prominent role. Edward W. Said's *Culture and Imperialism* (1993)[65] was a good example. Said suggested that in *Heart of Darkness* Conrad posits two visions: one is a conventional imperialist view, but the other sees an end to imperialism, and Said felt that although Conrad was unable to picture a postcolonial world he pointed the way for his readers to envision such a world. Like Said, Andrea White's *Joseph Conrad and the Adventure Tradition* (1993)[66] considered the question of Conrad's relationship to colonialism and imperialism, but she focused on his use of the adventure tradition to do so. White suggested that Conrad admired the discoveries resulting from the adventure tradition, as well as the capacity to dream that it embodied. At the same time, by working within this tradition Conrad could use irony to question the imperialist ideology that typically accompanied the tradition. While still focusing on colonialism, Christopher GoGwilt's *The Invention of the West* (1995)[67] took a different approach, arguing that the concept of a unified West is an invention created to justify the West's treatment of the non-Western world. Like many other commentators on Conrad's relationship to the colonial world. GoGwilt saw a divided response, Conrad both supporting and rejecting an invented West. Continuing the trend toward poststructuralist commentary, Daphna Erdinast-Vulcan's *Joseph Conrad and the Modern Temper* (1991)[68] contended that Conrad struggled against the modern temper and resisted Nietzsche's tendency toward ethical and epistemological relativity, searching instead for morality and stability. In the process, however, Conrad finds himself longing to believe in these values while finding he cannot do so. Jeremy Hawthorn's *Joseph Conrad: Narrative Technique and Ideological Commitment* (1990)[69] was similarly informed by poststructuralist views, but his emphasis was on narrative, which he saw as closely connected to content. In Conrad's strongest works, Hawthorn found Conrad's ideological and moral commitment tied to his narrative mobility.

A largely new debate appeared during this period. Although Conrad's attitude and treatment of women had been touched upon many times previously, Ruth Nadelhaft's *Joseph Conrad* (1991)[70] was the first extended inquiry into the topic. Nadelhaft posited that contrary to usual assumptions women play prominent roles in Conrad's fiction and that the negative attitudes toward them are typically those of Conrad's narrators rather than Conrad himself, who often sympathizes with the plight of women. Susan Jones's *Conrad and Women* (1999)[71] concurred, suggesting women play a prominent role in Conrad's works.

Jones further argued that Conrad's later career represents a shift in direction rather than a decline.

Other important studies include Mark A. Wollaeger's *Joseph Conrad and the Fictions of Skepticism* (1990),[72] Robert Hampson's *Joseph Conrad: Betrayal and Identity* (1992),[73] and Yves Hervouet's *The French Face of Joseph Conrad* (1990).[74] Wollaeger placed Conrad in a skeptical tradition and contended that his works consistently exhibit a tension between skepticism and a desire for shelter from such skepticism. Wollaeger also believed that Conrad was reluctant to abandon transcendent truths and while recognizing their illusory nature nevertheless adhered to systems of order to escape the abyss of nihilism. While Wollaeger looked at the prominent issue of skepticism, Hampson considered the equally prominent aspect of psychology. Working from the ideas of R. D. Laing, Hampson argued that Conrad presents an evolution of the self: from the isolated self to the socialized self to the sexual self. In the process, Hampson contends that Conrad's career is one of a movement toward maturity rather than decline.

Hervouet, however, moves in a very different direction, countering conventional thinking about the influences on Conrad and arguing instead that along with the well-documented influence of Polish literature Conrad was also strongly influenced by French literature. Two biographies appeared during this period, Jeffrey Meyers's *Joseph Conrad: A Biography* (1991)[75] and John Batchelor's *The Life of Joseph Conrad* (1994).[76] Both relied heavily on documentation, but they were very different, Batchelor's being a literary biography.

The New Millennium of Commentary

The new millennium has seen a return to many areas of debate and approaches to Conrad's fiction, while at the same time branching out into markedly new fields of inquiry. As with much previous commentary, poststructuralist and other contemporary literature theory has continued to influence critics. For example, Michael Greaney's *Conrad, Language, and Narrative* (2002)[77] looked at the relationship of narrative to speech and writing, arguing that Conrad's writing moved from speech communities, which involved storytelling, to the Marlow narratives, which represented a struggle between authentic and inauthentic language, to political communities, which employed modernist techniques of narrative. Somewhat differently, Stephen Ross's *Conrad and Empire* (2004)[78] considered issues of imperialism in light of poststructuralism, arguing that globalization and empire result in imperialism in Conrad's works, with globalization replacing the nation-state. In contrast, Robert Hampson's *Cross-Cultural Encounters in Joseph Conrad's Malay Fiction* (2000)[79] approached the idea of empire through postcolonial views, suggesting that Conrad's Malay fiction emerges from his own experience as well as from Western constructs of the Malay world. For Hampson, Conrad recognized these constructs and often undermined them.

Gender issues have also been prominent during this time. Along with feminist studies, the first studies of masculinity have also appeared. Andrew Michael Roberts's *Conrad and Masculinity* (2000),[80] for instance, insisted that masculinity is culturally constructed and that Conrad both reinforces those constructed images while also questioning them. Related to this has been an increasing interest in homoeroticism in Conrad's works, as evidenced by Jeremy Hawthorn's *Sexuality and the Erotic in the Fiction of Joseph Conrad* (2007),[81] which argued that sexuality and eroticism are more pervasive in Conrad's works than has typically been thought. In addition, Hawthorn argued for the presence of homosexuality and homoeroticism in Conrad's works.

Along with these areas of study, debates concerning Conrad and philosophy and Conrad and psychology have been prominent. My own book, *Conrad and Impressionism* (2001),[82] considered Conrad's works in light of impressionist epistemology, arguing that perception and experience in Conrad's works are a relative phenomenon determined by the relationship between subject, object, and context. I worked from this concept to argue for a similar view of Conrad's social and political views. As with philosophy, psychological inquiries have made their impact. Martin Bock's *Joseph Conrad and Psychological Medicine* (2002)[83] looked at Conrad's works in the context of pre-Freudian psychology, suggesting that Conrad narrates the mental illness of his characters and in the process narrates his concerns about his own mental stability. Bock also argued that Conrad's post-breakdown novels helped him come to terms with his own illness.

Perhaps more than any other period, the new millennium has seen commentators move in entirely new directions. For example, Stephen Donovan's *Joseph Conrad and Popular Culture* (2005)[84] argued that Conrad is often viewed as hostile toward popular culture, but in fact images and ideas from popular culture permeate his works. Donovan contended that one needs to understand Conrad's use of popular culture to fully appreciate his works. Similarly, Richard Hand's *The Theatre of Joseph Conrad* (2005)[85] considered Conrad's theatrical works, which had received little previous attention. Unlike other commentators, Hand saw value in these works and argued that they must be considered within the context of contemporary melodrama, realism, and Grand Guignol. Hand argued as well that Conrad's drama anticipated the work of such dramatists as Samuel Beckett and Eugene O'Neill, as well as expressionism and Theater of the Absurd. Richard Niland, in *Conrad and History* (2010),[86] moved in a different direction but one no less lightly traveled, arguing that Conrad was influenced by both Polish romanticism and Polish positivism, as well as other nineteenth-century views on history and politics. Niland also considered Conrad's response to the First World War and how it affected his views of Napoleon. Peter Lancelot Mallios moved in yet another direction in *Our Conrad* (2011),[87] as he suggested that American authors and thinkers appropriated Conrad for their own various ends, often coming to antithetical conclusions concerning his works. Finally, Jeffrey Mathes McCarthy's "'A Choice of Nightmares': The Ecology of *Heart of Darkness*" (2009)[88] looked at Conrad's *Heart of Darkness* in light of ecological issues. McCarthy argued that the story rejects the idea that nature is simply part of imperial trade but instead investigates the relationship between humanity and nature.

One major biography has appeared during this period: John Stape's *The Several Lives of Joseph Conrad* (2007).[89] Stape's was not a literary biography; basing his work on new documentary sources, he looked to dispel errors and misinterpretations by previous biographers and commentators. In particular, Stape focused on Conrad's roles of father, husband, and friend as opposed to his life as Pole, sailor, and writer, which so many other biographers have privileged.

PART II

Critical Approaches to Heart of Darkness

"The great demoralization of the land"

Postcolonial Ecology in *Heart of Darkness*

GREG WINSTON

In the early critical reception of *Heart of Darkness*, geography was secondary to psychology. The natural world was generally regarded as atmospheric backdrop to the story of devolutionary insanity of the European in Africa. As Graham Huggan and Helen Tiffin summarize, "In the orthodox modernist reading of Conrad's novel—an interpretation exported via education curricula throughout the English-speaking colonial world in the first half of the twentieth century—*Heart of Darkness* is about the primitive instincts always lurking in the human heart, and the danger of atavistic reversion."[1] If Conrad's landscapes were seen to have any sort of role, it was one that caused outsiders like Kurtz to lose their ethical bearing or mental grip. The converse effect, of European intruders on the African environment, was not generally addressed in a period when the subjugation of local people and exploitation of natural resources were widely accepted cultural norms for the vast majority of English readers.

Such a view was reified by canonizing critic F. R. Leavis's 1948 reading of the novella. While Leavis argued for Conrad's inclusion in his Great Tradition of English literature, it was despite *Heart of Darkness* and not because of it. For Leavis, Conrad's novella forms an "art of vivid essential record" wherein the natural world is an antagonistic agent: "Ordinary greed, stupidity and moral squalor are made to look like behaviour in a lunatic asylum against the vast and oppressive mystery of the surroundings, rendered potently in terms of sensation."[2] When reconfigured alongside intellectual or moral shortcomings as a cause of human dissolution and insanity, nature itself becomes denaturalized in Leavis's metaphor of the asylum. Moreover, this reading manages an inversion of the colonial power structure, as the surroundings become "oppressive," even when, after all, it is European invaders like Kurtz who oppress the people and despoil the resources of the Congo, not the other way around. Such displacement of the novella's geography not only ignores key elements of its writing and historical context but it also sequesters Conrad's environmental descriptions from his portrayals of imperialism, even though, in many instances throughout the book, the two occur in close proximity and intricate relation.

A little over sixty years later, the entangled political and environmental issues of the text have become for many readers as compelling as the personal insight of Marlow or primal regression of Kurtz. The burgeoning theoretical alliance between postcolonial and ecocritical studies now affords a useful perspective for tackling the essential, recurring parallel between imperial subjugation and ecological degradation in *Heart of Darkness.* The novella frequently states their connection through an economy of style that features intersecting tropes of imperialist and ecological significance. Take, for example, the following passage from Marlow's account of his journey to Africa: "We called at some more places with farcical names, where the merry dance of death and trade goes on in a still and earthly atmosphere as of an overheated catacomb; all along the formless coast bordered by dangerous surf, as if Nature herself had tried to ward off intruders."[3]

The sequence of metaphors conjoins nature and culture at the interface of commercial and political power. Europe's role in Africa and humankind's relationship to the natural environment are unified in the anthropomorphized image of Mother Nature fending off invasion. The sentence resumes, extending the ecological description to suggest that incursion and conquest are inherent to both natural ecosystem and human political system: "in and out of rivers, streams of death in life, whose banks were rotting into mud, whose waters, thickened into slime, invaded the contorted mangroves, that seemed to writhe at us in the extremity of an impotent despair."[4] Power and subjection run through the jungle and coastal zones, where water and earth, growth and decay contest for supremacy in a battle of the biosphere that mirrors the contested enterprise of colonial occupation.

Like the murky description, Marlow's account of his new surroundings is marked by ambiguity: "Nowhere did we stop long enough to get a particularized impression, but the general sense of vague and oppressive wonder grew upon me."[5] Due to the fleeting first encounters of the coast, it remains remarkably indeterminate whether for Marlow this "vague and oppressive wonder" emanates from the African surroundings or from the colonizers' behavior. Perhaps it derives from their interrelation, as Marlow's initial vision of the immense continent is virtually indistinguishable from the European efforts to subdue it. This is apparent, for instance, in the puzzling and reckless deployment of fresh troops and customhouse clerks, one of the careless routines of national efficiency that shows little regard for moral or economic costs: "Some I heard got drowned in the surf. . . . They were just flung out there and on we went."[6] So intent on reaching the next outpost of progress, colonial pilgrims fail to form a deep or abiding understanding of their territory for military and commercial conquest. For his part, Leavis seems to have taken this "oppressive wonder" to mean something inherent to the African landscape. His subsequent references to "the oppressive mystery of the surroundings"[7] and, soon after, to "the oppressive mysteriousness of the Congo"[8] eliminate the equivocality the original phrasing lends to Marlow's reading of the European presence in the African environment.

These remarks would greatly influence how *Heart of Darkness* was read and taught for several decades from the mid-twentieth century onward. Their privileging of individual psychology over cultural and environmental conditions inadvertently duplicates the very sort of imperialist attitudes to nature and people that the novella critiques. Like the processes of colonial subjection and environmental depredation, Leavis's reductive reading of the African setting centers on the material and psychological fortunes of the invader, to the exclusion of most everything else, including an ecosystem that faces as grave a threat to existence as did its colonized subjects. Moreover, it looks past many significant formal and thematic elements in the novella that speak to the intersecting issues of colonization and environment.

Within a couple of decades, various writers began to remedy the first of these omissions. In the novel *Things Fall Apart,* Chinua Achebe offered a tacit response to Conrad's depiction of the Congo in *Heart of Darkness* through an internal portrayal of Nigerian village life in the face of changes wrought by the religious and commercial waves of European colonialism in Africa.[9] A landmark lecture and essay by Achebe in the late 1970s issued a more explicit renouncement of Conrad's portrayal of Africans.[10] Two generations of postcolonial scholarship produced fresh readings that foregrounded issues of African marginalization and political oppression in the novella amid the broader frames of nineteenth-century imperialism, bringing increased historical relevance and multicultural scope to the Conrad critical project.[11] Much of this work makes the general case for *Heart of Darkness* as a critique of colonialism, in many instances still responding to Achebe's fictional assertions and critical claims. Perhaps for this reason many of these efforts tend to focus on the social, economic, and political collisions of African and European societies, with only tangential reference to the natural contexts in which the colonizing process takes place.

In recent years, another group of critics has found in *Heart of Darkness* a compelling narrative of natural resource issues and environmental abuse. Where postcolonialism focuses on the Europeans' treatment of the African people, ecocriticism highlights a parallel subjugation of the African setting and resources, also a prevalent theme in the novella's many moments that underscore the toll that humans, particularly the European ivory hunters, are taking on the landscape and wildlife. The most productive efforts in this regard have been those that align such ecological readings with postcolonial perspectives to consider their essential interconnection. Such scholarship has proven a boon to literary criticism in general and Conrad studies in particular since it offers revitalized readings and a new frame of reference for the novella while also serving to legitimate the growing interdisciplinary project of postcolonial ecocriticism.

Several recent editions have proclaimed the arrival of this theoretical fusion.[12] Until quite recently, however, ecocriticism and postcolonialism remained separate, and at times even antagonistic, enterprises in literary and cultural studies. In their introduction to *Postcolonial Green,* Bonnie Roos and Alex Hunt characterize the mutual distrust: “Scholars associated with postcolonialism see ecocritics as furthering an often unself-conscious settler or colonialist project; scholars associated with ecocriticism see postcolonial critics as alarmingly blind to environmental degradation or unreasonably suspicious of ecological discourse.”[13] The welcome cooperation of these previously competing approaches, while hardly complete, nonetheless provides a remarkable opportunity to balance the concerns and coordinate the critical efforts of the two disparate camps. The emergence of postcolonial ecology stems from the recognition that “our world is locked in a dance of cultural, economic, and ecological interdependence. This interdependence calls for a multiplicity of voices to address the problems that our world faces today.”[14] As it provides new ways to consider contemporary global issues, the interdisciplinary partnership can also offer fresh insight on classic texts, allowing us to reconsider old works of literature for their relevance to the current interplay of political and environmental conditions. In this regard, there seems no better candidate than *Heart of Darkness.* Its twin depictions of imperialism and resource exploitation in the Congo Free State a century ago illuminate the inseparable nature of the political sphere and the biosphere that remain relevant today.

Some of this valuable work is already underway, as two recent essays have concentrated on the interrelation of ecology and imperialism in *Heart of Darkness.* Building upon the race-oriented criticism of Conrad found in Achebe’s aforementioned novel and essay, and in the postcolonial theory of Edward Said, Jeffrey Meyers asserts the importance of seeing the connection between colonial and environmental concerns in the novella when he recognized “the European self that attempts . . . ‘acts of mastery’ not only over other peoples but over the ecology of Africa as a whole.”[15] He notes several mid-nineteenth- to mid-twentieth-century perspectives—from the evolutionary ecology of Charles Darwin to the deep ecology of Arne Naess—that can inform a reading of Conrad’s novella. With a slightly different emphasis, Jeffrey McCarthy, reading *Heart of Darkness* for its “destabilization” of Victorian cultural and scientific perspectives, concludes that the story is “about repositioning human beings within a new understanding of nature” (620). In this view, colonial domination and environmental exploitation reveal themselves as tandem forces so that "*Heart of Darkness* shows us a link between the moral and ecological limits of imperialism."[16] McCarthy and Meyers share the premise that any discussion of the colonial degradation of Africa in the book must also consider the environmental destruction of the continent. Their move toward a hybrid approach to enfold the political with the ecological is especially effective not just for reading one text but for realigning and connecting two fields. As effective criticism should generally do, this new postcolonial-green partnership appears all of a sudden to illuminate themes that were always present in the text but awaiting more specific and deliberate thinking.

A century prior to this theoretical alliance, *Heart of Darkness* of course intertwined themes of colonial oppression and environmental depredation. Such symbiosis is present in the formal devices of imagery and metaphor, of structure and of style; it is announced as well in the paralleling of disparate characters and the integration of distant settings. All of these aspects show the human costs of imperialism as inseparable from the environmental ones, since both are directly linked through the moral and material activities of the colonizing process. Conrad often has Marlow depict them in overlapping, inextricable relation. From linking images to layered metaphors, from narrative framework to sentence structure, interconnectivity is a recurring aesthetic in *Heart of Darkness.* A postcolonial-ecological perspective on the story can help illuminate this interconnectivity of natural resources with the historical circumstances of cultural conquest, a logical interplay of human activities and natural environments whose interconnection and impact was often denied or ignored by those who managed and took part in the processes of colonization and resource exploitation.

I do not mean to suggest here that in *Heart of Darkness* Conrad was bent on writing a proto-environmentalist argument or an anticolonialist manifesto. To project either authorial intention upon him would mean ignoring his own complicity in the contemporary system of global commerce and conquest. Conrad was certainly moved by the destructive abuses that he witnessed firsthand in the Belgian Congo in the 1890s; however, he also made a living from working in the nautical network that provided a direct link and support to the European colonial enterprise. Calling attention to anomalous problems or evils of colonization might well be more a localized gesture of fiction than a universal plea to overhaul or dismantle an entire economic system. What Conrad's African narrative does suggest, with its intermingling of imperialist agendas with ecological contexts and consequences, is the significant recognition that the political and the environmental in fact flow together along the same great waterways of the earth. For readers then and now, such interdisciplinary thinking at the very least forges links between the oft-divided notions of the human and natural worlds.

Moreover, it reflects the new science of modern ecology whose emergence coincided with Conrad's journey to the Congo and writing of the novella.

Hydrologic

From its outset, *Heart of Darkness* establishes a sense of political and ecological interconnectedness in its layered tropes and linked narratives. In the opening scene, the frame narrative speaks to such seamless interrelation on multiple levels: "The sea-reach of the Thames stretched before us like the beginning of an interminable waterway. In the offing the sea and the sky were welded together without a joint."[17] As metaphors join river to sea, and human industry to natural surroundings, the narrator prepares the reader to see the seemingly infinite interrelations of the biosphere: the apparent endlessness of all water on earth, the seamless connection of sea and sky. The vehicle of the latter metaphor, like the *Nellie,* offers a nod to the technological process (that is, welding, shipbuilding) that makes human transportation and enterprise possible in maritime environments.

The frame narrative is itself welded without a joint to the interior one, as the men on board the *Nellie* prepare "to hear about one of Marlow's inconclusive experiences."[18] As language and tide begin to flow, the narrator comments generally on stories and storytelling in figurative terms that unite cultural artifacts with biological resources. Doing so, he prepares us for a story in which such commingling will be a certainty, even if the significance of events might seem inscrutable or the morality of characters unclear. As the narrator states, "The yarns of seamen have a direct simplicity, the whole meaning of which lies in the shell of a cracked nut. But Marlow was not typical (if his propensity to spin yarns be excepted), and to him the meaning of an episode was not inside like a kernel but outside, enveloping the tale."[19] Marlow tells stories like any other sailor, but to understand their significance, an audience must consider the form as inseparable from the content. In other words, the moral or meaning of the narrative to come will emerge as much from the shell, or surface language of the story, as from any sort of hermeneutical nut it contains.

These first two metaphors—of yarns for stories, of nutshells for meaning—collectively initiate the sense of reading and meaning-making as taking place at distinct intersections of human culture and natural resources. To spin a yarn (tell a story) and to crack a nut (decode a story's meaning) are both, appropriately enough, rooted in the production and consumption of natural resources. These metaphors of storytelling and interpretation align such cultural work with the economic activities of animal husbandry and agriculture. If we read the passage as the narrator advises we hear Marlow's tale, with attention to the outer "shell" of the narrative, that is, with focus on the vehicles of the metaphors—the spinning of wool or harvesting of nuts—we see the overture to issues of natural resource consumption that will extend across the story. Yarn appears in literal form soon after in the mythological image of the two women at Company headquarters in Belgium, "guarding the door of Darkness, knitting black wool as for a warm pall, one introducing, introducing continuously to the unknown, the other scrutinizing the cheery and foolish faces with unconcerned old eyes. '*Ave!* Old knitter of black wool. *Morituri te salutant.*'"[20] Amid Greco-Roman metaphors of knitting Fates and gladiatorial combatants, yarn appears in its raw material, wool, as questions of corporate efficiency, resource consumption, and sheer survival are figuratively woven into the fabric of individual and collective experience.

A subsequent detail from the narrator's diversion about narration—"misty halos"—joins notions of narrative interpretation and environmental conditions. In that same mid-century critique of *Heart of Darkness,* Leavis also rendered a critical judgment of what he deemed the inferior quality of the writing. In particular, he spoke of Conrad's tendency for vague language and repetitive word choice. He cited a remark made some two decades earlier by E. M. Forster that Conrad's writing contained "a central obscurity, something noble, heroic, beautiful, inspiring half-a-dozen great books, but obscure, obscure. . . . [H]e is misty in the middle as well as at the edges."[21] Forster had in fact been referring to the essays he was reviewing in Conrad's *Notes on Life and Letters* (1921), but Leavis applied the comment to the stylistic opacity he found in *Heart of Darkness.* Still, given the predominance of ecological imagery and environmental themes in the text, the obscuring mists at the center of the story in fact lend a certain degree of clarity and focus to a reading. For beyond the analogy of nutshell and nut, the narrator's extended metaphor continues, emphasizing how the meaning of Marlow's yarns—including, presumably, the one he is about to tell—might be perceived as "enveloping the tale, which brought it out only as a glow brings out a haze, in the likeness of one of these misty halos that sometimes are made visible by the spectral illumination of moonshine."[22] The significance of the story becomes clear through the interplay of moonlight and mist, the combined effect of luminosity and obscurity; to look for one without the other is to miss the truthful and illuminating nuance of the tale.

This meteorological analogy for the interpretation of texts is already an atmospheric reality as the frame narrative gives way to the tale of Africa. For when the narrator suggests readers look to the "misty halos" for the meaning of Marlow's yarn, he draws upon his immediate surroundings, as just beyond the rails of the *Nellie,* "the very mist on the Essex marshes was like a gauzy and radiant fabric, hung from the wooded rises inland, and draping the low shores in diaphanous folds."[23] The metaphor is freighted with associations of economic commodity and national community, suggesting, on the one hand, the finished goods of human industry made from the raw materials of nature (such as wool);

it also suggests the proverbial social fabric, knit across the English landscape through the intersecting lives and interwoven stories. Beyond cognitive and social interconnectivity, the mists suggest the holistic ecology across geographic and biospheric regions. At the boundary of liquid and gas, river and land, the mists emphasize geographical connections even as they blur visual distinctions. Indeed, the Essex fens, and soon, the African mangroves, over which they condense are themselves liminal zones of water and earth. Thus, alongside the moonlit halos of literary interpretation or cognitive comprehension, the mists suggest the ecological connection between air, water, and land.

Such fluid boundaries in turn characterize Marlow's first glimpse of Africa: "The edge of a colossal jungle, so dark-green as to be almost black, fringed with white surf, ran straight, like a ruled line, far, far away along a blue sea whose glitter was blurred by a creeping mist."[24] An active, personified nature confronts the technology and geography of imperialism. The phrase "like a ruled line" suggests the human science and industry, including carpentry, shipbuilding, cartography, and architecture, so instrumental to the nineteenth-century project of colonial conquest of which Marlow's mission belongs. A ruled line might be a chalk line, outline, or blueprint; in cartographic and administrative terms, it suggests that the colonized territories of ruled subjects are inscribed on the "large shining map, marked with all the colours of a rainbow"[25] that hangs on the wall at the Company offices. The clearly demarcated boundaries and distinct colors for each national project represented on the map contrast with the blurred shades and distorted edges of the actual colonized spaces. Idealized cartography of imperialism begins to show itself as incongruent with its spatial reality.

The "creeping mist" of the African coast is also one of several personifications of nature found throughout *Heart of Darkness.* As a persistent literary trope, these contribute to an overall ecological vision, a sense of the entire natural world as a living organism. In Marlow's depiction, the African wilderness has agency and a capacity for vocalization: "The bush around said nothing and would not let us look very far either."[26] "The bush began to howl."[27] At times, it becomes a full-fledged character and personified natural force, as when he wonders whether "the stillness on the face of the immensity looking at us two were meant as an appeal or as a menace."[28] Along with the biblical echo, such description recalls another mythic personification, the classical notion of the earth mother Gaia. Seeing the complex ecosystems of earth as an integrated whole and unified organism harkens back to this classical idea but also anticipates such later twentieth-century perspectives as the holistic science and environmental ethics combined in the Gaia hypothesis of James Lovelock, which of course also drew upon the mythic personification.[29]

Nineteenth-century geologists had much to do with shaping this perspective. From 1885 to 1908, the same years Conrad was visiting the Congo and composing *Heart of Darkness,* Austrian geologist Edouard Suess published his three-volume *Das Antlitz der Erde* (*The Face of the Earth*), which became a mainstay among geology textbooks for a generation. Like Conrad, Suess posited many ideas about the links between Europe and Africa, including the supercontinent of Gondwanaland. He coined the term "biosphere" to refer to the regions of the planet—namely land, water, and sky—in which all the interconnected processes of life take place. It is worth remembering that *Heart of Darkness* emerged during a scientific age that, in the wake of Charles Darwin, was informed by the emerging theories of modern ecology that emphasized the essential interconnectedness of all life.

Within that framework, the mists that hover over English marsh and African jungle in the first pages of Conrad's novella suggest the inherent universality of the water cycle. As compositional structure and biological factor, they join to frame the narrative of Marlow's tale and provide, like the historical parallels of Roman legions and English seadogs to contemporary colonial conquest, an early link between two distant climates and countries, an underlying sense of global interconnectedness. The mists demonstrate the ubiquity of water throughout the biosphere, and, as basis for English and African rivers joined by the Atlantic Ocean to form the "interminable waterway"[30] linking all parts of the globe, they demonstrate the interrelation of biology and geography, culture and psychology. While they might cast a gloomy pall of obscurity over the scene for some early readers, these mists and rivers suggest a unifying element of ecology, the water cycle that binds people, rivers, wildlife, and distant landscapes.[31]

The hydrologic aspect of Conrad's environment joins every person and location, from England's Thames to Africa's unnamed river, and of course the vast Atlantic Ocean in between. As part of the pattern of global conquest and human history, water—and rivers in particular—invoke parallel ecological and colonial histories. This is first established in the narrator's personification of the Thames as a faithful servant to a fading empire: "The old river in its broad reach rested unruffled at the decline of day, after ages of good service done to the race that peopled its banks, spread out in the tranquil dignity of a waterway leading to the uttermost ends of the earth. We looked at the venerable stream not in the vivid flush of a short day that comes and departs forever but in the august light of abiding memories."[32] The day is rapidly fading for that golden era of the seadogs Sir John Franklin, Sir Francis Drake, and other "great knights-errant of the sea," and of the entire naval and commercial establishment that ruled the waves for Britannia—"the adventurers and the settlers; kings' ships and the ships of men on 'Change; captains, admirals, the dark 'interlopers' of the Eastern trade, and the commissioned 'generals' of East India fleets."[33] All those that sailed this river are faint and fading memories, as despite the old adage, the sun quite literally sets on the British Empire and twilight descends around its capital city and the upper reaches of the Thames: "The sun set; the dusk fell on the stream, and lights began to appear along the shore."[34] The passage conveys the sense of the gradual decline and fall of British greatness. As loyal vassal and subaltern of colonial conquest, the Thames is nearing the end of its "service" to England and to the "ends" of colonialism.

Marlow's subsequent digression about the river as well as the swamps, forests, and encampments of Roman Britain resets the imperial clock and reframes the perspective of his listeners onboard the *Nellie.* As prelude to his tale of contemporary European invasion of Africa, he reminds them of the human and ecological conquest of Britain: "And this also . . . has been one of the dark places of the earth."[35] At this point, the "dark" suggests the untamed landscapes and uncivilized people of Britain in the eyes of Marlow and of the commander of a trireme that sails north: "Imagine him here, the very end of the world, a sea the color of lead, a sky the color of smoke, a kind of ship about as rigid as a concertina—and going up this river with stores, or orders, or what you like. Sandbanks, marshes, forests, savages—precious little to eat fit for a civilized man, nothing but Thames water to drink. . . . They were men enough to face the darkness."[36] As means of transportation and sustenance, as well as the cyclical process of history and empire, water continuously joins humankind to the environment and colonizer to colonized.

Soon after, the Thames is juxtaposed with the unnamed African river of Marlow's narrative. The word "Congo" never appears for river or region, a geographical anonymity that, like the unspecified people and continent, reflects the inequality of the colonial project. Instead, the river is described through the analogy of the charming snake, then ultimately as an "infernal stream, stream of darkness."[37] This is reiterated in the last glimpse at the English river in the novella's final line, suggesting the symbolic confluence between the two, as "the tranquil waterway leading to the uttermost ends of the earth flowed somber under an overcast sky—seemed to lead into the heart of an immense darkness."[38] The Thames, finally, does not merely hold dark memories of an uncivilized past; in its service to the modern project of imperialism, the river maintains an ominous global connection to the twin evils of cultural and environmental conquest. In Marlow's words, "the conquest of the earth which mostly means the taking it away from those who have a different complexion or slightly flatter noses than ourselves, is not a pretty thing when you look into it too much."[39]

Geologic

After water, the second largest component of the biosphere also receives prominent treatment in *Heart of Darkness.* The novel makes frequent reference to the land; earth, along with the terms "heart" and "darkness," is among the most repeated words in the novella, occurring forty-six times. Such repetition, whether in paradoxical remarks ("the earth seemed unearthly")[40] or personifying phrases ("may it last as long as the old earth keeps rolling!"),[41] helps establish it as dynamic character and natural presence, much like the oft-mentioned Kurtz, as an elusive focal point to the narrative. Such geologic personification effectively challenges the Company's notion that the land is simply a territory for conquest or target for aggressive resource extraction.

Some critics have questioned the novella's ecological consciousness due its lack of awareness of land, suggesting for instance that Marlowe's narrative becomes complicit in the colonial and ecological domination. Robert Marzec argues that Marlow deliberately ignores the land, so that, consequently, "the novel takes on an oppressive force characteristic of Western narratives that recoil from anything outside their domestic system of representation: the aesthetic and the political potential of the land of the other is simply eliminated."[42] Yet Marlow gradually displays both a growing concern for the unethical treatment of the landscape and a recognition of the limits to his understanding of the African environment. In his initial geographic descriptions, Marlow's perspective sees the land in the abstract terms of the colonizer's map, perhaps the most overt representation of what Jeffrey Meyers reads as the text's "Cartesian separation of the self from the natural world."[43] Marlow's boyhood penchant for geography seems to have led him directly to the "shining map" at company headquarters, which depicts the earth in the various hues of colonial conquest: "There was a vast amount of red—good to see at any time, because one knows that some real work is done in there, a deuce of a lot of blue, a little green, smears of orange, and, on the East Coast, a purple patch, to show where the jolly pioneers of progress drink the jolly lager beer. However, I wasn't going into any of these. I was going into the yellow. Dead in the center."[44] Marlow's perspective generally accepts this territorial mapping with a mixture of national pride and individual cynicism.

On the one hand, his view tends to uproot humans from their ecological contexts. He exclaims at one point, "The earth for us is a place to live in, where we must put up with sights, with sounds, with smells too, by Jove!"[45] Meyers, following the lead of Neil Evernden, sees this "erasure of their personal subjectivity and anxiety over reincorporation into the body of nature driv[ing] the seemingly motiveless atrocities that Kurtz and others commit."[46] On the other hand, this psychological and sensory disconnection from nature seems at odds with Marlow's growing sense of sympathy for the senseless harm being done to the land. Increasingly, he expresses a rich awareness and deepening ecological connection to the landscapes, as when he recalls how "The silence of the land went home to one's very heart—its mystery, its greatness, the amazing reality of its concealed life."[47] This conflicts with the ideal cartographic control and corporate efficiency dedicated to returning the greatest profit margins the land and its resources will yield. Not much further upriver, Marlow concedes an inability to understand the enigma of the landscape: "We were cut off from comprehension of our surroundings."[48] Such conflicting perspectives on the land suggest an attempt to reconcile modernity's competing impulses to dominate or be immersed in the biosphere. This problematic relationship of the individual to his environment forms the paradoxical core to Marlow's ultimate perception of Kurtz: "He had kicked himself loose of the earth—confound the man, he had kicked the very earth to pieces."[49] Kurtz's experience in Africa is thus transformed into fundamental questions about humanity's connection with or control over its natural surroundings.

Environmental domination is most vividly portrayed by direct attacks on the land itself. This occurs by military methodologies, then through techniques of engineering, demolition, and waste disposal. As Marlow makes his way down the African coast, one of the first sights he witnesses is the French man-of-war "shelling the bush . . . incomprehensible, firing into a continent."[50] The symbolic weight of this moment emphasizing humanity at war with the environment recurs twice across the text. First, at the lower station, Marlow witnesses what he calls the "objectless blasting" of the construction crews, and he makes a deliberate connection for his listeners and for Conrad's readers, saying how it "made me think suddenly of that ship of war I had seen firing into a continent. It was the same kind of ominous voice."[51] Similarly, the pilgrims traveling upriver on the steamer take aim and fire into the jungle as a show of force that seems to pit them against the land itself rather than any identifiable enemy. While Achebe noted, with good reason, the simplification or outright omission of African faces in the text, on an environmental level at least, such lack of human visibility achieves an effect of privileging the colonizers' exploitation of the wilderness rather than the people of Africa.

Where African identities do emerge in greater detail, they are strongly linked to the landscape. The clearest instance of this comes in the woman at the Inner Station, referred to by some critics as Kurtz's mistress, whose description establishes a reciprocal comparison between herself and the landscape. She appears "savage and superb, wild-eyed and magnificent. And in that hush that had fallen suddenly upon the whole sorrowful land, the immense wilderness, the colossal body of the fecund and mysterious life seemed to look at her, pensive, as though it had been looking at the image of its own tenebrous and passionate soul."[52]

She is the mirror image of the land, at least to European eyes, its core mystery and creative power reflected back on itself: "she stood looking at us without a stir, and like the wilderness itself, with an air brooding over an inscrutable purpose."[53] These brief but resonating depictions invite an ecofeminist reading or other interpretation that might, if at all possible, disentangle her from the essentializing male European gaze of Marlow. Whatever one sees projected upon her, the woman is a character who merits reading for her reflective link to the land itself, as well as her divided subject position with regard to the colonial power structure. She registers an emotional potency and localized agency while incorporating the foreign male’s coterminous desires for territorial dominion and sexual conquest. Her experience at the hands of Kurtz, and the corrupted imperial enterprise he represents, embodies the desirability and devastation of the African land itself.

Mistreatment of the earth also occurs as a seemingly routine byproduct of engineering techniques. The Belgian “pioneers of progress” cut into the earth with the regressive methodology and destructive effects of colonial development. Here, the treatment of African landscape parallels the treatment of African people. Marlow notices this first when he passes “a vast artificial hole,” the purpose of which “might have been connected with the philanthropic desire of giving the criminals something to do.”[54] The chain gang he has just passed “walked erect and slow, balancing small baskets of earth on their heads”: their overworked, emaciated bodies dissect and cart away an equally broken landscape. Marlow nearly falls into a ravine beside the station that he calls “a scar in the hillside,”[55] a phrase that carries connotations of intrusive injury suffered by the land. The medical metaphor also sets up the intense description of human suffering in the grove-of-death scene, where the bodies of the overworked and the dying seem to be piled up with no more care than the discarded and broken pipes in the rubbish heap.

The narrative renders clearly that the hierarchy of the Company enterprise inflicts damage on the bodies of the African landscape and people alike. However vague and illogical this image of forced labor and environmental destruction might be, it exists within a logical corporate structure, as evidenced by a description of the native subaltern charged with propelling their meaningless march: “Behind this raw matter one of the reclaimed, the product of the new forces at work, strolled despondently, carrying a rifle by its middle. He had a uniform jacket with one button off, and seeing a white man on the path, hoisted his weapon to his shoulder with alacrity.”[56] Even the possibility that this public works project might be born of good intentions and for some rehabilitative purpose offers little consolation within a repressive power structure that renders certain local people complicit in the brutal domination of their own culture and landscape.

The description of human suffering in the grove of death solidifies their link to the landscape: “Black shapes crouched, lay, sat between the trees leaning against the trunks, clinging to the earth. . . . They were not enemies, they were not criminals, they were nothing earthly now.”[57] The value of these overworked and wasted bodies to the Company seems about the same, as human beings and the earth itself receive parallel treatments under the colonial presence. Later, the remark on the Eldorado Exploring Expedition likens the rapacious mining of the landscape for fossil ivory to an even more aggressive assault on the body: "To tear treasure out of the bowels of the land was their desire, with no more moral purpose at the back of it than there is in burglars breaking into a safe."[58] The doubling metaphors link the notions of physical vulnerability and aggressive criminality.

After leaving all the human devastation and earthly destruction of the grove of death, Marlow first meets the chief accountant. In remarking on the man's kempt clothing and style, Marlow's rather backhanded compliment of his first contact effectively points to the environmental contexts of colonialism: "I respected the fellow. Yes. I respected his collars, his vast cuffs, his brushed head. His appearance was certainly that of a hairdresser's dummy but in the great demoralisation of the land he had kept up his appearance."[59] The ambiguity at the heart of the observation evinces an awareness of the two-way relationship of humans and their natural surroundings. Given all that Kurtz has witnessed just thirty miles into his upriver journey, "the great demoralization of the land" seems to be not just the impact of Africa on one refined European sensibility, as the skull-measuring doctor at corporate headquarters would have one believe; rather, the phrase can also be read to refer to the unethical effects of European intrusion on the African landscape that are facilitated by such a refined and calculating presence as the kempt accountant. The pioneering eco-critic Lawrence Buell has argued that in order to bring about a shift in human concern for the land and a recommitment to the environment it is necessary to ensure the "extension of moral and sometimes even legal standing to the nonhuman world."[60] It marks a first step towards raising human consciousness and bringing humans back in line with the natural world. Marlow's equivocal phrasing does as much by advancing the observation that the African landscape is itself mistreated and demoralized from having been exploited for monetary gain and territorial power. The success of both processes depends on doing precisely the opposite of what Buell recommends, of stripping the land of its moral status as well as its physical resources.

Zoologic

While the human presence and impact, especially of the foreigner, is evident in the African wilderness, *Heart of Darkness* presents the flora and fauna of the continent in relative scarcity. The dearth of wildlife has upset expectations of readers past and present who had grown accustomed to abundant images of African wildlife in everything from Victorian hunting memoirs and modernist novels to documentary films. As Meyers notes, "the myriad species of African wildlife do not appear in this narrative of Africa, not even mosquitoes."[61] But when plants and animals do show up, they contribute significantly to the colonial subtext. Jungle trees and vegetation do make an appearance, "but these are not individual species, just a solid undifferentiated mass."[62] In this anonymity, they resemble the seldom specified African people.

Marlow's descriptions of plant life, if they do not offer Linnaean classifications, relate a hierarchal and politicized version of Edenic nature: "Going up that river was like traveling back to the earliest beginnings of the world, when vegetation rioted on the earth and the big trees were kings."[63] Given the Central African setting, the royal reference gives a tacit allusion to Belgium's King Leopold, whose national agenda and commercial interests are ultimately driving the enterprise in which Marlow has enlisted. It reiterates a prior suggestion that these lord it over an unruly and potentially volatile kingdom: "The great wall of vegetation, an exuberant and entangled mass of trunks, branches, leaves, boughs, festoons, motionless in the moonlight, was like a rioting invasion of soundless life, a rolling wave of plants, piled up, crested, ready to topple over the creek, to sweep every little man of us out of his little existence."[64]

This powerful hold of the great trees is also a tenuous one, considering how Leopold's exploitation of the Congo by the 1890s depended on his monopoly of the global market for rubber. Tree tapping and plantation activity for that forest resource grew exponentially in the final decade of the century, chiefly in response to the growing European demand for bicycle and automobile tires.[65] Therefore, the arborous monarchs Marlow sees looming over the African interior are themselves subjects to a more distant ruler, one whose political power manifests itself through technological and, ultimately, commercial control of colonial territory.

A similar sense of instability emerges with the first actual animal in the text, the nuisance hippopotamus at the Central Station: "There was an old hippo that had the bad habit of getting out on the bank and roaming at night over the station grounds."[66] This portrait of a rebellious colonial subject contrasts with the image of more peaceful and poetic coexistence wherein "[o]n silvery sandbanks hippos and alligators sunned themselves side by side."[67] The harmonious zoological image suggests again a primeval time that predates human, or at least western, intrusion.

Besides these few exceptions, animals do not otherwise appear in literal form; instead, they typically occur as metaphor, as when the steamboat is "hauled up on the slope like the carcass of some big river animal."[68] Or the first time the cartographic image of the great African river is described as "resembling an immense snake uncoiled, with its head in the sea, its body at rest curving afar over a vast country, and its tail lost in the depths of the land."[69] And also, when he sees it in the map hanging in company headquarters: "And the river was there—fascinating—deadly—like a snake."[70] This doubling of visual and metaphoric representation exhibits a sense of the layered distance between humans and nature. The image of the boyhood map is, significantly, depicted in a doubly framed perspective, perceived through a shop window on Fleet Street that suggests the transformation of the African environment by British media and commercial interests.

At the same time, however, Marlow infiltrates the cultural divide by inserting himself directly into the equation when he notes how that first map of Africa had "fascinated me as a snake would a bird—a silly little bird."[71] The inherent power of a Cartesian European bird's-eye view of Africa is destabilized and potentially overturned by the insertion of the qualifiers "silly" and "little" which effectively rewrite the predator-prey relationship and, by extension, destabilize the power of colonizer over colonized territory. It appears the snake might, after all, get the better of the silly little bird. Whatever the outcome, Marlow has written himself into the ecological system that was distorted by the colonial map.

One species of animal is referenced reductively and almost exclusively as a commodity in the system of colonial resource extraction. Ivory, the major animal-based economic resource of the Congo Free State, is one of the most commonly recurring words in the text. Marlow consciously remarks on its dialogic repetition at the Central Station, giving deliberate animation to the signifier by associating it simultaneously with the ritual of religious devotion and the stench of mortal decomposition: "The word 'ivory' rang in the air, was whispered, was sighed. You would think they were praying to it. A taint of imbecile rapacity blew through it all, like a whiff from some corpse."[72] It is a part of the air, perceived through multiple senses and on multiple levels. It is the major objective of commerce that parallels the natural flow of the river: "a stream of manufactured goods—rubbishy cottons, beads, and brass wire—set off into the depths of darkness and in return came a precious trickle of ivory."[73] In turn, its currency translates into the sole emotional obsession for the pilgrims: "The only real feeling was a desire to get appointed to a trading post where ivory was to be had, so that they could earn percentages."[74] Marlow shows how he quickly comes under the spell of this directive in his anticipation of journeying to the region upriver: "I could see a little ivory coming out from there, and I had heard Mr. Kurtz was in there."[75] The balanced grammar of the sentence foreshadows the merger of the materially obsessed Kurtz with the very commodity he seeks: "The wilderness had patted him on the head, and behold it was like a ball—an ivory ball."[76] The image ties directly to European consumerism, since, as McCarthy notes, billiard balls were high on the list of finished goods derived from the African ivory trade.[77]

With so much ivory—"Heaps of it, stacks of it. The old mud shanty was bursting with it"[78]— it is no wonder there are so few elephants. Perhaps this best explains the overall dearth of references to the animal itself. Their tusks have been so prized and their species so butchered that their scarcity can only be represented by metonymic substitution. The metaphor keeps readers' encounter with the actual creature always distanced or deferred, just as Marlow does not see the animal on his journey upriver, presumably due to its being so overhunted. He suggests as much when, still describing the overflowing shanty, he speculates on the species' possible extinction: "You would think there was not a single tusk left either above or below ground in the whole country."[79] Graham Huggan and Helen Tiffin describe elephants, much like Chinua Achebe said of Africans, as having the status of "absent referents"[80] in *Heart of Darkness*, while Jeffrey Mathes McCarthy remarks on the "word elephant having been hunted to extinction."[81]

This is almost, though not entirely, the case. There is in fact one appearance of the word in the text. It occurs in the description of the African woman whose adornments suggest something of her wealth and status in the tribe and her intimate link to the natural world when Marlow recalls how "she must have had the value of several elephant tusks upon her."[82] The moment illustrates the woman's close affinity with the African environment (particularly as seen through Marlow's European eyes), restraining her natural power by framing her in the male gaze and situating her in the continental network of goods and trade. That economy, in turn, relies on the diminished and dismembered source of ivory. The overhunted species is at last granted some linguistic visibility, albeit partial and minimal. The word "elephant" assumes only a subordinate, adjectival, and comparative form, modifying its own missing parts to underscore the economic value of the trade beads and charms that adorn the woman. This grammatical chain of dismembered parts and displaced values encircles the woman and the several elephants whose value adorns her, mirroring the economic system to which all are joined as well. Of course, no actual elephant ever appears. Severed appendages, not living animals, are what translate into currency and commodity, as the zoological is reappraised and reproduced as the monetary.

The ecological vision of *Heart of Darkness* developed at least in part from Conrad's own firsthand experience of the Congo Free State in the 1890s. He referred to the work, along with "An Outpost of Progress," as part of the "loot" he brought back from Central Africa,[83] a term that suggests a literary value even while it acknowledges complicity in environmental and imperial exploitation. The term more famously appears in his essay "Geography and Some Explorers," when Conrad recalls his realization that the Belgian enterprise in the Congo was "the vilest scramble for loot that ever disfigured the history of human conscience and geographical exploration."[84] As he wrote to editor William Blackwood, Conrad composed the novella with a conscious, deliberate motive for social justice: "The title I am thinking of is 'The Heart of Darkness' but the narrative is not gloomy. . . . The criminality of inefficiency and pure selfishness when tackling the civilizing work in Africa is a justifiable idea."[85] These pre- and post-composition remarks suggest a perspective on Africa that takes in the human and environmental costs of the European colonial enterprise. The text presents "inefficiency and selfishness" in equal measure as it portrays European treatment of African landscapes and people. The narrative style and structure of the novel frequently demonstrate the interconnected nature of cultural systems and ecosystems. *Heart of Darkness* in effect presents a merged vision of colonial and environmental depredation that is best understood through the recent fusion of these theoretical approaches; reciprocally, it can help us better understand the usefulness of such a theoretical alloy. Like the novella, the argument of this new interdisciplinarity is of the necessity of restoring a holistic vision. Read with such a comprehensive view of nature and culture, the story ultimately becomes, as Conrad described it, "something quite on another plane than an anecdote of a man who went mad in the Centre of Africa."[86]

Postcolonial ecocriticism affords a binocular view that can take in the full vista of Conrad's account of human and natural resource abuse in the Congo. It offers a useful approach to a text that interweaves the strands of colonialism with those of environmental degradation. The novella presents these strands as an organic whole, demonstrating how imperialism functions as much on the landscape and natural resources as on the people and cultural resources of Central Africa. *Heart of Darkness* effectively articulates this new theoretical partnership through a portrayal of imperialism and its consequences to the flora, fauna, people, and landscape of the continent. Its narrative design, figurative language, and geographic descriptions assert a sense of the inseparability of nature and culture. The ecological picture that develops is one that encompasses the biological and the economic processes, the human and the environmental, showing how Conrad's novella, over a century from its first publication, retains its relevance amid the increasing complexity of the global landscape.

The Elephant in the Text

Toward a Post-Humanist Reading of *Heart of Darkness*

WILLIAM ATKINSON

I: Haze

Shortly before the tale begins, the narrator of *Heart of Darkness* tells us that to Marlow "the meaning of an episode was not inside like the kernel but outside, enveloping the tale which brought it out as a glow brings out a haze in the likeness of one of those misty halos that, sometimes, are made visible by the spectral illumination of moonshine."[1] In a gloss on this figure, Ian Watt distinguishes between centripetal and centrifugal narratives. The former invite the reader to look inside the story for its meaning, whereas centrifugal stories, such as Marlow's, "make the reader go outside it in search of a circumambient universe of meanings that are not normally visible."[2] We could take these meanings as being inaccessible to the quotidian world, more or less numinous. Or they might be inaccessible because they are not born within a symbol but sit beyond the symbolic. I propose to take a more prosaic approach. If the meaning of the story is outside and therefore not to be found within the text, then *Heart of Darkness* becomes something of a riddle, and as Borges asks, what is the one word that is never used in a riddle? The word never used is the answer to the riddle. There are a number of words that the text never utters—Congo, Brussels, King Leopold—that could be taken to be the answer. Much of the late-twentieth-century scholarship that put the story back into its original African context can be taken to have resolved the riddle. However, while Marlow never names names, he is *in* Brussels, *in* the Congo, working *for* Leopold. And the narrator has told us that the meaning is not *in* the story. So we need to double up the riddle. The meaning of the tale is not to be found in the narrative, but standing just beyond it, in the haze that it lights up. The question is now this: what is evidenced *by* the text but is not *in* the text?

Five men are on the deck of the *Nellie.* The accountant has taken out a box of ivory dominoes. That the moneyman should be toying, playing with them is surely significant. It is the play, the jouissance of capital that drives Conrad's dark tale. And the sentence gestures toward the moment later in the account when the narrator tells us that the wilderness, caressingly, toyingly, had patted Kurtz on the head, "and behold it was like a ball—an ivory ball."[3] The story is about Kurtz, and Kurtz has become the commodity that is his overwhelming preoccupation, his fetish. Ivory is potentially money, which itself probably enables something else—in infinite regress. What it fails to represent is what it comes from: elephants. Human beings have always been more interested in ivory than in elephants, so much so that the elephant becomes a very absent referent behind, or before, its ivory.[4]

II: Ivory

When Conrad landed in the Congo in the summer of 1890, the Free State's principal export was ivory. As such, it was part of a long history that placed Africa at the center of a world trade in the commodity. Even before the first millennium BCE, ivory had been a key luxury item in China, India, Europe, and in Africa itself, where Egyptian royal tombs have revealed considerable quantities of ivory goods.[5] Initially, the Asian source was the indigenous elephant. But elephants soon became very rare in China[6] and were preserved as work animals in South Asia. So the Asian market started looking to Africa, and merchants took advantage of the monsoon to take ships back and forth between the coasts of East Africa and West India, with stop-offs on the Persian Gulf. South Asian carvers found they preferred African ivory to that from the Asian animals. The tusks were larger, and the ivory tended to be softer and therefore easier to work.

Ivory was greatly valued in Europe from the earliest times. In Athens, it was considered a medium fit to represent a goddess's complexion. So the skin of the statue of Athena in the Parthenon was of ivory. Pygmalion carved his ideal woman from the same material, the dead elephant's shadow quickening his Galatea. Elephants were found in North Africa, but there was pressure on the populations from early times. Pliny the Elder expressed concern in 77 CE, and well he might since elephants had been wiped out in Syria towards the middle of the first millennium BCE.[7] Roman demand was even more exigent. So many elephants were slaughtered for their ivory and for the delight of the crowds in the amphitheaters of Rome and Byzantium that, by the end of the sixth century, there were no more elephants to be found north of the Sahara. In the middle ages, ivory became ever more rare in Western Europe.[8]

Ivory was so heavily traded to Asia out of East Africa that elephants were disappearing from the coast by the fifteenth century. Collectors began to push inland. Meanwhile, Europeans began sailing to West Africa, where they took ivory as well as slaves and gold from the coast; the memory is preserved in the name of a West African state—Côte d'Ivoire (Ivory Coast). In the first quarter of the eighteenth century, Dutch and English ships carried away twenty-five hundred tons of ivory,[9] the tusks of more than forty-three thousand elephants (allowing sixty-five pounds per tusk). But pressure soon built up on the supply. The Vili people of Loango, above the mouth of the Congo, had been trading with Europeans since the end of the sixteenth century, at which time they could find ivory in their own country. A hundred years later, they had to organize expeditions of three months or more further upriver.[10]

The economics of the trade took a major turn at the very end of the eighteenth century. Up until this time, ivory was a rare and precious material, and even more value was added by highly skilled craftsmen who transformed it into unique luxury items. In 1799, a U.S. patent was filed for an ivory comb–making machine. "From now on," writes John Frederick Walker, "tusks were fed like logs into indefatigable machines."[11] Industrial production meant that luxury items could be produced in almost infinite quantity. But without a substantial and reliable supply, the machines would soon fall silent. Indeed, it is unlikely that they would have been built had that supply not been in place.

Africans had been killing elephants, primarily for meat, since time immemorial. But their techniques were dangerous and did not provide ivory at anything like an industrial level. The Portuguese Duarte Lopez in 1587 describes the Congolese people digging pits to catch elephants. Broad at the top and narrow at the bottom, they were covered with the such leaves and grasses as would attract the animals. George Frederick Kunz reports that travelers in the late nineteenth and early twentieth century described the same technique in operation in their own day.[12] Such a procedure would not take many animals, if only because a single pit could not be used again until the elephant had died and been butchered. Kunz also cites Belgian ethnographic reports of weighted lances being suspended above elephant trails that were released when an animal passed beneath. An illustration from an early twentieth-century Congolese line drawing on ivory shows men dropping heavy spears from trees onto elephants that others are driving toward the trap with drums.[13] A riskier approach, again illustrated in indigenous art, is to run behind the elephant and hamstring it with a long-bladed knife.[14] The simplest way of hunting elephants is with spears, and a one-franc postage stamp issued by the Congo Free State in 1894 shows a single African about to throw a spear at an elephant.[15] The line drawings make it very clear that hunting elephant is dangerous: in three out of five scenes, the elephant has a hunter in its trunk and is about to dash him to the ground.

A late-nineteenth-century gourd from the Kongo people shows an important development. The African is about to shoot the elephant with a gun.[16] While men sought to trap elephants in huge pits or kill them with spears, they had but small advantage over their prey. With guns, everything changed. John A. Van Couvering writes, "Almost as soon as muskets were put into the hands of West African native hunters, [. . .] the loxodont herds in the coastal regions and interior agricultural districts were quickly reduced to a few stragglers."[17] West Africans seem to have got hold of long-barreled "Dane guns" as early as the end of the eighteenth century.[18] The industrial machines cranked up soon after, and the European and American appetite grew with the century.

While ivory was not cheap, objects made of ivory were now luxuries that most middle-class people could afford: brush, knife, and teapot handles, toothpicks, tablecloth sweepers, shaving brushes, pistol grips, buttons, cufflinks, letter folders and letter openers, dominoes (such as the accountant was playing with), dice, gambling chips, cigarette cases and cigarette holders. The cutlery trade had grown with the shift to dining à la russe, separate courses served consecutively, each with its own set of flatware. In 1878, Joseph Rodgers and Sons of Sheffield were using twenty-six tons of ivory every year.[19] And that was just one manufacturer. Ivory was used in high-tech items too: telegraph transmitter keypads (it insulates against electric current), urethral syringes, artificial legs and noses, fracture pins, and hip replacements. It even featured in various parts of H. G. Wells's fictional time machine. And there were the piano keys and billiard balls.

A billiard table called for only three balls. But snooker, invented in 1875, requires twenty-three balls. Pool uses sixteen. As the nineteenth century wore on, the piano in the middle-class parlor became ever more common. By the end of the century, some half a million were being manufactured every year, and those that used ivory veneer required one-and-a-half pounds of it. In 1913, the US was importing nearly 200 tons of ivory for piano keys alone.[20] Clearly, capitalist production could use as much ivory as could be found. The growth of British imports alone gives an idea of demand: between 1800 and 1820, about 125 tons a year were making their way to the United Kingdom; in the mid-1830s, the figure had risen to 275 tons;[21] between 1850 and 1910, the average was 500 tons a year.[22] By the end of the nineteenth century, the United States was the world's largest consumer of ivory. The business was centered in Connecticut, where the two leading companies processed well over 1,000 tons in the dozen years between 1891 and 1903.[23] With the average Congolese tusk now reduced to a mere forty pounds,[24] this meant the death of more than thirty thousand elephants. Was such devastation sustainable?

Africa as a whole seems to have been widely regarded as inexhaustible. When one region was emptied out, another was found. When West African elephant herds were thinned over the course of the eighteenth century, collection shifted to Cameroon.[25] To the east, ivory acquired in the Mombasa hinterland fell from almost 44 tons in 1849 to barely 8 in 1887,[26] an almost six-fold decline in less than forty years. In 1858, Richard Burton in Unyamwezi, south of Victoria Nyanza, reported that elephants were common. By 1871, Henry Morton Stanley found otherwise.[27] During the same period, the area south of the Zambezi was hunted out.[28] By the 1870s, people were looking to Maniema, an area new to the trade. It is the region to the south of Kisangani/Stanley Falls (the Inner Station) and was spoken of as a place where tusks were so common that they were used as doorposts and prices were ridiculously low.[29]

The Zanzibari traders, Tippu Tip preeminent amongst them, began the exploitation of Central Africa, using slave labor to carry the tusks east from Nyangwe to the entrepôt of Zanzibar. Nyangwe, about four hundred kilometers south of Stanley Falls, has been described as "one of the greatest market places in Africa. . . . All roads led to Nyangwe."[30] But the Zanzibaris, coming from the east, soon encountered King Leopold's Belgians, coming from the west. The Belgians reached an accommodation with Tippu Tip in the late 1880s, but in 1892 fighting broke out for complete control of the ivory trade. By the middle of the 1890s, the Belgians had prevailed, and "this frontier region, pioneered by the Zanzibaris, was gradually sucked into a new commercial and political domain oriented to the west."[31] With its river steamers, King Leopold's company was able to transport large quantities of ivory to the coast without slave labor, which was inefficient and slow, as Conrad makes very clear in his account of Marlow's overland trek to the Central Station.

Extraordinarily enough, ivory prices had remained stable for much of the second half of the nineteenth century. But between 1895 and 1905, the price of ivory doubled.[32] It would appear that the trade was reaching a crisis. And let us remind ourselves that Conrad's story was first published in 1899 and then again in 1902. Conrad referred to it in a letter to William Blackwood as very much "of our time."[33] It is unlikely that he had a crisis in the ivory trade in mind, even though from the 1860s a number of observers were proposing what would now be called "peak ivory." An item in the *Journal of the Society of Arts* in 1864 even calculates the number of elephants that were dying in order to satisfy England's consumption alone—8,333 a year.[34] Robert Friedel, writing in 1983, describes "the ivory problem" as "largely a myth."[35] Myth or no myth, the largest extant tusks in the world—236 and 228 pounds, known as the Kilimanjaro tusks—were taken from an elephant that was killed in 1898. The very fact that none larger has ever been found makes the year an important marker in the history of ivory—and of elephants. That Friedel feels able to dismiss the ivory crisis as a myth is to a great extent because of the subject of his study, *Pioneer Plastic: The Making and Selling of Celluloid.* A substitute for ivory was being actively sought at least as early as the 1860s.[36] By the 1890s, synthetic ivories—celluloid—began to gain acceptance.

In the early twentieth century, plastics rapidly replaced ivory in all but the most deluxe circumstances. The best known of these early plastics was Bakelite, invented in 1907 by Leo Baekeland, a Belgian chemist. It is hard to know how long the ivory trade could have continued before the last elephant in Africa would have given up its tusks. As it was, the Elephant got a last-minute reprieve—the Elephant with a capital E, not the estimated 44,000 thousand individuals that were slaughtered every year to satisfy global demand between 1850 and 1914[37]—a total of almost three million.[38]

Heart of Darkness quite explicitly concerns itself with ivory. "The word ivory rang in the air, was whispered, was sighed. You would think they were praying to it."[39] Ivory is a truly fetishized commodity. We are told in "An Outpost of Progress" that the hut where the trade goods and the ivory are kept is called the fetish. *Heart of Darkness* is in no way evasive about what the white men are there for. Nor is it particularly squeamish about how they treat the Africans involved. But when we ask where ivory comes from, the text is silent. Where are the elephants? So far as *Heart of Darkness* knows, the last one may just as well have died in 1890. In this story, ivory is gathered, it is collected; it could grow on trees for all we hear of the animals who must die in giving it up. The accountant at the Central Station tells Marlow that Kurtz is in charge of a trading post "in the true ivory country"[40]—Maniema. And the Manager later reveals that there's "Lots of it—prime sort—lots."[41] So, as Marlow concludes, Kurtz "had collected, bartered, swindled or stolen more ivory than all the other agents together."[42] But where does he get it from? Marlow speaks of "Kurtz grubbing for ivory in the wretched bush,"[43] as if he were wandering about alone with a digging stick. No glamour here. Nor much when we hear how he took some of it from the Russian, at gunpoint. The Russian himself had been given it by the chief of the village near his house, downriver. Presumably Kurtz traded beads and cloth for ivory from the villagers. When he ran out of trade goods, "he raided the country" with the help of a local tribe over whom he had established ascendancy. There are plenty of cartridges left. The Russian calls it an "ivory hunt," not an elephant hunt. The cartridges are to be used against the natives, to force them to give up their ivory.[44] Constantly, the real origin of this pale, smooth commodity is deferred. The word *elephant* occurs just once. "A wild and gorgeous apparition of a woman": she is wearing brass leggings and gauntlets, "innumerable necklaces of glass beads on her neck. . . . She must have had the value of several elephant tusks upon her."[45] The elephant is in no way present either as itself or even as ivory. The ivory has been exchanged for other luxury items. And the word "elephant" is functioning as a modifier of tusk, not as a substantive.

Where do the natives get it? The text is silent, and we might assume they collect it from the corpses of elephants that have died of natural causes, gathering it up rather as they might collect sticks and fallen branches for firewood.

The forest will make more wood, but elephants do not shed their tusks and do not give them up unless they are dead. The manager dismisses Kurtz's ivory as "mostly fossil."[46] "It was no more fossil than I am," says Marlow, "but they call it fossil when it is dug up."[47] The Africans sometimes bury it, presumably to keep it from the likes of Kurtz.[48] Earlier, the Manager acknowledged that Kurtz's ivory was of the best, so he is using the word "fossil" to disparage the man, but the effect is again to suggest that ivory does not come from anything that has been alive in the recent past. But as we have seen, Africans hunted elephants. The ivory was coming from very recently killed animals, animals almost certainly killed by Africans.[49]

The text's silence on the subject of elephants is strange. There is no reason to exclude elephants from the story. Everyone knew where ivory came from. People were worried that the elephant population might not survive the depredations of the trade. In British colonies, tusks weighing less than sixty pounds per pair were becoming contraband.[50] In 1910, a similar ordinance came into effect in the Belgian Congo[51]—by which time, rubber was the key commodity. Furthermore, elephants were becoming popular animals.[52] Not so strange is that *Heart of Darkness*'s silence regarding elephants has been so little remarked upon. Two exceptions in particular stand out. Jeffrey Myers writes, "While 'ivory' seems to be everywhere in this text, the elephants from which the tusks are severed do no appear at all."[53] Jeffrey Mathes McCarthy wryly observes, "the elephant in the room, for all the novel's talk of ivory, is the distinct lack of elephants."[54] Both of these scholars approach the text from an ecocritical perspective. They are explicitly distancing themselves from a humanist anthropocentrism that sees the story as being largely about conflicts between human beings and between human cultures.[55]

III: Africans

More than thirty-five years ago, Chinua Achebe accused Conrad of being "a bloody racist."[56] Having no truck with Marlow's vaunted sympathy for the African workers, he writes, "Marlow comes through to us not only as a witness of truth, but as one holding those advanced and humane views appropriate to the English liberal tradition which required all Englishmen of decency to be deeply shocked by the atrocities in Bulgaria or the Congo of King Leopold of the Belgians or wherever."[57] Achebe himself had been educated in that same liberal humanist tradition but as an African was deeply sensitive to the racism manifested in *Heart of Darkness*. The critical community ignored the issue of race for so long because "white racism against Africa is such a normal way of thinking that its manifestations go completely unremarked."[58] The kind of active racism of which Achebe convicts Conrad was probably not very widespread in the academy of 1975, but the critical community for whom *Heart of Darkness* was a cultural beacon, a high point in the canon of literature written in English, had certainly been overlooking the casual and unquestioned racism that underlies the novella's representation of Africans. Students of Conrad, writes Achebe, coolly reduce Africa to "a metaphysical battlefield devoid of all recognizable humanity."[59] The novel, he declares, is "a story in which the very humanity of black people is called into question."[60] For Achebe, this was a profound failing. If great literature celebrates the values of humanism, as he seems to believe, any text that excludes oneself and one's people would deserve exclusion from a humanist canon.

After Achebe, nothing was quite the same. The issue of race would not go away and is now part of everyone's reading of the text. The consensus of critical opinion—mostly white, or course—is that Achebe is right but overstates his case. Having perceived the text's racism, he could see little else and regarded all the Africans in the story as equally dehumanized. But there is an important difference between those who are Kurtz's followers and all the rest.

"Rebels! What would be the next definition I was to hear," asks Marlow when the Russian explains the heads on the posts surrounding Kurtz's house.[61] "There had been enemies"—the men whose camp a French man-of-war was shelling from off the coast;[62] there had been "criminals," ganged up in chains;[63] and there were the "workers," whom Marlow sees reduced to a cluster of acute angles and left to die in a clump of shade.[64] And there are those "cannibals" with their mysterious restraint. "They had been engaged for six months [. . .] and of course, as long as there was a piece of paper written over in accordance with some farcical law or other made down the river, it didn't enter anybody's head to trouble how they would live."[65] The piece of paper, the law, has transformed them from anonymous Africans to Marlow's "cannibals," men he can work with and with whom he can exchange a word or two of English. The law, such as it is, finds a name and a place for them, includes them, albeit at the extreme margin of Western civil life. The question of inclusion and exclusion has been exhaustively examined by Giorgio Agamben, who writes that "the fundamental categorical pair of Western politics is not that of friend/enemy but that of bare life/political existence, *zoë/bios,* exclusion/inclusion."[66] Once contracted, Marlow's "cannibals" move from bare life to a minimal political existence. This is not to say that their own culture is without political reality, but its political reality is not acknowledged by Europe. It has no points of communication, no common principles of documentation or of juridical reality.

Marlow's expressions of outrage regarding rebels, criminals, and workers show that he sees clearly what is going on. There cannot be any rebels or criminals unless there is something to rebel against or a legal system to contravene. The rebels may not know that they are rebelling or that there's anything to rebel against, but the state knows rebels when it sees them; the criminals may not know what laws they have broken, but ignorance of the law is no defense. Labeling men draws them into the realm of western "political existence," whether they like it or not, and they can be controlled, legally punished, or killed. Farce is based upon characters acting in ignorance of a state of affairs of which other characters and the audience are fully aware. So "farcical" is precisely the right word for the laws made down the river. The "cannibals" know nothing of such laws or their meaning, so they are operating within a farce.[67] From the pilgrims' point of view, and possibly Marlow's, too, the "cannibals" are marginal to the European political and moral system. But before they can be marginalized, they must at the very least be seen and acknowledged from that system, from civil life. In order to be marginalized, they have to be briefly included—the better to be excluded.

As the steamer and its passengers move ever deeper into the heart of darkness, it moves away from political existence into bare life. The forest, nature itself, is represented as a single bare life: "the amazing reality of its concealed life,"[68] "could we handle that dumb thing or would it handle us? I felt how big, how confoundedly big was that thing that couldn't talk and perhaps was deaf as well."[69] One of the perennial features that western thinking finds to distinguish humans from animals is that the latter can't talk. Another, probably emanating from the same observation, is that they have no political life, only bare life. The animal may have some intention, but it is "inscrutable." All the adjectives that Leavis so deprecated—"impenetrable," "implacable," "hidden," "incomprehensible" —are exact. Conrad is not fumbling for the right word, not groping about in a semantic fog or generating any "hypnotic stupor."[70] Bare life is that whereof we cannot know and therefore cannot speak. Marlow often feels "its mysterious stillness watching" him.[71] What it makes of what it sees cannot be known because it does not speak.[72] If it did, it would no doubt be like the lion that Wittgenstein imagines: "If a lion could talk, we could not understand him."[73] The lion's experience of the world is so alien to ours that we would not understand its terms of reference, its base experience of life. In due course, "the bush began to howl. [. . .] I saw vague forms of men running bent double, leaping, gliding, distinct, incomplete, evanescent."[74] The people he sees are part of the wilderness and only nominally real human beings. Later, a group of men appear, "as though they had come up from the ground. . . . And as if by enchantment streams of human beings, of naked human beings with spears in their hands, with bows, with shields, with wild glances and savage movements, were poured into the clearing by the dark-faced and pensive forest."[75] These Africans, whom Marlow never speaks with, never really approaches, are one with the forest, are pure, bare life. Kurtz himself is also one with the wilderness, which drew him to its breast.[76] When Marlow comes upon him, he rises from the ground, "like a vapour exhaled from the earth."[77]

There is no law here, farcical or otherwise. There is only raw life and power. This part of Conrad's tale is not a story out of civil life. The text acknowledges as much when the narrator writes of "this narrative that seemed to shape itself without human lips."[78] Achebe would come straight back and say that Conrad is representing the Congolese as not human. But they are not necessarily the worse for that. The novella's declared human beings are a sorry lot. Kurtz's humanity is unclear. We may well read him as having been dehumanized by an entirely human obsession, by the ivory fetish—the commodity at the heart of darkness: ivory, then rubber, copper, gold, diamonds, coltan. All the horrors that have been visited upon the people of the Congo—forced labor, rape, mutilation, mass murder—have devolved from other people's desire for these commodities. We have learned to use *Heart of Darkness* to remind ourselves of such horrors.

IV: Elephants

There is a hippopotamus living near the Central Station, and it makes a practice of coming ashore at night. During the day, it lives, largely invisible, in the river. It can be scarcely more visible at night; nonetheless, when they hear it blundering about, the pilgrims regularly open up at it. They regard such a response as entirely appropriate when an "incomprehensible" entity from the forest, from the realm of the "hidden," blunders across into the not-yet-quite-civil space of the station. But the pilgrims always fail to kill the animal just as they fail to enact the "glorious slaughter" of Kurtz's followers in the bush.[79] In this, they are like the French warship that fires into the bush to no effect or the blasting that leaves no mark on the cliff face.[80] Bare life and human life in this narrative are incommensurable, so there is no communication between them. They are shadow realms with regard to each other.

Elephants, unlike the hippo, remain just outside the text. They cannot be said to be hidden because they are not fully manifested. But their ivory has a strong textual presence. Once separated from the elephant, the tusk becomes ivory and a commodity. As a tusk, it is part of bare nature; as ivory, it is part of the human world. When Marlow compares Kurtz's head to ivory, it is to an ivory ball, a product of human manufacture. The text, like the culture that produced it, prefers not to think about ivory and elephants as part of a single organism. Elephants are excluded from *bios,* from human life; tusks, ivory, are included.[81] Dr W. S. Rainsford, a one-time elephant hunter, shows why the entire Congo ivory project depended on this separation. In 1909, he wrote about a epiphanic moment: "I should not greatly care to kill any more elephants. They are too big, too old, and too wise to classed any more as game. As I stood by the side of that vast fallen bulk I realized I had extinguished a life perhaps three times as old as my own. What had that great beast not seen and survived? What comings and goings of the tribes? What changes among the petty bands of men? It was probably a full-grown elephant when Livingstone first resolutely set his face towards Africa's unknown interior. I felt small and a little guilty."[82]

Quite a lot is going on in this short passage. Africans themselves are already humanized. The "comings and goings of the tribes" are clearly something important—something worth seeing. Rainsford moves on to bring elephants within the human story and thereby give them value. He is not moved—or does not expect to move his reader—by thinking about the generations of elephants the dead animal may have seen. He does not see the elephant as what it is but values it for what it has seen of humanity, and particularly for its connection with the sainted Livingstone, a man more humane and therefore more human than most. The elephant is almost one of us. It is no longer other, so we can feel for it and with it. He has included the elephant within the circle of human sympathy. The elephant is a creature entirely of bare life. In watching the comings and goings of men, it enters the realm of human life.

Marlow's response to the men in the grove of death works the same issue of inclusion and exclusion. In some ways, he shows less feeling for them than Rainsford does for his dead elephant. Marlow abstracts the dying men, who are "nothing but black shadows of disease and starvation lying confusedly in the gloom"; "The black bones reclined at full length."[83] They are reduced to the result of their sufferings, to bare death. But it is not clear whether Marlow himself is so reducing them, perhaps in an effort to neutralize his horror, or whether his description is an ironic realization of the reduction that Leopold's system has wrought. "His brother phantom rested its forehead as if overcome with a great weariness; and all about others were scattered in every pose of contorted collapse as in some picture of a massacre or a pestilence."[84] This is a quite extraordinary description, suggesting that the dying men are posing for a tableau. "As if" implies imitation of the weariness that is such a monstrous understatement of the sufferer's own condition. The others are figuring something as bad as what they have actually experienced, but something different. What Marlow sees cannot be described in itself but only gestured at through images of things which are parallel but not the same. In this, the passage is entirely typical of the novella. *Heart of Darkness* constantly avoids naming things. The river, the Congo Free State, Brussels, King Leopold: all are indicated but never named, as if naming something would make it less real. The final reality, the horror, is not only not named but not named through someone whose name we never learn. Marlow's closing lie is that Kurtz's last words were "your name"—the Intended's name, which we do not know. The meaning of the story, we were told before we began listening, is not hidden within the tale, to be revealed at the very end with a whisk of narrative silk. The story brings out meaning, and the meaning is mist, which becomes all the more hazy the further away it is from the light. Meaning is at the point where the light fades into darkness. There lies the dead elephant, the mutilated skull, blood showing where the tusk grew and ivory was pulled through into the human world of commerce.

The elephant is not in the text because Conrad cannot see it. Why would he? He was, as McCarthy styles him à la Achebe, "a bloody anthropocentrist."[85] Like Achebe, Conrad is a humanist, "a bloody humanist" perhaps, not that the Achebe of 1975 would countenance the modifier. Indeed, at a literal level, there is no blood—no blood on the ivory, at least, no elephant blood. *Heart of Darkness* is ostensibly concerned with examining the boundaries of Kurtz's humanity, to push to the edge of the human. As a humanist text it has no space for the elephants who provide the ivory that motivates the narrative. But the image of the light in the mist figures humanism's faint understanding of its own limitations. The meaning, we remember, is outside the story itself. Elephants are thus the unseen meaning of the tale, made all the more real by the narrative's spectral illumination. Although we know they are not there, they become insistent by their absence. Once acknowledged, they can no longer be ignored. They are out there, in the glow of the text.

Conrad and Coppola

Rendering Empire Visible

JONATHAN ELMORE

In his 2004 study *Conrad and Empire,* Stephen Ross notes that his book "differs from much prominent recent work on Conrad in that it does not accord pride of place to questions of nation-state imperialism, colonialism, or race in Conrad's work."[1] He goes on to contend that "it is time to expand our scrutiny of Conrad's work. However crucial the insights and critiques of postcolonial criticism have been to our developing understanding of Conrad's engagement with modernity, they are ultimately inadequate to the scope and complexity of that engagement."[2] While not dismissing "much of the best criticism" done on Conrad since Achebe's "remark heard round the world," Ross simply calls for a reorientation in the critical engagement with Conrad's work.[3]

Ross then enacts this reorientation himself: "Conrad's failure to be sufficiently critical of imperialism—whatever that might have meant in the first quarter of the twentieth century—is less a symptom of his complicity with imperialism than a consequence of his grander, more oblique, and less articulate concern with what we might now call incipient globalization. Put another way, Conrad's engagement (or lack thereof) with imperialism as imperialism, though interesting and worthy of study, should no longer be taken as sufficient grounds for critique. Rather, it must be read as a symptom of his engagement with the emerging post-imperialist modernity that Michael Hardt and Antonio Negri have christened Empire."[4] For Ross, then, Conrad is neither critical of, nor complicit with, European imperialism. Rather "Conrad's works function as early detection devices, obliquely registering the impending supersession of imperialism with Empire. [. . .] Conrad is what Hardt and Negri identify late in their study as one of the 'voices crying out in the desert,' announcing the advent of a new world order even when they lack the vocabulary and conceptual apparatus to name or conceive it."[5]

There are far-reaching implications to a move that positions Conrad as a kind of prophet or pioneer repeatedly gesturing toward a conceptualization of Empire that was just coalescing and that he himself could not name. Since *Conrad and Empire* was published, other scholars have begun echoing Ross's assertion that the questions of nation-state imperialism, race, or colonialism are not adequate to account for Conrad's full engagement with the world in which he lived. These writers have not, however, followed out the implications of Empire in Conrad's work. For example, in *Under Conrad's Eyes: The Novel as Criticism,* Michael John DiSanto offers "a way of reading Conrad that differs from the dominant discussion pervading at the time. Postcolonial readings of Conrad's works have all but monopolized the critical discussion in recent years."[6] Likewise, Evelyn Cobley argues in her *Modernism and the Culture of Efficiency: Ideology and Fiction* that what is at stake "is the impact that our increasing commitment to efficiency has on our individual consciousnesses and our cultural self-understanding." Her assertion implicitly follows suit in not affording pride of place to the postcolonial questions that have dominated recent Conrad criticism.[7]

Certainly many contemporary scholars working on Conrad's writings continue to focus on his engagement with imperialism. For example, Glenn Willmott's *Modernist Goods: Primitivism, the Market, and the Gift* or Robert Hampson's "Joseph Conrad—Postcolonialism and Imperialism" both remain grounded in the postcolonialism that has been the pervasive discourse of Conrad studies. Indeed, these are examples of important and meaningful work that should continue. However, it is time to reorient the approach to Conrad's writing with an eye toward the distinction between imperialism and Empire that Ross, via Hardt and Negri, draws. One of the implications of Ross's work is its suggestion to reconceive the relationship between *Heart of Darkness* and *Apocalypse Now.* Exploring *Heart of Darkness* as an early engagement with then-nascent Empire leads to an understanding of Coppola's film as a rendering visible of Empire fully formed.

Empire Succeeds Imperialism

Hardt and Negri's *Empire* examines the current and past status of sovereignty. Their book challenges the idea that Empire declined during the modernist period. According to them it was imperialism that receded to extinction, while Empire thrived: "The declining sovereignty of nation-states and their increasing inability to regulate economic and cultural exchanges is in fact one of the primary symptoms of the coming Empire. The sovereignty of the nation-state was the cornerstone of the imperialisms that European powers constructed throughout the modern era. By 'Empire,' however, we understand something altogether different from 'imperialism.'"[8] They will go on to define "Empire" as "sovereignty" that "has taken a new form, composed of a series of national and supranational organisms united under a single logic of rule"; it is a "new global form of sovereignty."[9] This sovereignty is literally "capital," which, as they argue, has become a "biopolitical production, the production of social life itself, in which the economic, the political, and the cultural increasingly overlap and invest one another."[10] They go on to identify three characteristics of Empire: First, Empire "is characterized fundamentally by a lack of boundaries: Empire's rule has no limits. By definition, then, the concept of Empire posits a regime that effectively encompasses the spatial totality, or reality that rules over the entire civilized world."[11] Second, "Empire presents its rule not as a transitory moment in the movement of history, but as a regime with no temporal boundaries and in that sense outside of history or at the end of history."[12] Third, "Empire not only manages a territory and a population but also creates the very world it inhabits. It not only regulates human interactions but also seeks directly to rule over human nature."[13]

Heart of Darkness as Early Detection of the Coming Empire

Reading *Heart of Darkness* as an engagement with, or early detection of, nascent Empire is necessarily fraught in that such an exploration involves reading what is not quite in the text, what is only suggested or implied. In fact such an exploration requires attention to imprecisions of the text as it attempts to render visible the succession of Empire over imperialism which is beyond the available vocabulary or conceptual apparatus. The text itself offers a kind of warning to this effect in its description of Marlow's atypical yarns, one of which constitutes the entire narrative of the novella: "to him the meaning of an episode was not inside like a kernel but outside, enveloping the tale which brought it out only as a glow brings out a haze."[14] Stephen Ross deals with this particular challenge by taking up the "confluence of the psychic and the social" as "the crux of [his] examination of Conrad's critique of incipient Empire and his conception of Imperial subjectivity."[15] Focusing on Hardt and Negri's three defining criteria of Empire as they appear in the novella and subsequently in the film highlights how the novella and film together render visible Empire.

The first of the criteria of Empire—its necessary lack of borders—manifests in *Heart of Darkness* as a tension between blankness, borders, and darkness. Marlow's oft-cited recollection of his childhood fascination with maps introduces this tension: "when I was a little chap I had a passion for maps. [. . .] At that time there were many blank spaces on the earth. [. . .] But there was one yet—the biggest—the most blank so to speak—that I had a hankering after. True, by this time it was not a blank space any more. It had got filled since my boyhood with rivers and lakes and names. It had ceased to be a blank space of delightful mystery [. . .] It had become a place of darkness."[16] In this quickly narrated transition from blankness, to names, to darkness the text gestures toward the succession of Empire over imperialism. As the colonial powers moved about the world labeling it with names and borders, imperialism was made manifest. And yet the novella gestures to a point beyond imperialism and its names and borders. It can only denote this point with darkness, with absence. And of course this is the image with which the text ends: the path forward leading into "the heart of an immense darkness."[17] Hence the text indicates that there exists something beyond imperialism, but that something is yet not apparent enough to be identifiable.

The text carries the image of darkness into its chronological positioning of Empire as a phenomenon for all time: "and this also [. . .] has been one of the dark places of the earth. [. . .] I was thinking of very old times, when the Romans first came here, nineteen hundred years ago."[18] Marlow invokes the image of the conqueror plunging into the darkness of the savage, uncivilized, and unknown land: "Imagine the feelings of a commander of a fine [. . .] trireme in the Mediterranean, ordered suddenly north. [. . .] Imagine him here—the very end of the world, [. . .] going up this river with stores, or orders, or what you like. Sandbanks, marshes, forests, savages, precious little to eat fit for a civilized man [. . .] land in a swamp, march through the woods, and in some inland post feel the savagery. The utter savagery had closed in around him."[19] The experience of the anonymous Roman foreshadows that of Marlow and of Kurtz. Certainly all three men acknowledge the power of the savage and the terrifying unknown of the lands in which they find themselves. Furthermore, this experience remains unchanged from the Romans on English soil to the Europeans plunging centuries later into the African jungle. Hochschild diagnoses the scope of the novella, saying, "We read it as a parable for all times and places, not as a book about one time and place."[20] It is not dependent on the rise or fall of a particular sovereignty or colonial power; it is outside the temporal borders of any sovereign power.

By contrast, though, the temporal boundaries of Empire described by Hardt and Negri exist outside of history itself. The image of the Roman stepping off his trireme into the dark, unknown of what would become England, necessarily situates Marlow's very conception of Empire inside history, having a beginning and an end, framed by something that came before and comes after, even if that something is only represented by the absence of light: "Light has come out of this river since [. . .] but it is like a running blaze on a plain, like a flash of lightning on the clouds. We live in the flicker—may it last as long as the old earth keeps rolling!"[21] Conceptually, then, Marlow's notion of Empire is but a brief flash in human history. However, due to the lack of the necessary conceptual apparatus or due to Empire's infancy at the end of the nineteenth century, the text never manages to articulate Empire outside of temporality altogether.

It is in the presentation of the "Company" as the governing force behind the actions of the text that the novella most clearly forecasts the coming Empire. As a thinly veiled stand-in for King Leopold II's International African Society, a private holding company which would eventually achieve international recognition for the king's sovereignty over the newly created Congo Free State, the Company offers an amorphous collusion of political, private, and commercial authorities capable not only of ruling territory and subjects but of creating the very subjectivities of those it manages. In fact, Marlow assures his companions that "none of us would feel exactly like" the Roman conquerors.[22] "What saves us is efficiency—the devotion to efficiency."[23] The project of Empire rests not on political allegiance, national origin, or even personal gain; it is an "idea only."[24] And by instilling this idea into its subjects, Empire perpetuates itself and its capital interests not the through the subjugation of people but through creating subjects themselves.

The point is not that the novella is blind to or complicit in the sovereignty of the European nations over the Congo. As Adam Hochschild remarks, "*Heart of Darkness* is one of the most scathing indictments of imperialism in all literature."[25] Certainly the novella itself quickly establishes a cynical outlook regarding the imperial project at the heart of the narrative: "the conquest of the earth, which mostly means the taking it away from those who have a different complexion or slightly flatter noses than ourselves, is not a pretty thing when you look at it too much."[26] The text is more than a condemnation of Leopold's activities in the Congo or even of European colonialism. The novella is a rendering visible of the early manifestations of Empire as it began to supersede imperialism.

Relationship between Novel and Film

Reorienting our engagement with *Heart of Darkness* as an early forecaster of Empire's succession over imperialism suggests that Coppola's later film offers a vision of Empire fully entrenched, which in turn changes our understanding of the relationship between novella and film. The dyad of Coppola's film(s) and Conrad's novella remains a node of critical interest and disagreement. Linda Cahir argues that the framing narration of the novella—that is, the unnamed narrator narrating Marlow's tale—functions cinematically and allows both the novella and the film to suggest the necessary mediation of narration itself: "the recording eye of the camera and Conrad's interposed voice [. . .] both function as a warning: No interpersonal communication can ever be fully unmediated."[27] Louis Greiff attends to the parallels between minor characters, arguing that it is in figures such as Chef, Chief, Lance, and Kilgore that the film finally delivers its "far darker rendering of *Heart of Darkness*."[28]

Margot Norris contends that "the folly both Conrad and Coppola underline in their criticism of colonial adventurism [. . .] is the senseless brutality, waste, and destructiveness of enterprises with misguided and hypocritical goals and inept and ill-conceived strategies."[29] On the other side, Keith Soloman argues that "while the making of *Apocalypse Now* can be seen as a physical extension of the American imperial or colonial enterprise, the film's content—far from expressing an antiwar stance—likewise promotes imperialism and war through technical effects, cinematography, narration, and dramatic structure."[30]

Pamela Demory suggests that *Apocalypse Now* and the subsequent *Apocalypse Now Redux* are simply further links in the narrative chain of which *Heart of Darkness* is a part and "can thus be read as yet another chapter in the ongoing story of the dangers of wielding 'imperial authority.'"[31] Yet where her analysis circulates around the narratological parallels between the novella and films, arguing that all three are warning of the same dangers of imperialism, I position *Apocalypse Now* as the later link in the narrative chain of the succession of Empire over imperialism. Where *Heart of Darkness* forecasts the stirrings of nascent Empire and the waning of imperialism even as it lacks "the vocabulary and conceptual apparatus"[32] to name or conceive of Empire, the film renders visible Empire fully realized and entrenched.

Apocalypse Now: Rendering Empire Visible

Apocalypse Now, at the outset, offers a vision of imperial power and then systematically strips away the trappings of the nation state in its rendering visible Empire's succession and the disappearance of imperialism. The film, even though it opens with a presentation of the power of the American nation state, renders visible the actual authority in the film as Empire, defined by the same three criteria articulated by Hardt and Negri: it blurs or obliterates both national and ontological boundaries; it shows authority that exists outside of historical time; and it reveals a power not granted by authority but immanent in people.

Coppola's film begins with a foreshadowing of the upending of American imperial power offered by the long introductory scene of Captain Willard's upside-down face superimposed over napalm fires, with *The Doors'* "The End" providing the only audio. In the setting of an American military base in Saigon, the audience sees an iconic image of American imperialism, augmented by a complex presentation of national sovereign power being exercised. On the one hand, the "finest officer"[33] America has ever produced is out there in the field commanding troops "totally beyond the pale of any acceptable human conduct."[34] On the one hand, here is the tip of imperial power's spear: Colonial Kurtz, authorized by the sovereign power of the United States and using that power to whatever ends he sees fit. This Colonel Kurtz cuts much the same figure as Agent Kurtz, one authorized by the king of Belgium, the other by the president of the United States. On the other hand, and reinforcing the imperial power of America, the same nation state that authorized Colonel Kurtz's power is now authorizing his "termination."[35] All power at work here, whether it be that of the General, Captain Willard, or Kurtz himself, exists as an extension of the sovereign power of the United States.

The national boundaries that literally define nations also serve to define their spheres of influence. The authority and rigidity of these boundaries appear meaningful as Captain Willard begins his trek up the river. He and the Chief briefly discuss their final destination, and the Chief underscores the importance and power of boundaries in his claim to not thinking: "My orders are I'm not supposed to know where I'm taking this boat, so I don't."[36] Their subsequent exchange confirms the circumscription of national power by national borders:

> "We're going up river about 75 clicks above the *Do Lung* bridge."
> "That's Cambodia, Captain."
> "That's classified. We're not supposed to be in Cambodia but that's where I'm going."[37]

It is the power of the nation state that has placed these two men in their boat and given them their assignment. American sovereign power is justified by the location of the boat in relation to a national boundary, and the nation state controls not only its interests within and outside that border but even the knowledge of the border's location. The veneer of imperial power grounded in the nation state begins to fracture as the river journey continues. The artificiality of these national borders manifests when the manufactured boundary of the Do Lung bridge, not the Cambodian border, proves the only discernible divide encountered by the men. The mise-en-scène as the boat approaches the bridge shows a vivid border that must be passed. The bridge, lit from end to end, stands out sharply against the black sky and jungle as it spans the river. Surrounded by activity, explosions, gunfire, unintelligible cries, and confusion, the bridge lives up to the ominous earlier discussions of the Cambodian border yet proves to be an entirely artificial boundary: "we build it every night. Charlie blows it right back up. Just so the generals can say the road's open."[38] The boat will later cross the Cambodian border without acknowledgment, the double irony being that the Cambodian border in reality is just as artificial as the bridge.

Not only is the bridge a manufactured boundary, the authority that maintains it (the American government) proves artificial as well. Willard's repeated request for the commanding officer is met with silence or obscure answers such as, "Beverly Hills."

> "What?"
> "Straight up the road there's a concrete fuckin' bunker called Beverly Hills! Where the fuck else you think it would be!?"[39]

Whether there is a bunker up the road or not, no authority is apparent. Finally asking a solider again, "Do you know who's in command here?," Willard receives a long and inscrutable stare followed by the one-word answer, "Yeah."[40] In this enigmatic reply, the film illustrates the absence and impotence of American sovereign power to create or maintain the borders that give the nation state its identity. The authority investing all the energy, power, and violence surrounding the bridge is futile at best. It maintains and defends a false border existing only to support the fiction of a sovereign power. Once the boat has passed the bridge, the film no longer attempts to maintain the fiction of borders, and the boat makes its way into an increasingly amorphous jungle.

As the geographic borders that define and empower nations reveal themselves to be fictional, so too are the chronological borders of national power. As Soloman contends, "America's involvement in Vietnam is conceivably erased altogether, as the movie possesses a surreal nightmarelike quality, and employs a metaphorical trip back in time."[41] National power is inevitably defined by historical time: the rise of a nation, the beginnings of wars or occupations, the taking of colonies, the reign of rulers, and so forth. As the landscape gives way to undefined jungle, chronology becomes less apparent as well. The boat passes ancient monuments and downed planes all looking as if they had been there for a comparable period. Attacked by arrows, the boat responds with gunfire. The arrows at first seem harmless, especially against the high-caliber, automatic fire from the boat; however, the most effective weapon in the encounter proves to be a spear that graphically kills the Chief. Increasingly the scenery of the jungle becomes more primal, complete with slow-moving water, fern-like trees, and fire. The boat and the men themselves become covered with foliage, seemingly blending into the jungle. Finally arriving at Kurtz's compound, Willard meets a formation of natives and soldiers. The appearance of this motley crew further smears the chronology of the scene and subsequently of the end of the film. They seem not so much from an earlier time as outside of time entirely.

The confluence of humanity in and around Kurtz's compound reveals an authority that has ceased to exist as a hierarchy where authority rests at the top and has come to emanate instead from the homogenous assembly. Apart from Kurtz, who clearly holds a privileged place among them, the people inhabiting the compound show no evidence of rank. All seem equally powerful or powerless within the depths of the jungle. Whatever their nationality, appearance, or dress, "Kurtz's people" exist outside of the constitutive hierarchies of nationally authorized power.

The remaining boat crew has also shed all vestiges of rank and appears no different from the mass of humanity in the compound—a point made sharply by Lance's later seamless integration into the group on the shore. The last conversation between Chef and Willard gives no evidence of Willard's authority as a captain. Issuing an order ceases to have meaning in this environment. Instead, it is Chef who sums up the situation, leaving Willard in the position of thc supplicant:

> "This colonel guy. . . . He's wacko, man!"
> "Then you'll help me?"
> "Help you, fucking A, I'll help you.[42]

The equal authority exercised by the men in this exchange gives evidence that the imperial authority that sent them here has ceased to wield power.

The killing of Kurtz is a primal act that demonstrates an authority driving his death that exists outside of the physical and chronological borders of the American occupation of Southeast Asia and thus outside of the sovereign power of the United States. As Willard reflects, "They were going to make me a major for this, and I wasn't even in their fucking army anymore. Everybody wanted me to do it. Him most of all. . . . Even the jungle wanted him dead, and that's who he really took his orders from anyway."[43] Willard, functionally and by his own admission no longer a part of the American military, rises from the primordial river as a creature outside of time. As Willard stalks his way toward Kurtz, the film juxtaposes his approach for the final "assassination" of the colonial with the ritualistic sacrifice of a water buffalo. The chilling "primal" dancing overlaid with Willard's movement toward Kurtz serves as prologue to Kurtz's death, mirrored by the violent death of the buffalo, both hacked apart in deference to an unnamed and unnamable authority. In the climax of the narrative, the violence of the piece is entirely outside of the authority of America or any nation state. When at the end of the narrative Willard, his face black and his body covered in Kurtz's blood, appears as a kind of authority to which many of the watching crowd kneel and drop their weapons, the effect is not to reestablish a locatable authority but rather to deepen the force of the film's conclusion.

"The horror" becomes an acknowledgment of an unnamable authority found outside of time, nationality, or setting. In essence, the film ends face-to-face with Empire. That a force motivates the actions of the later film is undeniable, but that force is evident only in the subjects it has created. The assortment of humanity assembled at Kurtz's compound after his death is not made up of subjects of particular national powers, historical conflicts, or apparent objectives. They exist as subjects to Empire drawn together by a sideshow conflict in a proxy war of Empire's global capital interests.

Stephen Ross has called for the field of modernist studies to reorient itself toward reading the works of Conrad as engagements with Empire, as articulated by Hardt and Negri, rather than as either critical of, or complicit with, imperialism. If Ross is correct that studying Conrad's writings as responses to imperialism is ultimately inadequate to understanding his writings and responses to the world he inhabited, then following his reorientation offers numerous possibilities for expanding our understandings of one of the most important and fascinating writers of the modernist period and, in fact, of all of literature.

Such work has implications beyond literary studies. As Hardt and Negri themselves argue, "The passage to Empire and its processes of globalization offer new possibilities to the forces of liberation. Globalization, of course, is not one thing, not unified or univocal. Our political task [. . .] is not simply to resist these processes but to recognize them and redirect them toward new ends. The creative forces of the multitude that sustain Empire are also capable of autonomously constructing a counter-Empire, an alternative political organization of global flows and exchanges."[44] If true, then what do Conrad's works have to teach about this "counter-Empire"? Following Ross's work with further explorations of Conrad's engagement with nascent Empire may well bear fruit far beyond literary studies.

Reinventing the Congo through Western Eyes

Echoes of Joseph Conrad's *Heart of Darkness* in Michaela Wrong's *In the Footsteps of Mr Kurtz*

MAWULI ADJEI

Joseph Conrad's *Heart of Darkness* (1902) is one of the most widely read novellas in the English language, noted particularly for its satirical critique of European imperialism in Africa and what many see as its demeaning depiction of Africa and Africans, as well as women. Set in the Belgian Congo in the heat of Europe's exploitative imperial presence in Africa, it is partly based on Conrad's own experiences. The novella tells the story of Marlow, who is dispatched by boat up the Congo River to relieve Kurtz, a trader who runs the most successful ivory business on behalf of the Belgian government. On this mission Marlow is confronted by the stark reality of colonialism and is appalled by the hypocrisy of Europe's so-called civilizing mission in Africa, which is only a thin veneer for exploiting the continent's wealth. Marlow is also confronted with knowledge that Kurtz, the hitherto highly respected man whom he has read and heard so much about, has degenerated into a greedy monster who brutalizes the natives. When Marlow eventually meets Kurtz, he is in a vegetative state, a complete wreck on the verge of death.

Many themes, symbols, images, and metaphors run through *Heart of Darkness,* and the novella still yields new and contentious interpretations. Key among these are the contrasting and alternating patterns of light and darkness to depict civilization and moral refinement on the one hand and moral degeneracy, depravity, and savagery on the other. As N. O. Orisabiyi points out, it is the morality of the characters in the tale that is put to the test, and it is their moral failure at different points that readers are to witness, a claim contested by Michael Lackey, who is of the view that, for Conrad, "the problem is not defining true morality. . . . [M]orality is an empty signifier, a semiotic vacuity that dominant political powers can strategically manipulate in order to justify crimes against humanity."[1] The novella has influenced many other literary works set in Africa, including Graham Greene's *The Heart of the Matter* (1948), Saul Bellow's *Henderson, the Rain King* (1959), John Updike's *Out of Africa* (1978), and V. S. Naipaul's "A New King for the Congo: Mobutu and Nihilism in Africa" (1975), *A Bend in the River* (1979), and *Congo Diary* (1980). Recent works include Helen Winternitz's *East Along the Equator: A Journey Up the Congo and into Zaire* (1987), Adam Hochschild's *King Leopold's Ghost* (1998), Jeffery Taylor's *Facing the Congo: A Modern Day Journey into the Heart of Darkness* (2001), and Michaela Wrong's *In the Footsteps of Mr Kurtz* (2000).

In the Footsteps of Conrad and Marlow

Unlike *Heart of Darkness,* Wrong's *In the Footsteps of Mr Kurtz* (hereafter referred to as *Footsteps*) is nonfiction, and the author is a British international journalist who covered extensively the political trajectory of the Congo/Zaire up to the death of Mobutu. The introductory chapter of Wrong's narrative reads very much like Conrad's introductory statements in *Heart of Darkness,* especially about the Thames, whose tidal current, "in its unceasing service," is "crowded with men and ships it had borne . . . men of whom the nation is proud, from Sir Francis Drake to Sir John Franklin [who] had all gone out on that stream, bearing the sword and often the torch, messengers of the might within the land . . . the dreams of men, the seed of commonwealths, the germs of empires."[2]

Like Conrad, Wrong's journey begins, quite predictably, by a river—the same old Congo River, now rechristened River Zaire. The narrator in *Footsteps* describes her journey by the River Zaire with trepidation: "When the motor-launch deposited me in the cacophony of the quayside, engine churning mats of water hyacinth as it turned to head back across the brown expanse of oily water that was the River Zaire, I was hit by the sensation that so unnerves first-time visitors to Africa."[3]

Thus, Wrong establishes the metonymic importance of River Zaire; it is representative of the continent of Africa, and the author stresses particularly how a journey across this most unfriendly passage reveals the continent's horrific primeval identity, an identity premised on the exotic or the Other. The River Zaire commands a predatory ambience, a world governed by darkness, invoking uncertainty, triggering a pulse of apprehension, stirring the alien Western mind into a gyroscope of wild imaginations. For the author, "It is that revelatory moment when white, middle-class Westerners finally understand what the rest of humanity has always known—that there are places in this world where the safety net they have spent so much of their lives erecting is suddenly whipped away, where the right accent, education, health insurance and a foreign passport—all the trappings of 'It Can't Happen to Me'—no longer apply, and their well-being depends on the condescension of strangers."[4] This introductory portrait of the passage into the heart of Africa is patterned on Conrad's portrait of Africa through Western eyes, and prepares the mind of the reader for descent into a world of darkness, whether of places, people, or systems.

Into the Heart of Darkness

The similarity between Wrong's quest and Marlow's is immediately striking. Marlow discovers Kurtz when Kurtz is in the throes of death. Wrong's story is set in the twilight of Mobutu Sese Seko's three-decade autocratic misrule. Under Mobutu's rule, Zaire was reduced to a failed (police) state. In the words of Wrong, "The ominous awareness of a world of infinite, sinister possibilities had become one of the dominant characteristics of the nation."[5] The narrative thus vividly captures spectacles of unmitigated horror symptomatic of a failed state. The streets and alleys are awash with marauding rebel soldiers toting machine guns, rotting bodies in the sun, and a brutal dictator dying slowly of prostate cancer. These gory spectacles, the author reminds us, are a replica of the macabre and murky setting of Conrad's *Heart of Darkness.* As she emphatically puts it, "Zaire was Joseph Conrad's *Heart of Darkness.*"[6]

In making the transition—from a colonial fiction based on the reality of European imperialism in the Belgian Congo, to a postcolonial journalistic travelogue based on postcolonial Zaire—Wrong draws the necessary historical linkages and parallels between the past and the present within the context of imperial brigandage and pillage in the name of civilization and post-independence political malaise in the guise of self-rule and unparalleled graft, personified by Mobutu. On one side of the divide is Europe's rape of the Congo; on the other side is Mobutu's rape of Zaire. In both works, decadence, decay, and metaphors of barbarism and plunder pervade the pages. Both authors attempt to probe systems, institutions, and individuals, if only to come to terms with what informs the inexplicable levels of horror one encounters. The parallels are many.

First of all, Wrong's four-page pseudo-review of Conrad's *Heart of Darkness* in her introduction to *Footsteps* is an enterprise in placing her own work in perspective; in effect, an attempt to establish the fact that nothing has really changed in the former Belgian Congo, now renamed Zaire by Mobutu. In Wrong's prefatory notes, she invokes Conrad and his enigmatic character Kurtz. Somewhere in between is Wrong herself—as an international journalist, pseudo-historian, political observer/analyst, narrator, and commentator. She and Conrad share a lot in common. Both of them are on a quest in the Congo: "For Conrad . . . *Heart of Darkness* was a book based on some very painful personal experience" which turned out to be "the most traumatic of his life."[7] Wrong on the other hand blends the history of the Congo and her personal experiences as a journalist into a kind of creative nonfiction. And both authors are appalled by what they experience. Wrong therefore allows Conrad to invade her narrative, trying hard—most times unsuccessfully—to dispel some of the racist undercurrents of *Heart of Darkness.* According to her, "The 'darkness' of the book [*Heart of Darkness*] refers to the monstrous passions at the core of the human soul, lying ready to emerge when man's better instincts are suspended, rather than the continent's supposed predisposition to violence. Conrad was more preoccupied with rotten Western values, the white man's inhumanity to the black man, than, as is always assumed today, black savagery."[8]

And yet, Wrong contradicts herself, falling foul of the very stereotyping or "Othering" that has, in part, blighted *Heart of Darkness* in the opinion of Afrocentric critics such as Chinua Achebe and Ngũgĩ Wa Thiong'o. In Wrong's view, the "darkness" in Conrad's title perfectly suits contemporary Africa: "The shift reflects, perhaps, the level of Western unease over Africa, a continent that has never disappointed in its capacity to disappoint: Hutu mothers killing their children by Tutsi fathers in Rwanda; the self-styled Emperor Bokassa ordering his cook to serve up his victims' bodies in Central African Republic; Liberia's rebels videotaping the torture of a former president—the terrible scenes swamp the thin trickle of good news, challenging the very notion of progress."[9]

The foundation for Wrong's tale having been clearly established with regard to the setting—the dark recesses of a disturbing continent—the author then proceeds to outdo Conrad, whose work she draws on heavily. In the main, Conrad's "Tarzan" setting in *Heart of Darkness* is replicated in *Footsteps.* It is a world dominated by the jungle, reflecting nothing but darkness, gloom, and doom. The African jungle, and the Western mind's pathological fear of and aversion to it, goes way back in time. Of the same setting, colonial British explorer Henry Morton Stanley once wrote:

> The trees kept shedding their dew upon us like rain in great round drops. Every leaf seemed weeping. Down the boles and branches, creepers and vegetable cords, the moisture trickled and fell on us. Overhead the wide-spreading branches in many interlaced strata, each branch heavy with broad thick leaves, absolutely shut out the daylight. We knew not whether it was a sunshiny day or a dull, foggy, gloomy day. . . . We had certainly seen forests before. But this scene was an epoch in our lives ever to be remembered for its bitterness . . . the slopping moisture, the unhealthy reeking atmosphere, and the monotony of the scenes; nothing but the eternal interlaced branches, the tall aspiring stems, rising from a tangle, through which we had to burrow and crawl like wild animals, on hands and feet.[10]

The extensive quotation of Stanley attests to Wrong's intention to use it to add support to the geographical context and background for her (his)story.

It does appear, then, that between Conrad and Wrong, Africans, particularly people of the Congo, are products of their geography and environment, which setting is complicit in their "savagery" and, by extension, why characters like Kurtz and Mobutu become so degenerate. Like Conrad, Wrong's emphasis is on the African jungle, for it is that which separates Africa from the rest of the world of civilization and which makes Africans "savage" and "barbaric." As Jean-Francois Bayart points out, "The theme of the isolation of Africa from the rest of the world . . . is a key one in the negation of their historicity," and this myth "persisted into the nineteenth and twentieth centuries, and culminated in the motifs of the Jungle and the Desert."[11] And it has been such a pervasive and contagious perception that even the great Muhammad Ali, noted for his radical Pan-Islamic and Pan-Africanist leanings, termed his epic battle with George Foreman in the Zairean capital Kinshasa in 1974 as "Rumble in the Jungle"—in sharp contrast to his third fight with Joe Frazier in the Philippines in 1975 which he termed "Thrilla in Manilla" (emphasis on the Philippines capital Manilla, not the terrain).

In *Footsteps,* as in *Heart of Darkness,* the exotic is not necessarily the alien and unfamiliar but the debilitating, obtrusive, and destructive Other. Therefore, in *Heart of Darkness,* Kurtz falls sick and disintegrates mentally because he has "gone native"—where going "native," according to Wrong, means: "Cut off from the Western world, inventing his own moral code and *rendered almost insane by the solitude of the primeval forest* [italics added], he has indulged in 'abominable satisfactions', presided 'at certain midnight dances ending with unspeakable rites.'"[12]

The jungle, "the solitude of the primeval forest," is, therefore, seen as critical in the creation of the "savage" universe of the Belgian Congo and now Zaire. No wonder, in Wrong's book, Mobutu, the dysfunctional state apparatus, and the sick and crumbling nation are constantly subsumed in the overawing canopy of impenetrable jungles and ecosystems, complete with the symbols and metaphors of the jungle. Wrong reminds the reader that Mobutu's appellation is "The Leopard"—in consonance with his being a product of the jungle. And when Mobutu decides to spend more time in his hometown, Gbadolite, away from the political turmoil of Kinshasa and Lubumbashi and his political opponents, Wrong sees it symbolically as a return to origins—the jungle. To the author's mind, the rainforest looms much larger than the all-encompassing political morass; it is where Mobutu feels most at home, transformed and purged by the cathartic and therapeutic efficacy of the jungle: "Looking out over the tree tops, an undulating expanse of giant broccoli heads, or driving through the simple villages with their thatched huts, the burden of office seemed less heavy, his spirits quietly lifted and he breathed more easily. He was, after all, an Ngbandi, and this was home."[13]

For Wrong, the jungle enclave of Gbadolite, paradoxically, becomes the only spot of brightness in a country enveloped in darkness. However, in the context of the total atmospheric decadence, Gbadolite also stinks of corruption and, in effect, accentuates the general darkness hovering over Zaire.

Engendering Decadence—the Masculinity of Graft and Depravity

In the general scheme of corruption, greed, barbarism, and depravity in *Heart of Darkness,* women operate on the margins. As far as the treatment of women in the novella is concerned, critics over the years have expressed different views. Kurtz's Belgian fiancée has no name—she is known simply as "The Intended"; his African mistress is "a wild and gorgeous apparition of a woman," and Marlow's aunt is referred to as "an enthusiastic soul." While some critics, such as Nina Straus (1987), Felicity Nussbaum, and Victoria Moffatt see the portrayal of women as negative and demeaning, others think otherwise. According to Kathryn Marie Smith, "Though the women in *Heart of Darkness* are often relegated to the margins of the text, they are simultaneously unimportant and vitally important." She posits that "[t]he Intended and the Mistress are not valued characters in terms of textual attention and spoken voice, but they are imperative to Marlow, for they represent functional symbolisms of colonialism. . . . As symbols, these two women are vital to colonialism in that they justify the racism, ideals, and false heroism of imperialist agendas."[14] Indeed, the "imperialist agenda" is what drives the novella's setting in a world dominated by men, engaged in the "rape" of Africa. Moffatt, for instance, sees the imperial West's presence in Africa as, in a conjugal sense, "penetrating into Africa upon whom it has imposed a maternal clitoric, feminine status and over whom it asserts its power and authority."[15] It evokes images of conquest and domination. The West derives its penetrative power from the coercive arsenal it possesses such as cannons, ships, infantry, and adventurists who, against all odds, are able to penetrate the continent. So sordid is this penetrative indulgence and its atavistic conquest, colonization, and plunder of the maternal Africa of her body and material wealth that Nussbaum likens it to pornography, describing it as "prostitution and sexual geography."[16]

Wrong's *Footsteps* operates on a similar scale. Apart from the female first-person narrator-author and references to a few women in Mobutu's life, particularly his mother, the narrative functions as a patriarchal and phallocentric discourse. The feminization of Africa is well established in the guise of the general acquiescence of the masses in a system where power is concentrated in the hands of a closely knit cabal of men, headed by Mobutu. In the torrid flux of looting and pillage by the establishment, it makes very little sense for the author to explore the feminine angle, unless there is compelling evidence of feminine complicity in the national malaise; or, better still, to highlight the official exclusion of women from the establishment.

On the basis of these considerations, feminist arguments against both *Heart of Darkness* and *Footsteps* may seem all the more misplaced. To insist on a masculine-feminine balance of hierarchy is not only to inflict an artificial binary opposition on the texts but to also deny the historical and sociocultural contexts in which both works were produced. The Victorian background of *Heart of Darkness* could only produce a work in which women are accorded peripheral roles. Similarly, the political space in Africa, deriving from a continent-wide culture of patriarchy, has been male-dominated. In both texts, the colonial and postcolonial project in Africa, for its sheer capacity for aggressive acquisitiveness and barbarism, can only be denominated in masculine sadomasochistic terms. It has to be conceived as a forced marital relationship between the West and Africa. The West assumes the posture and attributes of male while Africa is female. In *Heart of Darkness,* Europe's flirtation with Central Africa begins as a "courtship"—under the guise of the "torch." The courtship blossoms into a bizarre "love affair," expressed in "carnal" gratification, leaving the "woman" (Africa), the object of "love," stripped naked, raped, and ravaged in a long night of orgy. In much the same way, in *Footsteps,* the young Joseph Désiré Mobutu "courts" the Congo with the sweet messianic promise of redemption and national pride. In *Footsteps,* Mobutu becomes the Belgian King Leopold and the Conradian Kurtz welded into one massive larger-than-life personage. Leopold's plunder of the Belgian Congo and Kurtz's harvest of ivory are transferred to the postcolonial canvas of Congo/Zaire where Mobutu perfects kleptocracy into a fine art.

Mobutu, Zaire, and Africa from Western Cold War Perspectives

In *Footsteps,* Wrong attempts to establish historical, political, and cultural continuities between King Leopold, the scramble for Africa, and contemporary Western economic and political maneuvers and disguises in Mobutu's Zaire through the latter's relationships with the West and its institutions such as the World Bank, IMF, CIA, and so forth. It is in this context that the comparison between Kurtz and Mobutu becomes even more compelling. Mobutu, like Kurtz, is presented as a pathologically corrupt monster, mentally and physically, surrounded by his "savage" native cohorts and Western allies. However, the two protagonists function in different contexts, for whereas Kurtz is alien to the Congo and almost a loner lost in the jungle, Mobutu is native, visible, and feels at home in the "primeval forest"; and whereas the former is destroyed mentally and physically by the jungle, the latter is enervated and sustained by it for more than three decades.

Perhaps it is in the convergence of Conrad's and Wrong's interest in highlighting human character, particularly its susceptibility to moral, spiritual, and physical decay, that Conrad's Kurtz and Wrong's Mobutu reinforce each other. *Heart of Darkness* may be a masterpiece in exploring the human heart—from which the novella derives its title. However, all the reference to Conrad's subtle and implicit criticism of European imperialism in the Congo to counter the racist undercurrents of the narrative (often ascribed to Marlow) is, in effect, subordinated to the "darkening" or "blackening" of Kurtz's heart as an individual. As Achebe notes, "Africa as a metaphysical battlefield devoid of all recognizable humanity, into which the wandering European enters at his peril," is only a "prop for the break-up of one petty European mind."[17] Similarly, *Footsteps* appears to be the story of the break-up of "one petty" African mind. Wrong chronicles the rise and fall of the typical African despot from an essentially Western perspective—one despot who has managed to outdo all the other African political dinosaurs combined. The inflections of her narrative discourse are thus geared towards first elevating Mobutu to the status of a demigod, a brutal dictator and master craftsman who is able to outlast successive American, French, and Belgian presidents and governments as well as CIA chiefs and operatives. Mobutu's superhuman portraiture reduces *Footsteps,* in all its literary configurations, to an African version of the Latin American dictator "novel." Michael Walonen draws our attention to the superhuman African dictator, the so-called "Big Man" syndrome, as an over-flogged motif in the African dictator literature. According to Walonen, many literary commentators, "native and non-native observer alike," have come to terms with "the complex interplay of repression, patriarchal authority, tribalism, nationalism, residual colonial power structures, Afrocentric and or third world socialist rhetoric . . . that undergirded the regimes of African dictators during the late Cold War period," and there are "multiple potential points of textual entry into the literary interrogation of this phenomenon."[18]

Of all the multiple entry points of "interrogation," Wrong chooses to focus on the "lone" African dictator plundering his country's resources and brutalizing his own people. In the process, the author-narrator, on the surface, subtly acts as a surrogate voice for the Western ideological, political, and economic perspective. This is a familiar narrative and rhetorical trope of expatriate (Western) literature set in Africa: "Even where they were aware of the devastating effects of imperialism on the subject peoples, as in Conrad's description of the dying victims of colonial adventurism in *Heart of Darkness,* they could not free themselves from the Eurocentric basis of their vision."[19] Evidently, in *Footsteps,* Zaire's institutionalized systemic malaise is grand, but even grander is the country's total eclipse by the overbearing presence and personality of Mobutu, a man cast in a shroud of mythology. In Mobutu's Zaire, all political actors, including the Western powers that installed him, become puppets in the hands of "a master manipulator, the student of Machiavelli who had taken the motto 'divide and rule' to heart."[20] Although, appropriately, both Mobutu and Zaire are projected as pawns on a Cold War chessboard, from the corpus of evidence assembled by the author, Mobutu is practically a nonentity in the context of Western imperialist interests and designs. As observed by Walonen, "The postcolonial African dictator was invariably a product of the Cold War. . . . They were generally propped in place, financially and/or militarily, by the CIA laboring under domino theory anxieties, or the USSR. . . . Accordingly, the literature they inspired, with the interrogation of worldly power and the possibilities of resistance to it, occupies a central place in the world of African letters from the nineteen seventies well into the twenty-first century."[21]

In capturing the Cold War scenario, Wrong, like Conrad, deploys sarcasm and veiled contempt for the Western powers that combined, in concert with their prized protégé Mobutu, to plunder Zaire. Wrong, like the multiple narrative voices in *Heart of Darkness*, shuffles through a range of points of view. She does it by speaking on behalf of the Western Cold War powers and at the same time strongly criticizing them. She presents a much more complex and larger picture beyond the East-West divide, making the West's ideological posturing sound like a hollow apologia. She stresses that the principal actors in Zaire—the United States, France, and Belgium—ideologically, politically, economically belong to the same Western axis, yet they are not seen working in concert against a common enemy (the Soviet bloc) but as fierce and cunning competitors for Zaire's resources. Recapitulating the American position, she reports: "For the Americans, the Afro-optimism of the 1960s had ebbed away, to be replaced by a pragmatic appreciation that it needed Zaire as an ally in the fight to stem Communism's spread. Even before Mobutu became head of state, the White House had signaled its regard by inviting the army chief to meet President John Kennedy in Washington. The White House welcome was to be repeated under every American president through the 1970s and 1980s. The US, using Zaire's bases as a conduit for arms destined for Angola's rebels, was determined to keep Mobutu on board."[22]

Her take on the French needs to be placed in a certain historical continuum, as far as the linkages between *Heart of Darkness* and *Footsteps* are concerned. Marlow's views about the French in *Heart of Darkness* are anything but noble. He recounts that, once, they came upon a French man-of-war anchored off the coast: "There wasn't even a shed there, and she was shelling the bush. . . . In the empty intensity of earth, sky, and water, there she was incomprehensible, firing into a continent," and, according to Marlow, there was "a touch of insanity in the proceeding, a sense of lugubrious drollery in the sight."[23] That "touch of insanity" is repackaged in *Footsteps* as follows:

> For the French, the motivation was different, but no less compelling. Despite its Belgian roots, Zaire had come to be regarded as forming part of what Paris had labelled "chasse gardee"—that "private hunting ground" of African allies whose existence allowed France to punch above its weight

> in the international arena. Part of the panoply of French-speaking African countries forming a bulwark against encroaching Anglophone influence, Zaire was a country where French businessmen, shored up by their belief that they—in contrast with the clumsy Anglo-Saxons—understood the African psyche, hoped to do business. The schools and media propagated the French language, culture and values. In return, Paris assured Mobutu, as it assured all its African dinosaur friends, of its undying support.[24]

Something, indeed, has changed over time between the two texts. First, no longer do the French see the natives as "enemies" but as "allies." Second, France does not appear to be dealing with a Cold War foe, but a Western competitor—the "clumsy Anglo-Saxons." Third, France wants a monopoly to do "business." Fourth, she does not want to do "business" with the people of Zaire, whose "psyche" she perfectly understands, but with her "African dinosaur" friend Mobutu.

In all of these circumstances, the author situates herself outside the narrative and sometimes inside it. As narrator, she is selective in what she puts out *verbatim,* what she *paraphrases* and what she *interprets* in the context of the hard facts. Her sarcastic tenor is embedded in such phrases as "private hunting ground," for its implied reference to exploitation and plunder; "encroaching Anglophone influence," for its allusion to a "scramble" or turf war over Zaire's resources; "clumsy Anglo-Saxons," for its deflationary connotations. And, finally, of the Belgians, she writes: "For the Belgians, it was a question of maintaining a toehold of influence in a former colony that was still home to several thousand Belgian expatriates. Their safety was of less importance than national prestige: however difficult the scars left by colonization made the task, Brussels was determined to maintain a historical link that allowed a small, not-too-impressive European nation to count as a significant world power."[25]

Again, in narrative technique the author-narrator dissociates herself from the real critical issues, or deliberately and sarcastically downplays their significance, such that the less compelling evidence is superimposed on the superior one. In so doing, Wrong is able to dismantle the oft-employed "inverted pyramid" format of reportage where the thesis statement is deployed as the opening paragraph. In Wrong's format, the thesis statement, which encapsulates the hard evidence and makes the earlier statements irrelevant, comes last—tucked somewhere at the bottom of the page: "All three nations want guaranteed access to Zaire's mineral reserves—especially, in the case of the US, the cobalt it needed to produce its fighter jets."[26] The above statement, in terms of the "rape" of Zaire's resources by external interests, approximates Nussbaum's "prostitution of sexual geography" and, in *Footsteps,* appears to be what Western presence in Zaire is all about—a reenactment of the scramble for Africa with Zaire as the ultimate trophy, a country which in the post-independence years, according to Wrong, "looked to the outside world like an oversized fruitcake about to crumble into a hundred tempting morsels."[27]

On the whole, Wrong's *Footsteps,* with its impressive compendium of facts and statistics, is a welcome politico-historical document, yet its disproportionate focus on Mobutu, with all the brutality, cunning, wiles, and near-magical charms attributed to him, does not shed any more light on the man than it does the real perpetrators of the plunder of Zaire. In *Heart of Darkness,* Conrad's Marlow is honest enough to make one of the most profound indictments of his own people in the following statement, imputing to the West nothing but barefaced armed robbery: "They were conquerors, and for that you need only brute force—nothing to boast of, when you have it, since your strength is just an accident arising from the weakness of others. They grabbed what they could get for the sake of what was to be got. It was just robbery with violence and aggravated murder on a grand scale, and men going at it blind. . . . The conquest of the earth, which mostly means taking it away from those who have a different complexion or slightly flatter noses than ourselves, is not a not a pretty thing when you look into it too much."[28] Perhaps Wrong, the omniscient narrator, is also an "incarnation" of Marlow, described by Watts as "sometimes unreliable as narrator," who is prone to making "generalizations which his own narrative variously subverts" and who "veers in judgement, giving with one hand and taking back with the other" and who also "oscillates between hyperbole and understatement."[29]

BEYOND A REPACKAGING of journalistic material, which has been in the public domain for decades, there is very little new information in *Footsteps,* except the fact that it draws openly on *Heart of Darkness* by invoking the name of Kurtz, one of the most popular characters in world literature. The author herself acknowledges her indebtedness to many earlier works, including *The Congo Cables* by Madeline Kalb (1982), *Les Derniers Jours de Mobutu* by Honore Ngbanda Ko Atumba (1998), *Dans la Cour de Mobutu* by Pierre Janssen (1997), and *Le Dinosaur: Le Zaire de Mobutu* by Colette Braeckman (1992). Thus, the Mobutu that dominates the pages of *Footsteps* appears to be a creature cloned from many sources. Conrad found himself in a similar situation, the atrocities of Belgium in the Congo Free State having been widely condemned across the world by human rights groups before he wrote *Heart of Darkness.* However, as Wrong herself concedes, "while *Heart of Darkness* is in part a psychological thriller about what makes man human, it had enough topical detail in it to carry another message to its readers."[30] This is where *Footsteps* and *Heart of Darkness* differ essentially. Whereas Conrad's novella, which, by the very nature of its density and deep-structure narrative tropes, continues to be received from feminist, psychoanalytical, racial, and political perspectives, Wrong's narrative, which is a mélange of journalese, creative nonfiction, and historical documentation, is, by and large, literal and lacking in metaphorical and philosophical depth. It is also weak and inconsistent in combining narrative, fact, conjecture, commentary, and critical analysis.

Notwithstanding all these, likening Mobutu to Kurtz, if only for the mystical capacity of both men to overreach themselves in megalomania, graft, and moral depravity, accords Wrong's story a refreshing sense of history, both characters having been used as mythical figureheads on behalf of certain powers; Kurtz on behalf of King Leopold and Mobutu on behalf of Belgium, France, and the United States. Wrong's forte lies in the linkages that she manages to draw between the Congo Free State of the 1900s and Zaire of the 1960s to the dawn of the twentieth-first century. As the author states in her introduction but, by design or accident, failed to explore satisfactorily: "No man is a caricature, no individual can alone bear responsibility for a nation's collapse. The disaster Zaire became, the dull political acquiescence of its people, had its roots in a history of extraordinary outside interference, as basic in motivation as it was elevated in rhetoric. The momentum behind Zaire's free-fall was generated *not by one man but thousands of compliant collaborators, at home and abroad.*"[31]

PART III

Critical Approaches to Other Major Texts

The Imitable Joseph Conrad

NISHA MANOCHA

In a 1907 letter to his agent, J. B. Pinker, Joseph Conrad muses on the likely success of his forthcoming *Chance* after the imminent publication of *The Secret Agent*: "I reckon I may make certain of the support of the Press for the next few years. The young men who are coming in to write criticisms are in my favour so far. At least all of whom I've heard are. I don't get in the way of established reputations. One may read everybody and yet in the end want to read me—for a change if for nothing else. For I don't resemble anybody; and yet I am not specialised enough to call up imitators as to matter or style. There is nothing in me but a turn of mind which whether valuable or worthless can not be imitated."[1] With the benefit of hindsight we might say that Conrad was both startlingly accurate and deeply mistaken in this self-assessment. Conrad was able to carve out a literary space for himself—that is, he did not tread upon the territory of the likes of empire writers Rudyard Kipling or H. Rider Haggard—but the implications of his singularity were far from what he imagined. Over a century on, the "imitators" of Conrad are many, appealing to each of his "matter," "style," and his elusive "turn of mind."

Although the point of Conrad's letter was not to offer a critical self-evaluation but to suggest the potential commercial success of *Chance* to settle his debts, Conrad's perfunctory remarks to Pinker about his literary status nonetheless managed to articulate a compelling hypothesis. Conrad developed a connection between an author's resemblances to his or her contemporaries and the question of the imitability of their work. According to Conrad, his distinctiveness prevents his imitation by others. With the vantage of the long view of his career, however, we might revise his formulation. Perhaps it is precisely the "change" Conrad alleged of his writing that incited the many "imitations" of his works. His inimitableness seems to have become a model for a range of writers.

Contemporary Reviews of *Almayer's Folly:* A Generic Misfit

The immediate difficulty of placing Conrad in a literary tradition would seem to contribute to his imitability. His arrival on the literary scene in 1895 with *Almayer's Folly* coincided with a burgeoning literary marketplace. With the creation of numerous periodicals and magazines and the advent of the literary agent, book reviewing reached new levels in numbers and significance.[2] There are recorded nearly fifty contemporary reviews of *Almayer's Folly* from the United Kingdom and the United States. As his correspondence with Pinker suggests, and numerous other letters he wrote across his writing career corroborate, Conrad monitored carefully the reviews of his fiction. He may have been incensed when he learned that a journalist credited him with too few novels in 1906: "Why the accurate newspaper press should credit me with 2 novels I don't know. It's one of these absurd misapprehensions of which journalists alone have the secret," but in another, later letter to Pinker, Conrad offers an alternative position on the utility of their commentary: "The *Set of Six* is out and looks tolerably well as to the get up. I have no cutting; but two people wrote to me saying they have seen some good reviews, especially in the *Dly News.* Could you send me that one? It isn't for the glory of the thing, you understand; and anyhow criticism as done in the daily press is of not much use to one; but all the same it is sometimes possible to get a hint of what pleases the general public and I am adaptable enough to profit by it."[3]

Although this excerpt points to Conrad's shrewd recognition of the paper as an index of popular opinion that he might use to his professional advantage, we might also speculate as to the degree to which the summary effect of years of reading reviews of his work that include analyses of his style and subject matter provided the terms for his account of his own practice to Pinker in 1907. Indeed, the reviews of *Almayer's Folly* seem to anticipate Conrad's evaluation of his singularity mid-career. Reviewers note almost unanimously the uniqueness of the Malay setting of Conrad's first novel in the introductory sentences of their reviews. In this respect, the Malay location appears to be the strongest indicator of Conrad's difference from his contemporaries, and his particular treatment of such "faraway" lands would become a source of imitation for writers to come. The critics are pleased to announce that a new author has discovered a fresh locale for English fiction. The Malay Archipelago is an "absolute novelty"; "a part of the world as yet, so far as our memory serves, unexplored by the writers of fiction"; "its very novelty gives it a certain attractiveness"; it has "the advantage of untrodden ground and characters of a new race."[4] With the same enthusiasm, Conrad is heralded as "the Kipling of the Malay Archipelago" and the "Mr. Becke" of "the Pacific islands."[5]

The periodicals' and papers' comparisons of Conrad to Kipling and Becke on the basis of the exotic locales of their fictions are revealing: Conrad's decision to write a novel set in a "far-off land" largely conditioned his readers' responses. By writing the Malay, Conrad recalled to his readers the adventure tales of G. A. Henty, R. M. Ballantyne, and Haggard. However, they would note almost immediately that Conrad was not, in fact, writing a story that relied on a set of assumptions about the European and the native that would manifest as a validation of expansionism through the imperial hero's mastery of the native and his land. The implications of this difference were not lost on reviewers, who responded in one of two ways. While some celebrated the novelty of Conrad's particular approach to the so-called exotic and its generic exigencies, others expressed disappointment in the novel's lack of heroism and romance—those indispensable elements of fictions that take place in distant lands amongst alien races.

Conrad's "Author's Note" offers, in part, an explanation for the generic disassociations of the novel, though it was not included in its initial publication; it first appeared in the Doubleday, Page "Sun-Dial" edition in 1921. In the "Note," Conrad takes issue with the essay "Decivilized" by the English writer Alice Meynell, published in 1891. Conrad quotes Meynell's argument that literature "which preys on strange people and prowls in far-off countries . . . amongst cannibals and the more sophisticated pioneers of our glorious virtues" produces tales that are "de-civilized."[6] According to Meynell's definition, Conrad, too, must be guilty of writing inferior literature. However, he exculpates himself from Meynell's charge by making the crucial claim that there is a "bond between us and that humanity so far away."[7] He frames this notion as an artistic imperative: "the picture of life, there as here, is drawn with the same elaboration of detail, coloured with the same tints."[8] As Robert Hampson observes, Conrad not only cites Meynell's essay to announce his novel as a departure from the adventure-fiction tradition, but also to suggest it will identify with the colonial subject.[9] In this, his first formal piece of literary criticism, Conrad takes an opportunity to deliver a polemic that will feature often in his fiction and the fiction of his imitators: the irreconcilability of multiple and competing systems of belief.

The omission of the "Author's Note" from the 1895 edition of the novel was clearly problematic. *The Literary World* complains: "One gets to the end of the story wishing there had been more characters in it with whom one could heartily sympathise, and more light and brightness to relieve the general gloom of the incidents narrated."[10] *The National Observer* describes "a feeling of disappointment that what promises to be a tale of sturdy adventure in an unfamiliar and picturesque world, should turn into a long-drawn story of despair."[11] As one

American reviewer put it: "It is difficult to understand just why this book should have been written. Whatever may have been the object of the author, Joseph Conrad, he has succeeded in giving us a decidedly unpleasant and apparently entirely aimless tale."[12] At its core, the bewilderment of this reviewer is an expression of the novel's generic disassociations. At the same time that its setting in the exotic East and cast of white and native characters announces its obligation to a certain extant narrative trajectory, it lacks bearers of Western morality and virtue, it presents a dystopic rather than idealized colonial landscape, and it is not committed to the triumphant racial superiority of its European characters.

Almayer, rather, is a representative figure of an altogether different kind; he belongs to that "class of petty-bourgeois colonials who hold power over a native population for purely contingent reasons, and who therefore exhibit all the symptoms of unearned self-esteem."[13] Of Dutch origin, Almayer resides in the fictional "Sambir" with his Malay wife whom he marries as a favor to the English trader Captain Lingard. Almayer is aggrieved daily by his marriage to an inferior, but Lingard's promise of riches is persuasive. With his new wealth, Almayer intends to relocate to Europe with his mixed-race daughter where he believes she will be accepted unreservedly as a member of that superior race to which he proudly belongs. Almayer, however, fails miserably in both his economic ventures and in securing the race loyalty of his daughter. Almayer's "folly" might be enlarged to include not only the house he builds to mark what he believes to be his inevitable and just success, but the foolishness of the very assumptions that underpin its construction. The narrative determinedly challenges the "romantic idealism" typical of the adventure novel.[14]

As Andrea White's and Linda Dryden's seminal studies of Conrad's colonial fictions in the context of imperial discourse at the turn of the century reveal, though Conrad was not the only writer to begin to question both the premises and promises of these popular genres, it is, perhaps, the depth of his repeated probing and revision that have instantiated his ideological distance from the likes of Kipling and Haggard.[15] Nevertheless, not everyone was attuned to Conrad's difference. *The Guardian* described his debut novel as "a romance in all senses of the word."[16] Perhaps the greatest misreading of the book can be attributed to the reviewer for *The Publishers' Circular,* who celebrates *Almayer's Folly* as a book that "will please readers who can appreciate the romance of adventure of wild life as a pleasant change from the 'problems' of 'modern' fiction."[17] The "problems" that feature in *Almayer's Folly,* which might be described as the uncontested racial superiority of Europeans, the unviability of expansion, and the exploitation of the resources and peoples in "far-off lands," were emphatically modern issues at the height of empire: issues as integral to the outposts of empire as to the metropolitan centers where the social and economic boons and costs of empire were debated daily in the press, among other public institutions.

If these responses largely address Conrad's peculiar "matter," this was not at the cost of discussions of his "style." Readers note repeatedly the novel's discretion with respect to divulging the precise thoughts and motivations of his characters. Moreover, the pacing and sequencing of events seem to be a departure from the linear, progress-driven action of the adventure tale. Much like the reaction to his unusual plots, the novelty Conrad introduces through the style of his writing is either celebrated or dismissed as detracting from what readers perceive to be his design. The thoroughgoing praise of the novel offered by the reviewer at *The Speaker,* who approves of Conrad's "delightful reticence and self-restraint" because it makes the tragedy of Almayer "more impressive," or *The Bookman*'s assertion that any summary of the events of the novel would be inadequate since it is "vague, and subtle, and mysterious" and its story "is rather told by suggestion than in asserted fact" is countered by what is described as the "inchoate method of composition which [Conrad] adopts" or his "laboured and muddle-headed involution."[18] For the irate critic at *The Sketch,* this novel's subtlety and suggestion is "a terrible offence": Conrad "forces his readers too often to turn back and re-read something of importance to the narrative . . . he had too slightly insisted on to command their attention and memory," which we might note, looking ahead, as one of the hallmarks of the modernist novel.[19]

Yet in another expression of the difficulty of placing Conrad in a tradition, according to E. M. Forster and Virginia Woolf, two self-styled practitioners of the modern novel, though Conrad was not a Captain Marryat or a James Fenimore Cooper, they would not go as far as claiming Conrad as one of their own. In her obituary for Conrad, first published in the *Times Literary Supplement* and later collected in *The Common Reader,* Woolf takes stock of Conrad's career. She admires the early sea fiction especially, but Conrad's later fiction proves he is unable to tackle effectively "this more crowded and complicated world" of contemporary life on land. The scenarios under which he developed his characters in his early fiction find no place in "drawing-rooms."[20] Conrad's "old nobilities and sonorities: fidelity, compassion, honour, service" are "now a little wearily reiterated, as if times had changed."[21]

If the first novel could be reduced to the work of a literary neophyte, Conrad's second novel suggested that he was invested in the subject matter of *Almayer's Folly* and the cultivation of a particular style, which Woolf would, in fact, imitate. Conrad explains that he only began *An Outcast of the Islands* (1896) when his reader Edward Garnett suggested he write another book. However, as Hans van Marle points out, the writing of *An Outcast of the Islands,* then titled "Two Vagabonds," was already well under way.[22] *An Outcast of the Islands* presents not only an opportunity for Conrad to develop the histories of a cast of characters he found compelling or to enlarge upon the economic rivalries of Sambir; it also allows him to pursue the themes of *Almayer's Folly* further.

Conrad's interest in the unequal distribution of power between races persists in this fiction.

Few critics were alert to this element of his text; instead, with another novel set in exotic lands, the comparisons to Kipling gained force. However, the perceived novelty of Conrad's fiction did not wear off entirely. Conrad's work was different from the "ordinary" novel. In making this distinction, the reviewer for *The Academy* recommends *An Outcast of the Islands* for the 1 percent of readers, the vast majority of the public being too incompetent to appreciate it. The reviewer continues: *An Outcast of the Islands* cannot be summarized in the space of a review as its "excellence lies in the way of telling it."[23] Again, the emphasis on how the particularity of the novel's form contributes to its meaning anticipates the structural experimentalism of modernist fiction. H. G. Wells's unsigned piece for *The Saturday Review* reiterates the idea that Conrad is writing pioneering fiction. According to Wells: "'An Outcast of the Islands' is, perhaps, the finest piece of fiction that has been published this year. . . . It is hard to understand how the respectable young men from the universities who are engaged in cutting out cheaper imitations of the work of Mr. Stanley Weyman and Mr. Anthony Hope can read a book like this and continue in that industry."[24]

Conrad the Imitable

It is only apt that Wells would go on to become one of Conrad's imitators. *Tono-Bungay,* published two years after Conrad's letter to Pinker, relies heavily on the imagined Africa of *Heart of Darkness.* This was not, of course, the only text published during Conrad's lifetime that might be described as imitative. Leonard Woolf's "Pearls and Swine" (1921) also draws on *Heart of Darkness,* as does Virginia Woolf's apprenticeship novel, *The Voyage Out* (1917). Woolf's novel takes place in the fictional port town of "Santa Marina" in South America where, among other organized activities, a group of British tourists venture out to observe natives. The description of their journey to the native village is strongly redolent of Marlow's trip to the inner station in *Heart of Darkness.* The singularity of Conrad's "matter" and "style" also offered itself up to less serious imitation. Max Beerbohm's "The Feast by J*s*ph C*nr*d," collected in his 1912 book of short stories, *A Christmas Garland,* mimics the language and so-called exotic locales of Conrad's early fiction. Beerbohm's short story is replete with repetitions and dense description. But perhaps it is the tale's irony that distinguishes it most as an imitation of Conrad. Conrad's ironic treatment of his disillusioned protagonists is, in the Beerbohm, applied disproportionately to objects: "Within the hut the form of the white man, corpulent and pale, was covered by a mosquito-net that was itself illusory like everything else, only more so."[25] Across the Atlantic, Willa Cather's 1912 "Behind the Singer Tower" invoked Conrad's anonymous frame narrator as one of her many borrowings from *Heart of Darkness.* The narrator of her short story, on a boat with a doctor, newspaperman, draftsman, lawyer, and engineer, recounts the yarn of the engineer as they cruise along New York's North River. The engineer tells an inconclusive story about the labor exploitation of foreigners in the city.

We do not know precisely what Conrad meant by "imitators" in this letter to his agent; that is, would he have acknowledged the works of authors as disparate as Wells, the Woolfs, Beerbohm, and Cather as imitators of his "style," "matter," or subtle "turn of mind"? In *Palimpsests: Literature in the Second Degree,* Gérard Genette, though ultimately rejecting the term "imitation" in favour of "mimetism," offers a definition of the imitative act in literature. For Genette, imitation, or mimetism, is a scenario in which an author borrows "from another author (in order to imitate his style)."[26] This borrowing could include "a figure of speech or a figure of thought or even a characteristic trope."[27] As a precondition of imitation, the figure being imitated must lend "itself to the process" of imitation.[28] Genette elaborates: "For to imitate a particular text in its particularity first means that one should establish that text's idiolect—i.e., identify its specific stylistic and thematic features—and then generalize them: that is, constitute them as a matrix of imitation, or a network of mimeticisms, which can serve indefinitely. No matter how individual and specific the corpus of extraction, an idiolect, by definition, is not a word, a discourse, a message, but rather a language: i.e., a code wherein the specificities of the message have been made fit for generalization."[29]

Virginia Woolf's imitation of *Heart of Darkness,* as one example, can therefore be understood as occurring on the condition of her recognition of the idiolect of Conrad's text—that which is imitable—which is itself dependent on the potentiality of those features of Conrad's text to be iterated. In the journey scene of *The Voyage Out,* the narrator explains that a group of six "English people" join an expedition to observe a native village. Though these characters have names, and by this stage, we are well acquainted with them, they are referred to as "the English."[30] With the prospect of meeting natives, the anxiety over their racial difference seems to manifest as repeated gestures to nationality. Though like Conrad, the imagined threat of defilement or contagion that attends proximity to natives is largely undermined in Woolf's novel. Instead, these foreign or uncertain circumstances facilitate the real difficulty: one's confrontation with the repressed or hidden self. The anxiety of the impending meeting with the natives (or moment of self-exposure) is also mirrored in the details of the group's movement upriver, where Conrad's idiolect in Woolf's idiom gains force: "They seemed to be driving into the heart of the night, for the trees closed in front of them . . . the great darkness had the usual effect of taking away all desire for communication by making their words sound thin and small . . . they clustered together, yawning deeply, and looking at the same spot of deep gloom on the banks. Murmuring very low in the rhythmical tone of one oppressed by the air."[31] The immediacy of "heart" and "darkness" in these sentences that describe a river journey at night, through thick vegetation, and in stifling air, recall the context of Marlow's trip to the inner station to meet Kurtz.

Woolf's ability to transpose Conrad's "darkness" to the colonized South America of her novel indicates the particularity of Conrad's conception of darkness. Contemporary invocations of darkness, typified by popular works, including Stanley's *Through the Dark Continent* (1878) and *In Darkest Africa* (1890), connote a continent not yet discovered, a part of the world devoid of the light of civilization. As an epithet for Africa, dark or darkness is entrenched to the degree that Marlow bypasses its naming. Marlow describes his fascination for maps and exploration as a child, and he remembers hankering after the "biggest—the most blank" space that has since "become a place of darkness."[32] "Africa" is never named as such. However, as Benita Parry and many other critics note, Conrad evokes darkness in many competing contexts in the novella, which serve to undermine its "established significations."[33] The word appears nearly thirty times across the text. It characterizes variously European history, Africa, Kurtz's heart, the Company's headquarters in Belgium, a moral void (largely attributed to European enterprises and characters), and the sky over the Thames and the Congo River.

In Genette's words then, Conrad's darkness is a feature "that seeks to emigrate and whose behaviour betrays them to the immigration authorities."[34] Insofar as this feature is "marked and identified, and capable of being reproduced, imitated, transferred, and in some way exported into another idiom," it will "unfailingly—and, to the trained ear, always perceptibly—preserve the stamp of its origin."[35] It is therefore possible to describe the journey scene in *The Voyage Out,* though occurring in a different geographical and temporal context, as an imitation of *Heart of Darkness.*

Genette's formulation of imitation offers, in part, an explanation for Conrad's miscalculation of his legacy. Conrad's lack of resemblance to his contemporaries—as the early reviews signal repeatedly—seems, in fact, to contribute to the potential for his imitation. As Woolf discerned in his particular usage of "darkness," or as Beerbohm recognized through his portrayal of a bloated colonialist in "The Feast," Conrad was doing something similar enough to his contemporaries that his singularity could be recognized as a "change." This particular "change" that his "subject," "style," and "turn of mind" offered can broadly be understood as a lack of fidelity to genre. Crucially, an iterative potential is borne with the perceptibility of this change: a potential that has led to a long history of imitative texts, up to and including current fiction.

Conrad's generic misfit suggests one factor in his imitability, though it would be slightly amiss to ignore the importance of his canonical status in this regard. The institutionalization of Conrad, facilitated most notably by the critic F. R. Leavis, contributed widely to Conrad's preeminent position in the history of English literature. Leavis's *The Great Tradition,* published in 1948, identifies Conrad as belonging to a tradition that includes Jane Austen, George Eliot, and Henry James. This book, in addition to a few other interventions, initiated the serious study of Conrad in the academy.[36] Today, Conrad is readily found on English literature course syllabi, and multiple editions of his works distributed by major publishing series including Penguin Classics and Oxford World's Classics only solidify his canonical status. In other words, Conrad's texts are widely accessible for imitation, and there are many "immigration authorities" able to recognize these imitations when they are written.[37] Padmini Mongia asserted that Conrad "is encountered—whether one wants to or not—in . . . college courses all over the world. Conrad has been everywhere before all of us who were schooled in English literature, whether we come from areas he wrote about or not." In the last fifty years, however, many of Conrad's imitators derive from the formerly colonized world, and they are not always admiring.[38]

Whether Conrad ascribed value to his possible imitation—that is, if he understood imitation as a classical virtue rather than the more recent premium placed on originality—is difficult to say with certainty. Genette describes the text that one is imitating as "a means of actualization—and possibly of derision."[39] Indeed, the contemporary turn to Conrad varies considerably. On the one hand, Conrad's fiction is invoked as part of a revisionary project. The term "writing back," for example, characterizes the adaptations of Chinua Achebe and Ngũgĩ Wa Thiong'o as they seek to dismantle the authoritative status of Conrad's Africa in *Heart of Darkness* in the colonial context. On the other hand, many of Conrad's fictions are rewritten by authors perceptibly less invested in imitating Conrad as a challenge to his formulation of the colonial encounter and from locations that are not referenced by his fiction.

The geographical reach of the sources of imitation is impressive. Works by Robert Kroetsch, Michael Ondaatje, J. M. Coetzee, Kim Scott, David Malouf, Arundhati Roy, and David Dabydeen are just some of the English-language writers who can be counted among what Peter Nazareth describes as Conrad's "descendants"; however, the capaciousness of the term "imitation," as it allows for deeply critical engagement in addition to deferential writing, seems preferable here in describing the sheer scope of literary responses to Conrad's *oeuvre.*[40] There appears to be no shortage of imitations of Conrad. Pulitzer Prize–winning author Richard Ford's recent offering, *Canada,* published in 2012, draws extensively on the iterative potential of the Marlow-Kurtz relationship.

For Arthur Remlinger—the American version of Conrad's Kurtz—it is the Canadian prairie that becomes a lawless frontier. Remlinger attempts to escape his troubled past by moving to a Saskatchewan prairie town where he effectively becomes the major business operator. It is here that the novel's protagonist and narrator Dell Parsons has a life-altering encounter with Remlinger. After Dell's parents are jailed for bank robbery, Remlinger becomes Dell's guardian. However, Remlinger will not turn out to be the surrogate parent that Dell expects. Dell's new caregiver and employer "did only what he wanted to do, within limits he alone recognized,"[41] recalling Marlow's description of Kurtz as a man who had "kicked himself loose of the earth."[42] The loquacious and declamatory Remlinger "*wanted* significance,"[43] but we are led to believe that, like Kurtz, he is a voice "hollow at the core."[44] On a day seemingly like any other, Remlinger forces the young Dell to accompany him on a planned trip to murder his American accusers. And yet, despite Dell's recognition of the absolute inappropriateness of his presence, and the horrific act of murder, Dell chooses not to report the crimes. Like Marlow's desire to preserve Kurtz's reputation contra the Company's allegations and especially when faced by Kurtz's Intended, Dell is "trapped and unable to resist" Remlinger.[45] Dell, too, will look back on his months with Remlinger, and this event in particular, as distasteful though formative: an experience that would change "the nature" of his life.[46]

At the point in the novel's narration, Dell is a sixty-six-year-old English teacher living in Ontario. In one of the narrative's most compelling moments, he names *Heart of Darkness* as a text he teaches his students because it is one of those "books that seem secretly about my young life."[47] It seems readers are being asked to consider how Dell's knowledge of *Heart of Darkness* has given shape to his experience with Remlinger. More broadly, how has Ford's recognition of the iterative potential of the Marlow-Kurtz dynamic—whose formulation is indebted to the colonial situation of Conrad's novel but can also, evidently, survive outside it—enabled the writing of *Canada*? Perhaps the more pertinent question is how the act of imitating Conrad can address present-day dilemmas. In other words, what is the purchase or profit authors obtain by imitating Conrad today?

Of *Heart of Darkness,* Benita Parry evocatively suggests that the novella's division between the mode of a "realist text" and the "opacity that . . . intensifies as the novel moves spatially and psychologically away from familiar terrains" is generative.[48] The "paradoxical connection between what can appear disjunctive, between a turn-of-the-century novel written in an era saturated in confident notions about cultural hierarchy and imperial destiny, but that concedes of its inability to speak of a world into which it has journeyed" might be distilled to the question of the novella's generic ambiguity.[49] For Parry, it is this paradox that has incited the widespread imitation of *Heart of Darkness.* In Conrad's novella, "a deliberated linguistic obscurity gestures toward meanings that the novel cannot understand, but that are perceived as *there* and awaiting a time when they will be spoken."[50] It seems thus that Conrad has uniquely, and yet unconsciously, availed himself to a future of imitation.

Well over a century after the first reviews of *Almayer's Folly,* conflicting appraisals of Conrad's generic associations and disassociations, political affiliations, and aesthetic commitments persist. The multiple responses of postcolonial authors especially to the colonial content of Conrad's early fictions—but, as the case of *Canada* would suggest, not exclusively so—indicate that the question of Conrad's "fit" with a particular tradition and, perhaps, concomitantly, the desire to imitate him, remain pressing.

Maternal Return

Lord Jim's Spectral Narrative

CAROLA M. KAPLAN

Although *Lord Jim,* with its multiple interpretations of Jim's story, is one of Conrad's talkiest novels, at its heart is a silence—a narrative hole as large as the abortive off-stage bombing of Greenwich Observatory in *The Secret Agent.* Perhaps Lord Jim's most eloquent story is one that is never told because it is, as Marlow and the larger text acknowledge, untellable. It is the story of Jewel's mother—that is, the mother of Jim's Malaysian mistress in Patusan. And behind the story of Jewel's mother is another untold and untellable tale—that of Jewel's mother's mother. Because they defy or exceed narration, these tales of silent, abandoned women call into question the meaning of Jim's story: in fact, they ask whether his story is meaningful at all. Ultimately, they underline the limitations of language and call into question the very nature of narrative itself.

On a narrative level, Jewel's mother is superfluous: she exists only in the form of "an unquiet grave," a reminder of betrayal and marital unhappiness that continues to exist in Jewel's life as an uneasiness about the trustworthiness of white men. Yet in her namelessness and silence, in her very extraneousness to the movement of the narrative, and in her displacement lies her significance. Jewel's mother is the visible sign of social injustice in the novel. Her misfortunes are reminders of the shortcomings of male-forged and male-dominated social institutions—marriage, the family, the state, the colony. The mother is thus the site of what Homi Bhabha terms "the unhomely."[1] Bhabha's concept of the "unhomely" derives from Freud's idea of the *unheimlich* or the "uncanny." By the "uncanny," Freud refers to a once-familiar thing that has been repressed in the past but that recurs in the present to frightening effect. There is of course a reason for this repression. The uncanny is "something which ought to have remained hidden but has come to light."[2] Thus an uncanny experience is one in which something one would wish to forget—something unpleasant or disturbing—returns to obtrude itself upon one's present existence.

In using the term "unhomely" in place of the "uncanny," Bhabha puns on the German word "heim" meaning "home." Applying Freud's term to a postcolonial context, he suggests that specific historical situations evoke the experience of the "unheimlich" or "uncanny," in particular the situation of colonization. For the colonized, home is unhomely for to be at home in a colonial context is also to be dispossessed, to live in a place at once familiar and strange. Thus, unhomeliness is not the same as homelessness. Rather, to be "unhomed" is to live in a condition of psychic and social displacement, a state of nonbelonging that destabilizes the categories and constructions upon which the civil state depends.

The recurrent character in Conrad's novels that I refer to as the "unhomely" mother reminds other characters—and, by extension, the reader—of an unpleasant reality they would prefer to forget. Because she precipitates a return of the repressed, she reveals that the apparently homey place she inhabits is in fact "unheimlich" or uncanny. By her very presence within it, the "unhomely" mother makes the home uneasy and unnatural for those around her.

In revealing the home to be unhomely, each of these mothers evokes as well a larger world, within which she also has her meaning but does not have a place—the world of social practice and political reality that exists outside the home. This world contains the repressed histories of subordinated peoples; in this instance, the repressed history of womankind: as Bhabha points out, "The 'unhomely' . . . dramatizes—in the figure of woman—the ambivalent structure of the civil State as it draws its rather paradoxical boundary between the private and the public spheres."[3] What makes this boundary paradoxical is that it reveals "the patriarchal, gendered nature of civil society and disturbs the symmetry of private and public which is now shadowed, or uncannily doubled, by the difference of genders which does not neatly map on to the private and the public, but becomes disturbingly supplementary to them."[4] "Woman" does not have her proper place in either realm, and so, makes this apparently "natural" division both excessive and inadequate. Thus the unhomely mother, like all women, belongs in neither the public nor private spheres; or, rather, she simultaneously belongs in both and neither. Her existence therefore calls into question the self-containment and separation of these two categories. Each of these mothers precipitates an unhomely moment in the life of one or more of the other characters—a moment of crisis in which the familiar becomes uncanny. Not only does the mother occasion these moments: she also offers a key to their meaning.

Such a moment occurs for Marlow when Jewel evokes for him the scene of her mother on her deathbed. In this unhomely moment, as Bhabha observes of all unhomely moments, "the recesses of the domestic space become sites for history's most intricate invasions. In that displacement, the borders between home and world become confused; and, uncannily, the private and the public become part of each other, forcing upon us a vision that is as divided as it is disorienting."[5] This is a vision of the disorder that underlies social systems, the shortfall in equity and public responsibility that disrupts the balance of domestic relationships. By evoking this vision, these martyred mothers become an instrument of social criticism in these novels. In *Lord Jim,* Jewel's mother, her unquiet grave a protest against her serial betrayals by white men, points up the abuses of colonialism. Winnie's mother in *The Secret Agent,* who seeks shelter in an almshouse, bespeaks the inadequacy of marriage to provide for women. Mrs. Haldin, in *Under Western Eyes,* manifests the toll on human lives exacted of its subjects by an autocratic state and registers the suffering inflicted upon their families by idealistic, impractical revolutionaries. The mother in these novels is therefore the silent victim and witness of the trauma of history about which the text cannot speak directly because it is imbedded in and supported by that history—and may even exist in part to justify that history.

In *Lord Jim,* two social systems fatefully intersect in the life of Jewel's mother: for her, the shortcomings of patriarchy are exacerbated by the abuses of colonialism. Having undone the life of the mother, these paired social evils will undo the life of the daughter as well. Marlow sketchily recounts at second-hand the relationship of Jewel's mother with a highly placed white official, an alliance that produced Jewel. When that relationship ended, Jewel's mother turned in desperation to another white colonialist, the ne'er-do-well Cornelius. When Jewel sees her mother die weeping, she vows not to repeat her mother's miserable history; but once she herself becomes involved in a cross-cultural love affair, she inevitably reenacts it.

Because the story of Jewel's mother is refracted through Marlow, the text can merely suggest rather than directly relate her history—and by extension the story of myriad women undone by the colonial enterprise: "How the poor woman had come to marry the awful little Malacca Portuguese—after the separation from the father of her girl—and how that separation had been brought about, whether by death, which can be sometimes merciful, or by the merciless pressure of conventions, is a mystery to me."[6] Whether her union with Jewel's father ended in death or in cruel abandonment, Marlow cannot say. His lack of knowledge on this crucial point both reminds the reader of the white, male, colonialist perspective from which her story is told and points up the ignorance of participants in the colonial enterprise regarding the lives of colonized people, including the injury they sustain at the hands of their colonizers. Further, Marlow's lack of knowledge confirms Gayatri Spivak's observation: "Within the effaced itinerary of the subaltern subject, the track of sexual difference is doubly [effaced]. . . . If, in the context of colonial production, the subaltern has no history and cannot speak, the subaltern as female is even more deeply in shadow."[7] If Marlow shows little understanding of colonized males, such as Dain Waris, whom he describes in exaggerated and stereotypic terms, he is truly ignorant about the lives of colonial women such as Jewel and her mother.

As Marlow, for all his limitations, correctly maintains, Jewel's love affair with Jim must be viewed and judged in light of her mother's history, for it is her mother's history that makes theirs a story for which "the ordinary standpoint" is not "adequate."[8] What makes their love affair different from "so many such stories," which "[f]or the most part we look upon as stories of opportunities: episodes of passion at best," is, Marlow insists, "the significant fact of an unforgotten grave": "there is visible in its background the melancholy figure of a woman, the shadow of a cruel wisdom buried in a lonely grave, looking on wistfully, helplessly, with sealed lips."[9] And, as evidence of Jim's "conscience" in the affair, Marlow points out that "Jim with his own hands had worked at the rustic fence"[10] enclosing—and symbolically sanctifying—the mother's grave site.

Jim himself attests to what Marlow terms "his seriousness" in his relationship with Jewel: "You take a different view of your actions when you come to understand, when you are *made* to understand every day that your existence is necessary—you see, absolutely necessary—to another person. I am made to feel that. Wonderful. . . . Well, it is a trust too. . . . I believe I am equal to it."[11] Yet this assertion is more closely allied with Jim's egotism than with his commitment to Jewel, as Marlow himself suggests: "He slapped his chest. 'Yes! I feel that, but I believe I am equal to all my luck!' He had the gift of finding a special meaning in everything that happened to him. This was the view he took of his love affair."[12] What is lacking in his relationship with Jewel is evident in his first stammering reference to it, when he assures Marlow that it is "exactly as if,"[13] that Jim's connection with Jewel is not a marriage but a simulation of one—"exactly as if"— is echoed in Marlow's description of Jim's name for her: "Jewel he called her, with a marital, home*like,* peaceful *effect.*"[14]

When Gentleman Brown persuades Jim to help him, in part through a racialist appeal—"You have been white once, for all your tall talk of this being your own people and you being one with them"[15]—the text confirms Jewel's deepest misgivings and fulfills her worst fears: "You always leave us for your own ends."[16] Jewel's tale and Jim's is the old story of colonial romance turned to ashes, after all. In fact, the novel suggests that all romances that bloom in the shadow of colonialism are doomed—Stein's marriage to "the princess," that ends in the death of his wife and daughter; as well as the "dark story" of Gentleman Brown's elopement with a missionary's wife, at whose death Brown "gave way to an outburst of sombre and violent grief."[17]

At the end of the novel, the difference between Jewel's assessment of Jim, "He was like the others," and Marlow's, "Not like the others";[18] between Jewel's condemnation, "He was false," and Stein's defense, "No! no! no! Not false! True! true!"[19] reveals an unbridgeable gulf between them. This gulf is the difference between the way the indigenous population experiences colonization and the way the white male participants view the colonial enterprise. The novel does not deal with these merely as conflicting perspectives, which produce rival claims, incapable of resolution. Rather, the narrative, by repeating the story of Jewel's mother in the abandonment of her daughter, suggests the loss that the colonized—in particular, women—sustain in being deprived of their own real lives. Through many examples, the text powerfully illustrates Marlow's assertion: "our common fate fastens upon the women with a peculiar cruelty."[20]

In retelling the story of Jewel's mother, Marlow first notes that, although she was "no ordinary woman," she "lacked the saving dullness—and her career ended in Patusan."[21] What career, the reader may well ask. Her so-called career—a liaison that ends unhappily—is certainly not analogous to that of Jewel's father, "a high official" known as "one of the brilliantly endowed men,"[22] who has both agency and choice, as she apparently does not.

Further, in recounting her daughter Jewel's story, Marlow makes even clearer the foreclosure of a woman's "career." Marlow indicates with a number of examples Jewel's bravery, independent spirit, and initiative—all of which she enlists on Jim's behalf: in fact, he owes much of his success to her. It is not Jim who rescues Jewel but rather she who protects and aids him. First, she rejects Jim's offer to kill Cornelius, declaring "that if she had not been sure he was intensely wretched himself, she would have found the courage to kill him with her own hands."[23] Then she gives Jim "a lot of useful hints as to Patusan affairs,"[24] loads and brings him his revolver so that he can defend himself, warns him about a planned ambush, holds the torch unwaveringly and at peril to herself while he defeats his would-be assassins, and watches over him in his sleep to protect him.[25] Unlike Jim, she makes no declarations but is unequivocally "true." In actuality, she gives up her own life for his: "She lived so completely in his contemplation that she had acquired something of his outward aspect, something that recalled him in her movements, in the way she stretched her arm, turned her head, directed her glances."[26]

In showing how pervasively women's careers are absorbed into men's, the text protests against the toll taken by patriarchy and colonialism on the lives of women. In fact, in its imagery, the novel suggests that Jewel is the final specimen in Stein's butterfly collection. When Marlow's responses to Jewel's questions fail to allay her anxiety about Jim, Jewel resembles a captured butterfly: "two wide sleeves uprose in the dark like unfolding wings, and she stood silent, holding her head in her hands."[27] And when she moves to Stein's house after Jim's death, Marlow reports, "the poor girl is leading a sort of soundless, inert life."[28] She is "soundless" and "inert" like one of the specimens in Stein's cases.

The moral import of Jewel's experience—and the experiences of all women whose lives are undone by patriarchy and colonialism acting in consort—is conveyed through Marlow's unhomely moment, in which he contemplates the scene of Jewel's mother, weeping on her death bed. He reflects: "It [the passive, irremediable horror of the scene] had the power to drive me out of my conception of existence, out of that shelter each of us makes for himself to creep under in moments of danger, as a tortoise withdraws within its shell. For a moment I had a view of a world that seemed to wear a vast and dismal aspect of disorder. . . . I seemed to have lost all my words in the chaos of dark thoughts I had contemplated a second or two beyond the pale. These came back too very soon, for words also belong to the sheltering conception of light and order which is our refuge."[29]

Marlow, for whom culture, class, and gender combine to make this moment intolerable, turns away from it. But the reader cannot fail to consider its implications. In sum, Jewel's martyred mother in *Lord Jim* is a crucial figure in the text. This figure serves to criticize patriarchal institutions and to undercut men's actions, including their heroic exploits. In her silence and immobility, she is a reminder of the wrongs suffered by women that are not generally represented within the masculine conventions and language of narrative. The unhomely mother thus points up the gaps and omissions in conventional narrative and suggests that any definition of subjectivity predicated on male action and masculine language is both overdetermined and incomplete.

The Other Side of the Page in Typhoon

THOMAS JACKSON RICE

Joseph Conrad concludes the first chapter of his novella *Typhoon* much as he concludes the sixth and final chapter of his story, with letters written by three of its principal characters, Captain MacWhirr, Mr. Solomon Rout the chief engineer, and Mr. Jukes the first mate of the steamer *Nan-Shan,* bound "from the southward to the treaty port of Fu-chau" on the journey that the tale describes.[1] By incorporating these letters into his work, Conrad evokes the formula of the epistolary novel, but only mildly and in passing, merely quoting a few passages from these letters in the opening and somewhat more of their contents in the close.[2] The first and final chapters follow the same order, citing the letters of MacWhirr, Rout, and Jukes in turn, and in both instances providing more extended extracts from Jukes's correspondence with a "former shipmate."[3] A further similarity between the book's opening and close is that in each case Conrad mediates the letters of MacWhirr and Rout through the responses of their recipients, both those intended—the men's wives respectively—and one unintended: MacWhirr's steward furtively reads his captain's letters when he is out of his cabin. The readers of *Typhoon,* however, receive no information about the response of Jukes's recipient, his "old chum,"[4] leaving them speculating at the book's close whether the narrator of the story has himself been Jukes's shipmate, which would explain why the text contains more of the first mate's letters, or perhaps leaving the readers with the final impression that they themselves have been inserted into the role of audience for Jukes's letters, much as they have witnessed his perspective throughout much of the story. More generally, Conrad's decision to begin and end *Typhoon* with these precisely parallel letter sequences (not to mention a few additional remarks on MacWhirr's letters to his parents and his wife earlier in chapter 1), testifies to his growing concern for fictional form as he completes his literary apprenticeship.

These letters structurally frame the action of *Typhoon* and, as a patterned repetition, contribute to the motifs of circularity in his book, mirroring the circular storm that gives Conrad his title and his story's central event. Yet in another sense his presentation of these letters seems asymmetrical, since the readers apparently learn little of significance from the letters of the most important character in the book, Captain MacWhirr, the figure who stimulated Conrad's conception of *Typhoon* and the center of his novella's attention,[5] notwithstanding the allocation of most of its story to the perspective of the first mate Jukes. But at least Jukes is preoccupied with his captain, both in his letters and through much of his experience in the book. Unfortunately, MacWhirr does not get anything like the same attention from his wife, who has long since tired of perusing his monthly letters to her because they are "so prosy, so completely uninteresting," and who lives in "abject terror of the time when her husband would come home to stay for good."[6] Ironically, the readers gain what little sense they have of MacWhirr's reaction to his experience in *Typhoon* only through what his wife does *not* read in his letter in the book's conclusion. Skimming her husband's letter "perfunctorily," Mrs. MacWhirr fails to notice that he has written on both sides of the page.[7] "It did not occur to her to turn back overleaf to look. She would have found it recorded there that between 4 and 6 a.m. on December 25, Captain MacWhirr did actually think that his ship could not possibly live another hour in such a sea, and that he would never see his wife and children again."[8] "No body was to know this," the narrator adds, except the steward who has once again spied on the captain's letters: "They interested him much more than they possibly could the woman for whose eye they were intended."[9]

This apparently minor moment in the novella, the steward's discovery of MacWhirr's words, will prove absolutely central to our understanding of *Typhoon* and its pivotal position in Conrad's career. This novella is remarkable for early Conrad not only in its formal discipline, but also because it offers a kind of meditation on the response to language that is exceptionally alert to the problems of attention, specifically demonstrating an awareness that indifferent and inattentive readers routinely fail to reciprocate the writer's attention. *Typhoon* marks Conrad's arrival at his literary maturity through his accommodation to this audience. In his conclusion to this tale, Conrad seems to disclose his realization that much of his readership is composed of "Mrs. MacWhirrs" who will not and cannot attend fully to his art. Or perhaps like the captain himself, who has "just enough imagination to carry him through each successive day, and no more," this readership may not even be able to respond to literary language.[10] Given this reality, Conrad seems to suggest in *Typhoon* that his future fictions would seek more compelling forms of appeal to the attention of his audience without pandering, without compromising his artistic convictions, by exploiting the conventions of popular literature without conventionality. In short, when he was writing *Typhoon,* Conrad was driven by the hope that, while he was again spinning "a bit of a sea yarn after all," he could create "a work that might be popular though not contemptible" and, above all, a work that would "capture the reader's attention."[11] One of the greatest ironies in the reception of this writer, himself so fond of irony, is that for most the century-and-more that has passed since the publication of *Typhoon,* Conrad's readers and critics have more nearly resembled Mrs. MacWhirr than the steward in their response to the captain's final letter, figuratively failing "to turn back overleaf to look" at its uncharacteristic confessional "disclosure," while those who have noted the time MacWhirr provides in his letter for the main action of the book, "December 25th," Christmas morning, have mostly done so in the manner of the captain, regarding this date as a logbook fact that has been entirely stripped of its cultural associations and literary significance.[12] The inattentive reading that Conrad feared and anticipated, it would seem, has been the fate of both Captain MacWhirr and the book that contains him, even though the book itself models the importance of giving attention to the apparently unprepossessing figure of the captain of the *Nan-Shan.*[13]

In his 1919 "Author's Note" for *Typhoon,* written nearly twenty years after he completed the novella, Conrad responded to those few discerning "critics" who had found a "definite symbolic intention" in the figure of Captain MacWhirr by claiming that such was not "exclusively my intention."[14] Rather than discounting the implication of symbolic significance for this character, Conrad opens the possibility that his creation may have multiple symbolic resonances by further acknowledging in his "Author's Note" that this tale has "more than one intention"[15] Among the many significances of MacWhirr, he functions as a representation both of the writer who remains unread *and* of the reader incapable of attention or discernment.[16] MacWhirr gets precisely what he deserves when his wife fails to read his letter completely, for he himself is skeptical of reading and repeatedly expresses his unresponsiveness toward the spoken and the written word through the story. In fact, he is the utter antithesis of his creator, who had extolled the "power" of the word "to make you hear, to make you feel, [and] to make you *see*" in his 1898 "Preface" to *The Nigger of the "Narcissus"* only two years earlier.[17] Conrad establishes the captain's limited grasp of the power of the spoken word in a series of comic scenes in the opening chapters of *Typhoon,* scenes in which he misunderstands his first mate's distress at sailing under the Siamese flag—"it looks queer to me"—as a question of the flag's design, or later wonders at Jukes's ability to chat with his fellow crewmen—"'I can't understand what you can find to talk about,' says he. 'Two solid hours. [. . .] Must be saying the same things over and over again'"—and most provocatively, given his status as a character in a work of literature, evidences a total inability to understand figurative language:

> "The weather's awful [said Jukes]. It would make a saint swear. Even up here I feel exactly as if I had my head tied up in a woolen blanket."
>
> Captain MacWhirr looked up. "D'ye mean to say, Mr. Jukes, you ever had your head tied up in a blanket? What was that for?"
>
> "It's a manner of speaking, sir," said Jukes stolidly.
>
> "Some of you fellows do go on! What's that about saints swearing? I wish you wouldn't talk so wild. [. . .]"
>
> Thus Captain MacWhirr expostulated against the use of images in speech [. . .][18]

Not only is it decidedly odd to find a creation of words like MacWhirr so dismissive of the power of language, but readers of *Typhoon* must contend with a literary character who repeatedly discounts the value of books. True, as a seaman who "had no experience of cataclysms," the captain does consult a navigation manual as the storm approaches, but only "with a conscious effort" and little profit, "becoming contemptuously angry with such a lot of words and with so much advice, all head-work and supposition, without a glimmer of certitude."[19] MacWhirr rejects the manual's advice to steer round the storm as cowardly nonsense—"You would think an old woman had been writing this"—and after assuring Jukes "you don't find everything in books," he returns the volume to its shelf.[20] Conrad emphasizes MacWhirr's rejection of the *book,* the very form of the written word that has given him existence, by having Jukes repeat it in the novella's penultimate sentence: "The skipper remarked to me the other day, 'There are things you find nothing about in books.'"[21]

For much of *Typhoon* it would appear that the tale is as uncomfortable with Captain MacWhirr as he is with language. The voice of the narrative emphatically differentiates itself from that of its central character, almost compulsively illustrating the powers of figurative language as if to expose and dispute the captain's literal-mindedness, especially in its descriptions of the storm. A typical illustration of how the narration engages in a kind of dialogue with its character is the image- and simile-laden paragraph that almost immediately follows MacWhirr's dismissal of figurative language: "At its setting the sun had a diminished diameter and an expiring brown, rayless glow, *as if* millions of centuries elapsing since the morning had brought it near its end. A dense bank of cloud became visible to the northward; it had a sinister dark olive tint, and lay low and motionless upon the sea, *resembling* a solid obstacle in the path of the ship. She went floundering towards it *like* an exhausted creature driven to its death. The coppery twilight retired slowly, and the darkness brought out overhead a swarm of unsteady, big stars, that, *as if* blown upon, flickered exceedingly and *seemed* to hang very near the earth."[22]

Mr. Jukes's opening letter dismisses MacWhirr as "too dense to trouble about," and he ends his latest letter by calling the captain "a stupid man."[23] It might seem that the narrator shares this opinion and covertly expresses Conrad's own contempt for the mass of inattentive readers by privileging Jukes's last words, making them the final words of the novella. But such a conclusion is wrong, and it illustrates precisely what is at stake in the question of attentive reading. More likely Conrad intends readers to retain the earlier, final words of the book's standard of wisdom, the significantly named *Solomon* Rout, whose opinion of the captain has changed. Given to saying, as Mrs. Rout reports, "give me the dullest ass for a skipper before a rogue," in his second letter he states that a remarkable, if small transformation has taken place in MacWhirr: "Solomon says, wonders will never cease," the dullest ass has "done something rather clever."[24] Time has also shown that few readers retain the telling detail of the Captain's latest letter to his wife that precedes Rout's, giving the Christmas date of the book's action and providing a key to the wondrous transformation that has occurred. At this point, however, it suffices to say that the narrative's compilation of points of view on its central character leaves the readers, at best, with an equivocal response to MacWhirr. I would argue that the book's ambivalence toward this man precisely matches the mixture of repulsion and attraction in Conrad's attitude toward his audience, the mass readership of periodical literature that he both despised and courted.

Virtually every introduction to the novelist retells the tale of Conrad's midlife decision to leave his maritime career and become a writer, in the English language no less. Somewhat less familiar but well documented is his sense of urgency about his new career, a profession with perhaps as much risk and uncertainty about it as his first. Already in his mid-thirties when his first novel, *Almayer's Folly,* was published in 1895, married shortly after in 1896 and a father by the beginning of 1898, Conrad reveals his anxiety about his choices toward the end of the century by flirting with the possibility of resuming his seafaring, by his recurrent episodes of nervous exhaustion, bordering on breakdown, as he strove to meet deadlines, by his obsessive preoccupation with marketing his work and with following his reviews, by his false starts and struggles with a novel-in-progress that he wasn't to complete until 1920 (*The Rescue*), and above all by his continuing searches for a subject and approach for his fiction that might promise popular and financial success. This anxiety seems to underlie the succession of his early masterworks that were critically well received but hardly best sellers, *The Nigger of the "Narcissus"* (1896–97; 1897), *Youth* (1898; 1898), *Heart of Darkness* (1898–99; 1899), *Lord Jim* (1898–1900; 1899–1900), and

Typhoon (1900–1901; 1902), each of which centers on—or in the case of *Lord Jim,* begins with—the hazards of the journey.[25]

Throughout this period Conrad, while driven to find a formula for popular success, was unstinting in his commitment to preserve the artistic integrity of his work, even should his aesthetic convictions militate against the very popularity he sought. What he seems most often to have found during these years, however, was more a formula for frustration than for popularity. For every expression of his ambition in his correspondence—"I must drive on. One decent success with a book would give me the chance to [financially] breathe freely. But will it ever come?"—there was a realization of its futility: "If only five thousand copies of [a "book of mine"] *could* be sold! If only! But why dream of the wealth of the Indies? I am not the man for whom Pactolus flows and the mines of Golconda distil priceless jewels[. . . .] I am *not* the man. And oh! [. . .] it *is* a fool's business to write fiction for a living. It is indeed."[26] Thus playing the role of MacWhirr's steward and enjoying access to Conrad's personal letters—edited and published in nine volumes (1983–2008)—we can observe and now appreciate Conrad's slow and painful progress toward the reconciliation of popular appeal and literary distinction that he ultimately achieved. *Typhoon,* a book that not only embodies the conflict of his ambition and despair in the equivocal portrayal of MacWhirr, also enacts this very struggle in content and in form.

As the steamship *Nan-Shan* perseveres through a typhoon in the China Sea for the tale's central action, "struggle" becomes a major motif. Struggles are both external and internal when Captain MacWhirr strives to maintain control of the ship and its crew, at one point even subduing the second mate, who has lost his nerve, while the first mate, Jukes, is challenged both to maintain his own self-control and to reestablish order in the ship's hold, where coolies, the ship's "cargo,"[27] have begun a very real physical struggle among themselves to secure their personal property during the typhoon. The *Nan-Shan,* the captain, and the first mate all succeed in their respective struggles with storms both without and within and above and below, as does the book that contains them, through the solidity of their construction, so to speak. The readers learn in the opening pages that the most salient fact about the steamship *Nan-Shan* is the soundness of her construction. An "exceptionally steady ship in a sea-way," to its builders the three-year-old *Nan-Shan* had been "finished in every detail" and perfect "from stem to stern," saving only one "defective lock" that they replaced after MacWhirr's inspection.[28] Not prone to superlatives, and given his indifference to language rarely moved to speak at all, MacWhirr is much like his ship. He is a solid, imperturbable, "undemonstrative" man who "betray[s] no sort of inward disturbance"—even at the dramatic "fall of a barometer" that presages the onset of the typhoon—nor will he tolerate any internal disturbance in the ship's hold during the storm: "Couldn't let that go on in my ship, if I knew she hadn't five minutes to live. Couldn't bear it, Mr. Jukes."[29] As the barometer falls in the opening pages, Jukes's exasperation with his captain rises, for his obtuseness over the Siamese flag, for his utter lack of imagination, and of course for his stubborn rejection of the storm strategies to be found in books and in the received wisdom of experienced mariners. Jukes's frustration is comically reflected in the "profane" curses of the second engineer, Harry, and even in a mild "Damme!" from the captain himself: "Here's temper, if you like," Jukes thinks. "Of course it's the weather; what else? It would make an angel quarrelsome—let alone a saint."[30] Likely Jukes himself is no angel either, let alone a saint, and Conrad's readers become privileged witnesses to the psycho-drama of Jukes's hesitating response to Captain MacWhirr's preposterous command, when the first half of the typhoon approaches its height, that he descend into the ship's hold and settle the disorder among the coolies.[31]

To heighten the tension within Jukes, at precisely this point Conrad inserts a six-page expository interruption to build suspense, describing the boatswain's descent into the hold and discovery of the "mound of writhing bodies" of the struggling coolies, and then he reiterates the captain's command at its close—"Captain MacWhirr had made Jukes understand that he wanted him to go down below.[32] Will Jukes obey this order or will he, like Lord Jim, rebel "against the tyranny of training and command"? [33] It is a question of Jukes's professionalism, his formation, his construction. "The absurdity of the demand made upon him revolted Jukes. He was as unwilling to go as if the moment he had left the deck the ship were sure to sink."[34] Though neither angel nor saint, Jukes nonetheless accepts the challenge imposed upon him—he "understood he would have to go"—demonstrating the ultimate soundness of his formation.[35] (Conversely, Marlow is both fascinated and appalled by the "unsoundness" of Jim, who has fled a ship that he believed was sure to sink.)[36] Conrad even invests the psychological drama of Jukes's obedience to his captain's demand with a kind of salvific spiritual significance, in a story uncharacteristically, for Conrad, laden with biblical imagery and echoes of Christian parables, appropriate to its Christmas setting.[37] Earlier when losing his footing on deck and fearing being swept overboard, Jukes has exclaimed "My God! My God! My God! My God!" before being grasped by the "stout arms" of MacWhirr: "He had found his captain."[38] Returning to his master, his task completed, and receiving his god-captain's commendation, Jukes experiences a Pentecostal "access of confidence, a sensation that came from outside like a warm breath, and made him feel equal to every demand."[39] Though worse is to come in the second half of the typhoon (perhaps a final judgment?), Jukes is at one with his "God."

It might seem counterintuitive to claim that the novella *Typhoon* is as much a model of aesthetic beauty and sound construction as the steamship *Nan-Shan* that carries MacWhirr and Jukes through the storm, and not simply because of the unbalanced focus on the letters of the secondary character Jukes, to the neglect of those of the central character MacWhirr. There is also a fundamental structural asymmetry in the story, given Conrad's extended treatment of the first half of the typhoon and total omission of the storm's second half, the "worst [. . .] to come" that he simply omits, sparing both his readers and the captain such an "annoyance."[40] This structural irregularity seems to indicate the author's ongoing difficulties with fictional form. He seems to have expended so much energy and verbiage on describing the first half of the typhoon that any treatment of the climactic second half would be repetitive and ironically anticlimactic. We might attempt to justify Conrad's method by pointing again to the theme of imagination in the narrative, so that the missing second half of the storm is left to the readers' imaginations, which are always more powerfully creative than what words may describe, and thus provokes in those readers what is singularly lacking in a central character that the narrator describes—in remarkably figurative terms—as incapable of grasping even figures of speech: "It was, in truth, as impossible for [MacWhirr] to take a flight of fancy as it would be for a watchmaker to put together a chronometer with nothing except a two-pound hammer and a whip-saw in the way of tools."[41] Yet the impression remains that, by lavishly describing the first half and then abruptly jumping over the second half of the storm and promptly ending his story, Conrad has once again lost control of his narrative, as he had with mild consequences in *Heart of Darkness*—"my infernal tale [. . .] grows like the genii from the bottle in the Arabian Tale"—and even more alarmingly with the "unexpected development" of the short story provisionally titled "*Jim: A sketch*" of 10,000 words that grew into a full-length novel of about 130,000 words, *Lord Jim*.[42] This loss of control would have been fresh in Conrad's mind as he began his composition of *Typhoon* in September 1900, only weeks after having finally completed *Lord Jim* in one feverish twenty-three-hour stint of composition that he protracted a bit longer to draft an apologetic letter to his remarkably patient serial publisher, William Blackwood.[43]

If Conrad was assured that he had solved his need for form to control his fictions through his discovery of the voice of Marlow, the garrulous mariner who narrates the shapely tale of "Youth" that he completes in the spring of 1898, this becomes a lost illusion in the wake of his increasing lapses of control in *Heart of Darkness* and *Lord Jim*. Whatever its strengths, and they are many, no one has credited *Lord Jim* with formal excellence, and Conrad was well aware of this, writing defensively about the book in his "Author's Note" (1917) and denying that his story had ever gotten "beyond the writer's control."[44] But his very defensiveness should tell us how acutely Conrad was concerned with narrative structure. As Ruth Franklin has recently remarked, to "constantly struggle against form is to be constantly aware of form."[45] Thus it is plausible to argue that Conrad intended the surface structural irregularities in *Typhoon,* an apparent struggle against form, to raise the discerning readers' awareness of the underlying formal patterns in his work. For his novella, Conrad has employed a most conventional literary mode, as his feint toward the epistolary narrative hints, but the mode is almost unnoticed—like the second page of MacWhirr's latest letter—because he has placed it in an unconventional setting. As the spiritual element seen in Jukes's pilgrimage and the religious imagery in the book suggest and as the overlooked words of MacWhirr's letter confirm, *Typhoon* is a uniquely Conradian adaptation of the Christmas story, a staple of popular literature through the Victorian era, but unexpectedly set in the China Sea and among men hardly in a festive mood. They have faced "the wrath and fury of the passionate sea" and the ultimate "of perfidy, of violence, and of terror" through the early morning hours of "December 25th."[46]

Briefly put—for I have fully discussed the convention of the Christmas story in Typhoon elsewhere[47]—the time indications in the narrative make it clear that Captain MacWhirr's confrontation with his mortality, "between 4 and 6 A.M. on December 25th," occurs when he withdraws into his chart room toward the close of the penultimate fifth chapter.[48] During this scene the captain experiences a far less dramatic change in his nature than that of Dickens's Scrooge but a transformation that, by being largely unnoticed, more nearly resembles that of the original Nativity in the Christian tradition. The unimaginative man imagines his end with startling and most uncharacteristic "vividness" of "thought."[49] The man who typically "betrayed no sort of inward disturbance" finds that the "hurricane had broken in upon the orderly arrangements of his privacy."[50] The man who is "unable to discover the message of a prophecy" finds in a matchbox that he might "never have occasion to use [. . .] any more," a "symbol of all these little habits that chain us to the weary round of life."[51] The man who has "found very little occasion to talk" begins to speak "out in the solitude and the pitch darkness of the cabin[. . . .] 'I shouldn't like to lose her,' he said half aloud."[52] MacWhirr's newfound loquacity and imagination, an imagination that we might even call literary ("symbol"), continue after he leaves his chart room and converses with Jukes. The second half of the storm "will come very sudden [. . .] and from over there, I fancy."[53] And when he commends Jukes for calming the coolies, the biblical imagery in the text for the first time turns to the New Testament—the Pentecostal surge of confidence in Jukes—a change effected by the Christmas transformation scene in the chart room.

None of this is meant to suggest that the outspokenly skeptical Conrad suddenly "found religion" while writing *Typhoon* or returned to the Catholic faith of his Polish upbringing. What it means is that Conrad is fully aware of the conventionally Christian world view of his audience and that he is appealing to this religious sensibility for what it shares with his own aestheticism: its appeal to the imagination. More than this, Conrad intended *Typhoon* to have the further topical appeal of being published during the Christmas season, encouraging his agent, J. B. Pinker, to place it in a popular journal: "it is quite the thing that finds room in Xmas numbers."[54] But lest we forget, this is Joseph Conrad and not Charles Dickens. While Conrad may have intended the comic moments of *Typhoon* as a remote tribute to Dickens—"This is my first attempt at treating a subject jocularly so to speak"[55]—we find no holly and ivy and punch, no one like Fezziwig or Cratchit or Tiny Tim, or for that matter no Scrooge who learns "how to keep Christmas well" in this author.[56] Although Conrad was writing an unconventionally conventional novella originally intended for the Christmas season of 1900, he was also writing a book with an undercurrent of Apocalypse for the nineteenth century, which would end on December 31. The second half of the storm approaches—but never arrives—with intimations of the Day of Judgment, the Second Coming, and the approaching century: "The mutter of the winds drew near apace. In the forefront could be distinguished a drowsy waking plaint passing on, and far off the growth of a multiple clamour, marching and expanding. There was the throb as of many drums in it, a vicious rushing note, and like the chant of a tramping multitude."[57]

If the form of *Typhoon* turns out to be topical as a consequence of Conrad's continuing search for popular appeal that would simultaneously satisfy his rigorous demand for artistic integrity—in fact he so secularizes this Christmas story that his readers, like Mrs. MacWhirr, seem never to have noticed its mode—it should not surprise us that the topicality of the novella goes beyond the season of its publication. Consistent with his desire for and ambivalence toward the popular audience, Conrad invests *Typhoon* with a contemporary political relevance that could hardly escape his readers, much as he had done by imbedding a subversive critique of empire in *Heart of Darkness* for the confidently imperial British readership of *Blackwood's Monthly*: "The subject is of our time distinc[t]ly—though not topically treated."[58] The political subtext of *Typhoon* is distinctly of its time of composition, in the fall of 1900, and directly topical, invoking the Boxer Rebellion in China that had reached crisis proportions in the late summer of 1900.[59]

Conrad manifests his equivocal relationship to his audience and their preconceptions in *Typhoon* by reflecting and simultaneously undermining contemporary political anxieties, racial fears, and even gender-based assumptions. Stephen Donovan has described the relative scarcity of commentary on Conrad's relation to contemporary popular culture,[60] and to this I would add that there is rather limited discussion of his allusions to current world events, despite the vast literature on his most overtly political fictions, *Heart of Darkness, Nostromo, The Secret Agent,* and *Under Western Eyes.* Hence it appears that almost no one has noticed the topicality of Conrad's tale of an insurrection of Chinese coolies or recognized that the political significance of Captain MacWhirr's stratagem in *Typhoon,* his settlement of the conflict among the coolies by the Solomonic "Equitable Division" of the workers' property among them, might constitute a critique of the European response to the Boxer uprising.[61] The bloodiest episode of the Boxer Rebellion occurred from June to August 1900, the months immediately preceding Conrad's composition of *Typhoon,* as the xenophobic rebels, with the acquiescence of the weak Chinese regime, besieged the legation quarter of Beijing and terrorized the Europeans, both inflicting and suffering numerous casualties. At the same time, and fully documented in the press, there were numerous massacres of Western missionaries and Chinese Christians throughout the provinces that, as the subtitle of Diana Preston's history of Boxer Rebellion puts it, "Shook the World in the Summer of 1900."[62] The Boxers only abandoned the siege in August, when an eight-nation Western military force approached Beijing. One of the most gruesome moments for the British public during the siege, made fully credible by the attacks in the countryside, was a "lurid account of a frightful massacre" of the white residents of Beijing, "including 147 women and 76 children," that appeared in Harmsworth's *Daily Mail.*[63] This massacre turned out to have been a "pure invention" after the "legations were relieved,"[64] but the truth did little to lessen the growing Western alarm at what was being called the "Yellow Peril." Surely these terrors were fresh in the minds of Conrad's readers and would seem to explain the intensity of the fear of the coolies that Jukes expresses in *Typhoon:* "I am convinced that if they had not been so unmercifully shaken, and afraid [. . .] to stand up, we would have been torn to pieces."[65]

The immediate aftermath of the relief of the European legations was a "carnival of loot[ing]" in Beijing that spread into the provinces, both by the expeditionary forces and among the Chinese themselves.[66] This orgy of looting that "caused a sensation" in the British press, would seem to have inspired Conrad's description of the mad struggle over property among the coolies, "all these bodies whirling like dust [. . .] a confused uproar, a tempestuous tumult, a fierce mutter, gusts of screams dying away, and the tramping of feet mingling with the blows of the sea."[67] Rebecca West recounts the popular horror at the rebellion's aftermath: "Shocking, it seemed at first, that many Chinese found it possible to loot the homes of other Chinese; and how much more shocking it appeared when many of the European forces, sent to restore civilization in the shattered East, decided that there was much more in looting than people owned. How unbearable it was when some time later Europeans who should have known better, and who were not very well-paid, returned to their native countries with quantities of beautiful Chinese objects which they could not have acquired by payment."[68] West tactfully fails to make clear that British troops were particularly active among the "Europeans" doing this looting.[69] In this light, Captain MacWhirr's nonviolent and diplomatic solution of the crisis on the *Nan-Shan,* his equitable division and return of the coolies' property, represents an exercise of power and discretion sorely lacking in the European response to the Boxer Rebellion.

Conrad establishes the smoldering racial tension on the *Nan-Shan* early in the story. When Jukes realizes that his captain intends to disregard the advice of navigation manuals and steer the *Nan-Shan* directly into the typhoon, the first mate attempts to dissuade him by appealing to MacWhirr's humane instincts: "'I was thinking of our passengers,' he said, in the manner of a man clutching at a straw."[70] Jukes's concern for the coolies is definitely not a sign of his racial attitudes. He is merely grasping for a conceivable reason to convince the captain to change course, and shortly before this Conrad has emphasized Jukes's assumption of "racial superiority" to the Chinese, when conversing in "mangled [. . .] pidgin-English" with the coolies' interpreter.[71] Nor is MacWhirr any different from the first mate in this regard, dismissing Jukes's appeal: "Never heard a lot of coolies spoken of as passengers before."[72] Akin to the captain's complacent racism, we have also seen sexism in his rejecting the idea of avoiding the typhoon as no more than the hysterical advice of "an old woman," "It's the maddest thing!"[73]

Nevertheless, in the book's conclusion MacWhirr's actions suggest a moderate enlightenment as he insists on dealing humanely with the Chinese coolies, allowing them to come back out on deck and instructing Jukes to equitably divide the scattered savings of the Chinese passengers among them: "he shared all the cash we had picked up equally among the lot."[74] He averts an armed confrontation between the crew and the coolies—"'For God's sake, Mr. Jukes,' says he, 'do take away these rifles from the men,'" rejecting a militaristic "masculine" response to the situation.[75] While the captain acts from mixed motives—"He wanted as little fuss made as possible, for the sake of the ship's name and for the sake of the owners," and demonstrates his newfound imaginative insight, doing as Solomon Rout says "something rather clever" by realizing that the coolies will prefer his division of their property to the greater risk of trusting the corrupt authorities in Fu-chau—his intentions are nonetheless unexpectedly egalitarian: "We must plan out something that would be fair to all parties."[76] No doubt MacWhirr's diplomacy would have appeared even more unexpected to a readership that likely shared Jukes's racial arrogance: "They had had a doing that would have shaken the soul out of a white man. But then they say a Chinaman has no soul."[77] Shocked by the Boxer uprising, certainly this readership would also have shared Jukes's fear of the alien coolies as well. Overtly, then, *Typhoon* would seem to replicate the gender and racial views that would predominate in the popular audience at the time of its publication, while subtly unsettling these attitudes in its resolution.

In his 1898 Christmas letter to Aniela Zagórska, his cousin's wife, Conrad writes scathingly of three of the most popular British novelists of the day, Grant

Allen, Marie Corelli, and Hall Caine: "Neither [*sic*] of these writers belongs to literature. All three are very popular with the public—and they are also puffed in the press. There are no lasting qualities in their work. The thought is commonplace and the style (?) without any distinction. They are popular because they express the common thought, and the common man is delighted to find himself in accord with people he supposes distinguished. This is the secret of many popularities."[78] These authors, and their admiring readers as well, resemble Captain MacWhirr, the man with an "ordinary" mind who, were it not for his experience of a typhoon, seemed destined to "go skimming over the years of existence to sink gently into a placid grave, ignorant of life to the last."[79] By exploiting literary convention and the conventional attitudes of the "common man," and subtly subverting both for the discerning few among his readers, Conrad arrives at a formula for the popularity he so much desires, believing that his readers' experience of *Typhoon* will, like MacWhirr's experience of the storm itself, effect an ever so modest transformation of their minds, their attitudes, and their knowledge of life itself. And while popular success would continue to elude him for another dozen years, it is a formula he returns to for his major fictions that would follow.

Ideas Have Consequences

Women in the Compromised World of *Nostromo*

RUTH NADELHAFT

Nostromo, like every novel by Joseph Conrad, is full of ideas; it is also richly populated by women who illuminate the consequences of ideas and implicitly or explicitly offer critiques of those ideas. Seven individual women play significant roles, ranging from the intellectual appeal of Martin Decoud's sister in Paris to the enforced passivity and suppressed desires of Giselle Viola, the love object of Nostromo in the final sections of the novel. There are legitimate numbers of developed women characters as well as uncounted numbers of upper-class women, so powdered and adorned, so still and rehearsed in their behaviors, that they seem unrecognizable when they emerge as alert, responsive, and ultimately brave in the sporadic and intense fighting in and around Sulaco in its time of revolution. Those women ordinarily adorned, powdered, painted, and immobilized behind their fans and in their black dresses manage to be present and absent at once, all in disguise yet all offering commentary to any person courteous or besotted enough to persevere beyond the obligatory exchange of postures. The author of the supposedly authoritative account of Sulaco's history, *Fifty Years of Misrule,* allows us the glimpse of these women, hidden in plain sight, who exemplify the way in which Conrad, so long misunderstood, made women individually and collectively central to the meaning of his work. At the heart of the novel are two women who, between them, fully live out the consequences of the ideas—capital investment in the underdeveloped world and the exploitation of material and human resources—that Conrad understood only too well at the time of *Nostromo*'s creation: Antonia Avellanos and Emilia Gould.

Since 1983, when Zdzislaw Najder published *Conrad Under Familial Eyes,* scholars and general readers have had the opportunity to encounter the sources of several richly observed and compelling women characters in Conrad's mature work. In this collection of important and revealing materials translated from their Polish originals, Najder made available to generations of Conrad scholars and interested readers the rich store of memory and emotion on which Conrad drew for much of his writing life. Academic critics who had struggled to categorize and assimilate Conrad as a writer of great but narrow capacity now had access to fragments of a personal history which enlarged all our conceptions of Conrad's preoccupations and his reach. The revelations of both the idealism and the dispassionate accounts of the costs of such idealism inform works as diverse as *Lord Jim, Nostromo, The Secret Agent,* and *Under Western Eyes.* As a writer, Conrad was a master of dissimulation, providing evidence at the same time that he concealed his own deepest emotional sources. The author of the supposed history of the modern state of Sulaco provides the glimpse of women's courage which has its own truth stemming from the courage and fortitude of Ewa Korzeniowska, Joseph Conrad's mother, an idealist and patriot who visited her husband in prison and lived frugally in exile. Identifying with the fortitude and suffering of peasants and the landless, she learned to conceal her tears and harness her strength of will as her body failed. Natalia Haldin, at the heart of Conrad's later novel, *Under Western Eyes,* derives from the same sources in Conrad's early life.

But these heroines of the great novels of Conrad's middle period did not suddenly appear as significant elements in the plots and themes of the novels. From the beginning of his career as a writer, Conrad created women characters who demonstrated that ideas have consequences, human and cultural consequences. One of the largest and most consequential ideas which flowers fully in *Nostromo* is the idea of capital expansion and exploitation, whether in the guise of "civilization" or the development of "natural resources." From the early stories of the East Indies to the compelling corruption of *Heart of Darkness,* Conrad was a scathing critic of ideas uncoupled from any awareness of the costs to indigenous peoples and cultures. *Nostromo* and the women of Sulaco are remarkable not because they are unprecedented in Conrad's work but because of their variety and because of the particularity of their commentary. In the early works, a woman such as Aissa, in *An Outcast of the Islands,* can scarcely express her sense of outrage and betrayal in intellectual terms. Like other women in the early novels, she embodies the humiliation and the despair of the native culture at the hands of white traders and empire builders.

In *Nostromo,* there are women such as Linda and Giselle Viola whose bodies and minds are in effect currency; like the silver which enslaves Nostromo, these women become commodities at the hands of their father, a true believer and hero worshiper. Giorgio Viola, the patriot of Italian unification, is one of the central characters in *Nostromo*; with his wife he has helped to invent the notion of Nostromo and to perpetuate the idea of his incorruptible fidelity. It is to this idea that Giorgio Viola pledges one of his daughters—the wrong one, as it happens. Almost blind, almost deaf, Giorgio Viola quite literally cannot perceive the difference between his daughters. These undifferentiated women, like the veiled and painted women of the upper classes, exemplify some of the most salient ideas at the heart of this novel. Both daughters have been brought up by both their parents to worship Nostromo. Though their individuality and individuated identities are made clear to the reader, and only too apparent to Nostromo as a man infatuated with one of them, their outlines are indistinct to their father who gives Linda, as the older daughter, to Nostromo with an authority only available to such an old and deluded ideologue. Georgio Viola's lack of sight and insight will in the end kill Nostromo.

Conrad differentiates the sisters from one another in a number of ways. Linda, the older, is dark and energetic; Doctor Monygham describes her as "that white-faced Linda, with her red mouth and coal-black eyes," making clear the difference between the sisters. Giselle, "the recognized beauty of the town," is fair and languid.[1] Their father, in love with ideals of political freedom and honor, described by Doctor Monygham as "the old Garibaldino," lives like an exiled king as the keeper of the lighthouse and a sometime innkeeper. His wife and his daughters represent his diminished dominion, and he presides over this tiny territory with a loaded shotgun across his bony knees. Like many women in Conrad's span of novels and stories, Linda and Giselle Viola are portrayed both as symbols and as specific personalities. A common accusation by critics used to be that there were no women characters of any significance. When some critics and scholars began to identify and explore the presence of women characters, other critics lurched to the opposite position and accused Conrad of sexism and even racism for his inclusion of native and indigenous women such as Aissa in *An Outcast of the Islands* or Kurtz's enraged native mistress in *Heart of Darkness.* A major critical approach, espoused by female writers as well as male, perceives Conrad as enmeshed in the colonialism and imperialism he portrays. The voices of indigenous people, especially women, are thus nullified regardless of the quality of their critical insights. The "hysterical female" dehumanizes individual women and denies their presence in the author's design, which is not to affirm but to subvert the colonial project. The presence of women characters persists, however, and their range of characterizations develops from text to text. By the time Conrad wrote *Nostromo,* even in the construction of minor characters such as Linda and Giselle Viola and their fiercely protective mother, Conrad was able to design women characters who both move the narrative forward and serve to comment on its themes as they serve instrumental purposes of others.

General readers and academic critics agree that the narrative construction of *Nostromo* presents difficulties. Beyond the early commitment to impressionism, a mode of presentation which immersed readers in the moment-to-moment experience and a delayed comprehension of events and their meaning, Conrad developed an apparent detachment which can be mystifying or may be mistaken for the irony so often attributed to his view of the world. From the outset in *Nostromo,* when Conrad explains the appearance of Antonia Avellanos in a tale of schoolboy adoration, the author removes his real self from the people and events of the world of Costaguana. The narrative itself is further displaced, since it purports to be based on the *History of Fifty Years of Misrule* and the tedious chatter of a surviving witness, Captain Mitchell, about the events and people who lived out the consequences of the North American capital investment into the abandoned silver mine whose treasure eventually led to the creation of the state of Sulaco and the personal tragedies of Antonia Avellanos and Emilia Gould.

As Conrad constructs the political and material world of Costaguana, it conforms to the notion that masculine or patriarchal principles routinely overcome the existing or natural world which is feminine in principle. It was the anthropologist Sherry Ortner who coined the memorable image which fixes in language the regular—if not inevitable—dichotomy: woman is to man as nature is to culture. Sherry Ortner posed this theory as a question in 1974.[2] *Nostromo* is just one of the novels in which Conrad seems to consider that question repeatedly, with individual women persistently identifying themselves with the natural world (in this case the site of the abandoned silver mine which has reverted to its wild state) while men regularly invade, conquer, and transform the natural world into plunder and precious metal. It is the masculine illusion that the transformation of nature into commodities brings with it all the benefits of modernity without any loss of inherent value. Charles Gould, the reluctant owner of the silver mine, believes that keeping himself scrupulously aloof from corruption will purify an enterprise which is at its heart plunder.

One of Conrad's last novels, *Victory,* uses the term "plunder" without embarrassment. In *Nostromo* the phrase "material interest" comes to stand for the entire colonial and capitalist enterprise which denatures nature and dehumanizes humans. The nature of Charles Gould's delusion allows him to participate in the enterprise while almost retaining his self-respect. But for his wife, Emilia, who is the moral and sensible touchstone of the novel, there is no such denial of reality. Conrad gives to Emilia Gould some moments of reverie after the silver has been lost which provide the summation of her fusion of personal and global understanding: "It had come into her mind that for life to be large and full, it must contain the care of the past and of the future in every passing moment of the present. Our daily work must be done in the glory of the dead, and for the good of those who come after. . . . There was something inherent in the necessities of successful action which carried with it the moral degradation of the idea. . . . An immense desolation, the dread of her own continued life descended upon the first lady of Sulaco. . . . In the indistinct voice of an unlucky sleeper, lying passive in the grip of a merciless nightmare, she stammered out aimlcssly the words—'Material interest.'"[3]

Emilia Gould's anguished and involuntary utterance stands as the clearest and most compressed example of the centrality of women's place in the world of *Nostromo.* It marks the end of chapter 11, but it does not by itself account for Emila Gould's importance; her lonely vision comes after a difficult and sensitive conversation with Doctor Monygham, who brings to her his understanding of the unfolding tragedy of the Viola household. Monygham occupies a critical position in the narrative of *Nostromo* and in the defining world of men and women. Having suffered torture and years of miserable imprisonment, the doctor has essentially been unmanned. Alone among the throngs of visitors and hangers-on, Doctor Monygham serves as a real companion to Emilia Gould, whom he adores and whose misery he perceives and understands. Doctor Monygham has lost the capacity for belief in himself as he has lost his willingness to believe in others. The exception that he makes for Emilia Gould has much to do with her silent suffering, which he sees and understands. Idealism, ideology, hero worship characterize the men of *Nostromo.* But Monygham has been tested and failed in his own estimation. In place of self-esteem, irrevocably lost to his experience of torture and his capitulation to unbearable pain, the failed doctor possesses the capacity for empathy, a distinguishing characteristic of the women who provide the political and moral commentary in all of Conrad's studies of European and North American expansion and imperialism.

Emilia Gould and Antonia Avellanos represent the most richly detailed and compelling examples of consequences for the women caught in the moment of capitalism's transformation of natural resources into wealth and modernism. The portrait of Emilia Gould is reminiscent of the shading and detail employed by Henry James in works such as *Portrait of a Lady,* which traces the development of Isabel Archer from her radiant and promising youth to her sophisticated and introspective sadness as a fully formed "modern" woman of the world. Emilia Gould is portrayed from great distances as well as intimate close-ups; the reader sees her early charm, her delight in the prospect of love and adventure, her sturdy constitution beneath her delicate appearance and deceptive air of fragility. From the first, like her beloved friend, Antonia, Emila Gould's emotional commitment is to a man who is himself committed to an idea. Charles Gould believes that in the reopening and development of the silver mine in partnership with the power and vision of American capitalism and Protestant expansionism he can redeem his father and bring the blessings of civilization to the premodern world of Sulaco. He reluctantly surrenders to the yoke of this idea without allowing himself to imagine that under it he will be transformed and consumed. In her great reverie, his wife summarizes her realization of the transformation of her husband: "Poor boy!" She thinks of his graying hair, his incorrigible devotion to the idea of the mine as benevolently transformative, his inability to recognize the personal and external destruction he has helped to bring about through his surrender to the forces of material interest.

Destructive dedication to an idea, Conrad suggests, is not limited to men lacking in introspection like Charles Gould or the great capitalist from San Francisco, Holroyd; Martin Decoud's capacity for introspection borders on solipsism and ultimately leaves him without the capacity to imagine any reality outside his own lonely existence. Emilia Gould and Antonia Avellanos, as Conrad develops their characterizations, represent alternative ways of understanding the force of ideas. They retain their ability to empathize even with those whose sense of self makes such empathy impossible to grasp or reciprocate. The survival benefits of empathy and intuitive observation for victims, slaves, prisoners, or any others caught in circumstances of unequal distribution of power are amply demonstrated in the characters of Emilia Gould, Antonia Avellanos, and the emasculated Doctor Monygham.

Nostromo is entirely consistent with the developmental history of Conrad's work in its illumination of women's capacity for and use of empathy as a survival mechanism and as a means of caring for the individuals and the causes to which they are devoted. As he did in previous explorations of imperialism, most notably in *Heart of Darkness* when Marlow asked for help from his well-placed aunt in his search for employment, Conrad invents European women of means and intellect to facilitate and to comment on the consequences of carrying out the colonial project of transforming human and natural resources into commodities and wealth. Like Charlie Marlow, Charles Gould's father turned to such a woman who reluctantly and presciently turned him down. When it became clear that the San Tome mine would be presented to the father of Charles Gould, he tried every expedient to rid himself of the burden that he knew would slowly destroy him.

> It would have been useless. Indeed, it would not have been a very safe proceeding. Such was also the opinion of a stout, loud-voiced lady of French extraction, the daughter, she said, of an officer of high rank . . . who was accommodated with lodgings within the walls of a secularized convent next door to the Minister of Finance. That florid person, when approached on behalf of Mr. Gould in a proper manner, and with a suitable present, shook her head despondently. She was good-natured, and her despondency was genuine. She imagined she could not take money in consideration of something she could not accomplish. . . . "No go," she had said with a cavalier, husky intonation which was natural to her.[4]

She was perhaps the only honest person, it seemed, of all those associated with the government of Costaguana or the redevelopment of the silver mine that came to dominate the lives of Charles and Emilia Gould. Realism bordering on cynicism allowed this woman to preserve her equanimity as she bobbed in the sea of corruption. The presence of such a woman provides another kind of evidence of Conrad's confidence in his own ability to integrate women into both the foreground and the background of his fiction. Indeed, he became so successful at this practice that such women may evade our notice, defined more by their function than by their gender. However sharply differentiated from one another, they might be unnoticed for their individuality by European and American readers, as the powdered women of Sulaco were invisible as individuals to the likes of Captain Mitchell until they materialized against the background of flames and gunfire in the brief and surprisingly successful revolution that made Sulaco a state and not a mere province.

The tragic destinies of Antonia Avellanos and Emilia Gould demonstrate the interplay between ideas and their consequences particularly as those larger-world forces work through men. Unlike the shrewd and self-aware functionary who sees the futility of bribery and her own limited sphere of influence, Charles Gould and Martin Decoud possess no such internalized awareness. Martin Decoud confides his grandiose vision for Sulaco to his sister in Paris, a useful narrative device that allows Conrad to expose Decoud's thoughts and feelings. At the same time, the invisible sister emerges indirectly, providing another portrait of a secular, skeptical, and politically sophisticated woman, the only person Decoud both respects and trusts to understand both his intellectual ideas and his human emotions. For, much as he loves and desires Antonia, Decoud confesses to his sister that he loves Antonia "with the heart, and with that alone."[5] A few moments earlier he characterized the women of Costaguana much as Captain Mitchell did in his tedious recital of the history of the successful revolution: "The women of our country are worth looking at during a revolution. The rouge and pearl powder fall off, together with the passive attitude towards the outer world which education, tradition, custom impose upon them from the earliest infancy." Immediately he contrasts them with his sister: "I thought of your face, which from your infancy had the stamp of intelligence instead of that patient and resigned cast."[6] Decoud's self-regard is immense. His belief in his own intellectual acumen allows him to confer intelligence upon his sister and to render judgments on everyone he has ever known. Martin Decoud represents the self-conscious Western intelligence to an extraordinary degree. He brings to Costaguana such extreme rationality that he disdains the very object of his love. His desire for political revolution is as pure and inhumane as the ambitions of the absurd anarchists of *The Secret Agent*. In the great trio of novels which focus directly on notions of revolution, women are the living emblems of the laws of unintended consequences. Emilia Gould and Antonia Avellanos are the foot soldiers who actually bring about the creation of the new state with its very real costs.

Decoud's letter to his sister, composed during the moments leading up to the doomed attempt to save the silver and deliver the constitution of the new state of Sulaco, gives no hint of the probable response of his sister. The clear implications are that from her safe and affectionate distance her habitual respect for her brother's philosophical pronouncements will provide the unquestioning support that he needs. He describes his calm and his sense of certainty even while he is under fire and writes: "I seemed . . . to hold my new State in the hollow of my hand." In this exalted visionary state Decoud perceives everyone and everything in and about Sulaco as a means to the glorious democratic end that exists in his mind and will be composed on paper. The women of Sulaco running with bandages and tending to the wounded, Emilia Gould carrying a bottle of disinfectant and wads of cotton, Father Corbelan tending to the wounded and hearing confessions all strike him as proper, even pleasing for the fate of the revolution, his revolution. For the sake of his plan, Emilia Gould and Antonia Avellanos are essential, however sentimental they may be in his radically skeptical view. For his own sake, Decoud has no room for the emotions of pity or grief. As for Antonia, whose father has been immobilized by a stroke, "I disregarded her sorrow. I would rather see her miserable than not see her at all, never any more. . . . She is more to me than his precious mine to that sentimental Englishman. I won't speak of his wife. She may have been sentimental once."[7]

What Decoud dismisses as "sentiment" he acknowledges as necessary to the accomplishment of his constitutional revolution. "Their sentiment was necessary to the very life of my plan; the sentimentalism of the people that will never do anything for the sake of their passionate desire, unless it comes to them clothed in the fair robes of an idea." All the human emotions, for Decoud, are abstractions to be harnessed for the sake of an idea; on their own, they have no value to him. Unself-consciously, he confides all this to his esteemed sister in Paris, counting on her intellectual capacity and her filial affection, presumably devoid of the "sentimentality" he perceives in Emilia Gould and Antonia Avellanos. Their alliance comes with the price of these emotions he disdains, but they are indispensable to the plan.

With deliberation, Conrad chose to conclude his "Author's Note" with a focus on Antonia Avellanos after laying a trail of misdirection worthy of his reputation as an ironist. Claiming to base his complicated tale on the *History of Fifty Years of Misrule,* the author anchors his tale in the depths of his own imagination. There, in memory well enough disguised to be securely unverifiable, he locates Antonia Avellanos, the beautiful schoolgirl, the aristocrat who, paired with the equally disguised man of the people, serves as the touchstone for the layered narrative of *Nostromo.*

Considering the vexed questions about male writers' depiction of female characters, some feminist critics came to understand that the privileged position of male authors might actually confer some benefits to women as characters and as readers. Their argument, posed by writers such as Rachel Brownstein and Nina Auerbach, might well apply to the character of Antonia Avellanos. Working from his own complicated perspective as the son of Polish idealists and failed revolutionaries, Conrad offers the character of Antonia Avellanos a presence and a voice that reach the reader all the more intensely through the mixture of reluctant passion and intellectual disdain of the deracinated Martin Decoud. In clandestine conversations with Antonia, in his hurried conversation with Emilia Gould, and above all in his outpouring to his sister in Paris, Decoud confers a present and a future upon Antonia. Without the voices of her father and her lover, Antonia would have remained trapped entirely in the customs and the costumes of her country. To some extent, what we see of Antonia in the recollections of the "Author's Note" and in the narrative itself confers upon her the status of exemplary devotion to the memory of her father and to Martin Decoud, even to the notion of revolution itself. Conrad, in the guise of the Author, writes:

> I long sometimes for another glimpse of the "beautiful Antonia" (or can it be the Other?) moving in the dimness of the great cathedral, saying a short prayer at the tomb of the first and last Cardinal-Archbishop of Sulaco, standing absorbed in filial devotion before the monument of Don Jose Avellanos, and with a lingering, tender, faithful glance at the medallion-memorial to Martin Decoud, going out serenely into the sunshine of the Plaza with her upright carriage and her white head; a relic of the past disregarded by men awaiting impatiently the Dawns of other New Eras, the coming of more Revolutions.[8]

The irony of this glimpse cannot be lost upon the contemporary reader. Antonia was more free, more poised on the brink of revolution, while Martin Decoud was infatuated with her physical and intellectual presence. Once he gave himself entirely to the idea of the new state, his brainchild, Antonia became an instrument, an objectified means, a postrevolutionary icon. Once more clad in black, her physical beauty transformed by age and abstinence, Antonia exemplifies the way in which revolutions may leave untouched those—particularly women—who desire and work for them on behalf of the ideas of others.

History in Ruins

Reading *Nostromo*

CAMELIA RAGHINARU

> There can be no evolution out of a grave. Another word of less scientific sound has been very much pronounced of late in connection with Russia's future, a word of more vague import, a word of dread as much as of hope—Revolution.
>
> Joseph Conrad, *Notes on Life and Letters*

Theodor Adorno ends his *Minima Moralia* with a messianic vision of our world as "[cracked and fissured]," "alienated from itself," and "distorted." [1] Such a political perspective, representing the distortions of the status quo from a quasi-messianic endpoint, is provided by Joseph Conrad's *Nostromo.* Not a messianic text *prima facie,* due to its contradictory political views, the novel does, however, expose the fissures in both reformist and revolutionary politics, deferring any specific endorsement for a political agenda.

Joseph Conrad is known to have avoided political commitment in either direction, whether on behalf of socialism or capitalism. Nor did he sympathize with revolutions and their bloody aftermaths. And yet, despite the fact that he conceived of revolutionary success in terms of caricature and betrayal, Conrad maintained a Romantic interest in revolutions. The import of such revolutions could be messianic, if the world could be slightly rearranged (as Walter Benjamin put it), so that a non-violent revolution would result in something other than moral anarchy and renewed tyranny.

Irving Howe establishes Conrad's contradictory approach to politics when he remarks on Cornad's outright hostility to "the life of politics," [2] on one hand, and his fascination with the world of anarchists and revolutionaries—be they British, Russian, or South American—on the other. Howe gets to the heart of this issue by analyzing the contradiction in Conrad's worldview: ostensibly outraged by Dostoevsky's mysticism and political messianism, as well as Dostoevsky's sense that salvation happens through community, Conrad counters with the skepticism and stoicism of solitude and "the solidarity with isolated victims."[3] This stoic mask, however, barely disguises the belief that one can only hang on to straws and crutches, because ultimately salvation is impossible when one is confronted with the terror of "*nada*."[4] However, Howe notes a romantic impulse at work in Conrad's oeuvre, in the stoic resistance and resignation of his characters. The tug of war between duty and resignation is unsustainable either way, and the pervasive sense is one of failure. This impossible commitment to any saving device leads to equivocation and ambiguity in Conrad's political representation. His hatred of anarchism is mitigated by a sense that in it he finds "a projection of an unrevealed self, of the desolation a modern ego fears to find beneath its domesticated surface."[5] Though mistrustful of the utopian impulses embedded in radical politics, he seems fascinated by the despairing romantic mood at work in them: "This kinship of apparent opposites may explain why Conrad kept returning to the dark corners of anarchist conspiracy."[6] The fugitive moral admiration for the revolutionary gesture is mitigated by its ultimate futility.

Nostromo enacts moral and political drama, and Paul Armstrong points out that the contradictions of the novel are reinforced by abrupt shifts in temporal structure. The fact that all the events are fixed in the past allows for a synchronicity (from the point of view of the present) that creates uncertainty and unpredictability for the reader. Digressions and temporal shifts call attention to the fact that the past dwells in the present but, most importantly, that "historical meaning is a teleological process."[7] Costaguana's political intricacies dramatize the contradictions in Conrad's political attitudes. Guzman Bento's tyranny is followed by an interval of chaotic political thievery which ends in the revolt staged by the new proletariat formed around the Blanco party and the San Tomé mine. The new regime headed by the moderate Don Vincente Ribiera fails to thrive in a political milieu that calls for radical measures and falls to the minister of war, General Montero, who leads a revolt of the barracks. The Monterist rebellion is defeated, and the San Tomé mine—symbol of prosperity, order, and lawfulness—reigns supreme in Mrs. Gould's terrible vision as a burden of wealth and vice ready to crush lives in its expansion. Another side effect of this structure is a suggestion that history is not necessarily progressive, but rather cyclical. The structural "disorder," however, seems to organize itself slowly toward the fulfillment of the prophecy regarding the deadly fate of the treasure-seekers, as Louise Knapp Hay points out.[8] As a story paralleling in some respects that of the Fall, *Nostromo* solves its consequences ambivalently, falling short of an overt messianic bent, yet yearning for it: "Though Conrad often pictured a future in which men may be made aware of the consequences of their social actions, he never implied that any radical change in human nature (such as a purging of ideologies would entail) could be achieved, or that warfare could cease."[9]

The paradox at the heart of Conrad's politics reinforces his pessimism about revolutionary failure: capitalism engenders the kind of progress that regresses into the chaos of civil war, calling forth a new revolution that restarts the vicious cycle. As Howe notes, imperialism and capitalism manufacture a false order that destroys the organic rhythms of native life and reinforces chaos and exploitation. Gould and Holroyd, the European and American symbols of imperialism, are left to dominate and exploit a land that is nonetheless groaning with the promise of a new revolution brewing in its entrails. The illusion of political change matches the illusion of meaningful heroic life. Nostromo's decline as a magnificent representative of the proletariat is concomitant with his increase in political awareness and individual consciousness, while Charles Gould's idealism is the very instrument that propagates the material interests that put an end to all political idealism in favor of the poor. Finally, Mrs. Gould, who seemed to possess the potential for humanity uncorrupted by material gain, retreats into a type of internalized suffering and devotion to her principles that severs her from the reality of Costaguana. The sense of failure structuring Conrad's view of revolutionary politics has to do with a reciprocal bond between colonizer and colonized, which cannot be ended through the predictable means of a repetitive pattern of futile revolutions. And yet, the vision at the heart of *Nostromo* is not completely hollow. The political vision in the novel does not have to do with an overt utopian revolutionary impulse, but consists rather in its repeated failure. I call this failure "messianic" in Walter Benjamin's sense of the term, in which the Messiah's coming is always imminent, and yet delayed. In Terry Collits's term, this is the visionary politics of the "*longue durée* . . . different in kind from the lazy and conservative habit of regarding the history of Latin America (or anywhere else) as merely a matter of endless repetition of the same."[10] *Nostromo*'s lack of closure is messianic in the sense in which "[i]t is too early to say"[11] how history in its synchronicity will turn out.

One important distinction to be made is between politics and history. "[I]f politics is fate, history is freedom,"[12] Avrom Fleishman notes, and this places messianism in the realm of synchronous history (where past and future give meaning to the present) rather than the politics of nationalism, socialism, anarchism, and their many revolutions. Messianism here does not refer to the history of revolutions that are bound to repeat themselves in a vicious cycle with no redemptive end. Rather, it is felt in Conrad's palpable sympathy toward the suffering of the common peasants, as in Mrs. Gould's vision: "a great land of plain and mountain and people, suffering and mute, waiting for the future in a pathetic immobility of patience."[13] Temporarily, Nostromo is the representative of this mass, and his trajectory traces the dehumanization of the common folk subjected to industrialization. All possibility of messianic redemption is denied when Nostromo's "social integration is eroded by personal preoccupations,"[14] and he is mistakenly and ironically shot by his revolutionary mentor, Viola. The contradiction at the heart of Nostromo—his inability to identify with his own people even as he experiences an increase in self-awareness and class consciousness—prevents the messianic restoration of the world. That, along with "a residual resistance to complete assimilation with the people"[15] points to a type of "heroic individualism"[16] common to Conrad's fables.

Ultimately, Conrad's story is about the impossibility of messianism in the world as it is. The fate of messianism is the fate of Nostromo at the end of the novel: his ascendance as a tragic hero is undermined by the "dialectical negation"[17] created by his failure to reconcile history with individuality. This same contradiction is found at the heart of Gould's motive in pursuit of the silver. It is this contradiction that twists and perverts any semblance of messianism: "the security which [foreign capital] demands must be shared with an oppressed people. A better justice will come afterwards."[18] In this instance Gould combines the types of the imperialist, the colonizer, the anarchist, and the nihilist—all perversions of the messianic revolutionary. In fact, as Fleishman records Conrad's expressed view, as a capitalist, Gould is the greatest anarchist, "and Gould's terrorism connects him with the subjects of the anarchist tales."[19] In sacrificing the veneer of his idealism, Gould reveals the hard steel of the bandit, the anarchist, and the terrorist underneath—according to the types of people with whom he has to make a pact. Thus, Nostromo and Gould are both perversions of the messianic ideal under the conditions of imperialism and capitalism. As Monygham predicts, "all that the Gould concession stands for shall weigh as heavily upon the people as the barbarism, cruelty, and misrule of a few years back."[20] Gould's fate is that of the revolution. Just like the Gould concession, the revolt ends up tightening the screw of oppression on the people. In fact, ironically, capitalism and revolt reinforce one another.

As Paul Armstrong put it, "Conrad" may seem revolutionary in his devastating critiques of imperialism and capitalism, but he has the doubts of a reactionary about the efficacy of revolutions and the motives of their advocates."[21] To the charge that Conrad's contradictory political attitudes cannot amount to a coherent political system of beliefs, Armstrong responds by noting a "fundamental metaphysical conflict between suspicion and faith"[22] swinging between demystification and affirmation of revolutionary nationalism, which tends to cause disagreements in Conrad studies. Lee Whitehead approximates a similar contradiction regarding the development of individuals: "For Conrad social process is tragic because, on the one hand, individuals discover themselves by pursuing an ideal, something beyond the immediate sensation of the moment, yet the pursuit of this ideal is self-contradictory; it destroys what it has made."[23]

The same could be said about the messianic ideal in *Nostromo.* Individuals—proletariat and capitalists alike—pursue a version of political redemption that destroys them. Yet, this is not to say that the novel does not aspire toward affirming redemption. In fact, failure gives meaning to the striving—akin to the paradox of the fortunate fall. Revolutions will not attain the messianic age, but the striving as well as the failure are paradoxically necessary in the development of individuals and historical processes.

Charles Gould exists at the intersection of capitalism, imperialism, and anarchism—a sovereign figure with the power to institute or suspend law and order in Costaguana. This places him and the silver in a quasi-messianic position. The question of identity formation in Gould, Nostromo, and Decoud is tied with the idea of catastrophe, each in a different way. The novel's despair of any political conviction does not completely inhibit its desire for change. It is, however, a messianism in the negative, especially since Conrad is "ambivalent about both evolution and revolution as vehicles of social improvement."[24] However, as Armstrong points out, evolutionary change (Ribiera's dictatorship) takes a more disastrous course than revolutionary change (the Sulacan revolt): "And so, although Conrad is for the most part dubious about revolutions, he cannot disallow the possibility that radical social change might serve the common good."[25] Finally, "*Nostromo* alternates between endorsing and demystifying the ideologies it portrays,"[26] and this is illustrated by Conrad's treatment of utopianism and messianism in the wake of a revolution. For the most part, they are mercenary affairs, but one has to take into consideration the minute chance that the potential for radical newness could be used for good as well. And because "any declaration of faith may harbor a mystification,"[27] then "*Nostromo* is both an endorsement and a demystification of democracy."[28]

Walter Benjamin's memorable image of history as a pile of debris envisions the end of history as victory for the oppressed. For Benjamin, the meaning of history is best perceived in its wreckages and fractures. Revolution is the expression of redemption, ushering in the messianic age that marks the end of history of oppression. Taking history as its object, *Nostromo* is an effect of incipient modernism owing to two types of crises at the end of the nineteenth century: revolutionary failure and capitalist success of the fin-de-siècle European postcolonial venture. In this historical context, in Conrad's *Nostromo* the continuum of exploitative history in the wake of all failed revolutions marks the catastrophic failure of messianism. Paradoxically, though, this same oppressive cycle gives rise to progress, which turns out to be the imperial impulse that drives the engine of history toward renewed revolution. Thus, Conrad's text could be read as a narrative of modernism. In the context of the cycle of failed revolutions in *Nostromo,* sovereignty and imperialism play a role in thwarting the messianic impulse at work in modernism.

The moment of danger—the catastrophe—bears tremendous political potential for Benjamin. It constitutes a moment of interruption, a concept essential to Benjamin's understanding of progress as a form of evil, insofar as progress perpetuates the tradition of oppression on which it depends in the first place. In the same way, the destruction of the San Tomé mountain could become an anti-capitalist and anti-imperialist ground zero that would finally end the cycle of failed revolutions—all begun in the pursuit of the San Tomé wealth—and turn the idea of catastrophe on its head. For Benjamin, the real catastrophe would be for the tradition of exploitation in the name of economic profit, on which prosperity in Costaguana is based, to go on uninterrupted and unchallenged, in all its "barbarism, cruelty, and misrule of a few years back."[29] Progress maintains the status quo; status quo is catastrophe. To invert this continuum is to interfere in the history of oppression, which rulers equate with progress.

States of Emergency

Temporarily, Charles Gould substitutes his position of sovereignty for one of anarchy. C. Brook Miller notes that Charles Gould is the instrument of legitimizing American economic imperialism, and the mountain is a symbol of tyranny and oppression, as Emilia Gould sees it: "hanging over the Campo, over the whole land, feared, hated, wealthy; more soulless than any tyrant."[30] Miller affirms that Gould believes his model of imperial progress fosters social change. However, his idealism develops into an obsession with and fetishization of the mine, and his desire to blow up the mountain is on a continuous line with this obsession. His anarchic gesture is not one of rebellion against capitalism and imperialism, but rather against competing forces that prevent his project from succeeding. This is, in fact, capitalism imploding on itself, and Sarah Cole places Gould's impulse on a line continuous with terrorism.[31] Gould and the mine work together toward producing the silver that is supposed to achieve the ideals of peace and political stability. Yet, penetrated by force, and taking the form of a gash in the side of the mountain, the mine is a constant proof of violence.[32] Ironically, as Cole points out, the success of the mine propagates profit that is not within the reach of a political act of violence. Gould's secret of ownership and perpetual success of the mine is violence as well, namely the threat of destruction. His gesture is akin to that of terrorism: the threatened explosion allows the mine to continue to render profit. Thus, "Charles Gould's use of dynamite as prophylactic against political upheaval represents a brilliant reimagining of the contemporary infatuation with dynamite as the material par excellence of anarchism and revolution."[33]

Sovereignty and anarchic subversion of the law are, paradoxically, related. Benjamin defines sovereignty in terms of Carl Schmitt's notion of the sovereign as the one who decides on the state of emergency. The emergency is a threat to the survival of the state. Sovereignty decides upon the state of emergency by suspending the state of law previously in force. The state and its survival are posited as superior to the law, and the state suspends the law in the name of self-preservation. The paradox consists in the fact that in order for the state to suspend its laws, it must appeal to the norms constituting it to justify its decision. Consequently, the state, the basis of law and order, is founded on a premise that evades considerations of law and order.

In *The Origin of German Tragic Drama,* Benjamin maintains that the sovereign represents history. Insofar as his gold mine makes history in Sulaco, Charles Gould is a type of sovereign. He has the ability to initiate a potential state of emergency in Costaguana. Ultimately, Gould chooses to go on with his counterfeit revolution, whose aim is to strengthen his hold on the mine, rather than annihilate it. Gould's determination to institute law and order in Costaguana through the agency of the mine makes the mine into a legal and economic instrument of the land. As the sovereign, Gould has the power to suspend the capitalist investments. However, he excludes this possibility and replaces it with a bogus interruption of the status quo—namely, the revolution. The utopian thrust of Benjamin's concept lies in the fact that the suspension of the law is the path to justice and the gate for the Messiah's coming. Instead of seeing the moment of suspension as a threat to be redressed (as does Schmitt), Benjamin sees it as the instance to be preserved and used for revolution. Conrad's dystopian vision is illustrated in the cyclical rise and fall of history through revolutions without redemption.

As Benita Parry notes, the novel's conflict is "presented as one of law against anomie,"[34] with Gould's silver holding the privileged place of law of the land in the legal system of Costaguana. The silver is endowed with the power to institute the law of material interests which, like every law, as Ursula Lord puts it, "is founded on expediency and is inhuman; it is without rectitude, without the continuity and the force that can be found only" in justice.[35] The implacability of law without justice seems embodied almost mystically in the San Tomé mine and its silver, beginning with the curse Gould invokes to explain his father's death and his own intricate involvement with the mine. A fatal curse is at work in the lives of most characters—Nostromo, Gould, Decoud, Linda, Emilia, Hirsch—who run into the very trap from which they are trying to escape, as Arnold Davidson points out.

Interruptions and Suspensions

Those held in the power of the silver undergo a schizophrenic split but, in this very fragmentation, justice emerges as a possibility. Ursula Lord argues that, through the theft of the silver, Nostromo becomes a divided man, "conscious of his criminality but also that society is the secret sharer in his guilt."[36] Nostromo also undergoes a reversed process of identity formation. He starts off as fully integrated in his community. He disintegrates as a self when he awakens from his metaphoric slumber under the weight of the law of the silver. Decoud, Gould, and Nostromo all have a hidden side, and they are split, schizophrenic, as Helen Funk Rieselbach also notes. In fact, Gould fashions his identity within the law of the silver as well. As the possessor of the silver and the mine, Gould is split between his role as lawmaker and bandit. In the realm of the *campo,* Gould and Hernandez "were equals before the lawlessness of the land."[37] They are doppelgangers, and the consequences of their actions become interchangeable, exposing lawlessness as the exception at the core of the law.

Conrad does not advocate political revolution in the conventional sense, because revolutions repeatedly fail in *Nostromo,* and there is no utopian vision as such in the novel. For a moment, however, the destruction of the mine could bring capitalist and imperial progress to a halt: "He was prepared, if need be, to blow up the whole San Tomé mountain sky high out of the territory of the Republic."[38] That moment embodies a number of realizations regarding the importance of the mine and its wealth for all those involved in its affairs. For Gould, the mine appears as a "weapon of wealth, double-edged with the cupidity and misery of mankind."[39] For Emilia Gould, in Monygham's words, "the Gould Concession stands for [something that will eventually] weigh . . . heavily upon the people."[40] For Nostromo, the wealth of the mine has the same hypnotic power he had predicted the treasure would have on Sotillo: "He will pray and blaspheme and still persevere, and will curse the day he ever heard of it, and will let his last hour come upon him unawares. . . . He will never forget it till he is dead—and even then—."[41] All these encounters with the silver result in failure because, paradoxically, each attempt at appropriating the wealth of the mine succeeds.

The idea of circularity evident in the rise and fall of endless revolutions reappears in the notion of progress as well. For Benjamin, progress is the eternal return of the perpetual catastrophe of human existence. The only way to counteract this cycle is to bring it to a standstill. To understand history as progress is to conform to the ideology represented by big companies like Gould's and Holroyd's, which claim that law and order ensure the chronological development of history toward a peak of achievement and success. This understanding of history enables the ruling classes to perpetuate the myth of progress and improvement, while continuing exploitation.

The notion of catastrophe is integral to the purpose of the mine in the narrative. From the beginning, the mine is identified with an ill-omened treasure that destroys Gould's father's life in Costaguana. The Gould Concession steps into the history of oppression of Costaguana, hoping to use the "material interests" attached to the mine to bring "law, good faith, order, [and] security" to

Costaguana.[42] This proclamation of faith in materialism is followed by disaster. Disillusioned, Charles Gould describes the mine as a "weapon of wealth, double-edged with the cupidity and misery of mankind."[43] His deception consists in insisting on pairing two distinct categories—justice and material interests—in an inextricable link: "Anyone can declaim about these things, but I pin my faith to material interests. Only let the material interests once get a firm footing, and they are bound to impose the conditions on which alone they can continue to exist. That's how your money-making is justified here in the face of lawlessness and disorder. It is justified because the security which demands it must be shared with an oppressed people. A better justice will come afterwards. That's your ray of hope."[44]

In Costaguana, Gould attempts his own materialistic revolution based on the condition of the oppressed. He views his involvement there as an adventure, a material for-profit adventure, but he endows it with revolutionary potential, not in the least because he is a son defying his father's death wish. Against his "English parentage and English upbringing, he perceived that he was an adventurer in Costaguana, the descendant of adventurers enlisted in a foreign legion, of men who had sought fortune in a revolutionary war, who had planned revolutions, who had believed in revolutions."[45] Thus, from the beginning, his revolutionary ideals are tinged with mercenary ambitions. In effect, his "revolution" fails precisely because it succeeds on these mercenary grounds. He assists in the planning of a revolution that will save and further his plans of enrichment. His "adventurer's easy morality"[46] does not have qualms about founding an idea of justice based on the perpetuation of oppression of the *mozzos* working in the mine. As long as Gould's plans for justicc are attached to the furtherance of "material interests," the path to justice is thwarted by the historical progress of capitalism and imperialism.

The moment charged with the potential for change is the blowing up of "the whole San Tomé mountain sky high out of the territory of the Republic,"[47] but the utopian potential of this gesture is thwarted by the resentment implicit in Gould's motivation. His resolution expresses "the spirit of a buccaneer throwing a lighted match into the magazine rather than surrender his ship."[48] The revolution that would bring about the end of history in this real state of emergency is a quasi-eschatological event. The nineteenth-century myth of progress is important to the narrative, and it is tied up with the dynamics of failure and hope. As Suresh Raval observes, in *Nostromo* history "recognizes the need for technological and scientific advance, but recognizes as well that social-historical forces do not harmonize with such advance. . . . In their contingency, these forces, however recurrent in man's history, are catastrophic. Thus the vision of hope puts into motion forces that tend to subvert that vision."[49] The narrative ends with the reign of stability and progress, yet remains skeptical of this progressive vision of history. *Nostromo* retains the bitterness of the failure of progress, and Conrad's protagonists are destined to failure. Gould repeats the disaster of his father's life. Decoud bows before the deterministic force that pushes him into suicide, and Nostromo's supposed liberated will renders him paralyzed by a bullet, while Linda remains emotionally paralyzed and thwarted. All the main characters are entangled in their own paralyzed histories, in one way or another.

The destruction of the mine could play the role of messianic catastrophe in the history of Costaguana. However, the messianic impulse is constantly frustrated in the text. Apart from Montero's corruption, Nostromo's counter-revolutionary appropriation of the silver and Gould's own obsession with it mock any legitimate attempts at revolution. Conrad's endless cycle of failed revolutions implies that messianism is not ushered in through political upheaval that is as self-interested and cynical as the forces it seeks to overthrow. Neither Decoud's isolation from the masses nor Nostromo's initial identification and solidarity with them points toward redemption in the end. As Ursula Lord argues, Conrad fails to endorse alternatives and "systematically discredits any option" for the political and economic freedom of Sulaco.[50] If there is a weak messianic impulse at work in the text, it can be solely understood in terms of possibilities: each missed possibility becomes an opening in the future, precisely because it has failed to find its fulfillment.

Women under Erasure

The failure of male potentiality has implications for the female characters as well, since the text fails to acknowledge the potential of the female body in modernity. Emilia, Linda, and Giselle are women whose lovers cheat on them with the silver. Doctor Monygham, for example, is loyal to the mine because it presents itself to him in the "shape of a little woman in a soft dress."[51] The female body and commodity intersect, as Christine Buci-Glucksman notes. Silver as courtesan prostitutes itself to different owners, who pay for it with the bodies of their female lovers (all childless). This is the ultimate vengeance of the commodity over the human. The modernist female body in Benjamin's analysis of Baudelaire appears as "the female body robbed of its maternal body, [which] becomes desirable only by going to the limits as dead-body, fragmented-body, petrified-body."[52] The prostitute, the modernist body par excellence, is "fragment, ruin of nature, disfigurement of the 'sublime body.'"[53]

The fragment as literary form disrupts this cycle and marks the only power of modernity: that of weakness, failure, and brokenness, as a sort of messianic harbinger of redemption. Conrad hints at this when, in the voice of Dr. Monygham, he marks Nostromo's triumph at the limit of Linda's final cry, a negative utopia that ends the story on a note of catastrophe: "'Never! Gian' Battista!' Dr. Monygham . . . heard the name pass over his head. It was another of

Nostromo's triumphs, the greatest, the most enviable, the most sinister of all. In that true cry of undying passion . . . the genius of the magnificent Capataz de Cargadores dominated the dark gulf containing his conquests of treasure and love."[54] Along with the failed explosion and destruction of the mine, Linda's unfulfilled expectation remains what Jameson calls "the interrogation of a hole in time," an impossible place of unfulfilled hope, a place of no return between the past and the failure of the present."[55]

Enchanting and intangible—a trope of femininity—the silver itself is a bearer of failure and unfulfilled hopes. Throughout the narrative, the silver is endowed with expectations it is unable to fulfill. On Gould's silver "rests the remnant of our hopes,"[56] according to the engineer-in-chief during the revolt. Charles Gould thinks he has no illusions when he fights "for life with such weapons as could be found at once in the mire of corruption."[57] But the moment he feels that "the worthiness of his life was bound up with success,"[58] the success of the mine, he gets sucked into the same mentality that motivates Holroyd—that of a simulacrum utopia, brought about by progress based on his thriving business: "Time itself has got to wait on the greatest country in the whole of God's Universe. We shall be giving the word for everything: industry, trade, law, journalism, art, politics, and religion. . . . And then we shall have the leisure to take in hand the outlying islands and continents of the earth. We shall run the world's business whether the world likes it or not. The world can't help it—and neither can we, I guess."[59] Along the lines of this vision of success, Gould constructs a false notion of justice: "The Gould Concession was symbolic of abstract justice. . . . The Gould Concession was a serious asset in the country's finance, and, what was more, in the private budgets of many officials as well. It was traditional. It was known. It was said. It was credible. Every Minister of Interior drew a salary from the San Tomé mine. It was natural."[60]

The gradual corruption brought about by the mine reinforces the idea of catastrophe in the wake of progress. *Nostromo's* vision is of a history that encrypts its own disaster in its boasting of success. The Goulds' marriage contains at its core the same object of disaster. The couple starts on the ruins of the life of the father, replacing it with the "splendour of hopeful love, which to the most sensible minds appears like triumph of good over all the evils of the earth. A vague idea of rehabilitation had entered the plan of their life."[61] The father's prohibition must be disregarded, for in *Nostromo* catastrophe goes hand in hand with success: "The very prohibition imposed the necessity of success,"[62] though the final disaster is precisely the success they predict and eventually achieve. Through this catastrophe, however, the prohibition gives way to changes anticipated by the father in his warning, the meaning of which Gould misreads: "Poor Father did not understand. He was afraid I would hang on to the ruinous thing, waiting for just some such chance, and waste my life miserably. That was the true sense of his prohibition, which we have deliberately set aside."[63]

The novel is about the tension between possibility and impossibility: "So the act happens—capitalism arrives in Sulaco—even though it is impossible."[64] It turns out, however, that the act never happened, because Decoud's and Nostromo's actions are "reabsorbed by the very stability and transindividuality of the institutions" [65] they founded. Their passions and values become "unwitting instruments for the construction of a new institutional space in which they fail to recognize themselves and their actions." Emilia Gould has a vision of this when she sees through the illusion of the mine's success to the disaster veiled beneath it: "He was perfect—perfect. What more could she have expected? It was a colossal and lasting success. . . . There was something inherent in the necessities of successful action which carried with it the moral degradation of the idea . . . but she saw clearly the San Tomé mine possessing, consuming, burning up the life of the last of the Costaguana Goulds. . . . A terrible success for the last of the Goulds. . . . With a prophetic vision she saw herself surviving alone the degradation of her young life, of love, of work—all alone in the Treasure House of the World."[66]

The "colossal and lasting success" of the mine is bound up with the degradation of Emilia's young life, itself in need of mortification. As feminist critics have observed, Emilia Gould perpetuates a vision of imperialist progress through the perfection of her Victorian womanhood. *Nostromo* dramatizes the wretched nature of the human attempt at progress and perfectibility on several levels: First of all because, as Monygham grimly observes, "There is no peace and no rest in the development of material interests. They have their law, and their justice. But is it founded on expediency, and it is inhuman."[67] Second, because as Gould has to admit eventually, he has both the spirit of a buccaneer and the lawlessness of the indomitable bandit Hernandez.

Catastrophe and Messianism

Just as humanity in Benjamin's allegory is seated in the world of the Edenic fall and baseness of human nature, ready to be admitted into the eternal life through redemptive grace, so is the corruption of the mine a venue and opening for the messianic, both for Gould and Nostromo. Nostromo's development throughout his dealings with the silver is a case in point. His metaphoric awakening from the deep slumber of lack of self-awareness is greeted by the appalling cry of the owl: "'Ya-acabo! Ya-acabo!—it is finished; it is finished'—announc[ing] calamity and death in the popular belief. . . . The cry of the ill-omened bird, the first sound he was to hear on his return, was a fitting welcome for his betrayed individuality."[68] Out of this sleep the formerly integrated Nostromo, a part of his community, a coherent self, disintegrates under the weight of his betrayal and becomes a split self—the potential of which is bound up with "the signs of death and corruption."[69] The break between history and salvation is only seemingly absolute. Even the fact that the law of material interests is inhuman and eventually returns to cruelty and misrule is complemented by the fact that, as Marx points out, capitalism itself turns out to be a revolutionary and anarchic force. Thus, history's pile of ruins, an image of the hopelessness and futility of earthly existence, points towards an eschatology that reverberates in Linda's final cry uttering Nostromo's name and Mrs. Gould's vision of herself as destitute.

The cycle of the rise and fall of revolutions and their constant failure in Conrad's text draws attention to the utopian value of history in *Nostromo* being bound up with its fallen state. Sulaco is never lifted out of fallen history. For Jameson, since the founding act of the new history and society in Sulaco is left to the imagination, the novel becomes profoundly utopian. Revolution fails in *Nostromo* because redemption is encrypted in an allegory. The silver occupies a privileged place in it, at the intersection between law and justice, corruption and redemption. It is on Gould's silver that the remnant of hopes rests, but of course, the political hope of revolution is shattered precisely because of the silver's absence. Silver functions both in its presence and absence to prevent the revolution. It fascinates by the fiction of its power. Through the explosion of the mine, the silver's absence would be complete and unable to exert a sick and binding fascination on Gould, Nostromo, and the members of the government. As long as hope is bound to the silver, it prevents the emergence of true politics. As Parry notes, politics is the "the agency of deliverance from the soulless materialism of a debased world."[70]

For Benjamin, utopia is discovered in ruins and fragments. Allegorical meaning is reconstructed from fragments. Jameson argues that *Nostromo* is "a meaningful narrative with a Utopian telos, which is the recuperation of the whole."[71] He finds utopias to be intricately bound to failure, loss, and weakness. We reconstruct the meaning of utopia from the fragmentariness and contradiction of doubting the Utopian enterprise to imagining its possibility. The revolt in Sulaco marks the crisis of modernity—the break with the old and the beginning of the new. In the ruins of the failed revolution, Conrad captures this aspect of modernity: the moment it opens to its utopian possibilities is also the moment of catastrophe. The island is spoiled for feudalism and capitalized. Therefore, it is ripe grounds for catastrophe, crisis, and change. Previously a closed system, now closure is an impossibility. Akin to a fallen demiurge, Gould brings mankind into a corrupted Eden said to have been inhabited solely by snakes—the San Tomé gorge. There, lawlessness meets material interest. In that sense, he is Benjamin's satanic force. He initiates men in the law, which then forms the basis of culpable behavior. This knowledge is best revealed by Nostromo, whose awakening is a consequence of the capitalistic law of the Master instituted by Gould.

Revolution and Failure

Nostromo's knowledge is sensuous. Since it is bound to its material counterpart, the silver, Nostromo brings together pleasure and work. Cesare Casarino discusses one of Marx's ideas according to which the questions of pleasure and crisis are related. Engaging in pleasure is a way to subvert capital and bring about a crisis, a state of emergency. This is precisely what Nostromo does once he takes possession of the silver—so in that sense, at least, he enacts a revolution of sorts. Borrowing from Hardt and Negri's *Empire,* Casarino calls this engagement in pleasure the sphere of non-work. Non-work produces both joy and crisis in capital.[72] At the end of the novel, Costaguana has entered a classic state of emergency, in which the government has more power and the people fewer rights. Ironically, this is the consequence of the Sulaco revolution. As a staple of crisis, the revolution that devastates Sulaco becomes the crisis that justifies a perpetual state of emergency, consisting of the expansion of economic and political capitalist powers. Derek Reveron and Jeffrey Stevenson Murer note, "While in most circumstances the 'state of emergency' ends and decision- and rule-making powers are restored to the legislature, many of the instruments of government depicted as 'temporary arrangements' eventually become lasting peacetime institutions."[73]

The failure of the revolt contains, at the very least, a promise that revolt and change are possible. Arnold Davidson notes that the groundwork for a new revolution is laid out in the last chapter, seeking to undo precisely what the previous revolution had accomplished.[74] Capitalism in Costaguana does what Marx predicted of capitalism all along: it acts as a revolutionary force. Ursula Lord points out, "Utopia does not loom on the horizon at the end of the novel, but rather further revolution based on class consciousness fueled by capitalist exploitation."[75] For Marx, "the alleged solidity of capitalist social structure depends upon constant disruption and integration."[76] Silver divides and disturbs the status quo, and capitalism destabilizes politics, society, and individuality just like a revolutionary force. It crushes the individual under the goals of production. Even though it seems as if Conrad had an aversion to revolution, Ursula Lord contends that this belief is at odds with the praise of the old Garibaldino. The problem is not revolution per se, but the way power is realigned afterwards.

Revolution, however, remains a problematic notion in *Nostromo.* Even for Walter Benjamin, revolution is a form of violence and terrorism. While Gould's potential explosion of the mine could count as the ideal moment of the Benjaminian interruption in the novel, rather than the failed revolutions that seem to go on in cycles, Benjamin's idea of messianism is ultimately outside historical change in chronological time. According to Anson Rabinbach, "Benjamin rejects both the natural right justification of revolutionary terrorism derived from the French revolution and the gradualism that seeks to replace one form of state power with another."[77] Yet there is a tension in Benjamin's messianisms: rejection of violence, on one hand, and "a radical affirmation of the new and creative destruction of the old order," on the other.[78] Messianism is otherworldly, yet perpetually attracted to revolution. Ultimately, Benjamin's utopia is marked by its impossibility to be transformed into a clear program of political emancipation.

Conrad demystifies progress along the same lines as Benjamin. The storm of progress carries us to a repetition of the past catastrophe—the expulsion from paradise. The eviction initiates chronological time, while paradise past and future remains outside temporality. He who attempts to undo a past catastrophe is doomed to repeat it.

A Simple Tale?

The Writing and Rewriting of *The Secret Agent*

ANDREW GLAZZARD

Conrad described *The Secret Agent,* in its dedication to H. G. Wells, as "THIS SIMPLE TALE OF THE XIX CENTURY," and added *A Simple Tale* as the novel's subtitle. The novel is, of course, far from simple structurally, thematically, and narratively. The writing of the novel was also a complex affair, and following its twists and turns helps us to notice points of ideology or technique, and shows that Conrad wrote and rewrote the story at different times for different purposes. The discipline of "book history,"[1] far from being an arid examination of matters of interest only to scholarly editors and antiquarians, can help us see familiar texts in new ways, and challenge our preconceptions about authorship and reading.

A Tale of the XIX Century: Conrad's Sources

In his "Author's Note," written in 1920, Conrad claimed that the novel's subject came about in a conversation with an unnamed friend we can confidently identify as Ford Madox Hueffer (later Ford Madox Ford, 1873–1939), with whom Conrad collaborated on numerous projects from 1898 to 1909. Their conversation began on the subject of "anarchist activities" in general before passing to the specifics of "the already old story of the attempt to blow up the Greenwich Observatory; a blood-stained inanity of so fatuous a kind that it was impossible to fathom its origin by any reasonable or even unreasonable process of thought."[2] The "blood-stained inanity" was an explosion in Greenwich Park at 4:50 p.m. on Thursday, 15 February 1894, that resulted in the death of Martial Bourdin, a tailor of French origin who lived and worked in an area immediately north of London's Oxford Street, and who was a member of the nearby Autonomie Club, an anarchist society.

Contemporary newspaper accounts agree that Bourdin initially survived the explosion, despite terrible wounds: his "legs were shattered, one arm was blown away, and the stomach and abdomen were torn open," yet he was able to ask the park keeper who found him to take him home.[3] He died shortly after his arrival at the Seamen's Hospital in Greenwich. Some accounts suggest that Bourdin was transporting the explosive device to France, and broke his journey at Greenwich because he believed he was being followed.[4] H. B. Samuels—brother-in-law to Bourdin's brother, editor of the anarchist newspaper *The Commonweal,* and believed by some to be a source for Conrad's Verloc—claimed in his obituary of Bourdin on *The Commonweal*'s front page that Bourdin chose the park to "test a new weapon of destruction."[5] However, the enduring version of events is the official one, given at the inquest into Bourdin's death by the British government's principal expert on explosives: Bourdin intended to attack the Greenwich Observatory.[6]

Writing privately in 1923 to Ambrose G. Barker—an anarchist who had sent him a contemporary pamphlet on the bombing by the former editor of *The Commonweal,* David Nicoll—Conrad denied being in Britain at the time of the bombing, and claimed not to have read any contemporary accounts.[7] Conrad's claim has been roundly rejected by literary historians, not least as Conrad was definitely in London when he claimed not to be;[8] Conrad has also been suspected of having drawn on Nicoll's pamphlet when writing the novel.[9] Conrad's "Author's Note" shows therefore that he preferred to acknowledge anecdotes from Hueffer rather than printed accounts as his source material for the bombing. Conrad goes on, however, to cast doubt on Hueffer's knowledge of the anarchist milieu: "It never occurred to me later to ask how he arrived at his knowledge for I am sure that if he had once seen in his life the back of an anarchist that must have been the whole extent of his connection with the underworld"; Conrad then suggests that Hueffer may have "gathered those illuminating facts at second or third hand."[10]

Again, there is good reason to doubt the reliability of Conrad's version: Hueffer was in fact very knowledgeable about anarchists, and knew several personally, including the Russian émigrés Sergei Kravchinsky—who wrote under the pseudonym "Stepniak" and had murdered the head of the tsar's secret police in St. Petersburg before fleeing to London—as well as Felix Volkhovsky and Peter Kropotkin.[11] George Gapon, the leader of the 1905 "Bloody Sunday" march on the tsar's Winter Palace in St. Petersburg, and the model for Father Zosim in *Under Western Eyes* (1911), was sheltered by Hueffer's mother in London after he escaped from Russia.[12] But it was Hueffer's cousins, Helen and Olivia Rossetti, who provided Conrad's most significant connection to anarchism prior to the writing of *The Secret Agent.* They were in fact child-anarchists, printing at the ages of twelve and sixteen respectively an anarchist newspaper called *The Torch* (in which they published Hueffer's first poem) in the basement of their London home while their father, William Michael Rossetti, senior civil servant and brother to Dante Gabriel and Christina, presumably turned a blind eye.[13] Conrad slyly acknowledges this connection with a reference at the very opening of the novel to "obscure newspapers, badly printed," with "rousing titles" such as *The Torch,* being on display in the window of Verloc's shop.[14]

Conrad met Helen Rossetti twice, possibly in 1903–4, and there is good reason to believe that he read the Rossettis' autobiographical novel, *A Girl Among the Anarchists* (1903), published under the pseudonym "Isabel Meredith."[15] Shortly before he began work on what became *The Secret Agent,* Conrad wrote a short story, "The Informer" (1905), which features a glamorous young woman whose anarchist activities are "gestures" rather than sincere expressions of commitment; the "Lady Anarchist" of that story is evidently based on the Rossettis, and the story draws material from their novel.[16] That novel also includes a thinly disguised account of the Greenwich bombing, transposed to London's Queen's Park, in which the bomber, Augustin Myers, dies in the explosion, and his brother, Jacob—described with blatant anti-Semitism by "Meredith"—is identified as an agent provocateur working for the Metropolitan Police who was instructed to provoke the incident in order to discredit the anarchists and justify repressive responses.[17] This fictionalized account, which closely follows the version of events presented in Nicoll's pamphlet, has obvious echoes in Conrad's plot, with one very significant difference: in *The Secret Agent,* the bombing is arranged not by the British police force but by a diplomat working for an unnamed foreign power that we clearly recognize as Tsarist Russia. This is an important ideological point: although Chief Inspector Heat operates his informer, Verloc, as a private source of information, he is far from being as politically manipulative and conspiratorial as his equivalents in *A Girl Among the Anarchists*; by shifting the blame for the horror of Greenwich Park from the British to the Russian authorities, the novel not only stigmatizes the tsarist regime, but also exonerates the British state.

This ideological purpose can also be detected in the novel's handling of another important source, acknowledged in the "Author's Note": about a week after his conversation with Hueffer, Conrad "came upon [. . .] the rather summary recollections of an Assistant Commissioner of Police," Sir Robert Anderson. Conrad was "arrested by a little passage of about seven lines" describing Anderson's encounter with Sir William Harcourt, the home secretary—the senior minister responsible in the British government for law and order, equivalent to Sir Ethelred in the novel—in which Harcourt accused Anderson of withholding information. In his memoirs, *Sidelights on the Home-Rule Movement* (1906), Anderson described his intelligence work undertaken against Irish republican terrorists in the 1870s and 1880s that involved the use of informants. Anderson wrote that this "was always a sore point with Sir William Harcourt. 'Anderson's idea of secrecy is not to tell the Secretary of State,' he once said to one of his colleagues, fixing his eyes on me as he spoke."[18] In his "Author's Note," Conrad comments that this passage "stimulated" his mind like a catalytic reaction, "the tiniest drop of the right kind, precipitating the process of crystallisation in a test tube containing some colourless solution."[19]

This passage precipitated some dialogue between the Assistant Commissioner and Chief Inspector Heat in chapter 6. Heat says, "There are things not fit for everybody to know," to which the Assistant Commissioner replies, "Your idea of secrecy seems to consist in keeping the chief of your department in the dark. That's stretching it a little too far, isn't it?"[20] The verbal resemblance is striking, but the difference between the two texts is also revealing. Anderson's defence of official secrecy, to the extent of withholding information from senior ministers, becomes Heat's defence of a private "system of supervision."[21] Two aspects of the change are worth noting. The first is that Anderson asserts he was acting on the principle of safeguarding his informants, while Heat's principle is the rather more self-serving one of "knowledge is power": "It's a private affair of my own," he tells the Assistant Commissioner. "Private friendship, private information, private use of it."[22] The second change is the switching of the actors in the scene: instead of the home secretary being kept in the dark by a senior official, later to become Assistant Commissioner, it is the Assistant Commissioner who is being kept in the dark, and actually misled, by a middle-ranking detective. This matters because the Assistant Commissioner comes to embody the only moral positive that this otherwise bleak narrative can offer: the maintenance of liberty. The Assistant Commissioner refuses to be obstructed by Heat's machinations, goes to Verloc's shop, and solves the crime; he provides a full account of his actions, and the secrets he has revealed, to Sir Ethelred; he foils Mr. Vladimir's plan to bring England "into line" and provoke "a universal repressive legislation," and strikes a blow for political freedom by ensuring Mr. Vladimir's expulsion.[23] He makes clear that his actions have a political purpose to Mr. Vladimir in chapter 10 in a passage that encapsulates the novel's ideology: "What pleased me most in this affair [. . .] is that it makes such an excellent starting-point for a piece of work which I've felt must be taken in hand—that is, the clearing out of this country of all the foreign political spies, police, and that sort of—of—dogs. In my opinion they are a ghastly nuisance; also an element of danger."[24]

What have we learned from examining the novel's sources? First, the novel draws on facts (that is, the facts of the 1894 bombing), but also narrative versions of these and other facts—Hueffer's anecdotes, the Rossettis' novel, Anderson's recollections. These narratives are not necessarily factually accurate, but they are useful to the novelist—and remind us that history as well as fiction is largely made up of stories. Second, in describing these sources, whether publicly (in the "Author's Note") or privately (to Ambrose Barker), Conrad remains a storyteller, his accounts providing invaluable directions but without being reliably accurate or definitive. Third, and appropriately for a novel whose interest in secrecy is declared in its title, Conrad covertly acknowledges sources in his text (for example, the reference to *The Torch* in the opening pages): the richness of our reading experience depends on the knowledge we bring. Fourth, and most significant, a detailed comparison of the sources with Conrad's handling of them provide clues to the novel's ideology, which we can broadly describe as "liberal"—as shown by the avoidance of the anti-Semitism found in the Rossettis' novel, and, most clearly, the endorsement of British liberal values that survive the political and domestic tragedies of the novel.

A Longish Story: Writing "Verloc"

The "Author's Note," simultaneously revealing and deceptive about the genesis of the novel, also omits one important fact: Conrad's original intention was not to write a novel at all. *The Secret Agent* began as a short story whose title remains to this day on the first page of the manuscript: "Verloc."[25] Conrad announced to his literary agent, J. B. Pinker (1863–1922), on 13 February 1906, that he was beginning work on "Verloc" while staying at the Riche et Continental Hôtel in Montpellier, France, with his wife, Jessie, a partial invalid since 1904, and eight-year-old son Borys.[26] Writing to Pinker on 21 February, Conrad stated that the story would be complete by the end of the month, and that he expected it not to be "unduly long"—not much more than the one he had just completed, "The Brute," a mere 8,200 words.[27] However, the story quickly grew, in a way not uncommon with Conrad's novels: *Lord Jim* (1900), *Nostromo* (1904), *Under Western Eyes* (1911), and *Chance* (1913) are all long novels that began as short stories.[28]

At the beginning of his writing career in the mid-1890s, Conrad was rather disdainful of the short-story form. However, it did not take him long to change his mind: beset by financial pressures, and recently married, Conrad discovered with the publication of stories such as "Karain" and "The Lagoon"—subsequently collected in *Tales of Unrest* (1898)—that short stories could be more lucrative than novels. Conrad received just twenty pounds for the copyright of his first novel, *Almayer's Folly* (1895), but earned more than twice that for each of his first short stories, giving him ten times the income per word than he received from his first novel.[29] Short stories also potentially generated income from both magazine and book publication: by the time he embarked on "Verloc," Conrad had three volumes of short stories or novellas to his name, nearly all of which had been previously published in magazines. A fourth volume of short stories, *A Set of Six*, published in 1908, contains two short stories that can be seen as companion pieces for *The Secret Agent,* "The Informer" and "An Anarchist." Both were written in 1905–6 for publication in the American magazine *Harper's* and take anarchism as a subject. "The Informer" is particularly close to *The Secret Agent* technically as well as thematically: it carries the subtitle "An Ironic Tale," and it was applying "the ironic method" to the subject of an anarchist bombing and the domestic tragedy it caused that Conrad identifies as the novel's "artistic purpose" in the "Author's Note."[30] "The Informer" also shares with the novel a trans-textual character, "The Professor," a former science student working on explosives and perfecting detonators. In fact, in the early stages of its composition, "Verloc" was planned to be part of a "special volume" of three anarchist stories, a project that might be seen as combining artistic unity in both subject and treatment.[31] It was also a potentially remunerative project: Conrad wrote to Galsworthy at the end of December 1905, less than two months before he embarked on writing "Verloc": "Yes I wrote the Anarchist story and now I am writing another of the sort [that is, "The Informer"]. I write these stories because they bring more money than the sea papers."[32]

"Verloc" did not remain a short story for long. On 2 March 1906 Conrad told Pinker that "Verloc is extending," adding: "It's no good fighting against it. It would take too much time. Any way I think the story is good."[33] Three days later he informed Pinker that during the week he would send a further and possibly final batch of pages: "Alas it'll be a longish story 18000 words or so—I fear."[34] By 9 April he had completed 14,000 words, approximately the first two-and-a-half chapters, and had probably completed the third chapter by the time he returned home to the Pent, a farmhouse near Hythe in Kent that he rented from Hueffer.[35] There, and possibly during a three-week stay at Hueffer's house in Winchelsea, East Sussex, Conrad wrote part or all of chapter 4 in May–June, before moving with his heavily pregnant wife to John Galsworthy's home in West London in July in order to be near medical assistance if Jessie required it.[36] By early September, after Jessie had recovered from the birth of John Conrad on 2 August and the family had returned to the Pent, Conrad had completed chapters 5 and 6, and most of chapter 7.[37] After this point, the composition of the novel becomes complicated by a very significant factor—its serial publication.

A short story, expected to take one or two weeks to complete, growing into what eventually became a novel of thirteen chapters is highly revealing about Conrad's method. We are accustomed to viewing Conrad as a technically accomplished modernist or proto-modernist whose novels, especially those of what has been labelled his "major phase," are finely wrought, *coherent* works of art.[38] Indeed, this impression of the inspired author was carefully nurtured by Conrad himself: his "Author's Note" describes the genesis of the novel as a chemical reaction, suggesting that once the influences had come together in the author's consciousness they were transformed into an artistic creation.

However, an awareness of Conrad's writing methods invites us to read his work as more improvisatory. This can be illustrated by the effect of Conrad's reading of Anderson's *Sidelights on the Home-Rule Movement,* published on 12 May 1906, by which point Conrad had already written the novel's first three chapters. The three characters suggested by Anderson's book, Chief Inspector Heat, the Assistant Commissioner, and Sir Ethelred, do not appear until chapter 5 (although Heat is mentioned in chapter 4), showing that Conrad incorporated substantial new material suggested by his reading when nearly a quarter of what became the published novel had already been written. Although we may now consider *The Secret Agent* to be a tightly organized, thematically unified, and carefully planned novel, that is not how it was written.

The Awful Rag: Serial Publication

When Conrad embarked on his writing career in the 1890s, he developed strategies for generating an income for himself and his family, at the same time establishing himself as an artistically serious literary figure.[39] Once he had accepted the need to publish in magazines, he was initially discriminating, preferring either the heavyweight, politically conservative magazines such as *Blackwood's Magazine* (often referred to at the time as "*Maga*") and the *New Review,* or new, avant-garde publications such as *The Savoy,* edited by the poet Arthur Symons, which published "The Idiots," and the *English Review,* created by Hueffer in 1908 with substantial help from Conrad. *The Secret Agent* did not, however, appear in one of these prestigious publications: it was serialized over eleven weeks, from 6 October to 15 December 1906, in a new but ultimately short-lived American newspaper-magazine called *Ridgway's: A Militant Weekly for God and Country.*[40] *Ridgway's* combined American current-affairs comment and reporting, some fiction, and photographic miscellanies. For a new publication, a serialized story by Conrad was clearly something of a coup, which it celebrated by lauding both writer and serial. The magazine described Conrad as "a story-teller who writes literature," whose "tales last because there is more of them than the bare bones of plot; there is the knowledge of men, the feeling for life. In his new novel, 'The Secret Agent', there is a deal of plot and life. It is a story of diplomatic intrigue and anarchist treachery."[41] Conrad's deal with the magazine was arranged by Pinker, possibly working through an agent in New York, Paul R. Reynolds.[42] Conrad's letters reveal nothing about negotiations for serialization, but once it was underway in late October, Conrad wrote to Pinker dismissively about both the magazine and its editing of his story: "Ridgways are sending me their rag. It's awful—and it don't matter in the least. I see they are editing the stuff pretty severely."[43]

Pinker, who represented some of the greatest writers of the period (including Conrad's friends Hueffer, Wells, and Henry James), has long been recognized as a significant figure in Conrad's development.[44] From September 1900, when Conrad engaged him to place *Romance,* until his death in 1922, Pinker not only placed Conrad's work and negotiated on his behalf with publishers and editors, but also became his friend, literary adviser, and, in effect, financial adviser and banker (Conrad's 1,300 letters to Pinker include many requesting loans and advances on future work). One effect of Pinker's relationship with Conrad appears to have been that the latter became more accepting of having his work published in mass-circulation magazines and newspapers such as *T.P.'s Weekly,* the magazine published by the Irish politician and editor T. P. O'Connor which carried the serial version of *Nostromo* (1904), and the *Daily Mail.*[45]

Prestigious publications such as the *New Review* shaped Conrad's fiction writing thematically and ideologically: Conrad sometimes wrote with the publication's reputation, audience, and political tendencies in mind.[46] Conrad's correspondence shows also that he was extremely sensitive to the commercial and reputational opportunities that different publications brought. In 1901, for example, he turned down an offer from *Blackwood's* to publish *Typhoon* in order to accept a lower offer from the *Pall Mall Magazine,* telling Pinker that he did not want to return to *Blackwood's* "for many reasons—one of them being that I wish to reach another public than *Maga*'s."[47] Conrad's dismissiveness about *Ridgway's* might suggest that, having assigned responsibility to Pinker, he felt less concerned about the effect on his literary reputation of where his work was placed, and his precarious finances might have caused him to prioritize income over reputation. It is also possible that Conrad cared less about the American scene, although the publication of "An Anarchist" and "The Informer" in the prestigious *Harper's* possibly suggests otherwise.

Whatever the reason for his acceptance of publication in *Ridgway's,* this apparently "awful" magazine shaped the composition of *The Secret Agent.* For a start, once serialization had been agreed upon, Conrad found himself working to deadlines. By mid-September 1906, Conrad was able to send pages 407–28 of his manuscript to Pinker, promising "the dramatic half of the last chapter" still to come, and a week later declared himself "anxious as to the last 30 pages."[48] However, even at this late stage the story was still growing beyond Conrad's own expectations—he was to write another two hundred pages of manuscript for the serial version.[49] However, once the serial began to appear, the deadlines—exacerbated by the time needed to send the manuscript from Kent to Pinker's office in London and then via ship to New York—forced a drastic reappraisal. In late October, Conrad told Pinker he was "doing the knifing scene over again," and on the last day of the month announced that the final pages would be ready for the mail boat due to sail from Southampton on 3 November.[50] The day before it sailed, however, Conrad sent Pinker a telegram that captures his frenetic pace of work: "38 pages leave by 10 train begin typing at once another 1500 words to end shall leave at noon by rail with you about 2.40 in time to be typed and catch Southampton mailboat please wire me at five oclock Conrad."[51]

The effect of this time pressure is plain to see in the serial version. It has six chapters (the completed novel has thirteen), and the serial's chapter 6, serialized in three instalments from 1 to 15 December 1906, and comprising material which appears in expanded form in chapters 8, 9, 11, 12, and 13 of the book version, shows how, despite Conrad's protestations to Pinker, the novel was still growing in his imagination as he claimed to be concluding it. However, the deadlines meant he simply did not have time to write the novel that he had conceived. The final 15 December instalment is at times barely more than a sketch of what became the final third of the novel, as this extract demonstrates:

> Next day, drinking a glass of beer at the Silenus, he pulled a paper our of his pocket and for the third time that day read the account of a "Suicide from a cross-Channel steamer." A lady. First-class passenger. He folded the paper thoughtfully and on going out left it on the table.
>
> A week later he sat there again. Opposite him the Professor, dark and moody, sipped his beer, talking in a contemptuous way.[52]

Serialization in *Ridgway's* also appears to have affected the tone and content of the later instalments. On 11 October Conrad assured Pinker that *Ridgway's* need not fear "something unsuitable for general reading" in the forthcoming pages: "You may assure them that I am safe."[53] Examining the text of the serial side-by-side with that of the first book editions, it is clear that the former is not only drastically truncated but also lacking some of the most disturbing content of the novel. The serial treatment of the murder scene, for example, remains powerful, but swathes of the impressionistic artistry, psychological penetration, and philosophical commentary that make this one of the most admired sequences in all of Conrad's fiction are absent. Verloc's attempt at sexual seduction of his anguished wife—the "note of wooing" that appears in his voice immediately before he is murdered—is only one of many such absences.[54] In addition, the editors at *Ridgway's*—possibly with Conrad's collusion[55]—excised materials, present in the manuscript, which add depth to the characters and provide much of the novel's celebrated imagery. A reader who had only the serial version, for instance, would have been denied the images of Chief Inspector Heat as a tightrope artist, and London as a "slimy aquarium."[56]

Editorial policy at *Ridgway's* led directly to the simplification and shortening of the narrative, while Conrad's acceptance of the magazine's commercial and editorial requirements led him to rush out to them an abbreviated and partly bowdlerized version of the narrative he would go on to expand in the book version. Perhaps the most significant effect of serialization is its presentation: reading Conrad's text in instalments, hemmed in by advertisements, and accompanied by Henry Raleigh's line-drawings is a qualitatively different experience from reading it in a scholarly edition accompanied by introduction, notes, and critical apparatus. Raleigh's illustrations also draw attention, as Watts has noted, to the narrative's "dramatic incidents": the serial is "less resonant and subtle" than the book version, "a graphic thriller for rapid reading."[57]

Putting in the Quality: Preparation for Book Publication

At around the time that he completed the serial version in November 1906, Conrad wrote to his English publisher, Algernon Methuen, offering him the novel's typescript "at once" and requesting "galley slips"—non-paginated printed proofs with wide margins—to facilitate revisions.[58] However, Methuen did not receive the typescript until 14 March 1907, by which time Conrad and his family had returned to Montpellier, the birthplace of "Verloc." *The Secret Agent* had by this time already reappeared in Conrad's plans, as he confessed to Pinker in mid-February that the prospect of revising it, which he projected to take six weeks, was "not pleasant."[59] He told Pinker in early May that he would finalize the manuscript "soon," but wished "to put as much 'quality' as I can in that book which will be criticised with some severity no doubt—or *scrutinised* rather."[60] In mid-May, after several postal delays—the Conrads had moved first to Geneva and then to the nearby resort of Champel in Switzerland on account of severe ill-health of both children, as well as Conrad's own "nervous collapse"—Conrad received from Methuen not galley slips, as requested, but paginated set-proofs. Conrad, already anxious and ill, was indignant, telling Pinker that he was "hurt at Methuen disregarding my perfectly reasonable wishes."[61] But it was not just the perceived "slight." Firstly, Methuen would charge more for corrections to set proofs than galley slips, and secondly the set-proofs had much smaller margins. As a result Conrad concluded that he would have to "curtail" his corrections.[62] By 25 May he had begun to return the corrected proofs, aspiring to have completed the new version by the end of the month.[63] On 1 June, Conrad told Pinker about "the additional stuff" he was inserting, and promised to have the new manuscript ready within two days.

As usual, Conrad hugely underestimated the time required and the expansive possibilities of his narrative: the manuscript was finally completed in late July and the proofs corrected in late August, a mere two weeks before publication in Britain on 12 September and in the United States a few days later.[64] Nevertheless, given the scale and scope of Conrad's reworking of the narrative, this was a major achievement under the circumstances: he told Pinker in late July that it was "the most awful time I've ever had."[65] In just over three months

Conrad made many alterations to the first two-thirds of the novel, including changing names of characters (he originally had Winnie as "Minnie," Stevie as "Steevie," Alexander Ossipon as "Andrew," and Karl Yundt as "Max Kling"). His major achievement was to rewrite the closing instalments of what had been published in *Ridgway's* to become the last third of the novel, adding by his own estimation 26,000 to 30,000 words.[66] The most sizeable expansion was the addition of the whole of chapter 10, in which the Assistant Commissioner reports back to Sir Ethelred and confronts Mr. Vladimir at the house of the "lady patroness." This latter episode is the ideological core of the novel—yet in the history of the novel's composition it is almost an afterthought. There is, of course, no way that Conrad could have written this chapter in a margin, whether of a galley slip or a set-proof. Perhaps Methuen's mistake in sending set-proofs did Conrad, and his readers, a favor: unable to expand his novel literally in the margins, he produced in the summer of 1907 a new manuscript (now lost) of the final third of the novel.

Conrad's preparation for the novel's book publication shows not only the narrative's continuing expansion but also that the process of writing can be contingent on such mundane factors as the width of margins. To ignore the presence of factors such as the requirements and practices of publishers, the influence of a literary agent, or even the exigencies of a writer's financial and family circumstances, is to accept uncritically the myth of the author as isolated genius, independent of everything but the inspiration of the Muse. Conrad's imagination was such that his stories could spill over the containers he expected to put them in, and anarchically subvert his own and others' expectations. To show that a novel is both a collaboration and the outcome of a series of contingent events is not to deny the author's agency: it is to set that agency in the richness of its context.

Conrad's Reevaluations

In 1919, Conrad began to reevaluate and in some cases to rework his novels. The reevaluation was necessitated by plans for a collected edition of his works, and, in line with the practice of other authors of the period who had an eye to posterity, such as Henry James, the volumes required prefaces. At the same time, Conrad renewed an interest in adapting his own work for stage, and became excited by the new medium of cinema.[67] In September he met Pinker and the actor and producer Frank Vernon, and the following month, with the latter's help, Conrad embarked on a dramatization of *The Secret Agent*. He completed the "Author's Note" for what became the Heinemann edition the following March, and later the same month completed the first draft of the dramatization. This was printed privately in 1921 and received its first performance on 2 November 1922 at the

Ambassadors Theatre in London to an "unfavourable reception."[68] Conrad made immediate cuts to the play, but these could not save it and it was taken off after just ten performances.

The preface and the play show Conrad interpreting and rewriting his novel. Both, for example, give particular prominence to Winnie: the play opens and closes with her—the final moments show her collapsing into madness—while in the "Author's Note" Conrad emphasises repeatedly that the novel is "Winnie Verloc's story."[69] The play and the preface rewrite *The Secret Agent* as a domestic tragedy, downplaying the "diplomatic intrigue and anarchist treachery" celebrated by *Ridgway's*. The play opens with Winnie, her mother, and Stevie in a scene exploring aspects of family life, and introduces the notes of domestic tragedy and social comment as Winnie and her mother reminisce about her childhood, growing up with a brutal, alcoholic father. The final scene powerfully expresses Winnie's love for her brother, giving her more of a voice than in the novel: "WINNIE (*dry sob*). [. . .] He was to me like my heart in my body. . . . And I can't find a tear for him. Not a tear. Not one!"[70] Writing for a world exhausted by the cataclysmic effects of great power rivalry, Conrad may have decided that the human factor was most important, while his experience of British theater, notably the socially engaged dramas of his friend Galsworthy and his acquaintance Granville Barker, no doubt conditioned his view of what would work on stage.

The "Author's Note" comments on the novel's most admired technical feature—its irony, which enables us to see its characters with "scorn as well as in pity"—and concedes that the play strips away that feature to leave the "bare bones."[71] For those critics who have noticed the play, that absence is its major weakness: "Removal of the narratorial voice is indeed a stripping of the flesh; and to fit the chronological and scenic requirements of stage-action the plot has been breathlessly compressed and the locations claustrophobically interiorised"; its finale is "almost a parody of the contrivances of theatrical thrillers."[72] What such criticisms overlook is that, irrespective of its dramatic merits,[73] the play enhances our rereadings of the novel: we can, for example, appreciate its irony by experiencing its absence, or use the play as a commentary on the novel by seeing what Conrad emphasized and omitted in a different medium and at a different time. Indeed, Conrad surprised himself by what he found in his own story when he subjected it to the "terribly searching thing" that is a stage adaptation: "I will confess that I myself had no idea what the story under the writing was till I came to grips with it in this process of dramatization."[74]

Furthermore, these rewritings remind us that a text such as a novel is not a stable and certainly not a simple entity. Conrad wrote three works called *The Secret Agent,* in 1906, 1907, and 1919–21. The differences between them are substantial, and reflect the circumstances of their production, and their audiences. Each of those three texts exists in multiple versions, with corrections, mistakes, and second thoughts, contributions by different collaborators—whether editors, illustrators, or even advertisers—and different impressions left by form as well as content. The *Ridgway's* editors made unilateral, unauthorized changes to Conrad's typescript; in 1920 the text of the novel acquired an "Author's Note"; in 1921 two different texts, both by Conrad, were performed in London on consecutive nights. The novel's writing and rewriting show that its title—"*The Secret Agent: A Simple Tale* by Joseph Conrad"—obscures the complexities of authorship. Recovering those complexities extends the possibilities of interpretation.

"The Secret Sharer"

When the Other Is the Self

Anna Krauthammer

Conrad's use of a double in "The Secret Sharer" creates an additional dimension to the main character, the captain, resulting in varied readings of the text. Barbara Johnson and Marilyn Garber in their essay "Secret Sharing: Reading Conrad Psychoanalytically" list several types of readings that have been and can be utilized to interpret the story: "The pathology of the author, the pathology of the protagonist, the pathology (or symptomology or symptomography) of the text, the text as a theory of a symptom or complex, the text as an allegory of psychoanalysis."[1] This list stresses a psychoanalytic lens, but historical, biographical, and social approaches are also used. These lenses of interpretation can address various layers of meaning for the captain's actions and thoughts as he leads dual lives and acts in more than one role.

In "The Secret Sharer," Conrad uses the captain/narrator's double, Leggatt, as a means of exploring the captain's conflicts in asserting leadership and adhering to the maritime codes of law he must follow. In choosing to allow Leggatt on board, hiding him, and letting him escape, the captain has to confront and resolve the conflicts of duty versus desire, morality versus legality, and individual need versus communal needs. Daniel Curley describes the captain's dilemma by suggesting that his problem is not perception or understanding, but rather a need to reconcile his conflicting feelings and dual lives and act in a manner that will not betray Leggatt, his crew, or himself. Curley is very specific about the captain's dilemma: "In shaping his material to the end he desired, Conrad was faced with two really difficult problems, he had to find a way to separate his protagonist's legal and moral responsibilities, and he had to invent for Leggatt an action that would be a crime in form but not a crime in fact."[2] Curley then describes the captain's very difficult choice: if the captain leaves Leggatt to drown, he betrays Leggatt and himself, because—according to Curley—Leggatt is himself, but if he wrecks the ship, he is disloyal to the crew.[3] Curley continues: "The captain must create out of the tradition of his life and profession an individual moral solution to meet the totally unexpected situation, and he must do it in the face of counter moral pressure of his own crew and the captain of the Sephora."[4] Curley also refers to this journey as a "ritual of initiation."[5] The site for the ritual is the sea. In the end it is the captain's ability to overcome its dangers, enabled by the hat of his double, that accomplishes three things: his assumption of command, his personality's integration, and his release of Leggatt, which not only helps Leggatt, but also frees the captain of his double. Furthermore, by letting Leggatt go, the captain stops the tension created by his constantly trying to find an appropriate role for that subconscious part of him that is authentic but interfering with his conscious life.

On the other hand, Leggatt, an actual physical presence on the ship, also represents the captain's subconscious self, which at first brings these conflicts to consciousness and then forces resolution. Albert J. Guerard's essay "The Journey Within" clearly delineates the captain's physical journey as a psychological one as well. He calls it a night journey: "I refer to the archetypal myth dramatized in much great literature since the Book of Jonah: the story of an essentially solitary journey involving profound spiritual change in the voyager. In its classical form the journey is a descent to earth followed by a return to light. . . . [M]ore often it is dramatized through an actual voyage and movement through space."[6] "I suspect the myth of the night journey is unusually conscious in "The Secret Sharer.'"[7] So there are two journeys: the one over the sea and the one into the interior of the captain's mind. And Leggatt is real as well as symbolic. For, as Guerard continues, "although psychological process was a major concern for Conrad, so too, was the remembered visible world."[8] For Guerard the psychological journey ends (it must) in integration of the captain's personality: "In Jungian terms . . . integration of personality cannot occur until the unconscious has been known, trafficked with and in some sense liberated."[9] "The conclusion," says Guerard, "is simply that of 'The Secret Sharer': we cannot be good seamen alone with our ships, until we have faced out, recognized and subdued those selves which interfere with seamanship"; "we cannot achieve wholesome integration of the personality until we have made the archetypal journey into self."[10]

Paul J. Emmett suggests this conflict of identifying with Leggatt and yet remaining separate as a form of suppression: "So the captain must be careful, he has to sail between Scylla and Charybdis, between being obliterated by difference and being lost in similarity."[11] The captain, by hiding Leggatt, leads two lives: one in the cabin and one on the ship. Once Leggatt leaves the ship, the captain no longer feels fragmented or conflicted, as illustrated by his ability to save the crew and the ship and assume command. The psychological journey of the captain in which he must confront his subconscious self and the actual journey during which he must assume leadership of his ship in his first command are linked primarily by Leggatt, who, as Daniel Schwarz notes, has a rather ironic relationship with the captain: "Paradoxically, Leggatt disrupts the captain's psychic health and hence the order of the ship, at the same time he is a catalyst for more efficient integration of both the captain's personality and his fitness to command."[12] These dual aspects of Leggatt's role in the captain's life drive the physical and the psychological journey in Conrad's and the captain's narrative.

Conrad wastes no time (or text) in establishing the sea as an important element of the narrative, not only as setting. The sea brings Leggatt to the captain and then bears him away. In the captain's initial encounter with him, Leggatt seems to be a headless, naked corpse. But Leggatt's nakedness also suggests infancy and innocence, so that by extension the water is the womb with the ladder as an umbilical cord.[13] The captain mentions the phosphorescent glow that illuminates the initial encounter, a lightening of the darkness of the sea, and one that will illuminate the captain's journey toward self-knowledge symbolized by a physical sign—the hat—which will light his way and save him and the ship. But this scenario also suggests a rebirth for them both; Leggatt escapes for a new life, the captain will assume command, no longer stranger to the ship or himself. This encounter will have significance for both men, as evidenced by the captain's almost immediate acceptance of Leggatt and the casualness of the dialogue before Leggatt ascends by the ladder. After the captain gets over the shock of seeing Leggatt in the water, there are a few preemptory comments during which the captain identifies himself and Leggatt hauls himself aboard. The immediate bonding is significant, and later in the story Leggatt remarks how it seemed as if the captain was waiting for him. Symbolically, he was.

Furthermore, the captain's initial description of the sea encompasses a number of distinctive boundaries, foreshadowing the boundaries the captain must adhere to as well as overcome in his struggle to maintain command of his ship: "On my right hand there were lines of fishing stakes resembling a mysterious system of half-submerged bamboo fences, incomprehensible in its division of the domain of tropical fishes. . . . To the left a group of barren islets suggesting ruins of stone walls, towers and blockhouses. . . . And when I turned my head . . . I saw the straight line of the flat shore joined to the stable sea, edge to edge, with a perfect and unmarked closeness."[14] It also illustrates the captain's keen sense of observation and his perception that will enable him to understand his conflicts and his feelings of isolation and connectedness with Leggatt.

The sea offers the captain moments of silence, solitude, and reflection, and in this mood he first encounters Leggatt. The sea allows the captain a space of his own so that the encounter can remain private. His description of the ship as she puts out to sea emphasizes the separateness of the ship in the immensity of sea and sky, and suggests the actual and psychological journey the captain will take: "She floated at the starting point of a long journey, very still in an immense stillness. . . . At that moment I was alone in her decks. There was not a sound in her and around her, nothing moved, nothing lived, not a canoe on the water, not a bird in the air, not a cloud in the sky. In this breathless pause at the threshold of a long passage we seemed to be measuring our fitness for a long and arduous enterprise, the appointed task of both our existences to be carried out far from human eyes with only sea and sky for spectators and for judges."[15] The captain's sense of communion with the sea, although ironic in the beginning of the narrative, because of the ensuing events, is true at the end of the novel when he finally feels not only in command of the ship, but also a contentment that stems from having resolved his conflicts: "And suddenly I rejoiced with the great security of the sea as compared with the unrest of the land, in my choice of that untempted life, presenting no disquieting problems, invested with an elementary moral beauty by the absolute straightforwardness of its appeals and by the singleness of its purpose."[16] It is a projected ideal which foreshadows the end of the narrative, when having let Leggatt go, he no longer leads a dual existence and he, too, feels a single purpose. At the end of his narrative, the cabin which had been both a hiding place and a tension-filled space because both the captain and Leggatt feared discovery, becomes simply the captain's cabin: a real, tangible space to sleep and eat.

The sea is immense and isolating with rules of its own, both natural and man-made and, because of these limits, the captain can either succeed or fail. The isolation it provides for the captain mimics the isolation he feels on the ship and serves to underscore his alienation from and contempt for Archbold. On the other hand, it provides space in which he can act almost unilaterally, away from land that is more chaotic and ambiguous, and it allows him to create a separate world inhabited only by himself and Leggatt. As captain he can control this environment and the environment of the ship. He can create a secret private space, by dint of being a captain, a world in which no one can intrude without permission—his own cabin. It is a world within the world of the ship within the larger world of sea and sky. These multiple spaces are not psychological, but environmental, reflecting several worlds he actually moves in, as does Leggatt, because he is the double, although Leggatt is unaware of the psychological aspects of his relationship to the captain and the effects they have on the captain's actions and conflicts.

The captain's personal journey to self-knowledge is connected to establishing his command within the maritime laws of the sea, where he must prove himself. The sea is both a threat and a place of safety. It is revelatory and mysterious. He can delve into his own conflicts in privacy and secrecy but, from a practical point of view, it can kill him and the crew if they can't handle the closeness to the shore when he aids in Leggatt's escape. Furthermore, his behavior in harboring Leggatt and going so close to the shore may well destroy his career: "I realized suddenly that all my future, the only future for which I was fit, would perhaps go irretrievably to pieces in any mishap in my first command."[17]

Throughout his narrative, the captain repeatedly mentions that he feels a stranger to the ship and crew: "All these people had been together eighteen months or so, and my position was that of the only stranger on board. I mention this because it has some bearing on what is to follow. . . . But what I felt most was being a stranger to the ship and if all the truth must be told, I was somewhat a stranger to myself."[18] He lacks self-knowledge and an awareness of his subconscious, conflicted self that has yet to emerge. He is not fully aware of what being a captain entails, nor is he prepared for how to meet the challenges that await him. He reacts rather than initiates commands and actions. He functions only on a conscious level. His reading of the emotions and motives of Archbold and his own comes later as he becomes more connected to Leggatt and perceives the dual lives he leads. His growing perception of his dilemma signals a need for integration which still needs to be resolved through an action he is not prepared to take until Leggatt suggest he must let him go. However, these feelings of isolation also prepare the captain for the encounter with Leggatt, and propel him to not only bond with Leggatt as a kindred spirit, but also to accept the strangeness of that initial encounter. His acceptance of Leggatt, his second self, alleviates his feelings of being a stranger to himself; Leggatt is that subconscious part of him that he has yet to confront in order to acquire a deeper knowledge of himself.

Beth Ash calls Conrad's style writing between the lines: "All of Conrad's most significant work is written 'in between'—between various necessary yet untenable options that can neither be realized nor abandoned . . . being in between impossible psychological options and/or social commitments is what drives Conrad's narratives even when the writing seems designed to obscure rather than illuminate the underwriting, blindly to enact rather than comprehend the reasons, the relations, that motivate irresolution."[19] The ambiguities in the text reveal several levels of the captain's consciousness. The experience appears to be alternately a dream, a nightmare, a challenge to morality, a connection to a kindred spirit, a subversive lie. The narrative is ambiguous because it is fluid, illustrating the fluid nature of the captain's experience and thus inviting varying readings of the story and of the role of Leggatt.

Leggatt is not only the captain's physical double, but he also represents aspects of his personality that are submerged in the captain's subconscious that must reveal themselves so that he may grow as a person and as a leader. These aspects are the more instinctive, aggressive, risk-taking traits that the captain admires in Leggatt, calling him a strong soul. The captain admires Leggatt for his control, calm, and conviction. Leggatt possesses a decisiveness as a man of action, whereas the captain seems stuck, unsure of himself, unsure of the crew, unable to act decisively until the end when he must finally allow Leggatt to leave and is willing to sacrifice the ship and the crew to make it happen. "Preoccupied with his unconscious thoughts, he is unable to function in the world, unable to exhibit the certain kind of unconsciousness crucial to everyday command."[20] Up until the end, very often, except for his attempt to hide Leggatt, he can neither reveal him nor let him go.

Ash suggests that Conrad views the world in terms of "irremediably opposing alternatives that can neither be embraced or given up" and describes Conrad's fiction as creating an "internal world conflict," in which "the mutually informing experience of otherness and sameness within the self becomes contradiction."[21] This analysis accounts for the captain's tensions and conflicting emotions as he alternately tries to be loyal to Leggatt, to maritime law, to his ship, and to his crew. The otherness of Leggatt and his sameness are almost unbearable for the captain, and it causes him to wear a mask with his crew and Archbold. "He was not a bit like me, really; yet as we stood leaning over my bed-place, whispering side by side with our dark heads together and our backs to the door, anyone bold enough to have opened it stealthily would have been treated to an uncanny sight of a double captain busy talking in whispers to his other self."[22] It also causes the captain to doubt his own sanity: "and all the time the dual working of my mind distracted me almost to the point of insanity. I was constantly watching myself, my secret self as dependent on my actions as my own personality. . . . It was very much like being mad, only it was worse because one was aware of it."[23] The dilemma is classic; he is facing two realities, both of which are true, but incompatible.

The dual lives he leads not only cause tension but also cause him to doubt his sanity, probably because he cannot yet discover his true self—which is a mixture of both lives. His separate statements of Leggatt being his double and yet not being like him reveal his conflict of identifying with Leggatt. However, although the captain needs Leggatt to draw out those characteristics that would make him a strong, effective captain, he does not need to *be* Leggatt in order to achieve this.

Conrad wants the reader to experience not only what the captain experiences, but *how* he experiences it. An example of this intent is the various ways the captain describes Leggatt. Furthermore, the text itself is a memory recounted through the lens of experience acquired over time and edited by the captain's changing perceptions of what happened. The captain revisits the anxiety of being young and inexperienced in his first command from the vantage points of later success and confidence. Critics speak of ambiguities in the relationship, related to the use of Leggatt as a double. But actually the relationship is made up of several layers of perception that create different realities that interface in the various contexts in which the captain must function both as an individual and in his role as commander, a role in which he must be successful if he is to retain command of the ship. This interface is obvious to the captain as he tries to balance the secret life with Leggatt, his command over his crew his encounter with Archbold—to the point where he doubts the actual existence of Leggatt. He refers to the non-physical existence of Leggatt several times, referring to him as "as noiseless as a ghost," being "haunted," Legatt saying something "a ghost might have said," Leggatt being visible to only him. These references point to his agitated state of mind, his mindfulness of the duality of his life in the cabin, and on the ship, his doubts about his sanity and his recognition that Leggatt might represent an unconscious or even supernatural element of himself. His perception is more layered, more problematic. He recognizes a separate aspect of his identity and finally the absolute connection between Leggatt and him alone. While he may be upset and fearful, he is functioning on a different level of consciousness that allows him to accept the part of him that cannot be seen by anyone else. This perception is triggered by the stress of hiding Leggatt and his recognition of their similarities.

Leggatt fulfills a purpose: to draw forth the qualities that will make the captain a true commander, resulting in the captain's ability to resolve his conflicts. But this must remain forever a secret, one of the mysteries the sea will hold. This secret is relevant to no one but the captain. Only its result is important. The question remains then why the narrative is at all important to the captain. Clearly, it is his recognition of his coming of age and a desire to reveal it as such. It is also a self-examination and affirmation; throughout the narrative the captain reveals himself to be a careful, introspective individual.

In consideration of the various conflicting feelings the captain has in the course of hiding Leggatt and the perception of those feelings, the encounter with Archbold is instructive. It almost runs the gamut of issues and doubts the captain has in the three major problem areas that will determine his future: hiding Leggatt, who is considered a criminal; doubting his own mental stability; and trying to figure out a way of dealing with his fellow captains who represent the laws of the sea:

> My lack of excitement, of curiosity, of surprise, of any sort of pronounced interest, began to arouse his distrust. But except for the felicitous pretense of deafness, I had not tried to pretend anything. I had felt utterly incapable of playing the part of ignorance properly, and therefore was afraid to try. It is also certain that he had brought some ready-made suspicions with him and that he viewed my politeness as a strange and unnatural phenomenon. And yet how else could I have received him! Not heartily! That was impossible for psychological reasons which I need not state here.

> My only object was to keep off his inquiries. Surlily? Yes, but surliness might have provoked a point-blank question. From its novelty to him and from its nature punctilious courtesy was the manner best calculated to restrain the man. But there was the danger of his breaking through my defense bluntly. I could not, I think, have met him by a direct lie, also for psychological (not moral) reasons. If he had only known how afraid I was of his putting my feeling identity with the other to the test! But strangely enough—(I thought of it only afterward)—I believe that he was not a little disconcerted by the reverse of that weird situation, by something in me that reminded him of the man he was seeking, suggested a mysterious similitude to the young fellow he had mistrusted and disliked from the first.[24]

This passage encompasses the captain's conflicts, his unease, and his enactment of a masquerade designed to protect him and Leggatt. At this point he is totally self-centered, wanting only to save himself and Leggatt. He is tense and is constantly wracked by needing to control, not to overplay his hand, and he is constantly afraid of his secret being discovered, not only by Archbold, but by a mistake of his own. His tension is palpable, but he is aided by Archbold's obtuseness and discomfort.

A notable aspect of this account is the repetition of words connoting mystery and strangeness. The captain recognizes the lack of precedents for his behavior and the almost unreality of his dilemma—from which he cannot yet free himself. The contradiction for him is that what is real has an air of unreality as does his relationship with Leggatt which is also real, but hidden to the world outside his cabin. The hidden bleeds into the revealed; the visible seems invisible; the invisible to everyone else is visible to the captain. There is a blending which he recognizes, and it is remarkable for his perception—and memory—of his state of mind at the time. He is clearly in a constant state of agitation but also in control of the dialogue, and he is strategizing while he is speaking to Archbold. He reads Archbold well.

In addition to illustrating the captain's conflicts, this encounter, although it shows him weak with worry, also presages his ability not only to command but also to navigate the sea. While he doubts his own ability to handle Archbold, he exercises control of his own feelings as he masquerades deafness. He knows his life is filled with dualities that overlap and interface. The captain's agitation during the journey is always present. He feels threatened by those outside the cabin as well as by the stress of hiding Leggatt: "Every day there was the horrible maneuvering so that my room and the bathroom should be done in the usual way. I came to hate the sight of the steward to abhor the voice of that harmless man. I felt that it was he that would bring on the disaster of discovery. It hung like a sword over our heads."[25] He says of his internal conflicts: "I was not wholly alone in my command; for there was that stranger in my cabin. Or rather I was not completely and wholly with her. Part of me was absent. That mental feeling of being in two places at once affected me physically as if the mood of secrecy had penetrated my very soul."[26] In addition to the agitation caused by hiding Leggatt, almost everyone in his crew poses a potential threat even as they fulfill their duties. Separation and strangeness are still there for him, even from his own crew. He mentions the sword over both their heads, connoting the bond between himself and Leggatt. In a possible choice between ship and career and Leggatt's safety and survival, it's clear he chooses Leggatt at this point. Everyone else is a stranger. And it is only when he attains command, and as he watches Leggatt swim away, that he can refer to him as a stranger as well as a second self. He rejoins his community and is truly part of the ship. He is no longer absent or in two places. There is integration in his personality.

Leggatt and the captain are bound by their backgrounds and training. Leggatt believes no one on land can judge him fairly and feels that he has an ally in the captain, although other than their similar backgrounds he cannot prove it. How does he know the captain will understand, and why does he understand? The captain is breaking the law of the sea by harboring a fugitive. This threatens all and will affect all on ship, but it also threatens the traditions and protocols that protect sailing vessels in the navy. The law is a way of protecting a whole community of which he must be a part if he is to remain a captain. He should be allied with Archbold, rather than obfuscate the issue. Why then doesn't he? Is he a law unto himself? Does he really understand Leggatt? Does he not consider Leggatt a criminal? Leggatt's explanation of extenuating circumstances is good enough for him.

Leggatt triggers the captain's actions because he realizes he had better remain dead, and so insists he has to go before he is discovered. Thus, if Leggatt represents the captain's subconscious desires, then it can be proposed that the subconscious saves him by insisting he has to escape. The captain in this way is moved from thought to action. His temporary disorientation and his inability to act finally dissolve. The community is the sea, not the land. He saves Leggatt, but Leggatt has also saved him. On the other hand, Edward Said suggests that "surely 'integration' in some manner is a feature of all fiction anyway; moreover this story possesses a number of deliberate details whose interest extends beyond their use as prescriptions for psychic good health."[27] He continues: "Leggatt is a direct reflection of the narrator; he is a person in whom the narrator can see himself clearly and directly."[28] He then strengthens this argument: "While Leggatt is a real person, he is also an image according to which the young narrator can see himself in an extreme moral and intellectual perspective."[29] So Leggatt may represent someone who can serve as an ideal example, someone the captain can aspire to be. Therefore, he is not a fragment of the captain's personality that lies dormant, waiting to be integrated. On the other hand, calling Leggatt a reflection does not mean an exact correspondence; mirrors reverse their images. Leggatt murdered someone; the captain did not. In fact, he saves Leggatt, and the ship and the crew.

Curley also supports the image of Leggatt as a part of the captain that is not realized till the story's end: "Leggatt is a manifestation of this instinctive nature, isolated and useless in the cabin, and it is only when Leggatt slips back into the sea that the instinctive nature of the captain slips into its proper place as part of an integrated personality."[30] He later notes more succinctly: "Specifically, the captain is carried through by that ideal conception of himself made manifest by Leggatt who is 'one of us' by birth and training and by acts."[31]

In a discussion of the different types of doubles and their roles in a text, which can be applied to Leggatt, Joan Steiner refers to Ralph Tymms's work on different types of doubling: "doubling by duplication, in which the counterpart appears as twin, or in its essential aspects a physical duplicate, and doubling by division, in which the counterpart represents one major facet of character customarily spiritual or psychological in nature." In addition, he describes the alternation between allegorical or ethical doubles, which express dualism in human nature in terms of good and evil, and realistic or psychological doubles, which depict dualism in terms of reason and emotion of the conscious or unconscious."[32] These representations of the double are all linked, although most critics separate the two physically, acknowledging they are separate characters from a narrative point of view regardless of the symbolic or psychological linkage, but not necessarily linked by intent or desire.[33] To deny this linkage would be to discard parts of the narrative—a point Said makes. The doubling that occurs in the story is critical to the interdependence of the captain and Leggatt, which transcends doubling by duplication and is hinted at by the various types of references the captain uses to describe Leggatt: "my second self," "my double," "my secret sharer." It is apparent that the captain recognizes both doubling by duplication and doubling by division by using these different names for Leggatt. And he has no problem with either type of doubling, except when they compromise his role as captain.

Furthermore, his admiration for Leggatt, his sensitivity to the choices he must make, and his analysis of his state of mind all point to categories other than duplication and division. Even though the captain made a moral choice by releasing Leggatt, this act is unacceptable to the larger maritime community of which Archbold is a part. Therefore, the captain cannot continue with his double indefinitely, and Leggatt must have his life back—as must the captain. Both need the separation, although for different reasons. That is, the captain cannot tolerate the physical incarnation of his other self; Leggatt must leave. The captain and Leggatt cannot exist in the same space. The sleeping suit Leggatt wears, his lack of clothing and uniform of rank, his nakedness all point to this; his actual physical existence is vulnerable and has a dreamlike quality. He is not part of anything except the captain. As a fugitive, he is isolated and his connection to the captain is primarily based on their mutual feeling of isolation. Leggatt's rejection of the hat is the final letting go of the link to the captain.

Clearly, Leggatt didn't intend to kill. So what motivates the captain? Not that the crime is ambiguous; a man is dead. But the captain puts his own interest above the law of the sea. What does he need from Leggatt? Or, perhaps more accurately, what does Leggatt provide for him? Whatever it is, it must be necessary to him either as a standard of behavior in the face of extenuating circumstances and/or that part of him which needs to be revealed because as yet it is buried in his subconscious. The captain is unprepared for the appearance of Leggatt, yet he is more familiar to him than his own crew and ship, and his whole life revolves around Leggatt while he is hiding him.

There is an instant sympathy between the two. Leggatt states: "As long as I know you understand . . . but of course you do. . . . You seem to have been there on purpose."[34] He calls the encounter "wonderful" and mentions earlier that it was as if the captain were expecting him. He, too, feels the meeting was somehow preordained and that there is a fit between himself and the captain. The fit is deeper than intellectual, and seems almost instinctive. From a practical viewpoint, that they have the same background and training may account for the understanding, but not completely for the depth and rapidity of the tie that forms. On the other hand, once the captain lets Leggatt go, he is whole again and not only does he refer to him as his second self but also as a stranger. There never is any question about giving Leggatt up, although the captain is violating maritime law by harboring a fugitive. By doing so, he is following his own moral compass, temporarily suspending maritime law. He also feels contempt for Archbold, which is mirrored by Leggatt's description of him. That and Leggatt's distaste for the laws of the shore also resonate with the captain's desire to let him escape.

The captain's sense of isolation on the ship is resolved once Leggatt leaves. Leggatt is both a support and a barrier. The captain has also resolved his conflict between duty and desire. Once that happens, Leggatt is no longer needed. The intimacy he feels with Leggatt is transferred to an intimacy he feels with the ship and crew and himself as he becomes more in touch with his feelings. He must let Leggatt go because both their positions are untenable and unsustainable in the world outside the cabin. While Leggatt feels a sympathy with the captain, he does not conceive of himself as a double, nor does he seem to see the captain's perception of him. His need is for freedom and physical survival. The captain's integration comes from suppression of Leggatt as other. He can finally act, and once he does act, he can recognize Leggatt as a separate entity in the real world, a world in which both their futures may be uncertain. His narrative frames his relationship with Leggatt as a thing of the past, signaling his ability to place Leggatt in a specific role at a specific time in his life, which has passed. Leggatt may have helped him, but the captain no longer needs him. So is the captain abandoning Leggatt, in effect abandoning part of himself? Or is he repressing the subconscious part of himself that places him in conflict? Leggatt helped the captain to resurrect those parts of him he needed to maintain command and act. He therefore becomes an intrinsic part of the captain's interior, subconscious life, but by letting Leggatt swim away, the captain no longer has to tolerate a duality that is inhibiting his ability to command.

At the end of the narrative Conrad suggests that each man has saved the other and is in command of his own destiny: "Walking to the taffrail . . . I was in time to catch an evanescent glimpse of my white hat left behind to mark the sport where the secret sharer of my cabin and of my thoughts as though he were my second self had lowered himself into the water to take the punishment of a free man, a proud swimmer striking out for a new destiny."[35] The captain's letting Leggatt go enables him to bond with his ship. He is no longer absent. This is an act of survival for both. Steiner describes the act like this: "Having demonstrated confidence and self control he hardly gives a thought to his 'other self,' and regards him now, not as a spiritual double, but as 'mere flesh.' . . . The hat not only suggests a transference and ultimate reintegration personality, but also, as it were, a transference of destiny. . . . By consciously facing danger and challenging his vulnerability, the captain overcomes his crippling sense of duality and demonstrates his ability to command."[36] She continues: "Metaphorically, the lowering of Leggatt into the water and 'passing out of sight into uncharted regions' suggest the reemergence of the captain's subconscious and the reintegration of his personality. Thus during his night journey, the narrator has moved, with the assistance of his double, from immature and naïve integration through a period of severe disorientation and disintegration to a more mature reintegration resulting from self-knowledge and self mastery."[37] The captain, finally, is no longer a stranger on his ship, and he makes this bonding clear: "And I was alone, with her. Nothing! No one in the world now should stand between us, throwing a shadow on the way of silent knowledge and mute affection, the perfect communion of a seaman and his first command."[38]

The captain can finally verbalize the relationship objectively and let go of Leggatt. He is not only whole by having developed a more mature confident self (thus completing the end of the journey he referred to at the beginning of the narrative), but also now he is truly a captain and part of the larger maritime community. The narrative comes full circle. He has sensed the import of his first journey; he has experienced the various conflicts resulting from having to choose in almost all cases between duty and desire, between wanting to assert himself and yet fit into the world of the career he has chosen, and he has emerged transformed confident and in command. The narrative is a record of his journey to self-knowledge, a painful one. He, too, is striking out for a new destiny, unencumbered and free.

Sensationalized Stories of Russian Revolutionary Terrorism in Under Western Eyes

JENNIFER MALIA

On 28 July 1904, the Party of Socialist-Revolutionaries assassinated Russian Interior Minister Vyacheslav von Plehve by throwing a bomb at his carriage. Reporting three days after the incident, the *Journal de Geneve* summed up the reaction to the assassination in various newspapers in England and Germany, which condemned the killing on moral grounds while suggesting that the Russian government was responsible or that Plehve deserved his fate. The *Journal de Geneve* also included telegraphed details of the assassination that came from an unspecified source:

> The explosion was tremendous, and the scene of carnage was indescribable. The coachman, missing his arms, lay dying on the ground. The body of the minister, projected into the air, fell among the debris of the car, his face battered, the right side of his figure mutilated, his right shoulder torn.
>
> Disemboweled horses were struggling in a pool of blood; wounded women were uttering terrible screams. . . .
>
> In all the houses, windows were shattering; shouts were resounding from all sides.[1]

This grotesque account was just one of many examples of how the Western media sensationalized the Plehve assassination at the time. The assassination in *Under Western Eyes* is loosely based on this assassination, as some critics have noted.[2] Conrad makes a direct allusion to it when he refers to the victim as "Mr de P——" in the novel. Andrzej Busza convincingly argues that the assassination scene in the novel seems to use the Plehve assassination as a model, but it is "simultaneously 'typical' (recalling the circumstances of other assassinations) and ahistorical."[3] Some of the details of the assassination in the novel are not consistent with the facts of the incident. One of the main differences is that the assassin was apprehended at the scene of the bombing in reality, but the assassin in Conrad's novel, Victor Haldin, is not caught until the informer, Razumov, gives him up. Other critics have suggested that Conrad based his novel on the 1881 assassination of Czar Alexander II, which supports Busza's claim that the assassination in the novel is typical of other assassinations that occurred at the time.[4] In his 1920 Author's Note, Conrad writes that *Under Western Eyes* is "a sort of historical novel dealing with the past" and that his characters are "not the product of the exceptional but of the general—of the normality of their place, and time, and race."[5] Conrad, then, suggests his interest in representing the general circumstances, rather than particular incidents, surrounding Russian revolutionary violence at the beginning of the twentieth century. The fictionalized assassination initiates the main plot of *Under Western Eyes,* as Victor Haldin's confession of the assassination to Razumov sets the story into motion and the subsequent press coverage of the incident contributes to the main conflict of the story.

The events that unfold as a result of the assassination in *Under Western Eyes* expose Conrad's distaste for sensationalized accounts of Russian revolutionary terrorism in the press. The way the narrator interprets the story for the reader reveals the problems Conrad finds with early twentieth-century journalism. In the novel, the Western press looks to Russia for shocking stories of revolutionary terrorism to fulfill its readership's desire for spectacles of violence. The narrator not only acknowledges accounts of Russian terrorism in the Western press but also provides journalistic accounts of Russian terrorism for the reader, such as the events surrounding the assassination of Plehve. As a consumer of sensationalized print media, the narrator lets his lust for sensation affect his narration. While the narrator provides the reader of the novel with his interpretation of Russian revolutionary terrorism, the newspapers provide the characters in the novel with reports of terrorism. The narrator's point of view as an Englishman and the accounts of the Western press within the novel provide the reader with multiple narrations that are told under Western eyes.

Critics have commented on Conrad's objections to early twentieth-century journalism. Matthew Rubery discusses Conrad's "frustrations with international reportage" and focuses on *Heart of Darkness,* in which the "most compromised character [is] a journalist."[6] Brian Artese also acknowledges Conrad's criticism of journalism, contending that "Conrad's famous break from prevailing narratological norms is inextricable . . . from his constantly reiterated loathing of the daily press."[7] He goes on to argue that, at the beginning of the twentieth century, journalism paraphrased and added commentary to testimonials in the press, and novels followed suit because "the promise of comprehension that had come to be demanded of the newspaper, the most popular and pervasive disseminator of narrative norms the modern world had known, would also henceforth be demanded of the novel."[8] But the novel influenced journalism as much as journalism influenced the novel. In fact, the novel used the techniques of sensationalism in the mid-1800s, before they were popular in journalism. In his novels, Conrad does not imitate the devices of journalism; rather, he exposes how early twentieth-century newspapers used the devices of fiction, especially the techniques of sensationalism.

The attempt of early twentieth-century print media to sensationalize violence for the reader is especially evident in Conrad's essay "Autocracy and War" (1905). Using the Russo-Japanese War as an example, Conrad highlights the effect that sensational reports of atrocities have on the readership and therefore provides a context for understanding his treatment of the press and the newspaper reader in *Under Western Eyes.*[9] Conrad suggests that the "printed page of the Press makes a sort of still uproar, taking from men both the power to reflect" on what they read "and the faculty of genuine feeling" so that they are left with "only the artificially created need of having something exciting to talk about."[10] Conrad exposes this artificial need for sensation in *Under Western Eyes* by revealing the reader's expectations for newspaper accounts of Russian revolutionary violence that are both pleasurable and fearful.

The Narrator's Point of View

Many critics have argued that the language teacher is an unreliable narrator in *Under Western Eyes.* The narrator draws on Razumov's diary for his story, but his narration is not a simple translation of the document. In *Under Western Eyes,* Conrad undercuts the language teacher in the beginning of the novel when he says the story is "based on a document; all I have brought to it is my knowledge of the Russian language."[11] Of course, "based on" leaves room for interpretation and implies that the story is not simply translated. The story that follows reveals the extent of Conrad's irony, as large sections of the novel are told from the point of view of the narrator, and Razumov is not even present in all of the scenes of the story. In addition, the description of the original document the language teacher draws on to tell the story does not leave the reader with the confidence that he or she will be reading an authentic account: "The document, of course, is something in the nature of a journal, a diary, yet not exactly that in its actual form."[12] The narrator goes on to say that "all the entries are dated" and that the beginning is "a retrospect, in a narrative form."[13] With a translation, you would expect the form to be maintained, whatever it might be. By organizing the story in parts and chapters, rather than dated entries, the language teacher does not provide the reader with the "marks of documentary evidence" that he claims to.[14] This uncertainty in describing the document leaves the form of the narration up to the narrator, and makes it easier for him to manipulate his translated version.

If the language teacher's translation were the novel itself, then he would not be a character in the novel. Therefore the reader cannot assume that the novel is simply the narrator's translation of the document. As Penn R. Szittya argues, *Under Western Eyes* is a double narration: "one is the novel as a whole, told by the language teacher, and the other is Razumov's diary, which is quoted at length with the primary narration as an authoritative document. . . . This narrative doubling gives to *Under Western Eyes* a schizoid character, in effect dividing the reader between two narrators, two stories, two points of view, two chronologies, two styles."[15] While I agree that the novel is a double narration of sorts, the lines are not drawn between these two different narrations. The language teacher draws on Razumov's diary, but it is not always "quoted," at least not in a way that the reader knows for certain which parts of the text are a translation of the diary. In fact, because of the way the double narration is handled, it is impossible to know how much of the novel is a translation of Razumov's diary, the narrator's interpretation and/or embellishment of the diary, and the narrator's own account that has nothing to do with Razumov. Allan Hepburn argues that "as a translator of documents and an assembler of information, the Professor enacts the role of the reader within the novel. As a surrogate, the Professor's errors dramatize our own potential misunderstandings."[16] But should we assume that the narrator's attempt to translate and assemble information results in errors, and in turn misunderstandings, that we as readers might have? Errors and misunderstandings assume that there is a right way to translate and assemble the information. The narrator's aim is not to simply translate and assemble information for the story because he includes his own interpretation of the events that occur. Conrad suggests that the reader should be skeptical of the narration serving as any sort of authentic account.

Conrad originally conceived the story with Razumov as the narrator before changing the point of view to the language teacher, which emphasizes the importance of the language teacher's role as a narrator. In his 1920 "Author Note," Conrad explains his reason for changing the narrator: "In my desire to produce the effect of actuality it seemed to me indispensable to have an eyewitness of the transactions in Geneva."[17] On the one hand, Conrad undercuts the narrator's claim of just translating the story. On the other hand, Conrad suggests that the language teacher's narration gives the "effect of actuality," which suggests that he wants the reader to vicariously experience the events in the novel as though he or she is actually witnessing them. In fact, the language teacher, who is not named, represents the reader of the novel. As a consumer of sensational accounts of Russian revolutionary terrorism, the narrator stands in for the early twentieth-century reading public.

The Assassination of Mr de P——

The language teacher and Razumov, whose story is filtered through the narrator, provide the two points of view in *Under Western Eyes,* but they are not eyewitnesses of all of the events that occur in the novel. The most important event that neither the narrator nor Razumov witnesses is the assassination in Saint Petersburg. Conrad leaves it up to the reader to question from where the sensational account of the assassination originated. Victor Haldin might have sensationalized the details of the assassination when telling Razumov about it. Razumov might have elaborated Victor Haldin's account with sensational details when he wrote his diary. We will assume that Nathalie Haldin did not change the diary when she passed it along from Razumov to the language teacher. The narrator may have embellished the story with his own sensational details when he translated the diary. Whether the narrator bases his description of Plehve's assassination on what he read in the newspapers or Razumov's diary is unclear. The description, though, seems to be based on the narrator's own sources since he prefaces his account by saying that "the origin of Mr. Razumov's record is connected with . . . the assassination of a prominent statesman," rather than indicating that the account that follows is based on Razumov's diary.[18] The account of the assassination, then, is told with at least three degrees of separation. This parallels our experience when reading newspapers because news stories are at least twice removed from the witness.

The assassination scene in the novel, then, is perhaps the best example of the narrator's opportunity to embellish the story. The narrator comments on the news coverage of Mr. de P——: "the newspapers made noise enough about that fanatical, narrow-chested figure" and "not a month passed without his portrait appearing in some one of the illustrated papers of Europe."[19] These comments applied to the actual news coverage of Plehve at the beginning of the twentieth century, as the 27 June 1903 article in *The Literary Digest* makes clear: "not for years has the personality of a Russian statesman been exploited in the European press to the extent now witnessed in the case of the Czar's Minister of the Interior."[20] Here is the narrator's sensationalized description of the assassination of Mr de P—— in the novel:

> In an instant there was a terrible shock, a detonation muffled in the multitude of snowflakes; both horses lay dead and mangled on the ground and the coachman, with a shrill cry, had fallen off the box mortally wounded. . . .
>
> A tall young man who had remained perfectly still within a carriage gateway, two houses lower down, stepped out in the street and walking up rapidly flung another bomb over the heads of the crowd. It actually

> struck the Minister-President on the shoulder as he stooped over his dying servant, then falling between his feet exploded with a terrific concentrated violence, striking him dead to the ground, finishing the wounded man and practically annihilating the empty sledge in the twinkling of an eye. With a yell of horror the crowd broke up and fled in all directions, except for those who fell dead or dying where they stood nearest to the Minister-President, and one or two others who did not fall till they had run a little way.
>
> The first explosion had brought together a crowd as if by enchantment, the second made as swiftly a solitude in the street for hundreds of yards in each direction. Through the falling snow people looked from afar at the small heap of dead bodies lying upon each other near the carcasses of the two horses.[21]

The assassination scene focuses on the actions of the crowd. The first bomb draws the crowd closer to the scene, suggesting that the "mangled" horses and the "mortally wounded" coachman provide a spectacle that piques the morbid curiosity of the crowd. The second bomb, though, has the opposite effect. While the narrator describes the bomb exploding in the "twinkling of an eye," he slows down the moment for the reader by describing in minute detail where the bomb hit (first the minister's shoulder, then between his feet) and the effects of the bombing on the minister ("striking him dead"), the servant ("finishing the wounded man"), and the carriage ("annihilating the empty sledge"). The language teacher also describes the chaos of the crowd with its "yell of horror" and people who "fled in all directions," unless they dropped dead. Moreover, the narrator uses the grotesque mode to describe the victims of the bombing who made up a "small heap of dead bodies." With this fictional account of the assassination, Conrad reveals the narrator's, and in turn the reading public's, desire for sensational accounts of Russian revolutionary violence.

Newspaper Accounts of the Assassination of Plehve in 1904

The description of the bombing in the novel is just as sensational as in the newspapers that reported the Plehve assassination in 1904. Here are some details describing the incident that appeared on 29 July 1904 in *The Standard,* the newspaper that Razumov reads to learn about the assassination of Mr. de P—— in the novel: "the explosion which followed, with a flash of blinding flame, was terrible," "the carriage was smashed to pieces," and "the Minister lay dreadfully mutilated and apparently lifeless amidst the *débris*."[22] This article included accounts of the incident told from the perspective of witnesses and multiple correspondents reporting from all over the world. These accounts were highly repetitious, recounting the events of the assassination with virtually the same information but using different shocking phrases to sensationalize the bombing. In its report of the incident, *The Guardian* described how the bomb "immediately exploded" and "the effects were terrible."[23] While the scene from the assassination in the novel describes the explosion as striking the Minister "dead to the ground," *The Guardian* provided an even more appalling description of his physical injuries: "the unhappy Minister was blown to pieces."[24] Immediately following its account of the bombing, *The Guardian* included another report of the incident written by the special correspondent from *The Standard* quoted above. Like *The Standard, The Guardian* repeated the same information concerning the incident in multiple accounts but used different sensational phrases to describe the scene. The early twentieth-century reader, then, vicariously experienced the assassination not once but multiple times when reading these newspapers. By shocking the reader with several versions of the bombing, these newspapers also created the illusion that there were multiple assassinations, which perpetuated anxiety about terrorist violence and inevitably resulted in more newspaper sales.

On 29 July 1904 *The Times* of London printed a column including time-stamped news of the incident, presumably based on telegrams sent from Saint Petersburg. This article claimed "the carriage and the horses were shattered to atoms," "the body of the Minister was terribly mutilated, the left arm and both legs being torn from it," and "the violence of the explosion was so great that splinters of the carriage were driven into M. de Plehve's body and his head was nearly severed."[25] Once again the newspaper piqued the morbid curiosity of readers by bombarding them with grotesque descriptions of terrorist violence. Two days after the Plehve assassination, *The Times* corrected some of the details of the bombing, blaming the "contradictory telegrams which hourly succeeded each other from Saint Petersburg" for its inaccurate report the previous day.[26] On 30 July 1904 *The Times* reported news that allegedly came from *The Official Messenger,* an organ of the Russian government. Unlike the 29 July article in *The Times,* which claimed that eighteen were injured in the bombing or the assassination scene in the novel which described a "heap of dead bodies," the 30 July article reported the facts of the incident without shocking details: the minister and coachman were victims, a captain traveling behind the minister was "severely injured," nine passersby were "slightly injured," and the assassin sustained "a few wounds" that were "not dangerous."[27] This matter-of-fact description of the assassination was quite different from other news reports of the incident at the time.[28]

Fictional Newspaper Articles on Russian Revolutionary Violence

Under Western Eyes alludes to a newspaper article covering the assassination of Mr. de P—— to reveal the public's waning interest in the subject. According to the narrator, a brief newspaper article revealing the name of the assassin,

Victor Haldin, and the details of the midnight arrest appear in the correspondence columns rather than the telegrams, which indicates that "the sensation from a journalistic point of view" is "well in the past."[29] This article reporting accurate news, then, is presumably less newsworthy than the shocking details reported earlier in the telegrams. Despite the lack of importance assigned to this story, the narrator assumes that the article is interesting enough to attract the attention of international presses, as it is likely to be "reproduced on the morrow by French and Swiss newspapers."[30] Conrad suggests that the public's appetite for sensational news is so great that this story revealing the assassin's name and the details of the midnight arrest will disappoint the public because it does not have the shocking details that readers have come to expect in reports of terrorist violence.

Despite the apparent lack of public interest in the story, Conrad will not let the reader of the novel forget it, as the allusion to the fictional article reappears throughout *Under Western Eyes.* Even the idiom "ferreted out" appears three times in the novel to emphasize the journalist's persistence in uncovering more details about the assassination of Mr de P——. When the narrator first learns about the fictional article, he tells us that "Mr. de P——'s death was no longer an actuality, but the enterprising correspondent was proud of having ferreted out some unofficial information about that fact of modern history."[31] Later Conrad reminds us of the effect of the article on Nathalie Haldin: "The action, the hopes came to an end with the details ferreted out by the English journalist."[32] Conrad alludes to the fictional news article once again when the narrator has a conversation with Razumov and ponders, "I don't think he was aware that the story of the midnight arrest had been ferreted out by an English journalist and given to the world."[33] Conrad makes his repetitive allusions to this fictional article obvious to emphasize how the Western reader has become jaded by accounts of Russian revolutionary violence. This repetition draws attention to the experience of the early twentieth-century newspaper reader. Despite the multiple allusions to the article throughout the novel, the reader is not privy to the account itself. By omitting this newspaper account, Conrad reveals that he is more concerned with the outcome and results of assassinations than with the rhetoric used to describe them.

With references to this fictional news article, Conrad also reveals the effect it has on the assassin's family. Conrad uses dramatic irony to emphasize the misfortune of learning about a personal tragedy in a public newspaper. The reader knows the name of the assassin, Victor Haldin, from the beginning of the novel, but the narrator, Mrs. Haldin, and Nathalie Haldin do not know this until much later. The reader has to anxiously await the revelation of the news, as it is slowly passed on. In *Under Western Eyes,* this story about the Plehve assassination in

Russia is picked up by *The Standard,* a newspaper that the English narrator has delivered to Geneva, and then he conveys the news he reads to the Russian women in the Haldin family. The news then goes full circle, traveling from East to West and back East. The irony is that the news that does not cause a sensation for the general public is shocking for Haldin's mother, Nathalie Haldin, and even the narrator. As Rubery suggests, the novel "brings the news even closer to personal experience through the sensation of reading not about strangers but about one's own circle."[34] Readers with a personal interest in the story are of course not the intended audience. Mrs. Haldin, though, considers contacting the reporter who wrote the story to learn more about her son: "If one knew what sort of man he was one could perhaps write to him."[35] She does not write to the journalist, leaving the reader to wonder how he would have reacted had she done so. Perhaps the "enterprising correspondent" would have taken advantage of her personal tragedy by interviewing her in hopes of obtaining more sensational material for the paper. As even she acknowledges, "The English Press is wonderful. Nothing can be kept secret from it, and all the world must hear."[36]

In the novel, Razumov changes what he says about news reports concerning Russian revolutionary activities, depending on whether he expresses his own views or the views of a revolutionary. With this contrast, Conrad emphasizes that both the Western reader and the Russian revolutionary look to the newspaper to be entertained by sensational accounts of Russian revolutionary activities. Razumov has a long conversation with the narrator about the news story on Victor Haldin in which he condemns the West for finding amusement in such stories: "What's going on with us is of no importance—a mere sensational story to amuse the readers of the papers—the superior contemptuous Europe. It is hateful to think of. But let them wait a bit!"[37] Even the narrator acknowledges that this is a "sort of threat addressed to the Western world."[38] Razumov's reaction to news reports about Russian revolutionary activities is quite different when he has a conversation with a revolutionary, Sophia Antonovna. When she wants to drink tea because she is tired, Razumov responds facetiously, "As to you being tired I can hardly believe it. We are not supposed to be. We mustn't. We can't. The other day I read in some paper or other an alarmist article on the tireless activity of the revolutionary parties. It impresses the world. It's our prestige."[39]

Posing as a revolutionary himself, Razumov suggests that he is amused by sensational accounts of revolutionary activities in the newspaper. He pokes fun at not only Sophia Antonova but also other Russian revolutionaries who seek worldwide recognition and prestige. Just as the Western reader looks to accounts of Russian revolutionary violence as a good read, revolutionaries look to these accounts to satisfy their need for self-importance.

Russian Revolutionary Émigrés in Geneva

In *Under Western Eyes,* Conrad depicts Russian revolutionary emigrants living in Geneva, Switzerland. In the early twentieth century, many Russian revolutionaries, such as Peter Kropotkin, Boris Savinkov, Sergei "Stepniak" Kravchinsky, George Plekhanov, Vera Zasulich, and Vladimir Lenin emigrated to Switzerland and other European countries.[40] In the novel, Peter Ivanovitch, the Russian revolutionary émigré and proclaimed feminist, is a satiric figure whose writings expose his need for self-importance. The narrator indicates the popularity of Peter Ivanovitch's memoirs: "at one time all Europe was aware of the story of his life written by himself and translated into seven or more languages."[41] He goes on to describe that "the sensational clink of these fetters is heard all through the chapters describing his escape—a subject of wonder to two continents."[42] The narrator describes Peter Ivanovitch's memoirs: "His naked tawny figure glimpsed vaguely through the bushes with a cloud of mosquitoes and flies hovering about the shaggy head, spread tales of terror through whole districts."[43] There are three degrees of separation from the writer of his memoirs and the reader of the novel. The story is presumably passed on from Peter Ivanovitch's memoirs to Razumov's diary to the narrator to the reader of the novel. Once again it is difficult to know the extent to which the narrator is responsible for the sensational details of the story. In *Under Western Eyes,* the narrator also describes how Peter Ivanovitch became known as a "heroic fugitive" when "this name was bestowed upon him in a review of the English edition of his book."[44]

The narrator does not seem impressed with Peter Ivanovitch's exploits, but he also expresses his reluctance to judge him: "it is not becoming for an obscure teacher of languages to criticize a 'heroic fugitive' of worldwide celebrity."[45] The reader should question why an escaped fugitive becomes so famous in the first place. Peter Ivanovitch seems to be a worldwide celebrity in this novel, not because of his participation in revolutionary activities but because of his sensational memoirs and the "tales of terror" that others spread about him. Conrad suggests that the terrorist is a publicity hunter and his revolutionary cause does not matter as much as his reputation.

In *Under Western Eyes,* the depiction of Madame de S——, another Russian revolutionary émigré, and her involvement in revolutionary violence goes beyond sensationalism by invoking the supernatural. Once again it is unclear whether Razumov's diary or the narrator's translation makes the implication. The description of her "mystic revolutionary salon" and her appearance is in the fantastic rather than the realist mode.[46] Madame de S—— is depicted as not one but many different supernatural beings: a "witch," a "grinning skull," a "galvanized corpse out of some Hoffman's Tale," and an "ancient, painted mummy."[47] The focus on Madame de S——'s physical appearance suggests that she is feared, not because of her connection to the assassination of Czar Alexander II, but rather due to her uncanny appearance. The narrator also draws attention to the supernatural elements of her writing: "Some of my readers may remember a little book from her pen, published in Paris, a mystically bad-tempered, declamatory, and frightfully disconnected piece of writing, in which she all but admits foreknowledge, more than hints at its supernatural origin, and plainly suggests in venomous innuendoes that the guilt of the act was not with the terrorists, but with a palace intrigue."[48]

Madame de S——'s suggestion that Alexander II's assassination has supernatural origins reveals her desire, and in turn the public's desire, for conspiracies. She creates an eerie narrative for the readers of her book, and in turn the readers of Conrad's novel, by implying that the assassination has supernatural causes. In *Under Western Eyes,* Westerners are apparently so interested in what Madame de S—— has to say that an Anglo-American journalist interviews her. Even though the reader of the novel is not privy to the interview, he or she can imagine that Madame de S—— provides the journalist with a fantastic, or at least a sensational, story, if the narrator's description of her own writing is any indication of her ability to tell a story that piques the curiosity of readers. Conrad reveals that ghostly narratives of Russian revolutionary violence arouse the public's desire for more and more shocking accounts.

In *Under Western Eyes,* the press's connection to stories of Russian revolutionary violence is taken to another level with Julius Laspara, who is both a Russian revolutionary émigré and a journalist. The narrator's description of him reads like a sensational novel: "The obscure celebrity of the tiny man was well known to Razumov. Polyglot, of unknown parentage, of indefinite nationality, anarchist, with a pedantic and ferocious temperament, and an amazingly inflammatory capacity for invective, he was a power in the background, this violent pamphleteer clamouring for revolutionary justice, this Julius Laspara, editor of the *Living Word,* confidant of conspirators, inditer of sanguinary menaces and manifestos, suspected of being in the secret of every plot."[49]

Here Conrad draws attention to the double meaning of plot to emphasize Laspara's roles as both a writer and an anarchist: he plots not only articles, pamphlets, and manifestos but also revolutionary activities. As an "obscure celebrity," Laspara is presumably not as well-known as Peter Ivanovitch or even Madame de S——. However, the narrator, or perhaps Razumov, exaggerates the exploits of this "celebrated subversive journalist," who cannot possibly be "in the secret of every plot," showing the extent to which he will go to shock the reader with sensational details.[50]

The distinction between the terrorist and the spy becomes so blurred that their political agendas become indistinguishable. Here is the narrator's, or perhaps Razumov's, sensational account of Nikita's exploits as a violent revolutionary:

> Razumov had heard of him. He had heard so much since crossing the frontier of these celebrities of the militant revolution; the legends, the stories, the authentic chronicle, which now and then peeps out before a half-incredulous world. Razumov had heard of him. He was supposed to have killed more gendarmes and police agents than any revolutionist living. He had been entrusted with executions.
>
> The paper with the letters N.N., the very pseudonym of murder, found pinned on the stabbed breast of a certain notorious spy (this picturesque detail of a sensational murder case had got into the newspapers), was the mark of his handiwork. "By order of the Committee.—N.N."[51]

With the parenthetical comment mentioning that the murder case was reported in the newspapers, Conrad reminds the reader that the press is a source for sensational material on Russian revolutionary violence. The reader first learns that Nikita is a terrorist who "killed more gendarmes and police agents than any revolutionist living" and who later maims Razumov when Razumov confesses to being a spy. Toward the end of the novel, the reader discovers that Nikita is in fact a double agent, revealing the irony of his brutality toward Razumov. By misleading the reader about Nikita's identity, Conrad emphasizes the unclear distinction between the terrorist and the double agent.

Nikita represents the double agent whose sensational exploits were all too familiar for the turn-of-the-twentieth-century reading public. In his 1920 "Author's Note," Conrad writes, "As to Nikita—nicknamed Necatorhe—he is the perfect flower of the terroristic wilderness. What troubled me most in dealing with him was not his monstrosity but his banality. He has been exhibited to the public eye for years in so-called 'disclosures' in newspaper articles, in secret histories, in sensational novels."[52]

As Busza notes, the early twentieth century was the "hey-day of the professional secret agent: of Yevno Azef, Peter Rachkovsky, Baron Arkady Harting, Cyprien Jagolkovsky, Alexander Evalenko."[53] With Nikita's character, Conrad probably had in mind Yevno Azef, the Socialist-Revolutionary Party leader who organized assassinations and was exposed as a spy for the Russian police in 1909. Fleishman convincingly argues that Conrad was aware of the Azef scandal when writing *Under Western Eyes*.[54] Conrad suggests the trivial nature of Russian revolutionary politics with Nikita, a double agent who is essentially a terrorist. Nikita stands in as the notorious double agent of the early twentieth century, just as the narrator of the novel stands in as the reader of the newspaper.

Toward the end of the novel, Conrad exposes the reader's waning interest in newspapers reporting Russian revolutionary conspiracies. According to the narrator:

> Later on, much later on, at the time of the newspaper rumours (they were vague and soon died out) of an abortive military conspiracy in Russia, I remembered the glimpse I had of that motionless group with its central figure. No details ever came out, but it was known that the revolutionary parties abroad had given their assistance, had sent emissaries in advance, that even money was found to dispatch a steamer with a cargo of arms and conspirators to invade the Baltic provinces. And while my eyes scanned the imperfect disclosures (in which the world was not much interested) I thought that the old, settled Europe had been given in my person attending that Russian girl something like a glimpse behind the scenes. A short, strange glimpse on the top floor of a great hotel of all places in the world: the great man himself; the motionless great bulk in the corner of the slayer of spies and gendarmes; Yakovlitch, the veteran of ancient terrorist campaigns; the womsn, with her hair as white as mine and the lively black eyes, all in a mysterious half-light, with the strongly lighted map of Russia on the table.[55]

The narrator reveals his own excitement to be not only a privileged spectator of these world-renown celebrities—Peter Ivanovitch as the "great man himself," Nikita as "the slayer of spies and gendarmes," and Yakovlitch as the "veteran of ancient terrorist campaigns"—but also a witness of revolutionaries plotting a military conspiracy. The allusion to a news story reporting this conspiracy "in which the world was not much interested" recalls the newspaper article that named Victor Haldin as the assassin earlier in the novel. Ironically, in *Under Western Eyes,* the public is indifferent toward accurate news, favoring sensational news instead. The rumors of a military conspiracy are apparently too ordinary for the reader in the novel because interest in this conspiracy with its "vague" rumors does not last very long. The press ultimately cannot meet the reader's expectations for shocking news. Conrad cautions the early twentieth-century reading public that looks to sensational accounts of terrorist violence in the paper as just a good read, expecting to be entertained.

In *Under Western Eyes,* the Western press trivializes Russian revolutionary politics and the Czarist Russian government by favoring sensationalized reporting. Even Councillor Mikulin's calculated secrecy is not enough to keep him safe from sensational accounts in the press. According to the narrator, "the larger world first heard of him in the very hour of his downfall, during one of those State trials which astonish and puzzle the average plain man who reads the newspapers, by a glimpse of unsuspected intrigues."[56] Mikulin's unsuspected intrigues recall another palace intrigue that the narrator mentions earlier in the novel, the events surrounding the assassination of Czar Alexander II that Madame de S—— talks about in her book. As a Western consumer of newspaper accounts, the English narrator describes intrigues to pique the morbid curiosity of the reader throughout the novel. In his accounts of revolutionaries and Russian government officials, the narrator reveals the influence of journalistic sensationalism on his narration, which once again serves to caution the reading public not to allow its lust for shocking news to go too far. The celebrity status of the Russian revolutionary emigrants in the novel suggests that the Western press is more interested in plotting sensational stories than informing the public about Russian revolutionary politics. In turn, the public is more interested in reading these stories than understanding international politics because of, in Conrad's own words, "the artificially created need of having something exciting to talk about."

Chance and Betrayal in Under Western Eyes

ROBERT MCPARLAND

Under Western Eyes is launched by a tragic event and a chance encounter that brings to the novel's chief character, Kyrilo Razumov, a new awareness of the complexity of the world. An assassin appears in Razumov's rooms, seeking refuge. An act of terrorism has disrupted the world. In its fierce, blunt horror, it jars even the most complacent life. Haldin has come into Razumov's residence, as if from out of nowhere. He intrudes into Razumov's life, bursting in like sudden chance. "Haldin means disruption," Razumov reflects.[1] "Fatality enters your rooms while your landlady's back is turned; you come home and find it in possession bearing a man's name, clothed in flesh—wearing a brown cloth coat and long boots—lunging against the stove."[2] For Razumov, security and the common world vanish. He is burdened. He has lost his life's direction.

Razumov is representative of humanity. He is an individual subject to fate, who can never live separate from the social context in which he lives. His identity—the very stability of his life—is impinged upon by the politics, the psychological pains and repressions, and the wild, revolutionary atmosphere of his environment. The assassin, fleeing from the scene of his desperate act to Razumov's rooms, draws Razumov into revolutionary conflict. Haldin's seemingly random appearance in Razumov's life changes him and underscores how no man or woman is ever isolated. Conrad reminds us that events may draw us into something we were not originally involved with. The environment that surrounds this character draws him inevitably into its conflicts. One hears in Razumov's narration the aching search for meaning: "What is this Haldin? And what am I? Only two grains of sand. But a great mountain is made up of just such insignificant grains. And the death of a man is an insignificant thing. Yet we combat a contagious pestilence."[3]

Razumov meditates within the epistemological crisis that has arisen from the implications of Darwinian evolution. He recognizes that his life is insignificant, a mere grain of sand. Gillian Beer has observed that revisions of existing knowledge like those set in motion by Darwin "are particularly vexatious when they shift man from the centre of meaning or set him in a universe not designed to suit his needs."[4] Conrad presents the observation that that our lives are affected by chance and that our time on earth is apparently insignificant within the scope of an evolutionary process that is indifferent to us. In our search for security, we fight against death and the winds of an inexorable fate shake these grains of sand that are the patterns of our lives. In a moment, chance sweeps away our certainties and the newly disrupted world eludes our efforts at rational control. He implies the fickle twists of fate in his text: After Haldin, running from justice, winds up in his rooms, Razumov is trying to control his life and how he will be perceived. In attempting to regain some control, he betrays Haldin. However, this betrayal weighs upon him. At first he thinks that he has done the proper thing. Haldin has assassinated someone; he has killed people and he is a threat to Russia. However, Razumov experiences a sense of guilt. He can no longer concentrate on his studies, so he gives them up. He turns to revenge, targeting all of those he thinks have disrupted his life. He asserts, "perdition is my lot."[5]

Razumov struggles with a sense that he has betrayed Haldin to the authorities: "Betray. A great word. What is betrayal? They talk of a man betraying his country, his friends, his sweetheart. There must be a moral bond first. All a man can betray is his conscience. And how is my conscience engaged here; by what bond of common faith, of common conviction, am I obliged to let that fanatical idiot drag me down with him?"[6] Razumov concludes, "In giving Victor Haldin up, it was myself, after all, whom I have betrayed most basely."[7] The reader is left to wonder if Razumov achieves a moral resolution. In what sense does he choose humanity in the end, rather than ideas and ideology?

It is only by such a choice, by moral resolve and the recognition of love, that Razumov is transformed from being merely a creature bound by the elements of nature into a person who expresses human dignity and value beyond politics. Conrad inherits the Darwinian vision, as George Levine has observed.[8] He struggles with Darwinian thought, as well as with the political landscape of his own time. Chance and necessity are central to Darwinian debates, and chance moves through this novel. If Ziemianitch had not been drunk, perhaps he would have taken Haldin away. How is it that Razumov and Haldin's sister, Natalia, happen to be in the same part of the same city and meet each other? Why is Nikita present when Razumov offers his confession of what he has done to Haldin? Why was that streetcar there at the moment that Razumov stepped out? Conrad's uses of these "coincidences" are unlike those of Victorian novelists like

Dickens, who imply a providential universe. Rather, Conrad suggests a world of randomness and he raises questions: Can people control their lives? What happens when events come along that affect them? How do political, economic, or social circumstances affect their lives? Conrad may be suggesting that people do not have control of many events. In examining the choices of this one man, Razumov, he is implying that our own choices in life are contingent. Throughout Conrad's stories, we see this theme arise again and again. In "The Secret Sharer," a story he wrote while writing this novel, the captain discovers a stranger on board who will have a great impact upon his life. In *Lord Jim,* the chance occurrence of the *Patna* hitting something that is adrift forces Jim to make a choice that has serious consequences. In *Under Western Eyes,* the sudden arrival of Haldin changes the course of Razumov's life.

Chance and change lurk within *Under Western Eyes,* a novel that is constructed as a frame narrative. A British teacher of foreign languages, who is never named, recalls the life experience of Kirylo Sidorovitch Razumov. The story starts with Razumov, who is a student at St. Petersburg University, writing an essay that he hopes will win a medal that will set him on the path toward success. Razumov has no family. He is the illegitimate son of Prince K——. He also has no connection with politics, but this soon changes. When he returns home one evening, he finds Victor Haldin, a fellow student, waiting for him. Haldin has just assassinated a political figure and has run away. He thinks that Razumov will be sympathetic toward him. Instead, Razumov finds what Haldin has done deeply disturbing. Razumov realizes that, if Haldin were caught, he might be considered a coconspirator. He agrees to help him to escape — mostly to get rid of him. Razumov makes an arrangement with a sleigh driver, Ziemianitch, to hurry him away. However, Razumov finds the driver in a drunken state, falling asleep. Bothered and annoyed, he decides that he is going to give Haldin up.

This experience pulls Razumov into the political world. He feels guilty about telling on Haldin and betraying his confidence. He will now work as a double agent, who will infiltrate a revolutionary cell in Geneva. He holds the view that he is now guarding Russia against revolutionary activities. He wants to get back at Haldin and the revolutionaries that Haldin has associated with. He is able to win the confidence of the revolutionaries. Then, in another life-changing encounter, he meets Victor's sister, Natalia Haldin, whom he finds honest and sincere. This moves him to confess what he has done to Victor. Learning of this, Nikita, a revolutionary, responds, destroying Razumov's eardrums. Because Razumov is unable to hear, he cannot detect a streetcar's approach and it runs him over. Injured seriously, he goes back to Russia and lives in the countryside for the rest of his days.

We are left to ponder one of the central questions that Conrad raises: how much of Razumov's life is a response to the random occurrences of chance?

These questions enter into areas of philosophical probing that extend beyond the inquiry of Darwinian issues. Conrad, with his innovations in narrative time, moves away from the patterns of the Victorian novel. As Gillian Beer points out, "Evolutionary ideas proved crucial to the novel during the [nineteenth] century, not only at the level of theme but at the level of organization."[9] Conrad, the modern, unfolds a different organizational design, one in which he tests the assumption that human language always corresponds with reason. He suggests that language's grasp of experience is limited. In exploring chance, he pursues a study of human relations. This is a story of Razumov and the people he interacts with. *Under Western Eyes* is a study of Razumov's interaction with Haldin's sister and the human sympathy that is summoned up inside him. Natalia is devoted and cares little for politics. She cares deeply about her brother and how her mother is despairing over him. One can explore the contrast between this familial devotion and the harsh political world that appears in the novel. Natalia represents humanity, emotion, and devotion in contrast with political and social ideas. Patriotism is bound up with revenge in Razumov. Yet, Natalia changes Razumov. His experience of Natalia's loving nature affects him and his orientation toward life. With the character Razumov, Conrad explores ideas like self-imposed isolation. Solitariness is not independence, and indeed no isolation is fully possible in this society. The individual must attempt to find some relationship with people and with values. Razumov, in his search, moves from principles based upon revenge or patriotism to ones based in love.

Clearly, Conrad's reflections upon Darwinism are only one of the many elements that dwell within *Under Western Eyes.* The novel is decidedly rich in political suggestion, and the existential situations of his characters find parallels in literary precursors. For example, Fyodor Dostoevsky's *Crime and Punishment* is a model for this novel. Razumov resembles Dostoevsky's Raskolnikov. He is a loner haunted by guilt and a troubled conscience who is affected by the love that he finds in a young woman. How is Razumov to define himself? Does he fit in anywhere? Can Razumov identify with anyone else? Like Raskolnikov, Razumov reflects upon his secret. He feels a need to talk about what he has done. In meeting Haldin, the assassin, it is almost as if he has met Raskolnikov, who, in Dostoevsky's novel, is a murderer. Will he shelter him, or give him up? Both characters tend to consider themselves superior to others and seek a calling. Both are existentially bereft of contact with others and are subject to tensions in their environments. In this, each of them tries to live apart from mankind. Both experience hate and appear misguided but are ultimately humanized.

The humanizing of Razumov occurs in a relationship. Conrad observes that socially and politically one cannot stand apart from the web of human interrelations. Man is indeed a political animal, as Aristotle once said, because men and women live in society. It is clear that Haldin's isolation is similar to that of

Razumov. Both are victims of cultural circumstances. In his double, Razumov senses Haldin's sincerity and the way Haldin gave himself for a cause. He acts in the shadow of Haldin, reflecting his idealism. In his betrayal of Haldin he annihilates himself. Tekla is also an isolated character. She is an outsider who gains identity by assisting others in their schemes. She recognizes this anonymity. "No one talks to me, no one writes to me," she says. "I have no use for a name." It is Tekla who would help Razumov after his confession results in a beating and his crippling.

One might also consider the divided character of Ziemianitch, the carriage driver. "Saint or devil, night or day is all one to Ziemianitch when his heart is free from sorrow."[10] We read that "Ziemianitch's passionate surrender to sorrow and consolation had baffled Razumov."[11] This character is not a romantic idealist or a revolutionary engaged in a political struggle. Instead, he is beset by love and the loss of it. In this, he might be contrasted with Haldin and the revolutionaries who are passionate about their political agenda. Meanwhile, Haldin grows as a figure of stature in the book. He does not fade away.

Conrad identifies with antirevolutionary attitudes, yet his conservative politics seem to be at odds with his innovative methods and technique. That is, his writing techniques are themselves revolutionary, disruptive of realist conventions. His story is discontinuous. Its language questions language, or distrusts it. The world has become a place of chance, a network of chance happenings. The way that things are often cannot be put into words. Little in this world is solid and sure, including how one may talk about the world in language. Peter Ivanovitch's chain, Mikulin's hat, and other objects are not signs of solidity, notes Levine.[12] They are tenuous, and daily life is not so certain a place as it once seemed. J. Hillis Miller writes: "Conrad shows such things wrested from their context in daily life and put before the spectator as mute, static presences."[13]

This story is told through several narrative devices. Along with the omniscient author, there is Razumov's diary, which tells a story, and there is the narrative of the language teacher. The diary sets up a time sequence. The confession scene is reported by Laspara, a revolutionary. The story of Razumov's confessions is told by Sophia Antonovna. The narrator gets his information from Razumov's diary. With these devices, Conrad practices a formalist rebellion against the conventions of realism. Conrad insists upon limited perspective, not omniscience. A Western rationalist understanding of experience is rejected by the Professor and by Natalia. Conrad recognizes the limitations of any single individual perspective.

The narrator of *Under Western Eyes* interprets experience to the reader. Indeed, the narrator offers attitudes that may represent those of Conrad. This novel is, at times, self-reflexive. Razumov says, "I am not a young man in a novel."[14] There is self-analysis in this text, in Razumov, and perhaps also in Conrad. Throughout the work, Conrad is highly conscious of the mechanics of novel writing. The novel as a construct, reflecting upon itself as a matter of words and language, is suggested by the presence of the old language teacher. "Words, as is well known, are the great foes of reality," says the Professor on the first page.[15] Razumov has decided to enter an essay contest; then Haldin enters his life. Does writing words, stating concepts, and applying reason in writing contrast with the strange, irrational event that happens: the breaking in of an assassin into Razumov's rooms? Razumov will try to find some logic in a world that seems now illogical.

Language is limited, and communication is challenged by these limitations. Communication, however, is central to human relationships. One may better communicate with words and with love than with bombs and ideology. In his relationship with Natalia, Razumov learns that revenge, patriotism, and other ideological notions do not mean as much as human connection and love. He learns the importance of humanity in his relationship. Natalia goes to meet Razumov, who—she has heard—has come to Geneva. Razumov begins with "I believed that I had in my breast nothing but an inexhaustible fund of anger and hate for you both. . . . And do you know what I said to myself? I shall steal his sister's soul from her."[16] To the contrary, Razumov's heart and soul are challenged by Natalia's presence. Natalia's genuine quality affects him. "I felt that I must tell you that I had ended by loving you," he says.[17] He claims that she was a light that saved him from ignominy, "from ultimate undoing."[18]

Despite this "light" of love, the impersonal indifference of the Darwinian world echoes in Conrad's text. Conrad challenges the idea that nature is compatible with human aspiration. Razumov affirms evolution over revolution. Natalia Haldin has also dreamt of an ideal society. She says, "Everything is inconceivable to the strict logic of ideas. And yet the world exists to our sense, and we exist in it."[19] However, this is hardly an ideal society that she and Razumov live in. The vast Russian wilderness is a fundamental reality. In its brute force, it has a rough solitude beyond human comprehension. How is human reason to work within this irrational context? It functions rather in an artificially constructed setting. Such a civilization is arbitrary. This reality is disrupted by chance. The narrative breaks.

This story is about finding humanity within conditions that include loneliness, darkness, and destruction. Daily life serves as a preoccupation, shielding some of the characters from the darkness that surrounds them. "The trivialities of daily existence were an armour for the soul," writes Razumov.[20] Irrationality and violence threaten this artificial order. Human interaction is affected by the environment. Tekla says, "I have been starving for, I won't say kindness, but just for a little civility, for I don't know how long."[21] Tekla is a revolutionary who has been mistreated by the other revolutionaries. He seeks a revolution that will bring about humane circumstances that will create a good life for people. This contrasts with Peter Ivanovitch, for whom revolution is a matter of utter seriousness. Conrad appears to ask how life, in these social conditions, can be humanized.

Thus, *Under Western Eyes* is filled with political issues. Conrad looks at the Russian government: at autocracy and revolution. This repressive government's efforts to preserve its power create an atmosphere of suspicion. While Conrad sharply critiques this government, he does not favor the revolutionaries. In rejecting the revolutionaries' position, he shows that they are wrong and ineffective. For example, the character of Peter Ivanovitch excels as a theoretical strategist. However, he treats Tekla poorly, even as he talks about improving humanity. Madame de S—— likewise appears strange. Haldin is described as a wild idealist, as is Kostia. Nikita is a brutal double-agent who likes to kill. These revolutionaries are engaged in an attack in which innocent people also die. Conrad here faces an issue that would have much importance in the twentieth century. The struggles between Poland and Russia occasioned this book. However, this story also reflects the history of the Russian revolution, the Mexican revolution, or other revolutionary situations and how the turmoil of these revolutions affected people. Following this line of questioning, one might trace through this novel to show that, when the autocratic and repressive government and the revolutionaries get into altercations, innocent people get hurt. In this novel, both the government and the revolutionaries are cast in a negative light. People are dehumanized and discarded, whether they are friends or enemies. Humanity is devoured by revolution.

Critical of revolution, Conrad portrays how people with misplaced ideals become fools; they become ridiculous. The novel suggests that such people need to be humanized. Razumov has played out a game with all seriousness. He has been like a marionette on strings. Mikulin, who represents Russian power, has a wisdom that is shortsighted. Haldin is a wild-eyed zealot full of energy. The cab driver is too drunk to drive. Peter Ivanovitch, the revolutionary guide, is an ideologue who cannot guide anyone, except into misery. The revolutionaries are not very efficient. Razumov's deception and his conflict about Haldin are played out amid their blindness. Engaging with the cause, Razumov assumes that he will become "a great reforming servant of the greatest of States . . . of the mightiest homogenous mass of mankind with a capability for logical guided development in a brotherly solidarity of force and aim such as the world has never dreamt of."[22] There is a warning here against overzealousness that may guide our response to terrorism in the world.

Conrad's novel is more than a dispassionate political reflection; it is also the product of a social and familial legacy. It embodies a Polish response to Russian autocracy that seems to have simmered within Conrad for years. "I carry in my head a great Polish novel on the corruption that has come to us from Moscow," wrote his father in 1869.[23] Conrad appears to have fulfilled this vision with *Under Western Eyes.* The novel, set in St. Petersburg and Geneva, is about the development of a political consciousness within a web of alienation. Like other Conrad novels, it is filled with the issues of the author's time. These include his attention to colonialism and the condition of European culture. Conrad is concerned with the decline of the individual and with the lack of an ethical code and moral laxity. He witnesses in this a recipe for social tragedy. Autocratic Russia reflects the modern bureaucratic state: an impersonal shadow under which humanity struggles for dignity and meaning.

Conrad had been thinking of the subject of this novel for a long time, Eloise Knapp Hay suggests, and he eventually "unburdened" himself of it.[24] Conrad never mentions Poland in this novel, yet many commentators say that the Polish nationalist experience lies behind it. They also say that Conrad was critical of "messianic" Polish nationalism. Jocelyn Baines claimed that Conrad repudiated Polish politics. Hay says that Conrad still sought "sparks of truth" in this legacy and sought reason, not just "a gesture of blind defiance."[25] In V. S. Pritchett's view, "the corruption that has come from Moscow [. . .] has a generalized quality" and may reflect Conrad's childhood.[26] He sees the evil in Conrad's novels, including that of *Lord Jim,* emerging from this childhood experience.

This evil repeatedly intersects with the theme of chance. Conrad began *Under Western Eyes* while he was working on the novel he called *Chance.* Zdzislaw Najder observes that the work on *Chance* was "very slow," and Conrad indicated in a letter to James Pinker that he was calling the new work that had emerged alongside that novel "Razumov." The new work, he said, was intended as "a contribution to a reading of the Russian character. . . . Here is given the very essence of things Russian. Not the mere outward manners and customs but the Russian feeling and thought." He adds, "The subject has long haunted me."[27]

Indeed, that haunting was personal, as Conrad perceived the shadow Russia cast upon Europe. Conrad writes of Russia: "Under the sumptuous immensity of the sky, the snow covered the endless forests, the frozen rivers, the plains of an immense country, obliterating the landmarks, the accidents of the ground, leveling everything under its uniform whiteness, like a monstrous blank page awaiting the record of an inconceivable history."[28] Najder describes *Under Western Eyes* as "a book about the real problems of the life and death of a huge empire, on whose fate also depended the fate of Poland."[29] Najder believes that Conrad, in writing *Under Western Eyes,* found himself face to face with a black wall of hopelessness raised by the real world."[30] Several of Conrad's concerns and themes during the time he wrote this novel are identified by Najder: responsibility, sense of duty, guilt, justice, freedom, honor, solidarity, anarchy, order.[31]

Conrad's perspective on Russia was deeply affected by the impact of Russia upon his parents. He did not like the revolutionaries he was writing about. However, he also saw that they might have the only means to change Russian autocracy. He dealt with these issues in his essay "Autocracy and War" (1905), asserting, "In whatever form of upheaval autocratic Russia is to find her end it can never be a revolution fruitful of moral consequences to mankind. It cannot be anything but a rising of slaves."[32] Jeffrey Meyers says Conrad derived his notion of the country from his father's "frightening conception of Russia" as "unrestrained, organized and ready to spew out millions of her criminals over Europe."[33] "[T]he Russians had enslaved his country, forbidden his language, confiscated his inheritance. Treated him as a convict, killed his parents and forced him into exile."[34] In his 1920 introduction, Conrad says that he seeks to illustrate "the psychology of Russia itself."[35] Conrad's "Author's Note" to the 1920 edition of *Under Western Eyes* is sharply critical of Russia. "The oppressors and the oppressed are all Russians together, and the world is brought once more face to face with the truth of the saying that the tiger cannot change his stripes nor the leopard his spots."[36]

The novel also summons up memories of the legacy of the French Enlightenment, the French Revolution, and one of its intellectual progenitors, Jean Jacques Rousseau. At the end of part 3, it is ironic that Razumov, in Geneva, retires to a place under the statue of Rousseau. Here he begins his diary, which is, in effect, his confession and his outline of his sense of social contract. He and the statue are near the bridge. Isolated, without human connection, Razumov, in front of the statue of Rousseau, listens to "an inner voice."[37]

Conrad's politics were rather different from those of Jean-Jacques Rousseau. Unlike Rousseau, he held to a personal moral code rather than to ideas of the social contract. He did not seek to release society toward unprecedented freedoms. Rather, Conrad, through his fiction, probed matters of conscience and pursued the moral imagination without offering a political solution. Even so, something is being said about humanity by positioning Razumov beside Rousseau's statue. One possibility is that Rousseau emphasized feeling, as opposed to sheer logic. Here Razumov is cut off from the company of other people and turns to feeling, or to sympathy.

This statue of Rousseau is reminiscent of Haldin the revolutionary. Returning to his room, Razumov sees Haldin "already at the door, tall and straight as an arrow, with his pale face and hand raised attentively; [he] might have posed for the statue of a daring youth listening to an inner voice."[38] Haldin is "youth," with its brash temerity and dreams. He is a reflection of the French Revolution, or any revolution, including that of the Polish revolutionaries.

The politics of European culture and history echo within the lives of Conrad's characters. *Under Western Eyes* is a psychological drama, dealing with the experience and choices of Razumov. Moral conflict and psychological conflict are at the center of this novel. There are issues of human relationship and there is politics: a look at the East (Russia) from the West. There is a pressing concern with chance and fate, a topic that Conrad had been exploring since his writing of *Lord Jim*. Razumov eventually experiences a "breakthrough" and chooses humanity over the political ideas that are swirling around him and through him. This character in becoming deaf and crippled is actually more whole in the end than he was earlier in the novel. Razumov has previously withdrawn from this society. He wants to be left alone. However, he cannot remain neutral in this atmosphere because the revolution comes in his door, in the form of Haldin. Razumov is sucked into the conflict, as by a vacuum. He is bounced about between sides and ultimately flattened in an accident. He is besieged by the impersonality of this situation in which he, an individual, is caught between these dialectical forces. In this Darwinian world—one of impersonal forces ever in conflict and struggle—the answer, if there is any, is in one's embrace of a moral code, an intention toward life that is alive in human connection and in human love.

Appendix

Sources for Further Reading

John G. Peters

Bibliography

Ehrsam, Theodore G. *A Bibliography of Joseph Conrad.* Metuchen, N.J.: Scarecrow Press, 1969.

Knowles, Owen. *An Annotated Critical Bibliography of Joseph Conrad.* New York: St. Martin's Press, 1992.

Peters, John G. *Joseph Conrad's Critical Reception.* Cambridge, U.K.: Cambridge University Press, 2013.

Teets, Bruce E. *Joseph Conrad: An Annotated Bibliography.* New York: Garland, 1990.

——. and Helmut E. Gerber. *Joseph Conrad: An Annotated Bibliography of Writings about Him.* De Kalb: Northern Illinois University Press, 1971.

Biography

Allen, Jerry. *The Sea Years of Joseph Conrad.* Garden City, N.Y.: Doubleday, 1965.

Baines, Jocelyn. *Joseph Conrad: A Critical Biography.* London: Weidenfeld and Nicolson, 1960.

Ford (Hueffer), Ford Madox. *Joseph Conrad: A Personal Remembrance.* Boston: Little, Brown, 1924.

Karl, Frederick R. *Joseph Conrad: The Three Lives, A Biography.* New York: Farrar, Straus, Giroux, 1979.

Meyer, Bernard C. *Joseph Conrad: A Psychoanalytic Biography.* Princeton, N.J.: Princeton University Press, 1967.

Najder, Zdzislaw. *Joseph Conrad: A Life.* Trans. Halina Najder. Rochester, N.Y.: Camden House, 2007.

Stape, John. *The Several Lives of Joseph Conrad.* New York: Pantheon, 2007.

Tennant, Roger. *Joseph Conrad.* New York: Atheneum, 1981.

Watts, Cedric. *Joseph Conrad: A Literary Life.* New York: St. Martin's Press, 1989.

Introductions

Karl, Frederick R. *A Reader's Guide to Joseph Conrad.* Rev. ed. New York: Farrar, Straus & Giroux, 1969.

Middleton, Tim. *Joseph Conrad.* New York: Routledge, 2006.

Peters, John G. *The Cambridge Introduction to Joseph Conrad.* Cambridge, U.K.: Cambridge University Press, 2006.

Simmons, Allan H. *Joseph Conrad.* New York: Palgrave Macmillan, 2006.

Watts, Cedric. *A Preface to Conrad.* 2nd ed. London, Longman, 1993.

Correspondence

Conrad, Joseph. *The Collected Letters of Joseph Conrad.* Ed. Laurence Davies et al. 9 vols. Cambridge, U.K.: Cambridge University Press, 1986–2008.

Knowles, Owen, ed. *"My Dear Friend": Further Letters to and about Joseph Conrad.* Amsterdam: Rodopi, 2008.

Najder, Zdzislaw, ed. *Conrad's Polish Background: Letters to and from Polish Friends.* Trans. Halina Carroll. London: Oxford University Press, 1964.

Stape, J. H., and Owen Knowles, eds. *A Portrait in Letters: Correspondence to and about Joseph Conrad.* Amsterdam: Rodopi, 1996.

Ecocritism

Clayton, Aaron. "*Victory* in Nature: An Ecocritical Reading of Joseph Conrad's Novel." *Conradiana* 42, nos. 1–2 (2010): 123–39.

Mayer, Michael. "When Trees Become Kings: Nature as a Decolonizing Force in Joseph Conrad's *Heart of Darkness.*" In *Local Natures, Global Responsibilities: Ecocritical Perspectives on the New English Literatures,* ed. Laurenz Volkmann, Nancy Grimm, Ines Detmers, and Katrin Thomson. 179–88. Amsterdam: Rodopi, 2010.

McCarthy, Jeffrey Mathes. "'A Choice of Nightmares': The Ecology of *Heart of Darkness.*" *Modern Fiction Studies* 55, no. 3 (Fall 2009): 620–48.

Mueller, William R. "Man and Nature in Conrad's *Nostromo.*" *Thought* 179 (Winter 1970): 559–76.

Myers, Jeffrey. "The Anxiety of Confluence: Evolution, Ecology, and Imperialism in Conrad's *Heart of Darkness,*" *Interdisciplinary Studies in Literature and Environment* 8.2 (summer 2001): 97–108

Sagar, Keith Sagar. *Literature and the Crime against Nature.* Hanover Township, Pa.: Chaucer Press, 2005.

Politics

Fleishman, Avrom. *Conrad's Politics: Community and Anarchy in the Fiction of Joseph Conrad.* Baltimore: Johns Hopkins University Press, 1967.

Hay, Eloise Knapp. *The Political Novels of Joseph Conrad: A Critical Study.* Chicago: University of Chicago Press, 1963.

Howe, Irving. "Order and Anarchy: The Political Novels Part I." *Kenyon Review* 15, no. 4 (Autumn 1953): 505–21.

——. "Order and Anarchy: The Political Novels Part II." *Kenyon Review* 16, no. 1 (Winter 1954): 1–19.

Schwarz, Daniel R. "Conrad's Quarrel with Politics in *Nostromo.*" *College English* 59, no. 5 (September 1997): 548–68.

Conrad and Gender

Austin, Mary. "Joseph Conrad Tells What Women Don't Know about Men." *Pictorial Review,* 24, no. 12 (September 1923): 17, 28, 30–31.

Casarino, Cesare. *Modernity at Sea: Melville, Marx, Conrad in Crisis.* Minneapolis: University of Minnesota Press, 2002.

Colbron, Grace Isabel. "Joseph Conrad's Women." *Bookman* 38, no. 5 (January 1914): 476–79.

DeKoven, Marianne. *Rich and Strange: Gender, History, Modernism.* Princeton, N.J.: Princeton University Press, 1991.

Hawthorn, Jeremy. *Sexuality and the Erotic in the Fiction of Joseph Conrad.* London: Continuum, 2007.

Jones, Susan. *Conrad and Women.* Oxford, U.K.: Clarendon Press, 1999.

Nadelhaft, Ruth L. *Joseph Conrad.* Atlantic Highlands, N.J.: Humanities Press, 1991.

Roberts, Andrew Michael. *Conrad and Masculinity.* New York: St. Martin's Press, 2000.

Ruppel, Richard. *Homoeroticism and Homosexuality in the Life and Fiction of Joseph Conrad: Love Between the Lines.* New York: Routledge, 2008.

Schneider, Lissa. *Conrad's Narratives of Difference: Not Exactly Tales for Boys.* New York: Routledge, 2003.

Straus, Nina Pelikan. "The Exclusion of the Intended from the Secret Sharing in Conrad's *Heart of Darkness.*" *Novel* 20, no. 2 (Winter 1987): 123–37

Narrative

Beach, Joseph Warren. *The Twentieth Century Novel: Studies in Technique.* New York: Appleton-Century-Crofts, 1931.

Brooks, Peter. *Reading for the Plot: Design and Intention in Narrative.* New York: Alfred A. Knopf, 1984.

Davidson, Donald. "Joseph Conrad's Directed Indirections." *Sewanee Review* 33, no. 2 (April 1925): 163–77.

Fernández, Ramón. "The Art of Conrad." Trans. Anne Luyat. In *Conrad in France,* ed. Josiane Paccaud-Huguet, 13–20. Boulder, Colo.: Social Science Monographs, 2006.

Lothe, Jakob. *Conrad's Narrative Method.* Oxford, U.K.: Clarendon Press, 1989.

——, Jeremy Hawthorn, and James Phelan, eds. *Joseph Conrad: Voice, Sequence, History, Genre.* Columbus: Ohio State University Press, 2008.

Hawthorn, Jeremy. *Joseph Conrad: Narrative Technique and Ideological Commitment.* London: Edward Arnold, 1990.

Henricksen, Bruce. *Nomadic Voices: Conrad and the Subject of Narrative.* Urbana: University of Illinois Press, 1992.

Richardson, Brian. "Construing Conrad's 'The Secret Sharer': Suppressed Narratives, Subaltern Reception, and the Act of Interpretation." *Studies in the Novel* 33, no. 3 (Fall 2001): 306–21.

Said, Edward W. "Conrad: The Presentation of Narrative." *Novel* 7, no. 2 (Winter 1974): 116–32.

Walpole, V. *Conrad's Method: Some Formal Aspects. Annals of the University of Stellenbosch.* Kaapstad, South Africa: Nasionale Pers Beperk, 1930.

Contemporary Critical Approaches

Bonney, William W. *Thorns & Arabesques: Contexts for Conrad's Fiction.* Baltimore: Johns Hopkins University Press, 1980.

Erdinast-Vulcan, Daphna. *Joseph Conrad and the Modern Temper.* Oxford, U.K.: Clarendon Press, 1991.

——. *The Strange Short Fiction of Joseph Conrad: Writing, Culture and Subjectivity.* Oxford, U.K.: Oxford University Press, 1999.

Fogel, Aaron. *Coercion to Speak: Conrad's Poetics of Dialogue.* Cambridge, Mass.: Harvard University Press, 1985.

Greaney, Michael. *Conrad, Language, and Narrative.* Cambridge, U.K.: Cambridge University Press, 2002.

Harpham, Geoffrey Galt. *One of Us: The Mastery of Joseph Conrad.* Chicago: University of Chicago Press, 1996.

Jameson, Fredric. *The Political Unconscious: Narrative as a Socially Symbolic Act.* Ithaca, N.Y.: Cornell University Press, 1981.

Levin, Yael. *Tracing the Aesthetic Principle in Conrad's Novels.* New York: Palgrave Macmillan, 2008.

Miller, J. Hillis. *Fiction and Repetition: Seven English Novels.* Cambridge, Mass.: Harvard University Press, 1982.

Said, Edward W. *Beginnings: Intention & Method.* Baltimore: Johns Hopkins University Press , 1975.

Conrad and Philosophy

Armstrong, Paul B. *The Challenge of Bewilderment: Understanding and Representation in James, Conrad, and Ford.* Ithaca, N.Y.: Cornell University Press, 1987.

Bohlmann, Otto. *Conrad's Existentialism.* New York: St. Martin's Press, 1991.

Johnson, Bruce. *Conrad's Models of Mind.* Minneapolis: University of Minnesota Press, 1971.

Peters, John G. *Conrad and Impressionism.* Cambridge, U.K.: Cambridge University Press, 2001.

Whiteley, Patrick J. *Knowledge and Experimental Realism in Conrad, Lawrence, and Woolf.* Baton Rouge: Louisiana State University Press, 1987.

Wollaeger, Mark A. *Joseph Conrad and the*

Fictions of Skepticism. Stanford, Calif.: Stanford University Press, 1990.

Colonialism and Imperialism

Achebe, Chinua. "An Image of Africa." *Massachusetts Review* 18, no. 4 (Winter 1977): 782–94.

Bongie, Chris. *Exotic Memories: Literature, Colonialism, and the* Fin de Siècle. Stanford, Calif.: Stanford University Press, 1991.

Brantlinger, Patrick. "*Heart of Darkness:* Anti-Imperialism, Racism, or Impressionism?" *Criticism* 27, no. 4 (Fall 1985): 363–85.

GoGwilt, Christopher. *The Invention of the West: Joseph Conrad and the Double-Mapping of Europe and Empire*. Stanford, Calif.: Stanford University Press, 1995.

Goonetilleke, D. C. R. A. *Developing Countries in British Fiction*. Totowa, N.J.: Rowman and Littlefield, 1977.

Hamner, Robert D., ed. *Joseph Conrad: Third World Perspectives*. Washington, D.C.: Three Continents Press, 1990.

Hampson, Robert. *Cross-Cultural Encounters in Joseph Conrad's Malay Fiction*. New York: Palgrave, 2000.

Harris, Wilson. "The Frontier on Which *Heart of Darkness* Stands." *Research on African Literatures* 12, no. 1 (Spring 1981): 86–93.

Hawkins, Hunt. "Conrad's Critique of Imperialism in *Heart of Darkness*." *PMLA* 94, no. 2 (March 1979): 286–99.

Kettle, Arnold. "The Greatness of Joseph Conrad." *Modern Quarterly*, n.s. vol. 3, no. 3 (Summer 1948): 63–81.

McClure, John A. *Kipling & Conrad: The Colonial Fiction*. Cambridge, Mass.: Harvard University Press, 1981.

Mongia, Padmini. "Narrative Strategy and Imperialism in Conrad's *Lord Jim*." *Studies in the Novel* 24, no. 2 (Summer 1992): 173–86.

Parry, Benita. *Conrad and Imperialism: Ideological Boundaries and Visionary Frontiers*. London: Macmillan, 1983.

Ross, Stephen. *Conrad and Empire*. Columbia: University of Missouri Press, 2004.

Said, Edward W. *Culture and Imperialism*. New York: Knopf, 1993.

Singh, Francis B. "The Colonialistic Bias of *Heart of Darkness*." *Conradiana* 10, no. 1 (Spring 1978): 41–54.

Szczeszak-Brewer, Agata. *Empire and Pilgrimage in Conrad and Joyce*. Gainesville: University Press of Florida, 2011.

Watts, Cedric. "'A Bloody Racist': About Achebe's View of Conrad." *Yearbook of English Studies* 13 (1983): 196–209.

White, Andrea. *Joseph Conrad and the Adventure Tradition: Constructing and Deconstructing the Imperial Subject*. Cambridge, U.K.: Cambridge University Press, 1993.

Conrad's Later Fiction

Geddes, Gary. *Conrad's Later Novels*. Montreal: McGill-Queen's University Press, 1980.

Palmer, John A. *Joseph Conrad's Fiction: A Study in Literary Growth*. Ithaca, N.Y.: Cornell University Press, 1968.

Schwarz, Daniel R. *Conrad: The Later Fiction*. London: Macmillan, 1982.

Wiley, Paul L. *Conrad's Measure of Man*. Madison: University of Wisconsin Press, 1954.

Conrad's Short Fiction

Billy, Ted. *A Wilderness of Words: Closure and Disclosure in Conrad's Short Fiction*. Lubbock: Texas Tech University Press, 1997.

Graver, Lawrence. *Conrad's Short Fiction*. Berkeley: University of California Press, 1969.

Reilly, Joseph J. "The Short Stories of Joseph Conrad." *Catholic World* 650 (May 1919): 163–75.

Said, Edward W. *Joseph Conrad and the Fiction of Autobiography*. 1966. Rpt. New York: Columbia University Press, 2008.

Conrad and the Sea

Bruss, Paul. *Conrad's Early Sea Fiction: The Novelist as Navigator.* Lewisburg, Pa.: Bucknell University Press, 1979.

Burgess, C. F. *The Fellowship of the Craft: Conrad on Ships and Seamen and the Sea.* Port Washington, N.Y.: Kennikat Press, 1976.

Reynolds, Stephen. "Joseph Conrad and Sea Fiction." *Quarterly Review* 432 (July 1912): 159–80.

Conrad and His Sources

Busza, Andrzej. "Conrad's Polish Literary Background and Some Illustrations of the Influence of Polish Literature on His Work." *Antemurale* 10 (1966): 109–255.

Gordan, John Dozier. *Joseph Conrad: The Making of a Novelist.* Cambridge, Mass.: Harvard University Press, 1940.

Hervouet, Yves. *The French Face of Joseph Conrad.* Cambridge, U.K.: Cambridge University Press, 1990.

Milosz, Czeslaw. "Joseph Conrad in Polish Eyes." *The Atlantic* 200, no. 5 (November 1957): 219–28.

Morf, Gustav. *The Polish Heritage of Joseph Conrad.* London: Sampson Low, Marston, [1930].

——. *Polish Shades and Ghosts of Joseph Conrad.* New York: Astra Books, 1976.

Sherry, Norman. *Conrad's Eastern World.* Cambridge, U.K.: Cambridge University Press, 1966.

——. *Conrad's Western World.* Cambridge, U.K.: Cambridge University Press, 1971.

Conrad and Morality

Cooper, Christopher. *Conrad and the Human Dilemma.* New York: Barnes & Noble, 1970.

Gekoski, R. A. *Conrad: The Moral World of the Novelist.* New York: Barnes & Noble, 1978.

Panichas, George A. *Joseph Conrad: His Moral Vision.* Rev. Ed. Mercer, Ga.: Mercer University Press, 2007.

Saveson, John E. *Conrad, the Later Moralist.* Amsterdam: Rodopi, 1974.

——. *Joseph Conrad: The Making of a Moralist.* Amsterdam: Rodopi, 1972.

Conrad and Language

Guetti, James L. *The Limits of Metaphor: A Study of Melville, Conrad, and Faulkner.* Ithaca, N.Y.: Cornell University Press, 1967.

Hawthorn, Jeremy. *Joseph Conrad: Language and Fictional Self-Consciousness.* London: Edward Arnold, 1979.

Pinsker, Sanford. *The Languages of Joseph Conrad.* Amsterdam: Rodopi, 1978.

Conrad and Film

Moore, Gene M., ed. *Conrad on Film.* Cambridge, U.K.: Cambridge University Press, 1997.

Phillips, Gene D. *Conrad and Cinema: The Art of Adaptation.* New York: Peter Lang, 1995.

Conrad and Religion

Lester, John. *Conrad and Religion.* New York: St. Martin's Press, 1988.

Purdy, Dwight H. *Joseph Conrad's Bible.* Norman: University of Oklahoma Press, 1984.

Conrad and Psychology

Ash, Beth Sharon. *Writing in Between: Modernity and Psychosocial Dilemma in the Novels of Joseph Conrad.* New York: St. Martin's Press, 1999.

Bock, Martin. *Joseph Conrad and Psychological Medicine.* Lubbock: Texas Tech University Press, 2002.

Hampson, Robert. *Joseph Conrad: Betrayal and Identity.* London: Macmillan, 1992.

Kirschner, Paul. *Conrad: The Psychologist as Artist.* Edinburgh, Scotland: Oliver & Boyd, 1968.

Other Useful Studies

Berthoud, Jacques. *Joseph Conrad: The Major Phase.* Cambridge, U.K.: Cambridge University Press, 1978.

Crankshaw, Edward. *Joseph Conrad: Some Aspects of the Art of the Novel.* London: John Lane, 1936.

Daleski, H. M. *Joseph Conrad: The Way of Dispossession.* London: Faber & Faber, 1977.

Donovan, Stephen. *Joseph Conrad and Popular Culture.* New York: Palgrave Macmillan, 2005.

Follett, Wilson. *Joseph Conrad: A Short Study of His Intellectual and Emotional Attitude toward His Work and of the Chief Characters of His Novels.* Garden City, N.Y.: Doubleday, Page, 1915.

Ford (Hueffer), Ford Madox. "Joseph Conrad." *The English Review* 10, no. 1 (December 1911): 68–83.

Guerard, Albert J. *Conrad the Novelist.* Cambridge, Mass.: Harvard University Press, 1958.

Hand, Richard J. *The Theatre of Joseph Conrad: Reconstructed Fictions.* New York: Palgrave Macmillan, 2005.

Hewitt, Douglas. *Conrad: A Reassessment.* Cambridge, U.K.: Bowes & Bowes, 1952.

Kaplan, Carola, Peter Lancelot Mallios, and Andrea White, eds. *Conrad in the Twenty-first Century: Contemporary Approaches and Perspectives.* New York: Routledge, 2005.

Leavis, F. R. *The Great Tradition: George Eliot, Henry James, Joseph Conrad.* New York: George W. Stewart, 1950.

Mallios, Peter Lancelot. *Our Conrad: Constituting American Modernity.* Stanford, Calif.: Stanford University Press, 2010.

Mencken, H. L. *A Book of Prefaces.* New York: Alfred A. Knopf, 1917.

Moser, Thomas C. *Joseph Conrad: Achievement and Decline.* Cambridge, Mass.: Harvard University Press, 1957.

Murfin, Ross C., ed. *Conrad Revisited: Essays for the Eighties.* University: University of Alabama Press, 1985.

Niland, Richard. *Conrad and History.* Oxford, U.K.: Oxford University Press, 2010.

Schwarz, Daniel R. *Conrad: "Almayer's Folly" to "Under Western Eyes."* Ithaca, N.Y.: Cornell University Press, 1980.

Warren, Robert Penn. "*Nostromo.*" *Sewanee Review* 59, no. 3 (Summer 1951): 363–91.

Watt, Ian. *Conrad in the Nineteenth Century.* Berkeley: University of California Press, 1979.

Yelton, Donald C. *Mimesis and Metaphor: An Inquiry into the Genesis and Scope of Conrad's Symbolic Imagery.* The Hague: Mouton, 1967.

Zabel, Morton Dauwen. "Editor's Introduction." *The Portable Conrad.* New York: Viking Press, 1947.

———. "Joseph Conrad: Chance and Recognition." *Sewanee Review* 53, no. 1 (January–March 1945): 1–22.

NOTES

All citations for Joseph Conrad's texts refer to the Cambridge University edition unless otherwise specified.

Notes to "Introduction"

1. "Chinua Achebe: 'Heart of Darkness' Is Inappropriate," Robert Siegel's interview with Chinua Achebe, *All Things Considered,* NPR, October 15, 2009, http://www.npr.org/templates/transcript/transcript.php?storyId=113835207. Chinua Achebe famously called Conrad "a bloody racist," while others defended him as an author exposing the atrocities of the empire. See Chinua Achebe's essay "An Image of Africa" in *Heart of Darkness & Selections from The Congo Diary* (New York: Random House, 1999). For a more detailed discussion of race and racism in Conrad's novella, see Mawuli Adjei's essay in this volume.
2. Joseph Conrad, *A Personal Record* (Cambridge, U.K.: Cambridge University Press, 2008), 26.
3. John Stape, *The Several Lives of Joseph Conrad* (New York: Pantheon, 2007), 250.
4. Qtd. in Norman Sherry, *Joseph Conrad: The Critical Heritage* (London: Routledge and Kegan Paul, 1973), 140. Qtd. from letter to Miss Collet, December 24, 1902, *Letters of George Gissing to Members of His Family,* ed. A. and E. Gissing (London: Constable & Co., 1927), 391.
5. Conrad, *A Personal Record,* 34.
6. John Batchelor, *The Life of Joseph Conrad: A Critical Biography* (Oxford, U.K.: Blackwell, 1994), 1.
7. Ibid., 11.
8. Ibid., 12.
9. Conrad, *A Personal Record,* 44.
10. Ibid., 92.
11. Ibid., 50.
12. Batchelor, *Life of Joseph Conrad,* 17.
13. Frederick R. Karl, *A Reader's Guide to Joseph Conrad* (New York: Noonday Press, 1960), 10.
14. Batchelor, *Life of Joseph Conrad,* 36.
15. For a complete list of Conrad's fiction, in chronological order, see "Chronological List of Works by Joseph Conrad" in this volume.
16. Conrad, *A Personal Record,* 23.
17. Peter Edgerly Firchow, *Envisioning Africa: Racism and Imperialism in Conrad's* Heart of Darkness (Lexington: University Press of Kentucky, 2000), 31.
18. Batchelor, *Life of Joseph Conrad,* 17.
19. To learn more about King Leopold's Congo, see Barry Morton's "Joseph Conrad: Historical and Cultural Contexts." Greg Winston, William Atkinson, and Mawuli Adjei will discuss Conrad in the context in his fictionalized account of Africa.
20. Zdzislaw Najder, *Joseph Conrad: A Life* (Rochester, N.Y.: Camden House, 2007), 130.
21. See Eliose Knapp Hay's *The Political Novels of Joseph Conrad* (Chicago:

University of Chicago Press, 1963), Avrom Fleishman's *Conrad's Politics* (Baltimore: Johns Hopkins University Press, 1967), and Richard Niland's *Conrad and History* (Oxford, U.K. Oxford University Press, 2010).

22. Lady Ottoline Morrell, *The Early Memoirs of Lady Ottoline Morrell,* ed. Robert Gathorne-Hardy (London: Faber and Faber, 1963), 240.
23. In *A Personal Record,* Conrad recalls the writing process of *Nostromo:* "Yes, I suppose I slept, and ate the food put before me, and talked connectedly to my household on suitable occasions. But I had never been aware of the even flow of daily life, made easy and noiseless for me by a silent, watchful, tireless affection." He adds that "The fortune of the house included a pair of gray-blue watchful eyes that would see to that" (93).
24. Joseph Conrad, Preface to *The Nigger of the Narcissus* (London: J. M. Dent, 1950), x.
25. The idea comes from a February 6, 1910, letter from Jesse to David S. Meldrum. My thanks go to John Peters, who pointed me to this reference and who offered generous comments on a draft of this introduction.
26. Conrad, *A Personal Record,* 94.
27. *The Collected Letters of Joseph Conrad,* ed. Frederick Karl et al. (Cambridge, U.K.: Cambridge University Press, 1986–2008), vol. 2: 90–91.
28. Stape, *Several Lives,* 98–99.
29. Ibid., 124.
30. *Collected Letters of Joseph Conrad* 6: 55.
31. Joseph Epstein, "Life Sentences: The Art of Joseph Conrad," *New Criterion* 12, no. 10 (June 1994). Accessed on Academic Search Premier EBSCO on October 16, 2012.
32. Edward Garnett, ed., *Letters from Joseph Conrad 1895–1924* (New York: Charter Books, 1962), 46.
33. Michael Gorra, "Joseph Conrad," *Hudson Review* 59, no. 4 (Winter 2007): 545.
34. Stape, *Several Lives,* 132.
35. Carola Kaplan, Peter Mallios, and Andrea White, eds., *Conrad in the Twenty-first Century: Contemporary Approaches and Perspectives* (New York: Routledge, 2005).

Notes to "Joseph Conrad: Historical and Cultural Contexts"

1. Cited in Monica M. Gardner, *Adam Mickiewicz: The National Poet of Poland* (New York: Dutton, 1911), 2.
2. Roman Koropeckyj, "Adam Mickiewicz as a Polish National Icon," in *History of the Literary Cultures of East-Central Europe: Junctures and Disjunctures in the 19th and 20th Centuries,* ed. Marcel Cornel-Pope and John Neubauer (Philadelphia: John Benjamins, 2010), vol. 4: 19–20.
3. Jerzy Lukowski and Hubert Zawadzki, *A Concise History of Poland* (Cambridge, U.K.: Cambridge University Press, 2001), 130.
4. Ibid., chap. 4; Norman Davies, *God's Playground: A History of Poland in Two Volumes* (New York: Columbia University Press, 1982), vol. 2: chap. 6.
5. Davies, *God's Playground,* chap. 6.
6. Gardner, *Adam Mickiewicz,* chap. 2.
7. Koropeckyj, "Adam Mickiewicz," 20–21.
8. Lukowski and Zawadzki, *Concise History of Poland,* 131–33.
9. Paul Soboleski, ed., *Poets and Poetry of Poland: A Collection of Polish Verse* (Chicago: Knight & Leonard, 1881), 32.
10. Ibid.
11. John Stape, *The Several Lives of Joseph Conrad* (New York: Pantheon, 2007), chap. 1.
12. Brian A. Porter, *When Nationalism Began to Hate: Imagining Modern Politics in Nineteenth-Century Poland* (New York: Oxford University Press, 2000), 10.

13. Owen Knowles, "Conrad's Life," in *The Cambridge Companion to Joseph Conrad,* ed. John Stape (Cambridge, U.K.: Cambridge University Press, 1996), 6.
14. Ailsa G. Zainu'ddin, *A Short History of Indonesia* (New York: Praeger, 1968), 3.
15. Bernard H. M. Vlekke, *Nusantara: A History of Indonesia* (rev. ed. Chicago: Quadrangle, 1960), 88–91.
16. Jonathan I. Israel, *Dutch Primacy in World Trade, 1585–1740* (Oxford, U.K.: Clarendon Press, 1990), 21–22.
17. Ibid., chap. 2.
18. Vlekke, *Nusantara,* 131.
19. David Bevan, Paul Collier, and Jan Gunning, *The Political Economy of Poverty, Equity, and Growth: Nigeria and Indonesia* (Oxford, U.K.: Oxford University Press, 1999), 197.
20. Vlekke, *Nusantara,* 288–96.
21. Ibid., 308–15.
22. Adrian Vickers, *A History of Modern Indonesia* (Cambridge, U.K.: Cambridge University Press, 2005), 60.
23. Jan Vansina, *Paths in the Rainforest: Toward a History of Political Tradition in Equatorial Africa* (Madison: University of Wisconsin Press, 1990).
24. Robert Harms, *Games Against Nature: An Eco-Cultural History of the Nunu of Equatorial Africa* (Cambridge, U.K.: Cambridge University Press, 1987), 28–56.
25. See Vansina, *Paths in the Rainforest,* 35–100.
26. The now-classic account of this process is Joseph B. Miller, *Way of Death: Merchant Capitalism and the Angolan Slave Trade 1730–1830* (Madison: University of Wisconsin Press, 1988), chap. 4.
27. See Ernest G. Ravenstein, *The Strange Adventures of Andrew Battell of Leigh in Angola and Adjoining Regions* (rpt. London: Hakluyt Society, 1901), regarding the experiences of an Englishman taken hostage by one of these groups in the late 1500s.
28. See Robert Harms, *River of Wealth, River of Sorrow: The Central Zaire Basin in the Era of the Slave and Ivory Trade, 1500–1891* (New Haven, Conn.: Yale University Press, 1981).
29. See discussion in Adam Hochschild, *King Leopold's Ghost: A Story of Greed, Terror, and Heroism in Colonial Africa* (New York: Houghton Mifflin, 1998), 232–33.
30. Henry Morton Stanley, *How I Found Livingstone: Travels, Adventures, and Discoveries in Central Africa* (London: Sampson Low, 1872), and *Through The Dark Continent* (New York: Harper Bros, 1878).
31. Hochschild, *King Leopold's Ghost,* 63–71, 95–100.
32. For a discussion of various concessions, see Bogomil Jewsewiecki, "Rural Society and the Belgian Colonial Economy," in *History of Central Africa,* ed. David Birmingham and Phyllis Martin (London: Longman, 1983), vol. 2: 95–125.
33. Robert Harms, "The End of Red Rubber: A Reassessment," *Journal of African History* 16, no. 1 (1975): 73–88.
34. See Edmund D. Morel, *The Congo Slave State: A Protest Against the New African Slavery* (London: John Richardson & Sons, 1903), and William R. Louis and Jean Stengers, eds., *E. D. Morel's History of the Congo Reform Movement* (Oxford, U.K.: Clarendon Press, 1968).
35. Mark Twain, *King Leopold's Soliloquy: A Defense of His Congo Rule* (Boston: P. R. Warren, 1905); Sir Arthur Conan-Doyle, *The Crime of the Congo* (New York: Doubleday, 1909).
36. Hochschild, *King Leopold's Ghost,* chap. 15.
37. Harms, *River of Wealth, River of Sorrow.*

Notes to "Conrad's Critical Reception"

1. [Edward Garnett], "Academy Portraits: Mr. Joseph Conrad," *Academy* 1380 (15 October 1898): 82–83.

2. [Hugh Clifford], "The Trail of the Book-Worm: Mr. Joseph Conrad at Home and Abroad," *The Singapore Free Press,* 30 August 1898, 3.
3. John Albert Macy, "Joseph Conrad," *Atlantic Monthly* 98, no. 5 (November 1906): 697–702.
4. John Galsworthy, "Joseph Conrad: A Disquisition," *Fortnightly Review,* n.s. vol. 83 (April 1908): 627–33.
5. Ford Madox Ford, "Joseph Conrad," *English Review* 10, no. 1 (December 1911): 68–83.
6. Stephen Reynolds, "Joseph Conrad and Sea Fiction," *Quarterly Review* 432 (July 1912): 159–80.
7. Frederic Tabor Cooper, "Representative English Story-Tellers: Joseph Conrad," *Bookman* 35, no. 1 (March 1912): 61–70.
8. Henry James, "The Younger Generation: Part II," *Times Literary Supplement* 637 (2 April 1914): 157–58.
9. Grace Isabel Colbrun, "Joseph Conrad's Women," *Bookman* 38, no. 5 (January 1914): 476–79.
10. Richard Curle, *Joseph Conrad: A Study* (London: Kegan Paul, Trench, Trübner, 1914).
11. Wilson Follett, *Joseph Conrad: A Short Study of His Intellectual and Emotional Attitude toward His Work and of the Chief Characters of His Novels* (Garden City, N.Y.: Doubleday, Page, 1915).
12. William Lyon Phelps, "The Advance of the English Novel: VIII," *Bookman* 43, no. 3 (May 1916): 297–308.
13. H. L. Mencken, *A Book of Prefaces* (New York: Alfred A. Knopf, 1917), 11–64.
14. [E. M. Forster], "The Pride of Mr. Conrad," *Nation and Atheneum* 28, no. 25 (19 March 1921): 881–82.
15. [Virginia Woolf], "A Disillusioned Romantic," *Times Literary Supplement* 963 (1 July 1920): 419.
16. [Virginia Woolf], "Mr. Conrad: A Conversation," *Nation and Atheneum* 33, no. 22 (1 September 1923): 681–82.
17. Ford Madox Ford, *Joseph Conrad: A Personal Remembrance* (Boston: Little, Brown, 1924).
18. Ramón Fernández, "L'art de Conrad," *La Nouvelle Revue Française* n.s. no. 135 (1 December 1924): 730–37.
19. Donald Davison, "Joseph Conrad's Directed Indirections," *Sewanee Review* 33, no. 2 (April 1925): 163–77.
20. G. Jean-Aubry, *Joseph Conrad: Life and Letters* (Garden City, N.Y.: Doubleday, Page, 1927).
21. Gustav Morf, *The Polish Heritage of Joseph Conrad* (London: Sampson Low, Marston, [1930]).
22. V. Walpole. *Conrad's Method: Some Formal Aspects* (Cape Town, South Africa: Nasionale Pers Beperk, 1930).
23. Joseph Warren Beach, *The Twentieth Century Novel: Studies in Technique* (New York: Appleton-Century-Crofts, 1931), 337–65.
24. Edward Crankshaw, *Joseph Conrad: Some Aspects of the Art of the Novel* (London: John Lane, 1936).
25. David Daiches, *The Novel and the Modern World* (Chicago: University of Chicago Press, 1939), 48–64.
26. John Dozier Gordan, *Joseph Conrad: The Making of a Novelist* (Cambridge, Mass.: Harvard University Press, 1940).
27. M. C. Bradbrook, *Joseph Conrad: Poland's English Genius* (Cambridge, U.K.: Cambridge University Press, 1941).
28. Morton Dauwen Zabel, "Editor's Introduction," *The Portable Conrad* (New York: Viking Press, 1947), 1–47.
29. F. R. Leavis, *The Great Tradition: George Eliot, Henry James, Joseph Conrad* (New York: George W. Stewart, [1948]), 17–23, 173–226.
30. Robert Penn Warren, "*Nostromo,*" *Sewanee Review* 59, no. 3 (Summer 1951): 363–91.
31. Douglas Hewitt, *Conrad: A Reassessment* (Cambridge, U.K.: Bowes & Bowes, 1952).

32. Paul L. Wiley, *Conrad's Measure of Man* (Madison: University of Wisconsin Press, 1954).
33. Irving Howe, "Order and Anarchy: The Political Novels Part I," *Kenyon Review* 15, no. 4 (Autumn 1953): 505–21; "Order and Anarchy: The Political Novels Part II," *Kenyon Review* 16, no. 1 (Winter 1954): 1–19.
34. Thomas Moser, *Joseph Conrad: Achievement and Decline* (Cambridge, Mass.: Harvard University Press, 1957).
35. Albert J. Guerard, *Conrad the Novelist* (Cambridge, Mass.: Harvard University Press, 1958).
36. Jocelyn Baines, *Joseph Conrad: A Critical Biography* (London: Weidenfeld and Nicolson, 1959).
37. Eloise Knapp Hay, *The Political Novels of Joseph Conrad: A Critical Study* (Chicago: University of Chicago Press, 1963).
38. Avrom Fleishman, *Conrad's Politics: Community and Anarchy in the Fiction of Joseph Conrad* (Baltimore: Johns Hopkins University Press, 1967).
39. J. Hillis Miller, *Poets of Reality: Six Twentieth-Century Writers* (Cambridge, Mass.: Harvard University Press, 1965), 13–67.
40. Edward W. Said, *Joseph Conrad and the Fiction of Autobiography* (1966; rpt. New York: Columbia University Press, 2008).
41. Andrzej Busza, "Conrad's Polish Literary Background and Some Illustrations of the Influence of Polish Literature on His Work," *Antemurale* 10 (1966): 109–255.
42. Norman Sherry, *Conrad's Eastern World* (Cambridge, U.K.: Cambridge University Press, 1966).
43. James L. Guetti, *The Limits of Metaphor: A Study of Melville, Conrad, and Faulkner* (Ithaca, N.Y.: Cornell University Press, 1967), 1–11, 46–68.
44. Donald C. Yelton, *Mimesis and Metaphor: An Inquiry into the Genesis and Scope of Conrad's Symbolic Imagery* (The Hague: Mouton, 1967).
45. John A. Palmer, *Joseph Conrad's Fiction: A Study in Literary Growth* (Ithaca, N.Y.: Cornell University Press, 1968).
46. Bruce Johnson, *Conrad's Models of Mind* (Minneapolis: University of Minnesota Press, 1971).
47. H. M. Daleski, *Joseph Conrad: The Way of Dispossession* (London: Faber & Faber, 1977).
48. Chinua Achebe, "An Image of Africa," *Massachusetts Review* 18, no. 4 (Winter 1977): 782–94.
49. Jeremy Hawthorn, *Joseph Conrad: Language and Fictional Self-Consciousness* (London: Edward Arnold, 1979).
50. Jacques Berthoud, *Joseph Conrad: The Major Phase* (Cambridge, U.K.: Cambridge University Press, 1978).
51. Ian Watt, *Conrad in the Nineteenth Century* (Berkeley: University of California Press, 1979).
52. Frederick R. Karl, *Joseph Conrad: The Three Lives, A Biography* (New York: Farrar, Straus, Giroux, 1979).
53. Norman Sherry, *Conrad's Western World* (Cambridge, U.K.: Cambridge University Press, 1971).
54. William W. Bonney, *Thorns & Arabesques: Contexts for Conrad's Fiction* (Baltimore: Johns Hopkins University Press, 1980).
55. Fredric Jameson, *The Political Unconscious: Narrative as a Socially Symbolic Act* (Ithaca, N.Y.: Cornell University Press, 1981), 206–80.
56. Aaron Fogel, *Coercion to Speak: Conrad's Poetics of Dialogue* (Cambridge, Mass.: Harvard University Press, 1985).
57. Jakob Lothe, *Conrad's Narrative Method* (Oxford, U.K.: Clarendon Press, 1989).
58. Benita Parry, *Conrad and Imperialism: Ideological Boundaries and Visionary Frontiers* (London: Macmillan, 1983).
59. Cedric Watts, *The Deceptive Text: An Introduction to Covert Plots* (Brighton, U.K.: Harvester Press, 1984).

60. Daniel R. Schwarz, *Conrad: The Later Fiction* (London: Macmillan, 1982).
61. Paul B. Armstrong, *The Challenge of Bewilderment: Understanding and Representation in James, Conrad, and Ford* (Ithaca, N.Y.: Cornell University Press, 1987), 1–25, 109–85.
62. Zdzislaw Najder, *Joseph Conrad: A Chronicle,* Trans. Halina Carroll-Najder (Cambridge, U.K.: Cambridge University Press, 1983).
63. Zdzislaw Najder, *Joseph Conrad: A Life,* trans. Halina Najder (Rochester, N.Y.: Camden House, 2007).
64. Cedric Watts, *Joseph Conrad: A Literary Life* (New York: St. Martin's Press, 1989).
65. Edward W. Said, *Culture and Imperialism* (New York: Knopf, 1993), 19–31.
66. Andrea White, *Joseph Conrad and the Adventure Tradition: Constructing and Deconstructing the Imperial Subject* (Cambridge, U.K.: Cambridge University Press, 1993).
67. Christopher GoGwilt, *The Invention of the West: Joseph Conrad and the Double-Mapping of Europe and Empire* (Stanford, Calif.: Stanford University Press, 1995).
68. Daphna Erdinast-Vulcan, *Joseph Conrad and the Modern Temper* (Oxford, U.K.: Clarendon Press, 1991).
69. Jeremy Hawthorn, *Joseph Conrad: Narrative Technique and Ideological Commitment* (London: Edward Arnold, 1990).
70. Ruth L. Nadelhaft, *Joseph Conrad* (Atlantic Highlands, NJ: Humanities Press, 1991).
71. Susan Jones, *Conrad and Women* (Oxford, U.K.: Clarendon Press, 1999).
72. Mark A. Wollaeger, *Joseph Conrad and the Fictions of Skepticism* (Stanford, Calif.: Stanford University Press, 1990).
73. Robert Hampson, *Joseph Conrad: Betrayal and Identity* (London: Macmillan, 1992).
74. Yves Hervouet, *The French Face of Joseph Conrad* (Cambridge, U.K.: Cambridge University Press, 1990).
75. Jeffrey Meyers, *Joseph Conrad: A Biography* (New York: Charles Scribner's Sons, 1991).
76. John Batchelor, *The Life of Joseph Conrad: A Critical Biography* (Oxford, U.K.: Blackwell, 1994).
77. Michael Greaney, *Conrad, Language, and Narrative* (Cambridge, U.K.: Cambridge University Press, 2002).
78. Stephen Ross, *Conrad and Empire* (Columbia: University of Missouri Press, 2004).
79. Robert Hampson, Cross-Cultural Encounters in Joseph Conrad's Malay Fiction (New York: Palgrave, 2000).
80. Andrew Michael Roberts, *Conrad and Masculinity* (New York: St. Martin's Press, 2000).
81. Jeremy Hawthorn, Sexuality and the Erotic in the Fiction of Joseph Conrad (London: Continuum, 2007).
82. John G. Peters, *Conrad and Impressionism* (Cambridge, U.K.: Cambridge University Press, 2001).
83. Martin Bock, *Joseph Conrad and Psychological Medicine* (Lubbock: Texas Tech University Press, 2002).
84. Stephen Donovan, *Joseph Conrad and Popular Culture* (New York: Palgrave Macmillan, 2005).
85. Richard J. Hand, *The Theatre of Joseph Conrad: Reconstructed Fictions* (New York: Palgrave Macmillan, 2005).
86. Richard Niland, *Conrad and History* (Oxford, U.K.: Oxford University Press, 2010).
87. Peter Lancelot Mallios, *Our Conrad: Constituting American Modernity* (Stanford, Calif.: Stanford University Press, 2010).
88. Jeffrey Mathes McCarthy, "'A Choice of Nightmares': The Ecology of *Heart of Darkness,*" *Modern Fiction Studies* 55, no. 3 (Fall 2009): 620–48.

89. John Stape, *The Several Lives of Joseph Conrad* (London: William Heinemann, 2007).

Notes to "'The great demoralisation of the land': Postcolonial Ecology in *Heart of Darkness*"

1. Graham Huggan and Helen Tiffin, *Postcolonial Ecocriticism: Literature, Animals, Environment* (London: Routledge, 2010), 142.
2. F. R. Leavis, *The Great Tradition* (New York: George Stewart, 1950), 176.
3. Joseph Conrad, *Heart of Darkness,* in *The Collected Works of Joseph Conrad,* ed. Owen Knowles (Cambridge, U.K.: Cambridge University Press, 2010), 55.
4. Ibid.
5. Ibid.
6. Ibid., 54.
7. Leavis, *The Great Tradition,* 176.
8. Ibid., 177.
9. Chinua Achebe, *Things Fall Apart* (New York: Anchor, 1994).
10. Chinua Achebe, "An Image of Africa: Racism in Conrad's *Heart of Darkness,*" *Massachusetts Review* 18, no. 4 (Winter 1977): 782–94.
11. Robert F. Lee, *Conrad's Colonialism* (The Hague: Mouton, 1969); Hunt Hawkins, "Conrad's Critique of Imperialism in Heart of Darkness," *PMLA* 94, no. 2 (March 1979): 286–99; Benita Parry, *Conrad and Imperialism: Ideological Boundaries and Visionary Frontiers* (London: Macmillan, 1983); Edward Said, *Culture and Imperialism* (New York: Random House, 1993); Peter Edgerly Firchow, *Envisioning Africa: Racism and Imperialism in Conrad's* Heart of Darkness (Lexington: University Press of Kentucky, 2000); Linda Dryden, *Joseph Conrad and the Imperial Romance* (New York: St. Martin's, 2000).
12. Bonnie Roos and Alex Hunt, *Postcolonial Green: Environmental Politics and World Narratives* (Charlottesville: University of Virginia Press, 2010); Huggan and Tiffin, *Postcolonial Ecocriticism;* Elizabeth DeLoughrey and George B. Handley, *Postcolonial Ecologies: Literatures of the Environment* (Oxford, U.K.: Oxford University Press, 2011).
13. Roos and Hunt, *Postcolonial Green,* 4.
14. Ibid., 3.
15. Jeffrey Myers, "The Anxiety of Confluence: Evolution, Ecology, and Imperialism in Conrad's *Heart of Darkness,*" *ISLE* 8, no. 2 (Summer 2001): 98.
16. Jeffrey Mathes McCarthy, "'A Choice of Nightmares': Ecology and *Heart of Darkness,*" *Modern Fiction Studies* 55, no. 3 (Fall 2009): 621.
17. Conrad, *Heart of Darkness,* 43.
18. Ibid., 47.
19. Ibid., 45.
20. Ibid., 51.
21. Leavis, *The Great Tradition,* 173.
22. Conrad, *Heart of Darkness,* 45.
23. Ibid., 44.
24. Ibid., 54.
25. Ibid., 50.
26. Ibid., 81.
27. Ibid., 90.
28. Ibid., 69.
29. Lovelock conveyed his integrative ecological theory via the classical personification of earth as a single living being. His titles include *The Ages of Gaia: A Biography of Our Living Earth* (New York: Norton, 1995); "The Earth is about to Catch a Morbid Fever" (*The Independent,* 16 January 2006); *The Revenge of Gaia* (London: Basic Books, 2007); and *The Vanishing Face of Gaia* (London: Basic Books, 2009).
30. Conrad, *Heart of Darkness,* 43.
31. Early theories of the water cycle can be found in ancient Greek natural philosophers, including Aristotle and Anaxagoras. French scientists Pierre Perriault and Marriotte advanced hydrological theory with studies of the River Seine in the seventeenth century.

By Conrad's time, hydrology had become a central concept in modern biology that extended into civil engineering, integrating theories of water evaporation, condensation, transpiration, and groundwater flow. See R. L. Nace, *General Evolution of the Concept of the Hydrological Cycle. Three Centuries of Scientific Hydrology* (Paris: UNESCO–World Meteorological Organization–International Association of Hydrological Sciences, 1974), 40–48.

32. Conrad, *Heart of Darkness*, 44.
33. Ibid., 44–45.
34. Ibid., 45.
35. Ibid., 45.
36. Ibid., 46.
37. Ibid., 125.
38. Ibid., 126.
39. Ibid., 47.
40. Ibid., 79.
41. Ibid., 46.
42. Robert Marzec, *An Ecological and Postcolonial Study of Literature: From Daniel Defoe to Salman Rushdie* (New York: Palgrave, 2007), 6.
43. Myers, "The Anxiety of Confluence," 98.
44. Conrad, *Heart of Darkness*, 50–51.
45. Ibid., 94.
46. Myers, "The Anxiety of Confluence," 99.
47. Conrad, *Heart of Darkness*, 68.
48. Ibid., 79.
49. Ibid., 113.
50. Ibid., 55.
51. Ibid., 57.
52. Ibid., 107.
53. Ibid.
54. Ibid., 57–58.
55. Ibid., 57.
56. Ibid.
57. Ibid., 58.
58. Ibid., 73.
59. Ibid., 59.
60. Lawrence Buell, *Writing for an Endangered World: Literature, Culture, and Environment in the U.S. and Beyond* (Cambridge, Mass.: Harvard University Press, 2001), 170.
61. Myers, "The Anxiety of Confluence," 103.
62. Ibid., 103.
63. Conrad, *Heart of Darkness*, 77.
64. Ibid., 73.
65. J. B. Dunlop invented the inflatable rubber tube for bicycle tires in 1887, and Andre Michelin used the first rubber pneumatic tires on an automobile in 1895.
66. Conrad, *Heart of Darkness*, 71.
67. Ibid., 77.
68. Ibid., 69.
69. Ibid., 48.
70. Ibid., 51.
71. Ibid., 48.
72. Ibid., 65.
73. Ibid., 60.
74. Ibid., 66.
75. Ibid., 69.
76. Ibid., 94.
77. McCarthy, "'Choice of Nightmares,'" 621.
78. Conrad, *Heart of Darkness*, 93.
79. Ibid.
80. Huggan and Tiffin, *Postcolonial Ecocriticism*, 144
81. McCarthy, "'Choice of Nightmares,'" 621.
82. Conrad, *Heart of Darkness*, 107.
83. John Peters, *A Historical Guide to Joseph Conrad* (Oxford, U.K.: Oxford University Press, 2010), 122.
84. Joseph Conrad, "Geography and Some Explorers," *Last Essays*, ed. Richard Curle (London: J. M. Dent & Sons, 1926), 16.
85. *The Collected Letters of Joseph Conrad*, ed. Frederick Karl et al. (Cambridge, U.K.: Cambridge University Press), vol. 2: 139–40.
86. Ibid., 417.

Notes to "The Elephant in the Text: Toward a Post-Humanist Reading of *Heart of Darkness*"

1. Conrad, *Heart of Darkness*, 45.
2. Conrad's manuscript was explicit as to the invisibility of the meaning's

location: "the meaning of an episode was not inside like the kernel but outside *in the unseen,* enveloping the tale" (Ian Watt, *Conrad in the Nineteenth Century* [Berkeley: University of California Press, 1979], 180).
3. Conrad, *Heart of Darkness*, 93.
4. The term "absent referent" is borrowed from Carol Adams, *The Sexual Politics of Meat: A Feminist-Vegetarian Critical Theory* (New York: Continuum, 1995), 40–46.
5. Alpers, "The Ivory Trade in Africa: An Historical Overview," in *Elephant: The Animal and Its Ivory in African Culture*, ed. Dora H. Ross (Los Angeles: Fowler Museum of Cultural History, 1992), 349.
6. Mark Elvin, *The Retreat of the Elephants: An Environmental History of China* (New Haven, Conn.: Yale University Press, 2004), 10.
7. We cannot be sure to what extent Egyptian demand was responsible, but it is known that there were no elephants left in the eastern Sahara after 2750 BCE, and they were gone from the central Sahara by 2000 BCE (Alpers, "Ivory Trade in Africa," 350).
8. John Frederick Walker, *Ivory's Ghosts: The White Gold of History and the Fate of Elephants* (New York: Atlantic Monthly P, 2009), 47–48.
9. Ibid., 64.
10. Alpers, "Ivory Trade in Africa," 354, 357.
11. Walker, *Ivory's Ghosts*, 83.
12. George Frederick Kunz, *Ivory and the Elephant in Art, in Archaeology, and in Science* (Garden City, N.Y.: Doubleday, 1916), 197.
13. Dora H. Ross, "Interleaf II: Elephant Hunters," in *Elephant*, ed. Ross, 61.
14. Ibid.
15. David A. Binkley, "The Teeth of the Nyim," in *Elephant*, ed. Ross, 278.
16. Ross, "Interleaf II," 61.
17. John A. Van Couvering, "Proboscideans, Hominids, and Prehistory," in *Elephant*, ed. Ross, 76.
18. Alpers, "Ivory Trade in Africa," 354.
19. Walker, *Ivory's Ghosts*, 95.
20. Ibid., 98.
21. Abdul Sheriff, *Slaves, Spices, and Ivory in Zanzibar* (London: James Currey, 1987), 87.
22. Walker, *Ivory's Ghosts*, 94.
23. Ibid., 87.
24. Kunz, *Ivory and the Elephant*, 419.
25. Walker, *Ivory's Ghosts*, 118.
26. Sheriff, *Slaves, Spices, and Ivory*, 171.
27. Ibid., 181.
28. Alpers, "Ivory Trade in Africa," 357; Martin Meredith, *Elephant Destiny: Biography of an Endangered Species in Africa* (New York: Public Affairs, 2003), 72.
29. Sheriff, *Slaves, Spices, and Ivory*, 189.
30. Ibid., 190.
31. Ibid.
32. Walker, *Ivory's Ghosts*, 138.
33. Joseph Conrad, *The Collected Letters of Joseph Conrad*, ed. Frederick Karl et al. (Cambridge, U.K.: Cambridge University Press, 1986–2008), vol. 2: 139–40.
34. Robert Friedel, *Pioneer Plastic: The Making and Selling of Celluloid* (Madison: University of Wisconsin Press, 1983), 30.
35. Ibid., 31.
36. Ibid., 13.
37. Walker, *Ivory's Ghosts*, 132.
38. The reprieve was temporary. The Convention on International Trade in Endangered Species of Wild Fauna and Flora (CITES) banned the international trade in ivory in 1989, but poaching and illicit trading have continued. Bryan Christy, in a *National Geographic* article from October 2012, "Ivory Worship," cites Kenneth Burnham, an official statistician for CITES, who estimates that at least 25,000 African elephants were killed in 2011—possibly twice as many (54). The same article reports that the total population of African elephants is thought to be between 470,000 and 690,000, down from 1.3 million in 1979 (44). Most of the ivory goes to Asia,

China and Hong Kong taking the largest share (45).

39. Conrad, *Heart of Darkness*, 65.
40. Ibid., 60.
41. Ibid., 74.
42. Ibid., 92.
43. Ibid., 87.
44. Ibid., 102.
45. Ibid., 107.
46. Ibid., 93, 108.
47. Ibid., 93.
48. Graham Huggan and Helen Tiffin. *Postcolonial Ecocriticism: Literature, Animals, Environment* (London: Routledge, 2010), cite Herbert Ward's *A Voice from the Congo* (1910), a white hunter's account of his experiences shooting elephants. Apparently Ward's African helpers—"ill-favored savages" and "cannibals" in his words (145)—take away the tusks "to be buried in a swampy region near the Bangala village in case they are needed to redeem villagers captured by Arab slave traders or neighbouring hostile groups" (146).
49. Jeffrey Myers ("The Anxiety of Confluence: Evolution, Ecology, and Imperialism in Conrad's *Heart of Darkness*," *ISLE* 8, no. 2 [Summer 2001]: 102) implies that, by the time of the narrative, there are very few elephants left, that Kurtz has taken to decorating his house with human heads because he has "decimated the Congo Basin's entire elephant population." Jeffrey Mathes McCarthy ("'A Choice of Nightmares': Ecology and *Heart of Darkness*," *Modern Fiction Studies* 55, no. 3 [Fall 2009]: 611) goes further and declares the animals to be "extinct."
50. Kunz, *Ivory and the Elephant*, 205.
51. Ibid., 208.
52. In 1882, P. T. Barnum purchased Jumbo, an African bull elephant, from the London Zoo. So popular had the creature become that questions were asked in the House of Commons and the *Daily Telegraph* campaigned to cancel the sale. A huge crowd saw Jumbo off from the London docks (Meredith, *Elephant Destiny*, 114–16).
53. Myers, "Anxiety of Confluence," 103.
54. McCarthy, "'Choice of Nightmares,'" 621.
55. Huggan and Tiffin, *Postcolonial Ecocriticism*, also remark on the elephant as an absent referent (144, 148), but they have little more to say about Conrad's text *per se*.
56. Chinua Achebe, "An Image of Africa: Racism in Conrad's *Heart of Darkness*," in *Joseph Conrad: Heart of Darkness*, ed. Paul B. Armstrong (New York: Norton, 2006), 343.
57. Ibid., 342.
58. Ibid., 343.
59. Ibid., 343–44.
60. Ibid., 346.
61. Conrad, *Heart of Darkness*, 105.
62. Ibid., 55.
63. Ibid., 57.
64. Ibid., 58.
65. Ibid., 84, 85.
66. Giorgio Agamben, Homo Sacer: Sovereign Power and Bare Life, trans. Heller-Roazen (Stanford, Calif.: Stanford University Press, 1998), 8. Of *zoë* and *bios*, Agamben writes that the Greeks used two different terms to express what we mean by "life": "*zoë*, which expressed the simple fact of living common to all living beings (animals, men, or gods) and *bios*, which indicated the form or way of living proper to an individual or a group" (1). *Bios* was used for "a qualified life, a particular way of life," distinct from simple, natural life, *zoë*, which Agamben translates as "la vita nuda"—"bare life" in Heller-Roazen's translation. I use "bare life" in preference to *zoë* because, as Agamben writes, "In the classical world, [. . .] simple natural life [*zoë*] is excluded from the *polis* [the city, the world of politics, of "qualified" life] in the

strict sense, and remains confined—as merely reproductive life—to the sphere of *oikos,* 'home'" (2). This suggests a level of domestication for *zoë* which is far from Conrad's idea of the forest. My principal debt to Agamben is in his insight that excluding something entails a preliminary inclusion. Conrad's text never fully includes "bare life" and thereby avoids excluding it.

67. Perhaps, the "cannibals" know more than Marlow gives them credit for. Their restraint might be a result of their understanding that they are indeed functioning in a state of *bios,* of political existence, rather than in bare life, that the world of the steamboat is not entirely dissimilar from the political world they come from.
68. Conrad, *Heart of Darkness,* 68.
69. Ibid., 69.
70. Achebe, "An Image of Africa," 338.
71. Conrad, *Heart of Darkness,* 77.
72. Jacques Derrida points out that the Western philosophical tradition makes of the animal "something seen and not seeing" (*The Animal That Therefore I Am,* ed. Marie-Louise Mallet, trans. David Wills [New York: Fordham University Press, 2008], 14). There is no space in the discourse for an animal to look back at the human observer. Derrida will not permit himself to project his own words onto the animal, but like Marlow, he will not allow that other "violence or *asinanity* [*bêtise*], that which would consist in suspending one's compassion and in depriving the animal of every power of manifestation, of the desire to manifest *to me* anything at all" (18).
73. Ludwig Wittgenstein, *Philosophical Investigations,* trans. G. E. M. Anscombe (Oxford, U.K.: Blackwell, 1978), 223.
74. Conrad, *Heart of Darkness,* 90.
75. Ibid., 105.
76. Ibid., 113.
77. Ibid., 112.
78. Ibid., 70.
79. Ibid., 97.
80. McCarthy sees the Congo as in the midst of an ecological disaster ("'Choice of Nightmares,'" 621). I would argue that Conrad represents the natural environment, absent elephants notwithstanding, as largely unaffected by European activity.
81. Walker observes that the Greek *elephas* originally meant simply ivory. The word was expanded to include the animal only after the Greeks encountered elephants as a result of Alexander's conquests (*Ivory's Ghosts,* 36).
82. Quoted in Kunz, *Ivory and the Elephant,* 207.
83. Conrad, *Heart of Darkness,* 58.
84. Ibid., 59.
85. McCarthy, "'Choice of Nightmares,'" 643.

Notes to "Conrad and Coppola: Rendering Empire Visible"

1. Stephen Ross, *Conrad and Empire* (Columbia: University of Missouri Press, 2004), 4.
2. Ibid., 5.
3. Ibid., 4. Achebe sees *Heart of Darkness* as an influential example of Europe's need to set Africa up as its foil, as the site of negation against which Europe can "manifest" its own "spiritual grace" (Achebe 2). Through his sharp analysis, Achebe famously decries Conrad as "a bloody racist" (2).
4. Ibid., 5–6.
5. Ibid., 14.
6. Michael John DiSanto, *Under Conrad's Eyes: The Novel as Criticism* (Montreal: McGill-Queen's University Press, 2009), 16.
7. Evelyn Cobley, *Modernism and the Culture of Efficiency* (Toronto: University of Toronto Press, 2009), 9.
8. Michael Hardt and Antonio Negri, *Empire* (Cambridge, Mass.: Harvard University Press, 2000), xii.

9. Ibid., xii.
10. Ibid., xiii.
11. Ibid., xiv.
12. Ibid., xiv.
13. Ibid., xiv.
14. Conrad, *Heart of Darkness*, 45.
15. Ross, *Conrad and Empire*, 31.
16. Conrad, *Heart of Darkness*, 48.
17. Ibid., 126.
18. Ibid., 45–46.
19. Ibid., 46.
20. Adam Hochschild, *King Leopold's Ghost: A Story of Greed, Terror, and Heroism in Colonial Africa* (Boston: Houghton Mifflin, 1998), 144.
21. Conrad, *Heart of Darkness*, 46.
22. Ibid., 47.
23. Ibid.
24. Ibid.
25. Hochschild, *King Leopold's Ghost*, 146.
26. Conrad, *Heart of Darkness*, 47.
27. Linda Costanzo Cahir, "Narratological Parallels in Joseph Conrad's *Heart of Darkness* and Francis Ford Coppola's *Apocalypse Now*," in *Joseph Conrad's Heart of Darkness: A Casebook*, ed. Gene M. Moore (Oxford, U.K.: Oxford University Press, 2004), 182.
28. Louis K. Greiff, "Soldier, Sailor, Surfer, Chef: Conrad's Ethics and the Margins of 'Apocalypse Now,'" *Literature Film Quarterly* 20, no. 3 (July 1992): 197.
29. Margot Norris, "Modernism and Vietnam: Francis Ford Coppola'a *Apocalypse Now*," *Modern Fiction Studies* 44, no. 33 (1998): 741.
30. Keith Soloman, "The Spectacle of War and the Specter of 'The Horror': *Apocalypse Now* and American Imperialism," *Journal of Popular Film and Television* 35, no. 1 (2007): 26.
31. Pamela Demory, "*Apocalypse Now Redux: Heart of Darkness* Moves into New Territory," *Literature Film Quarterly* 35, no. 1 (January 2007): 349.
32. Ross, *Conrad and Empire*, 14.
33. *Apocalypse Now*, produced and directed by Francis Coppola (Paramount Pictures, 1979; DVD, 1999), chapter 2.
34. Ibid., chapter 2.
35. Ibid., chapter 2.
36. Ibid., chapter 10.
37. Ibid., chapter 10.
38. Ibid., chapter 12.
39. Ibid., chapter 12
40. Ibid., chapter 12.
41. Soloman, "The Spectacle of War," 29.
42. *Apocalypse Now*, chapter 16.
43. Ibid., chapter 26.
44. Hardt and Negri, *Empire*, xv.

Notes to "Reinventing the Congo through Western Eyes"

1. Michael Lackey, "The Moral Conditions for Genocide in Joseph Conrad's *Heart of Darkness*," *College Literature* 32, no. 1 (2005): 21.
2. Joseph Conrad, *Heart of Darkness and Other Tales*, ed. Cedric Watts (Oxford, U.K.: Oxford University Press, 1990), 5.
3. Michaela Wrong, *In the Footsteps of Mr Kurtz* (London: Fourth Estate/Collins Publishers, 2000), 3.
4. Ibid.
5. Ibid.
6. Ibid., 7.
7. Ibid., 8.
8. Ibid., 9–10.
9. Ibid., 10.
10. From Henry Morton Stanley, *Through the Dark Continent* (1878), qtd. in Wrong, *In the Footsteps of Mr Kurtz*, 213.
11. Jean-Francois Bayart, *The State in Africa: The Politics of the Belly* (London: Longman, 1993), 3.
12. Wrong, *In the Footsteps of Mr Kurtz*, 9.
13. Ibid., 213.
14. Kathryn Marie Smith, "Revis(it)ing Joseph Conrad's 'Heart of Darkness': Women, Symbolism, and Resistance," MA thesis, Faculty of Arts and Letters, Atlantic University, Boca Raton, Fla., 2009, 2.
15. Victoria Moffatt, "Othering Through Gendering Discourses and Patriarchal Hegemonies in Joseph Conrad's *Heart of Darkness* and Barbara Kingsolver's

The Poisonwood Bible," *Legon Journal of the Humanities* 21 (2010): 174.

16. Felicity Nussbaum, "One Part of Womankind: Prostitution and Sexual Geography in Memoirs of a Woman of Pleasure," *Differences: A Journal of Feminist Cultural Studies* 7, no. 2 (1995): 19.
17. Chinua Achebe, "An Image of Africa: Racism in Conrad's *Heart of Darkness*," in *Heart of Darkness*, Norton Critical Edition, ed. Paul B. Armstrong (New York: W. W. Norton & Co., 2006), 343–44.
18. Michael Walonen, "Power, Patriarchy and Postcolonialism in the African Dictator Novel," *ALA Bulletin* 16, no. 1 (Summer–Fall 2011): 105.
19. Ngũgĩ wa Thiong'o, *Moving the Centre: The Struggle for Cultural Freedoms* (London: Heinemann, 1993), 4.
20. Wrong, *In the Footsteps of Mr Kurtz*, 196.
21. Walonen, "Power, Patriarchy and Postcolonialism," 104.
22. Wrong, *In the Footsteps of Mr Kurtz*, 196.
23. Conrad, *Heart of Darkness*, 151–52.
24. Wrong, *In the Footsteps of Mr Kurtz*, 196.
25. Ibid.
26. Ibid., 147.
27. Ibid.
28. Conrad, *Heart of Darkness*, 140–41.
29. Ibid., xxii.
30. Wrong, *In the Footsteps of Mr Kurtz*, 9.
31. Ibid., 11, emphasis added.

Notes to "The Imitable Joseph Conrad"

1. *The Collected Letters of Joseph Conrad*, ed. Frederick Karl et al. (Cambridge, U.K.: Cambridge University Press, 1986–2008), vol. 3: 459–60.
2. See Allan H. Simmons's introduction to the first volume of *Joseph Conrad: Contemporary Reviews*, ed. Simmons (Cambridge, U.K.: Cambridge University Press, 2012), vol. 1: 1–8. All the newspaper and periodical reviews referred to in this chapter are quoted from this volume.
3. *Collected Letters of Joseph Conrad* 3: 381 and 4: 101. By 1906, Conrad had published *Almayer's Folly, An Outcast of the Islands, The Nigger of the "Narcissus," Lord Jim*, and *Nostromo*.
4. See *The Glasgow Herald*, 25 April 1895, 9; *The Publishers' Circular*, 4 May 1895, 474; *The Academy*, 15 June 1895, 502; and *The Illustrated London News*, 25 July 1895, 98, as examples. Many more reviews invoked the same language in their recognition of Conrad's choice of the Malay as the site of his novel. However, the reviewer for *The Literary World* in Boston is one of the few to regard this decision as a gimmick: "Borneo is a new field for literature, but probably there will soon be no spot on the world's surface which the enterprising fiction-monger has not utilized in his search for novelties of local color" (18 May 1895, 155).
5. See *The Spectator*, 19 October 1895, 530, and *The Athenaeum*, 25 May 1895, 671.
6. Joseph Conrad, *Almayer's Folly* (Oxford, U.K.: Oxford University Press, 1992), 3.
7. Ibid., 3.
8. Ibid.
9. Robert Hampson, *Cross-Cultural Encounters in Joseph Conrad's Malay Fiction* (New York: Palgrave, 2000), 113.
10. *The Literary World*, 31 May 1895, 505.
11. *The National Observer*, 14 September 1895, 513–14.
12. *The San Francisco Call*, 23 June 1895, 21.
13. Jacques Berthoud, "Introduction," *Almayer's Folly*, by Conrad, xxx–xxxi.
14. Linda Dryden, *Joseph Conrad and the Imperial Romance* (New York: St. Martin's, 2000), 53.
15. See Dryden's *Joseph Conrad and the Imperial Romance* and Andrea White's *Joseph Conrad and the Adventure Tradition* (Cambridge, U.K.: Cambridge UP, 1993).
16. *The Guardian*, 3 July 1895, 1001.

17. *The Publishers' Circular,* 4 May 1895, 474.
18. See *The Speaker,* 29 June 1895, 722–23; *The Bookman,* September 1895, 176; *The Realm,* 10 May 1895, 966; and *The National Observer,* 14 September 1895, 513–14, respectively.
19. *The Sketch,* 4 September 1895, 314.
20. Virginia Woolf, "Joseph Conrad," *The Common Reader I,* ed. Andrew McNeillie (London: Hogarth Press, 1984), 229.
21. Ibid.
22. See "Notes" in *An Outcast of the Islands,* ed. J. H. Stape (New York: Oxford University Press, 2002). See also Conrad's letter to his aunt Marguerite Poradowska. Conrad describes his continuation of the Malay theme as unavoidable: "You see how Malays cling to me! I am devoted to Borneo" (*Collected Letters of Joseph Conrad* 1: 171).
23. *The Academy,* 27 June 1896, 525.
24. *The Saturday Review,* 16 May 1896, 509–10.
25. Max Beerbohm, *A Christmas Garland* (New York: E. P. Dutton & Co., 1918), 126.
26. Gérard Genette, *Palimpsests: Literature in the Second Degree,* trans. Channa Newman and Claude Doubinsky (Lincoln: University of Nebraska Press, 1997), 75.
27. Ibid., 75.
28. Ibid., 75.
29. Ibid., 83.
30. Virginia Woolf, *The Voyage Out,* ed. Lorna Sage (New York: Oxford University Press, 2001), 309.
31. Ibid., 309–10.
32. Conrad, *Heart of Darkness* (Cambridge: Cambridge University Press, 2010), 48.
33. Parry, *Postcolonialism,* 136.
34. Genette, *Palimpsests,* 76.
35. Ibid., 76.
36. F. R. Leavis, *The Great Tradition: George Eliot, Henry James, Joseph Conrad* (New York: George W. Stewart, 1950). See also John Dozier Gordan, *Joseph Conrad: The Making of a Novelist* (Cambridge, Mass.: Harvard University Press, 1940), and Morton D. Zabel, *Craft and Character: Text, Method and Vocation in Modern Literature* (New York: Viking Press, 1958).
37. Genette, *Palimpsests,* 76.
38. Padmini Mongia, "Between Men: Conrad in the Fiction of Two Contemporary Indian Writers," in *Conrad in the Twenty-first Century: Contemporary Approaches and Perspectives,* ed. Carola M. Kaplan, Peter Mallios, and Andrea White (New York, Routledge, 2005), 87.
39. Genette, *Palimpsests,* 82.
40. See Peter Nazereth, "Conrad's Descendants," *Conradiana* 2 (1990): 101–9.
41. Richard Ford, *Canada* (New York: HarperCollins, 2012), 577.
42. Conrad, *Heart of Darkness,* 113.
43. Ford, *Canada,* 581.
44. Conrad, *Heart of Darkness,* 104.
45. Ford, *Canada,* 555.
46. Ibid., 577.
47. Ibid., 593.
48. Benita Parry, "The Moment and After-Life of *Heart of Darkness,*" in *Conrad in the Twenty-first Century,* ed. Kaplan, Mallios, and White, 40–41.
49. Ibid., 50.
50. Ibid., 40–41.

Notes to "Maternal Return: *Lord Jim*'s Spectral Narrative"

1. Homi Bhabha, *The Location of Culture* (London: Routledge, 1994), 9.
2. Sigmund Freud, "The Uncanny," in *The Standard Edition of the Complete Psychological Works of Sigmund Freud,* ed. James Strachey (London: Hogarth Press, 1955), vol. 17: 241.
3. Bhabha, *The Location of Culture,* 10.
4. Ibid., 11.
5. Ibid., 9.
6. Joseph Conrad, *Lord Jim,* ed. J. H. Stape and Ernest W. Sullivan II (Cambridge, U.K.: Cambridge University Press, 2012), 208.

7. Gayatri Spivak, 1995, 28.
8. Conrad, *Lord Jim,* 208.
9. Ibid.
10. Ibid.
11. Conrad, *Lord Jim,* 229.
12. Ibid.
13. Ibid., 209.
14. Ibid. (emphasis mine).
15. Ibid., 287.
16. Ibid., 262.
17. Ibid., 265.
18. Ibid., 263.
19. Ibid., 264.
20. Ibid., 208–9.
21. Ibid., 208.
22. Ibid.
23. Ibid., 218.
24. Ibid., 219.
25. Ibid., 223–25.
26. Ibid., 212–13.
27. Ibid., 232.
28. Ibid., 313.
29. Ibid., 236.

Notes to "The Other Side of the Page in *Typhoon*"

1. Joseph Conrad, *Typhoon*, in *The Nigger of the "Narcissus" and Typhoon & Other Stories* (London: Dent, 1950), 6.
2. Jeremy Hawthorn considers *Typhoon's* relationship to the epistolary novel tradition in his *Joseph Conrad: Narrative Technique and Ideological Commitment* (London: Arnold, 1990), 223–33.
3. Conrad, *Typhoon* 16.
4. Ibid., 16.
5. See Conrad's "Author's Note" to *Typhoon,* vi.
6. Conrad, *Typhoon,* 93, 14.
7. Ibid., 93.
8. Ibid., 94.
9. Ibid., 94, 14. Contributing to the circular motifs in *Typhoon*, one of MacWhirr's earliest letters to his parents, quoted in the opening pages, introduces the Christmas date found in his latest letter: "On Christmas day at 4 P.M. we fell in with some icebergs" (5). The captain's log-book factuality in both letters is consistent both with his generally "undemonstrative" nature (8) and with the "distinctly weak" spirit of the holiday on shipboard that Conrad describes in "Christmas Day at Sea" (in *Last Essays*, in *Tales of Hearsay and Last Essays* [London: Dent, 1955], 29). My own early article "*Typhoon*: Conrad's Christmas Story" (*Cithara* 14, no. 2 [March 1975]: 19–35) was the first critical study to find significance in the date of the action. For subsequent discussions of the Christmas setting, see William W. Bonney, *Thorns & Arabesques: Contexts for Conrad's Fiction* (Baltimore: Johns Hopkins University Press, 1980), 44–48; Keith Carabine, "Introduction," *Three Sea Stories: "Typhoon," "Falk" and The Shadow-Line* (London: Wordsworth, 1998), xvi–xvii; and Stephen Donovan, *Joseph Conrad and Popular Culture* (New York: Palgrave Macmillan, 2005), 179–80.
10. Conrad, *Typhoon,* 4.
11. Conrad, *Typhoon,* vi, vii; Frederick R. Karl and Laurence Davies, "Introduction to Volume Two," *The Collected Letters of Joseph Conrad,* vol. 2: *1898–1902* (Cambridge, U.K.: Cambridge University Press, 1986), xxiv.
12. Conrad, *Typhoon,* 94.
13. Although *Typhoon* has remained one of Conrad's most popular stories, until discerning readings and reassessments of the book began to appear in the 1980s, the standard view among critics seems to have been that the novella was among his least interesting creations, one of his "simplest" tales (Jocelyn Baines, *Joseph Conrad* [London: Weidenfeld and Nicholson, 1960], 257), a work that "requires no elaborate interpreting" (Albert J. Guerard, *Conrad the Novelist* [Cambridge, Mass.: Harvard University Press, 1958], 294), or just boring: "as dull as its hero" (Frederick R. Karl, *A Reader's Guide to*

Joseph Conrad, rev. ed. [New York: Farrar, Straus, and Giroux, 1969], 144). Ian Watt (*Conrad in the Nineteenth Century* [Berkeley: University of California Press, 1979], 357) and T. A. Birrell, among more recent critics, see *Typhoon* as "mark[ing] a new phase in Conrad's development" ("The Simplicity of *Typhoon*: Conrad, Flaubert and Others," *Dutch Quarterly Review* 10, no. 4 [1980]: 294).

14. Conrad, "Author's Note" to *Typhoon*, vi–vii.
15. Ibid., vii.
16. Captain MacWhirr seems to have inspired a remarkable variety of both positive and negative views among recent critics, ranging from commendation as "an admirable hero" (Leo Gurko, *Joseph Conrad: Giant in Exile* [New York: Macmillan, 1962], 86) or a "celebration [. . .] of ordinariness" (Carolyn Brown, "Creative Combat in 'Typhoon,'" *The Conradian* 17, no. 1 (Autumn 1992): 13), to outright condemnation as an "imperceptive clod" and "psychic cripple" (Bonney, *Thorns & Arabesques*, 35, 37).
17. In *The Nigger of the "Narcissus" and Typhoon & Other Stories* [London: Dent, 1950], x; emphasis in the original. Conrad began composing *Typhoon* shortly before 13 September 1900 and completed the tale late the evening of 10–11 January 1901; see *The Collected Letters of Joseph Conrad*, vol. 2: *1898–1902*, ed. Frederick R. Karl and Laurence Davies (Cambridge, U.K.: Cambridge University Press, 1986, 293–94 and 318 n1.
18. Conrad, *Typhoon*, 10, 17–18, 25.
19. Ibid., 20, 32–33.
20. Ibid., 33, 34.
21. Ibid., 102.
22. Ibid., 26; emphases mine. Carolyn Brown similarly notes the "burgeoning 'as if's'" of the narrative (6) and contends that the voice of the narrative is not so much a narrator's as that of Conrad himself, the "creator" of "a storm of words" in direct "opposition" to MacWhirr (7). Also see Hawthorn, *Joseph Conrad*, 233–34.
23. Conrad, *Typhoon*, 18, 102.
24. Ibid., 16, 96.
25. The dates in the parentheses provide the date(s) of composition, followed by date(s) of first British periodical publication. *The Nigger of the "Narcissus"* was first published in book form in 1897, *Youth* and *Heart of Darkness*, together with *The End of the Tether*, in 1902, *Lord Jim* in 1900, and *Typhoon* together with four other stories in 1903.
26. *Collected Letters of Joseph Conrad* 2: 254, 205; emphases in original.
27. Conrad, *Typhoon* 99. One of Conrad's rejected early titles for *Typhoon* was "*Skittish Cargo*" (*Collected Letters of Joseph Conrad* 2: 237).
28. Conrad, *Typhoon*, 7–9.
29. Ibid., 8, 6, 88.
30. Ibid., 23–24, 25.
31. Ibid., 54, 59.
32. Ibid., 51–59, 58, 59.
33. Ibid., 53.
34. Ibid., 60.
35. Ibid., 60.
36. Joseph Conrad, *Lord Jim: A Tale* (London: Dent, 1946), 89.
37. See Rice, "*Typhoon*," 27–32.
38. Conrad, *Typhoon*, 42.
39. Ibid., 89.
40. Ibid., 85, 90.
41. Ibid., 4.
42. *Collected Letters of Joseph Conrad* 2: 146, 274, 67, 166, and 271.
43. Ibid., 281.
44. Conrad, *Lord Jim*, vii.
45. Ruth Franklin, "Imp of the Perverse," *New Yorker*, 30 July 2012, 77.
46. Conrad, *Typhoon*, 19, 94.
47. See Rice, "*Typhoon*," 19–35.
48. Conrad, *Typhoon*, 94.
49. Ibid., 85.

50. Ibid., 6, 85.
51. Ibid., emphasis mine.
52. Ibid., 9, 86.
53. Ibid., 87; emphasis mine.
54. *Collected Letters of Joseph Conrad* 2: 295. Pinker ultimately succeeded in placing *Typhoon* in the middle-brow *Pall Mall Magazine*, although it did not in fact appear until the end of the following year's Christmas season, from January to March 1902. For discussion of Conrad's move to the popular-magazine audience, see Donovan, *Joseph Conrad and Popular Culture*, 175–82, and Linda Dryden, "'The Times Indeed Are Changed': Conrad, 'Typhoon,' and *Pall Mall Magazine*," *Conradiana* 41, no. 2–3 (Fall–Winter 2009): 133–43.
55. *Collected Letters of Joseph Conrad* 2: 304.
56. Charles Dickens, *A Christmas Carol*, in *Christmas Books* (London: Oxford University Press, 1954), 76.
57. Conrad, *Typhoon*, 89–90.
58. *Collected Letters of Joseph Conrad* 2: 140.
59. Since Conrad expressed his increasing dismay at the deteriorating situation of the British military in South Africa in his letters while he was writing *Typhoon* in the fall of 1900, particularly in his correspondence with R. B. Cunninghame Graham, it is tempting to suggest that he was seeing the crisis on the *Nan-Shan* through the lenses of both the Boxer uprising and the Boer War, which "Graham regarded as a struggle between two burglars" (*Collected Letters* 2: 206 n4). In this light, it is significant that Conrad dedicated the book publication of *Typhoon and Other Stories* to Graham.
60. See Donovan, *Joseph Conrad and Popular Culture*, 8.
61. "Equitable Division" was another of Conrad's rejected early titles for *Typhoon* (*Collected Letters of Joseph Conrad* 2: 169).
62. See Diana Preston, *The Boxer Rebellion: The Dramatic Story of China's War on Foreigners that Shook the World in the Summer of 1900* (New York: Walker, 2000).
63. Robert C. K. Ensor, *England, 1870–1914* (Oxford, U.K.: Clarendon, 1936), 315.
64. Ibid., 315.
65. Conrad, *Typhoon* 97.
66. James L. Hevia, "Looting and Its Discontents: Moral Discourse and the Plunder of Beijing, 1900–1901," in *The Boxers, China, and the World*, ed. Robert Bickers and R. G. Tiedemann (Lanham, U.K.: Rowman and Littlefield, 2007), 94.
67. Ibid., 102; Conrad, *Typhoon*, 77.
68. Rebecca West, *1900* (New York: Viking, 1982), 82.
69. Preston, *The Boxer Rebellion*, 284.
70. Conrad, *Typhoon* 31.
71. Ibid., 13.
72. Ibid., 31.
73. Ibid., 33.
74. Ibid., 101.
75. Ibid., 100.
76. Ibid., 98, 96, 99.
77. Ibid., 101.
78. *Collected Letters of Joseph Conrad* 2: 137.
79. Conrad, *Typhoon*, 3, 19.

Notes to "Ideas Have Consequences: Women in the Compromised World of *Nostromo*"

1. Joseph Conrad, *Nostromo*, ed. Ruth L. Nadelhaft *Nostromo* (Ontario: Broadview, 1997), 353, 352.
2. Ortner, Sherry B. "Is female to male as nature is to culture?" *Women, Culture, and Society*. Edited by M. Z. Rosaldo and L. Lamphere (Stanford: Stanford University Press, 1974), 68–87.
3. Conrad, *Nostromo*, 355–56.
4. Ibid., 77–78.
5. Ibid., 190.
6. Ibid., 187.
7. Ibid., 190.
8. Ibid., 41.

Notes to "History in Ruins: Reading Joseph Conrad's *Nostromo*"

1. Theodor Adorno, *Minima Moralia: Reflections on a Damaged Life,* trans. E. F. N. Jephcott (New York: Verso, 1978), 247. Joseph Conrad is known to have avoided political commitment in either direction, whether on behalf of socialism or capitalism. Nor did he sympathize with revolutions and their aftermaths: "A violent revolution falls into the hands of narrow-minded fanatics and of tyrannical hypocrites at first," Conrad wrote in *Under Western Eyes.* And yet, despite his writing, in the same novel, that "[h]opes grotesquely betrayed, ideals caricatured—that is the definition of revolutionary success," Conrad maintained a Romantic interest in revolutions. The import of such revolutions could be messianic, if the world could be slightly rearranged (as Walter Benjamin puts it), so that a non-violent revolution would result in something other than moral anarchy and renewed tyranny.
2. Irving Howe, *Politics and the Novel* (New York: American New Library, 1987), 76.
3. Ibid., 80.
4. Ibid., 81.
5. Ibid., 82.
6. Ibid., 84.
7. Paul Armstrong, *The Challenge of Bewilderment* (Ithaca, N.Y.: Cornell University Press, 1987), 172.
8. Louise Knapp Hay, *The Political Novels of Joseph Conrad* (Chicago: University of Chicago Press, 1963), 179.
9. Ibid., 214.
10. Terry Collits, "Conrad in the Time of Globalization: A Latin American *Nostromo*?" *Yearbook of Conrad Studies* (Kraków: Jagiellonian University), vol. 3 (2007): 171.
11. Ibid.
12. Avrom Fleishman, *Conrad's Politics: Community and Anarchy in the Fiction of Joseph Conrad* (Baltimore: Johns Hopkins University Press, 1967), 161.
13. Conrad, *Nostromo*, 88.
14. Fleishman, *Conrad's Politics,* 175.
15. Ibid.
16. Ibid.
17. Ibid.
18. Conrad, *Nostromo*, 84.
19. Fleishman, *Conrad's Politics,* 181.
20. Conrad, *Nostromo*, 511.
21. Armstrong, *The Challenge of Bewilderment,* 152.
22. Ibid.
23. Lee Whitehead, "The Tragic 'Idea,'" *Nineteenth-Century Fiction* 23, no. 4 (1969): 464.
24. Armstrong, *The Challenge of Bewilderment,* 170.
25. Ibid., 171.
26. Ibid., 175.
27. Ibid., 183.
28. Ibid., 160.
29. Conrad, *Nostromo,* 511.
30. Ibid., 521.
31. Sarah Cole, *At the Violet Hour: Modernism and Violence in England and Ireland* (Oxford, U.K.: Oxford University Press, 2012), 125.
32. Ibid., 126.
33. Conrad, *Nostromo*, 511.
34. Benita Parry, *Conrad and Imperialism: Ideological Boundaries and Visionary Frontiers* (London: Macmillan Press, 1983), 112.
35. Ursula Lord, *Solitude versus Solidarity in the Novels of Joseph Conrad* (Montreal: McGill Queen's University Press, 1998), 208.
36. Conrad, *Nostromo*, 360.
37. Ibid., 365.
38. Ibid.
39. Ibid., 511.
40. Ibid., 460.
41. Ibid., 84.
42. Ibid., 365.

43. Ibid., 84.
44. Ibid., 365.
45. Ibid.
46. Ibid.
47. Ibid., 366.
48. Ibid., 366.
49. Suresh Raval, *The Art of Failure: Conrad's Fiction* (Boston: Allen & Unwin, 1986), 92.
50. Lord, *Solitude versus Solidarity,* 286.
51. Conrad, *Nostromo,* 431.
52. Christine Buci-Glucksman, "The Utopia of the Feminine. Benjamin's Trajectory," in *Walter Benjamin: Critical Evaluations in Cultural Theory,* ed. Peter Osborne (London: Routledge, 2005), 249.
53. Ibid., 250.
54. Conrad, *Nostromo,* 566.
55. Fredric Jameson, *The Political Unconscious: Narrative as a Socially Symbolic Act* (Ithaca, N.Y.: Cornell University Press, 1981), 264.
56. Conrad, *Nostromo,* 309.
57. Ibid., 85.
58. Ibid., 85.
59. Ibid., 85.
60. Ibid., 402–3.
61. Conrad, *Nostromo,* 74.
62. Ibid., 74.
63. Ibid., 73.
64. Jameson, *The Political Unconscious,* 268.
65. Ibid., 269.
66. Conrad, *Nostromo,* 521–22.
67. Ibid., 511.
68. Ibid., 418.
69. Ibid., 413.
70. Parry, *Conrad and Imperialism,* 109.
71. Jameson, *The Political Unconscious,* 254.
72. Cesare Casarino, *Modernity at Sea: Melville, Marx, Conrad in Crisis* (Minneapolis: University of Minnesota Press, 2002), 179.
73. Derek S. Reveron and Jeffrey Stevenson Murer, *Flashpoints in the War on Terrorism* (New York: Routledge, 2006), 310.
74. Arnold E. Davidson, *Conrad's Endings* (Ann Arbor, Mich.: UMI Research Press, 1984), 52.
75. Lord, *Solitude versus Solidarity,* 279.
76. Ibid.
77. Anson Rabinbach, *In the Shadow of Catastrophe: German Intellectuals Between Apocalypse and Enlightenment* (Berkeley: University of California Press, 1997), 61.
78. Ibid., 147.

Notes to "A Simple Tale? The Writing and Rewriting of *The Secret Agent*"

1. Book history evolved from the study of "the physical materiality of books" to "incorporate work on the social and cultural conditions governing the production, dissemination and reception of printed texts" (David Finkelstein, and Alistair McCleery, eds., *The Book History Reader,* 2nd ed. [London: Routledge, 2006], 7).
2. Joseph Conrad, *The Secret Agent: A Simple Tale,* ed. Bruce Harkness and S.W. Reid (Cambridge, U.K.: Cambridge University Press, 1990), 5.
3. Mary Burgoyne, "Conrad among the Anarchists: Documents on Martial Bourdin and the Greenwich Bombing," *The Conradian* (Amsterdam: Rodopi), 2007: 165.
4. "Anarchism in London," *The Graphic,* 24 February 1894; David Mulry, "Popular Accounts of the Greenwich Bombing and Conrad's *The Secret Agent,*" *Rocky Mountain Review,* Fall 2000: 45.
5. Burgoyne, "Conrad among the Anarchists," 182. For more on Samuels as a possible model for Verloc, see Norman Sherry, *Conrad's Western World* (Cambridge, U.K.: Cambridge University Press, 1971), 314–19, and Michael Newton, "Four Notes on The Secret Agent: Sir William Harcourt, Ford and Helen Rossetti, Bourdin's Relations, and a Warning Against Δ," *The Conradian* 32, no. 1 (Spring 2007): 136–41.
6. Burgoyne, "Conrad among the Anarchists," 148.

7. *The Collected Letters of Joseph Conrad*, ed. Frederick Karl et al. (Cambridge, U.K.: Cambridge University Press, 1986–2008), vol. 8: 165.
8. Zdzislaw Najder, *Joseph Conrad: A Chronicle*, trans. Halina Carroll-Najder (Cambridge, U.K.: Cambridge University Press, 1983), 164.
9. Sherry, *Conrad's Western World*, 239–44.
10. Conrad, *The Secret Agent*, 5.
11. Ian Watt, *Essays on Conrad* (Cambridge, U.K.: Cambridge University Press, 2000), 116, 118–19.
12. Keith Carabine, *The Life and the Art: A Study of Conrad's Under Western Eyes* (Amsterdam: Rodopi, 1996), 178–79.
13. Sherry, *Conrad's Western World*, 210–12.
14. Conrad, *The Secret Agent*, 9.
15. Sherry, *Conrad's Western World*, 213.
16. Ibid., 212–14.
17. Isabel Meredith, *A Girl Among the Anarchists* (London: Duckworth and Co., 1903); Mulry, "Popular Accounts of the Greenwich Bombing," 52–54.
18. Robert Anderson, *Sidelights on the Home Rule Movement* (New York: E. P. Dutton and Co., 1906), 89.
19. Conrad, *The Secret Agent*, 6.
20. Ibid., 103.
21. Ibid., 159.
22. Ibid., 100.
23. Ibid., 28.
24. Ibid., 171.
25. The manuscript was sold by Conrad to the American collector John Quinn in 1912, and is now at the Rosenbach Museum and Library in Philadelphia (Bruce Harkness and S. W. Reid, "The Texts: An Essay," in *The Secret Agent*, by Joseph Conrad [Cambridge, U.K.: Cambridge University Press, 1990], 236).
26. The first reference to "Verloc" in Conrad's letters is on 13 February 1906; eight days later, he had written "a good bit more" than the first thirteen pages, which he was happy to send to Pinker (*Collected Letters of Joseph Conrad* 3: 316–17).
27. *Collected Letters of Joseph Conrad* 3: 317.
28. Cedric Watts suggests "the predominant reason for this tendency was his imaginative integrity and originality [. . .], an imaginative resistance to conventional plotting, being concerned with the thematics and the wider implications of the narrative" (*Joseph Conrad: A Literary Life* [New York: St. Martin's Press, 1989], 60–61).
29. Peter D. McDonald, *British Literary Culture and Publishing Practice, 1880–1914* (Cambridge, U.K.: Cambridge University Press, 1997), 25–26.
30. Conrad, *The Secret Agent*, 7.
31. *Collected Letters of Joseph Conrad* 3: 338, 346. Conrad may even have had a quartet in mind: during the composition of "Verloc" he alluded in a letter to Pinker to having begun a story about "a bomb in a hotel" which has not survived (*Collected Letters of Joseph Conrad* 3: 326). "Razumov," the short story begun in 1907 that became *Under Western Eyes*, was a fifth story on an anarchist theme.
32. *Collected Letters of Joseph Conrad* 3: 300. The "sea papers" are the sketches that became *The Mirror of the Sea* (1906).
33. *Collected Letters of Joseph Conrad* 3: 318.
34. Ibid., 320.
35. Ibid., 327; Harkness and Reid, "The Texts: An Essay," 241–42.
36. *Collected Letters of Joseph Conrad* 3: 323, 335; Owen Knowles, *A Conrad Chronology* (Basingstoke: Macmillan Press Ltd., 1989), 63–64.
37. Harkness and Reid, "The Texts: An Essay," 244–47.
38. Jacques Berthoud uses the phrase in the title of his influential study of six of Conrad's novels from 1897 to 1911 (*Joseph Conrad: The Major Phase* [Cambridge, U.K.: Cambridge University Press, 1978]).
39. McDonald, *British Literary Culture*.
40. Watts describes *Ridgway's* as "downmarket" (*A Literary Life*, 103), which

is an exaggeration. Its first front cover proclaimed a magazine carrying "good fiction" as well as news sections informing Americans about what the U.S. government was doing in their interest.

41. *Ridgway's*, 6 October 1906, 12.
42. Harkness and Reid, "The Texts: An Essay," 251.
43. *Collected Letters of Joseph Conrad* 3: 369.
44. See for example Watts, *A Literary Life*, 85–89.
45. For a brilliant analysis of Conrad's association with the *Daily Mail* and other titles owned by the magnate Alfred Harmsworth (Lord Northcliffe), see Stephen Donovan, "Conrad and the Harmsworth Empire: *The Daily Mail, London Magazine, Times, Evening News,* and *Hutchinson's Magazine*," *Conradiana* (Texas Tech University Press), vol. 41, nos. 2–3 (2009): 153–77. For *T.P.'s Weekly*, see Watts, *A Literary Life*, 97–103.
46. McDonald in *British Literary Culture* shows how the *New Review*'s editor, W. E. Henley, his circle, and the magazine's reputation shaped the writing of *The Nigger of the "Narcissus"* (1898).
47. *Collected Letters of Joseph Conrad* 2: 320–32.
48. Ibid., vol. 3: 358, 360. It is not clear which chapter Conrad is referring to (see Harkness and Reid, "The Texts: An Essay," 247); however, the novel's continuing expansion suggests that Conrad had the murder scene in mind, and that he originally conceived this as the narrative's climax.
49. Harkness and Reid, "The Texts: An Essay," 236.
50. *Collected Letters of Joseph Conrad* 3: 369.
51. Ibid., 370.
52. *Ridgway's*, 15 December 1906, 47.
53. *Collected Letters of Joseph Conrad* 3: 365.
54. Conrad, *The Secret Agent*, 197.
55. Emily K. Dalgarno ("Conrad, Pinker, and the Writing of The Secret Agent," *Conradiana*, 1977: 53–54) argues that Conrad may have "actually attempted a style which could be simply dismantled to suit a magazine." Conrad's late October letter to Pinker about *Ridgway's* editing of the novel suggests otherwise (*Collected Letters of Joseph Conrad* 3: 369). Harkness and Reid ("The Texts: An Essay," 253) provide a more balanced and convincing case that the *Ridgway's* editors made numerous deletions "in order to make the tale fit not only their pages but their conception of audience" but that the alterations to the manuscript text that appear in both serial and book versions were Conrad's.
56. Conrad, *The Secret Agent*, 92, 114; Dalgarno, "Conrad, Pinker, and the Writing of *The Secret Agent*," 55.
57. Watts, *A Literary Life*, 105. The *Ridgway's* serial can be viewed and studied at Stephen Donovan's ground-breaking *Conrad First* (www.conradfirst.net), an online archive of magazines and newspapers featuring first and early publications of Conrad's works.
58. *Collected Letters of Joseph Conrad* 3: 371. The typescripts that must have been used for both the serial version and the book edition are lost, necessitating some detective work to infer what they must have contained. Harkness and Reid's account is authoritative.
59. *Collected Letters of Joseph Conrad* 3: 411.
60. Ibid., 434.
61. Ibid., 435.
62. Ibid., 439.
63. Ibid., 441.
64. Harkness and Reid, "The Texts: An Essay," 268.
65. *Collected Letters of Joseph Conrad* 3: 457.
66. Ibid., 458, 459.
67. In 1920 Conrad and Pinker produced a film scenario of "Gaspar Ruiz" entitled

Gaspar the Strong Man, completing it at the same time as the British release of *Victory*, the first film adaptation of a Conrad novel. The same year Conrad adapted "Because of the Dollars" for the stage as *Laughing Anne*.

68. Knowles, *A Conrad Chronology*, 119.
69. Conrad, *The Secret Agent*, 8.
70. Conrad, *Three Plays: Laughing Anne, One Day More and The Secret Agent* (London: Methuen & Co. Ltd., 1934), 179.
71. Conrad, *The Secret Agent*, 7–8.
72. Watts, *A Literary Life*, 108.
73. Richard J. Hand gives a fine and persuasive account of the play's artistic merits and technical skill in *The Theatre of Joseph Conrad: Reconstructed Fictions* (New York: Palgrave Macmillan, 2005), 136–64.
74. *Collected Letters of Joseph Conrad* 6: 520, qtd. in Hand, *The Theatre of Joseph Conrad*, 127.

Notes to "The Secret Sharer": When the Other Is the Self"

1. Barbara Johnson and Marjorie Garber, "Secret Sharing: Reading Conrad Psychoanalytically," *College English* 33 (October 1987): 629–30.
2. Daniel Curley, "Legate of the Ideal," in *Conrad*, ed. Marvin Mudrick (Englewood Cliffs, N.J.: Prentice-Hall, 1996), 77.
3. Ibid., 78.
4. Ibid., 79.
5. Ibid., 81.
6. Albert J. Guerard, *Conrad the Novelist* (Cambridge, Mass.: Harvard University Press, 1958), 15.
7. Ibid., 16.
8. Ibid., 18.
9. Ibid., 26.
10. Ibid., 31.
11. Paul J. Emmett, "Conrad's Secrets Shared: Narrative Suppression and Dream Distortion in 'The Secret Sharer,'" *Journal of Evolutionary Psychology* 25 (2004): 154.
12. Daniel R. Schwarz, *Rereading Conrad* (Columbia: University of Missouri Press, 2001), 160.
13. Johnson and Garber, "Secret Sharing," 638.
14. Joseph Conrad, "The Secret Sharer," in *'Twixt Land and Sea*, ed. J. A. Berthoud et al. (New York: Cambridge University Press, 2008), 81.
15. Ibid., 82.
16. Ibid., 85.
17. Ibid., 113.
18. Ibid., 82–83.
19. Beth Sharon Ash, *Writing in Between: Modernity and Psychosocial Dilemma in the Novels of Joseph Conrad* (New York: St. Martin's Press, 1999), 3.
20. Johnson and Garber, "Secret Sharing," 634.
21. Ash, *Writing in Between*, 15.
22. Conrad, "The Secret Sharer," 91.
23. Ibid., 97–98.
24. Ibid., 102.
25. Ibid., 108.
26. Ibid, 106.
27. Edward Said, *Joseph Conrad and the Fiction of Autobiography* (1966; rpt. New York: Columbia University Press, 2008), 127.
28. Ibid., 128.
29. Ibid., 127.
30. Curley, "Legate of the Ideal," 81.
31. Ibid., 82.
32. Joan Steiner, "'The Secret Sharer': Complexities of the Doubling Relationship," in *Joseph Conrad*, ed. Harold Bloom (New York: Chelsea House Publishers, 1986), 102.
33. See Steiner, "'The Secret Sharer,'" for a more comprehensive discussion of double types.
34. Conrad, "The Secret Sharer," 111.
35. Ibid., 119.
36. Steiner, "'The Secret Sharer,'" 110.
37. Ibid., 112.

38. Ibid., 119.

Notes to "Sensationalized Stories of Russian Revolutionary Terrorism in *Under Western Eyes*"

1. This is my own translation. Here is the original French version from "L'Assassinat de M. Plehve," *Journal de Genève*, 31 July 1904, 1, www.letemps archives.ch:

> L'explosion fut formidable, et la scène de carnage indescriptible. Le cocher, les bras emportés, gisait expirant sur la chaussée. Le corps du ministre, projeté en l'air, retomba parmi les debris de la voiture, le front défoncé, le côté droit de la figure en bouillie, l'épaule droite arrachée.
>
> Les chevaux, éventrés se débattaient dans une mare de sang; des femmes, blessées, poussaient des hurlements affreux. . . .
>
> Dans toutes les maisons, les vitres tombaient en éclats; des clameurs retentissaient de tous côtés.

2. Roger Griffin, *Terrorist's Creed: Fanatical Violence and the Human Need for Meaning* (Basingstoke, U.K.: Palgrave Macmillan, 2012), 76. Alex Houen, *Terrorism and Modern Literature: From Joseph Conrad to Ciaran Carson* (Oxford, U.K.: Oxford University Press, 2002), 72–73.
3. Andrzej Busza, "*Under Western Eyes* and the 'Theatre of the Real,'" in *Under Western Eyes: Centennial Essays*, ed. Allan H. Simmons, J. H. Staple, and Jeremy Hawthorn (Amsterdam: Rodopi, 2011), 132.
4. Adrian S. Wisnicki, *Conspiracy, Revolution, and Terrorism from Victorian Fiction to the Modern Novel* (New York: Routledge, 2007), 158. Avrom Fleishman, *Conrad's Politics: Community and Anarchy in the Fiction of Joseph Conrad* (Baltimore: Johns Hopkins Press, 1967), 219–20.
5. Joseph Conrad, *Under Western Eyes* (London: J. M. Dent and Sons Ltd., 1955), vii, x.
6. Matthew Rubery, "The Foreign Correspondence: Joseph Conrad's 'Wild Story of a Journalist,'" in *The Novelty of Newspapers: Victorian Fiction after the Invention of the News* (Oxford, U.K.: Oxford University Press, 2009), 142–43.
7. Brian Artese, "'Speech Was of No Use': Conrad, a New Journalism, and the Critical Abjection of Testimony," *Novel: A Forum on Fiction* 36, no. 2 (Spring 2003): 176, www.jstor.org/stable/1346125.
8. Ibid., 177.
9. For further analysis of "Autocracy and War" as well as Conrad's other essays that reveal his opinions on the press, see Rubery, "The Foreign Correspondence," 143–44.
10. Joseph Conrad, *Notes on Life and Letters* (New York: Doubleday and Page, 1923), 90.
11. Conrad, *Under Western Eyes*, 3–4.
12. Ibid., 4.
13. Ibid., 4.
14. Ibid., 3.
15. Penn R. Szittya, "Metafiction: Double Narration in *Under Western Eyes*," *ELH* 48, no. 4 (Winter 1981): 821, www.jstor .org/stable/2872963.
16. Allan Hepburn, "Above Suspicion: Audience and Deception in *Under Western Eyes*," *Studies in the Novel* 92, no. 4 (Fall 1992): 282.
17. Conrad, *Under Western Eyes*, ix.
18. Ibid., 7.
19. Ibid., 7.
20. "Viatcheslav von Plehve," *The Literary Digest*, 27 June 1903, 932, www.unz.org/ Pub/LiteraryDigest-1903jun27-00932.
21. Conrad, *Under Western Eyes*, 9–10.
22. "Assassination of M. de Plehve," *The Standard*, 29 July 1904.

23. "A Russian Minister Assassinated," *The Guardian*, 29 July 1904.
24. Ibid.
25. After this account, *The Times* included reports from correspondents in Paris, Berlin, Vienna, and New York, which, unlike *The Guardian*, did not recount details of the assassination, but rather focused on public opinion on the assassination ("Assassination of M. de Plehve," London *Times*, July 29, 1904, 3).
26. "The Assassination of M. de Plehve," London *Times*, 30 July 1904, 5.
27. Ibid., 5.
28. The shocking accounts of the Plehve assassination were not the only reports of terrorist violence that were sensationalized in turn-of-the-twentieth-century English newspapers. Alarming reports of the Greenwich bombing of 1894 inspired Conrad to write another novel concerning terrorist violence, *The Secret Agent*. See my "Media Sensationalism and Terrorism in *The Secret Agent*," *The Conradian*, Autumn 2013.
29. Conrad, *Under Western Eyes*, 110.
30. Ibid., 110.
31. Ibid.
32. Ibid., 140.
33. Ibid., 188.
34. Rubery, "The Foreign Correspondence," 145.
35. Conrad, *Under Western Eyes*, 114.
36. Ibid., 114.
37. Ibid., 189.
38. Ibid., 189.
39. Ibid., 247–48.
40. For more on Russian revolutionary emigrants in Britain and British fiction depicting these emigrants from 1880 to 1914, see John Slatter, "Bears in the Lion's Den: The Figure of the Russian Revolutionary Emigrant in English Fiction, 1880–1914," *Slavonic and East European Review* 77, no. 1 (Jan 1999): 30–55, www.jstor.org/stable/4212794.
41. Conrad, *Under Western Eyes*, 120.
42. Ibid.
43. Ibid., 122.
44. Ibid., 125.
45. Ibid., 126.
46. Ibid., 131.
47. Ibid., 215.
48. Ibid., 163.
49. Ibid., 285.
50. Ibid., 288.
51. Ibid., 266.
52. Ibid., ix.
53. Busza, "*Under Western Eyes* and the 'Theatre of the Real,'" 132.
54. Avrom Fleishman suggests that Conrad used David Soskice's "The Russian Spy System: The Azeff Scandals in Russia" as a source for *Under Western Eyes* (*Conrad's Politics: Community and Anarchy in the Fiction of Joseph Conrad* [Baltimore: Johns Hopkins University Press, 1967], 219–20).
55. Conrad, *Under Western Eyes*, 330.
56. Ibid., 305.

Notes to "Chance and Betrayal in *Under Western Eyes*"

1. Joseph Conrad, *Under Western Eyes* (London: Folio, 2000), 40. See also *Under Western Eyes* (New York: Harper and Brothers, 1911), chap. 2.
2. *Under Western Eyes* (London: Folio, 2000), 69–70.
3. Ibid., 42–43.
4. Gillian Beer, *Darwin's Plots: Evolutionary Narrative in Darwin, George Eliot, and Nineteenth-Century Fiction* (Cambridge, U.K.: Cambridge University Press, 2000), 14.
5. Conrad, *Under Western Eyes*, 362.
6. Ibid., 44–45.
7. Ibid., 361.
8. Levine, 263.
9. Gillian Beer, *Darwin's Plots*, 6.
10. Conrad, *Under Western Eyes*, 29.
11. Ibid., 31.
12. Levine, 266.
13. Levine, 267.
14. Ibid., 100.
15. Ibid., 1.

16. Ibid., 358–59.
17. Ibid., 361.
18. Ibid.
19. Ibid., 89.
20. Ibid., 44.
21. Ibid., 233.
22. *Under Western Eyes* (New York: Harper and Brothers, 1911), 299.
23. Czeslaw Milosz, "Apollo Nalecz Korzeniowski," *Kultura* (Paris), February 1956, 79.
24. Eloise Knapp Hay, *The Political Novels of Joseph Conrad* (Chicago: University of Chicago Press, 1963), 265.
25. Hay, 267.
26. V. S. Pritchett, "The Exile," *The News Statesman*, 24 August 1957, 229.
27. Zdzislaw Najder, *Joseph Conrad: A Chronicle*, trans. Helena Carroll-Najder (Cambridge, U.K.: Cambridge University Press, 1983), 333.
28. Conrad, *Under Western Eyes*, 32.
29. Najder, 358.
30. Ibid., 359.
31. Ibid., 362.
32. Joseph Conrad, *Notes on Life and Letters* (1921; Cambridge, U.K.: Cambridge University Press, 2004), 102.
33. Jeffrey Meyers, *Joseph Conrad: A Biography* (New York: Charles Scribner's Sons, 1991), 21.
34. Ibid., 29.
35. Joseph Conrad, "Author's Note," *Under Western Eyes* (London: Methuen, 1926), vii.
36. Ibid., x.
37. Conrad, *Under Western Eyes*, 134.
38. Frederick R. Karl, *A Reader's Guide to Joseph Conrad* (New York: Farrar, Straus, and Giroux, 1969), 215–16.

Works Cited

Achebe, Chinua. "Chinua Achebe: 'Heart of Darkness' Is Inappropriate." Robert Siegel's interview with Chinua Achebe. *All Things Considered.* NPR. October 15, 2009.

——. "An Image of Africa." *Massachusetts Review* 18, no. 4 (Winter 1977): 782–94.

——. "An Image of Africa: Racism in Conrad's *Heart of Darkness.*" In *Joseph Conrad: Heart of Darkness*, ed. Paul B. Armstrong, 336–49. New York: Norton, 2006.

——. "An Image of Africa." *Research in African Literature* 9 (1978): 1–15.

——. *Things Fall Apart.* New York: Anchor, 1994.

Adams, Carol J. *The Sexual Politics of Meat: A Feminist-Vegetarian Critical Theory.* New York: Continuum, 1995.

Adorno, Theodor. *Minima Moralia: Reflections on a Damaged Life.* Trans. E. F. N. Jephcott. New York: Verso, 1978.

Agamben, Giorgio. *Homo Sacer: Sovereign Power and Bare Life.* Trans. Heller-Roazen. Stanford, Calif.: Stanford University Press, 1998.

Allen, Jerry. *The Sea Years of Joseph Conrad.* Garden City, N.Y.: Doubleday, 1965.

Alpers, Edward A. "The Ivory Trade in Africa: An Historical Overview." In *Elephant,* ed. Ross, 349–63.

Anderson, Robert. *Sidelights on the Home Rule Movement.* New York: E. P. Dutton and Co., 1906.

Anonymous. "Anarchism in London." *The Graphic,* 24 February 1894.

——. "Something New in Weeklies." *Ridgway's: A Militant Weekly for God and Country,* October 6, 1906: 1.

Apocalypse Now. Produced and directed by Francis Coppola. Paramount Pictures, 1979. DVD, 1999.

Armstrong, Paul. *The Challenge of Bewilderment.* Ithaca, N.Y.: Cornell University Press, 1987.

Artese, Brian. "'Speech Was of No Use': Conrad, a New Journalism, and the Critical Abjection of Testimony." *Novel: A Forum on Fiction* 36, no. 2 (Spring 2003): 176–97. www.jstor.org/stable/1346125.

Ash, Beth Sharon. *Writing in Between: Modernity and Psychosocial Dilemma in the Novels of Joseph Conrad.* New York: St. Martin's Press, 1999.

"L'Assassinat de M. Plehve." *Journal de Genève,* 31 July 1904, 1. www.letemps archives.ch.

"Assassination of M. de Plehve." London *Times,* 29 and 30 July 1904.

"Assassination of M. de Plehve." *The Standard,* 29 July 1904.

Auerbach, Nina. *Communities of Women: An Idea in Fiction.* Cambridge, 1978.

Baines, Jocelyn. *Joseph Conrad: A Critical Biography.* London: Weidenfeld and Nicolson, 1960.

Batchelor, John. *The Life of Joseph Conrad: A Critical Biography.* Oxford, U.K.: Blackwell, 1994.

Bayart, Jean-Francois. *The State in Africa: The Politics of the Belly.* London: Longman, 1993.

Beach, Joseph Warren. *The Twentieth Century Novel: Studies in Technique.* New York: Appleton-Century-Crofts, 1931.

Beer, Gillian. *Darwin's Plots: Evolutionary Narrative in Darwin, George Eliot, and Nineteenth-Century Fiction.* Cambridge, U.K.: Cambridge University Press, 2000.

Beerbohm, Max. *A Christmas Garland.* New York: E. P. Dutton & Co., 1918.

Bellow, Saul. *Henderson, the Rain King.* New York: Penguin Group, 1959.

Benjamin, Walter. *The Origin of German Tragic Drama.* Trans. John Osborne. London: NLB, 1977.

Berthoud, Jacques. "Introduction." *Almayer's Folly,* by Conrad.

——. *Joseph Conrad: The Major Phase.* Cambridge, U.K.: Cambridge University Press, 1978.

Bevan, David, Paul Collier, and Jan Gunning. *The Political Economy of Poverty, Equity, and Growth: Nigeria and Indonesia.* Oxford, U.K.: Oxford University Press, 1999.

Bhabha, Homi. *The Location of Culture.* London: Routledge, 1994.

Billy, Ted. A *Wilderness of Words: Closure and Disclosure in Conrad's Short Fiction.* Lubbock: Texas Tech University Press, 1997.

Binkley, David A. "The Teeth of the Nyim." In *Elephant,* ed. Ross, 277–91.

Birrell, T. A. "The Simplicity of *Typhoon*: Conrad, Falubert and Others." *Dutch Quarterly Review* 10, no. 4 (1980): 275–95.

Bock, Martin. *Joseph Conrad and Psychological Medicine.* Lubbock: Texas Tech University Press, 2002.

Bongie, Chris. *Exotic Memories: Literature, Colonialism, and the* Fin de Siècle. Stanford, Calif.: Stanford University Press, 1991.

Bonney, William W. *Thorns & Arabesques: Contexts for Conrad's Fiction.* Baltimore: Johns Hopkins University Press, 1980.

Bradbrook, M. C. *Joseph Conrad: Poland's English Genius.* Cambridge, U.K.: Cambridge University Press, 1941.

Brantlinger, Patrick. "*Heart of Darkness*: Anti-Imperialism, Racism, or Impressionism?" *Criticism* 27, no. 4 (Fall 1985): 363–85.

Brown, Carolyn. "Creative Combat in 'Typhoon.'" *The Conradian,* Autumn 1992: 1–16.

Brownstein, Rachel. *Becoming a Heroine: Reading About Women in Novels.* New York, 1982.

Bruss, Paul. *Conrad's Early Sea Fiction: The Novelist as Navigator.* Lewisburg, Pa.: Bucknell University Press, 1979.

Buci-Glucksman, Christine. "The Utopia of the Feminine. Benjamin's Trajectory." In *Walter Benjamin: Critical Evaluations in Cultural Theory,* ed. Peter Osborne. London: Routledge, 2005: 243–60.

Buell, Lawrence *Writing for an Endangered World: Literature, Culture, and Environment in the U.S. and Beyond.* Cambridge, Mass.: Harvard University Press, 2001.

Burgess, C. F. *The Fellowship of the Craft: Conrad on Ships and Seamen and the Sea.* Port Washington, N.Y.: Kennikat Press, 1976.

Burgoyne, Mary. "Conrad among the Anarchists: Documents on Martial Bourdin and the Greenwich Bombing." *The Conradian* (Amsterdam: Rodopi), 2007: 147–85.

Busza, Andrzej. "Conrad's Polish Literary Background and Some Illustrations of the Influence of Polish Literature on His Work." *Antemurale* 10 (1966): 109–255.

——. "*Under Western Eyes* and the 'Theatre of the Real.'" In *Under Western Eyes: Centennial Essays,* ed. Allan H. Simmons, J. H. Staple, and Jeremy Hawthorn, 127–40. Amsterdam; New York: Rodopi, 2011.

Caminero-Santangelo, Byron. *African Fiction and Joseph Conrad: Reading Postcolonial Intertextuality.* Albany, N.Y.: State University of New York Publishing, 2005.

Carabine, Keith. "Introduction." *Three Sea Stories: "Typhoon," "Falk" and The Shadow-Line.* London: Wordsworth, 1998.

——. *The Life and the Art: A Study of Conrad's Under Western Eyes.* Amsterdam: Rodopi, 1996.

Casarino, Cesare. *Modernity at Sea: Melville, Marx, Conrad in Crisis.* Minneapolis: University of Minnesota Press, 2002.

Christy, Bryan. "Ivory Worship." *National Geographic,* October 2012, 28–61.

[Clifford, Hugh]. "The Trail of the Book-Worm: Mr. Joseph Conrad at Home and Abroad." *Singapore Free Press,* 30 August 1898, 3.

Colbron, Grace Isabel. "Joseph Conrad's Women." *Bookman* 38, no. 5 (January 1914): 476–79.

Cole, Sarah. *At the Violet Hour: Modernism and Violence in England and Ireland.* Oxford, U.K.: Oxford University Press, 2012.

Collits, Terry. "Conrad in the Time of Globalization: A Latin American *Nostromo*?" *Yearbook of Conrad Studies.* Kraków: Jagiellonian University, vol. 3 (2007): 165–80.

Conan-Doyle, Sir Arthur. *The Crime of the Congo.* New York: Doubleday, 1909.

Conrad, Joseph. *Almayer's Folly.* Oxford, U.K.: Oxford University Press, 1992.

——. *The Collected Letters of Joseph Conrad,* ed. Frederick Karl, Laurence Davies, Owen Knowles, J. H. Stape, and Gene M. Moore. 9 vols. Cambridge, U.K.: Cambridge University Press, 1986–2008.

——. "Geography and Some Explorers." *Last Essays,* ed. Richard Curle. London: J. M. Dent & Sons, 1926.

——. *Heart of Darkness and Other Tales.* Ed. Cedric Watts. Oxford, U.K.: Oxford University Press, 1990.

——. *Heart of Darkness & Selections from The Congo Diary.* New York: Random House, 1999.

——. *Heart of Darkness.* 4th edition. New York, N.Y.: Norton & Co., 2006.

——. *Heart of Darkness.* In *The Collected Works of Joseph Conrad,* ed. Owen Knowles. New York: Cambridge University Press, 2010.

——. *Lord Jim.* Ed. J. H. Stape and Ernest W. Sullivan II. Cambridge, U.K.: Cambridge University Press, 2012.

——. *The Nigger of the Narcissus.* London: J. M. Dent, 1950.

——. *Nostromo, a Tale of the Seaboard.* Cambridge University Press, 1988.

——. *Nostromo.* Ed. Ruth L. Nadelhaft. Ontario: Broadview, 1997.

——. *Notes on Life and Letters.* 1921. Cambridge, U.K.: Cambridge University Press, 2004.

——. *Notes on Life and Letters.* New York: Doubleday and Page, 1923.

——. *An Outcast of the Islands,* ed. J. H. Stape. New York: Oxford University Press, 2002.

——. *A Personal Record.* Cambridge, U.K.: Cambridge University Press, 2008.

——. *The Secret Agent: A Simple Tale.* Ed. Bruce Harkness and S. W. Reid. Cambridge, U.K.: Cambridge University Press, 1990.

——. "The Secret Agent." *Ridgway's: A Militant Weekly for God and Country,* 6 October and 15 December 1906: 12–15.

——. *The Secret Sharer and Other Stories.* Ed. Shane Weller. New York: Dover, 1993.

——. *Tales of Hearsay and Last Essays.* London: Dent, 1955.

——. *Three Plays: Laughing Anne, One Day More and The Secret Agent.* London: Methuen & Co. Ltd., 1934.

——. *'Twixt Land and Sea.* Ed. J. A. Berthoud et al. New York: Cambridge University Press, 2008.

——. *Typhoon,* in *The Nigger of the "Narcissus" and Typhoon & Other Stories.* London: Dent, 1950.

——. *Under Western Eyes.* Ed. Jeremy Hawthorn. Oxford, U.K.: Oxford University Press, 2003.

——. *Under Western Eyes.* London: Folio, 2000.

——. *Under Western Eyes.* London: J. M. Dent and Sons Ltd., 1955.

——. *Under Western Eyes.* London: Methuen, 1926.

——. *Under Western Eyes.* New York: Harper and Brothers, 1911.

——. *Youth, Heart of Darkness, The End of the Tether.* Ed. Owen Knowles. Cambridge, U.K.: Cambridge University Press, 2010.

Cooper, Christopher. *Conrad and the Human Dilemma.* New York: Barnes & Noble, 1970.

Cooper, Frederic Taber. "Christmas Day at Sea" in *Tales of Hearsay and Last Essays.* London: Dent, 1955.

——. *The Nigger of the "Narcissus" and Typhoon & Other Stories.* London: Dent, 1950.

——. "Representative English Story-Tellers: Joseph Conrad." *Bookman* 35, no. 1 (March 1912): 61–70.

Corbett, Peter David. "Make it New: Laurence Binyon, Pound and Vorticism." *Paideuma* 26 (1993): 2–3.

Crankshaw, Edward. *Joseph Conrad: Some Aspects of the Art of the Novel.* London: John Lane, 1936.

Curle. Richard. *Joseph Conrad: A Study.* London: Kegan Paul, Trench, Trübner, 1914.

Curley, Daniel. "Legate of the Ideal.'" In *Conrad,* ed. Marvin Mudrick. Englewood Cliffs, N.J.: Prentice-Hall, 1966.

Daiches, David. *The Novel and the Modern World.* Chicago: University of Chicago Press, 1939.

Daleski, H. M. *Joseph Conrad: The Way of Dispossession.* London: Faber & Faber, 1977.

Dalgarno, Emily K. "Conrad, Pinker, and the Writing of The Secret Agent." *Conradiana,* 1977: 47–58.

Davidson, Arnold E. *Conrad's Endings.* Ann Arbor, Mich.: UMI Research Press, 1984.

Davidson, Donald. "Joseph Conrad's Directed Indirections." *Sewanee Review* 33, no. 2 (April 1925): 163–77.

Davies, Norman. *God's Playground: A History of Poland.* 2 vols. New York: Columbia University Press, 2001.

DeLoughrey, Elizabeth, and George B. Handley. *Postcolonial Ecologies: Literatures of the Environment.* Oxford, U.K.: Oxford University Press, 2011.

Demory, Pamela. "*Apocalypse Now Redux: Heart of Darkness* Moves into New Territory." *Literature Film Quarterly* 35, no. 1 (January 2007):342–49.

Derrida, Jacques. *The Animal That Therefore I Am.* Ed. Marie-Louise Mallet. Trans. David Wills. New York: Fordham University Press, 2008.

Dickens, Charles. *A Christmas Carol.* In *Christmas Books.* London: Oxford University Press, 1954.

DiSanto, Michael John. *Under Conrad's Eyes: The Novel as Criticism.* Montreal: McGill-Queen's University Press, 2009.

Donovan, Stephen. "Conrad and the Harmsworth Empire: *The Daily Mail, London Magazine, Times, Evening News,* and *Hutchinson's Magazine.*" *Conradiana* (Texas Tech University Press), vol. 41, no. 2–3 (2009): 153–77.

——. *Joseph Conrad and Popular Culture.* New York: Palgrave Macmillan, 2005.

——. ed. "Conrad First." www.conradfirst.net (accessed 1–22 October 2012).

Dryden, Linda. *Joseph Conrad and the Imperial Romance.* New York: St. Martin's, 2000.

——. "'The Times Indeed Are Changed': Conrad, 'Typhoon,' and *Pall Mall Magazine.*" *Conradiana* (Fall-Winter 2009): 133–43.

Ehrsam, Theodore G. *A Bibliography of Joseph Conrad.* Metuchen, N.J.: Scarecrow Press, 1969.

Elvin, Mark. *The Retreat of the Elephants: An Environmental History of China.* New Haven, Conn.: Yale University Press, 2004.

Emmett, Paul J. "Conrad's Secrets Shared: Narrative Suppression and Dream Distortion in "The Secret Sharer." *Journal of Evolutionary Psychology* 25: 3–4 (Aug 2004): 154.

Ensor, C. K. Robert. *England, 1870–1914*. Oxford, U.K.: Clarendon, 1936.

Epstein, Joseph. "Life Sentences: The Art of Joseph Conrad." *New Criterion* 12, no. 10 (June 1994): 16–26.

Erdinast-Vulcan, Daphna. *Joseph Conrad and the Modern Temper*. Oxford, U.K.: Clarendon Press, 1991.

Fenollosa, Ernest. *The Chinese Written Character as a Medium for Poetry*. Ed. Ezra Pound. San Francisco: City Light Books, 1936.

Fernández, Ramón. "L'Art de Conrad." *La Nouvelle Revue Française*, n.s. no. 135 (1 December 1924): 730–37.

Finkelstein, David, and Alistair McCleery, eds.. *The Book History Reader*. 2nd ed. London: Routledge, 2006.

Firchow, Peter Edgerly. *Envisioning Africa: Racism and Imperialism in Conrad's* Heart of Darkness. Lexington: University Press of Kentucky, 2000.

Fleishman, Avrom. *Conrad's Politics: Community and Anarchy in the Fiction of Joseph Conrad*. Baltimore: Johns Hopkins University Press, 1967.

——. "*Nostromo*: Class Struggle as Tragedy." *Conrad's Politics*. Baltimore: Johns Hopkins University Press, 1967.

Fogel, Aaron. *Coercion to Speak: Conrad's Poetics of Dialogue*. Cambridge, Mass.: Harvard University Press, 1985.

Follett, Wilson. *Joseph Conrad: A Short Study of His Intellectual and Emotional Attitude toward His Work and of the Chief Characters of His Novels*. Garden City, N.Y.: Doubleday, Page, 1915.

Ford, Ford Madox. *Joseph Conrad: A Personal Remembrance*. Boston: Little, Brown, 1924.

——. "Joseph Conrad." *English Review* 10, no. 1 (December 1911): 68–83.

Ford, Richard. *Canada*. New York: HarperCollins, 2012.

[Forster, E. M.]. "The Pride of Mr. Conrad." *Nation and Atheneum* 4742 (19 March 1921): 881–82.

Franklin, Ruth. "Imp of the Perverse." *New Yorker*, 30 July 2012, 77.

Freud, Sigmund. "The Uncanny." In *The Standard Edition of the Complete Psychological Works of Sigmund Freud*, ed. James Strachey, vol. 17: 217–56. London: Hogarth Press, 1955.

Friedel, Robert. *Pioneer Plastic: The Making and Selling of Celluloid*. Madison: University of Wisconsin Press, 1983.

Galsworthy, John. "Joseph Conrad: A Disquisition." *Fortnightly Review* n.s. vol. 83 (April 1908): 627–33.

Gardner, Monica. *Adam Mickiewicz: The National Poet of Poland*. New York: Dutton, 1911.

Garnett, Edward, ed. *Letters from Joseph Conrad 1895–1924*. New York: Charter Books, 1962.

Geddes, Gary. *Conrad's Later Novels*. Montreal: McGill-Queen's University Press, 1980.

Gekoski, R. A. *Conrad: The Moral World of the Novelist*. New York: Barnes & Noble, 1978.

Genette, Gérard. *Palimpsests: Literature in the Second Degree*. Trans. Channa Newman and Claude Doubinsky. Lincoln: University of Nebraska Press, 1997.

Gissing, A. and E., eds. *Letters of George Gissing to Members of His Family*. London: Constable & Co., 1927.

GoGwilt, Christopher. *The Invention of the West: Joseph Conrad and the Double-Mapping of Europe and Empire*. Stanford, Calif.: Stanford University Press, 1995.

Goonetilleke, D. C. R. A. *Developing Countries in British Fiction*. Totowa, N.J.: Rowman and Littlefield, 1977.

Gordan, John Dozier. *Joseph Conrad: The Making of a Novelist*. Cambridge, Mass.: Harvard University Press, 1940.

Gorra, Michael. "Joseph Conrad." *Hudson Review* 59, no. 4 (Winter 2007): 545.

Graver, Lawrence. *Conrad's Short Fiction*. Berkeley: University of California Press, 1969.

Greaney, Michael. *Conrad, Language, and Narrative.* Cambridge, U.K.: Cambridge University Press, 2002.

Greene, Graham. *The Heart of the Matter.* New York: Viking Press, 1948.

Greiff, Louis K. "Soldier, Sailor, Surfer, Chef: Conrad's Ethics and the Margins of "Apocalypse Now," *Literature Film Quarterly* 20, no. 3 (July 1992): 188–97.

Griffin, Roger. *Terrorist's Creed: Fanatical Violence and the Human Need for Meaning.* Basingstoke, U.K.: Palgrave Macmillan, 2012.

Guerard, Albert J. *Conrad the Novelist.* Cambridge, Mass.: Harvard University Press, 1958.

——. *Joseph Conrad.* New York: New Directions, 1947.

Guetti, James. *The Limits of Metaphor: A Study of Melville, Conrad, and Faulkner.* Ithaca, N.Y.: Cornell University Press, 1967.

Gurko, Leo *Joseph Conrad: Giant in Exile.* New York: Macmillan, 1962.

Hamner, Robert D., ed. *Joseph Conrad: Third World Perspectives.* Washington, D.C.: Three Continents Press, 1990.

Hampson, Robert. *Cross-Cultural Encounters in Joseph Conrad's Malay Fiction.* New York: Palgrave, 2000.

——. *Joseph Conrad: Betrayal and Identity.* London: Macmillan, 1992.

——. "Joseph Conrad: Postcolonialism and Imperialism." *EurAmerica* 41, no. 1 (2011): 1–46.

Hand, Richard J. *The Theatre of Joseph Conrad: Reconstructed Fictions.* New York: Palgrave Macmillan, 2005.

Hardt, Michael, and Antonio Negri. *Empire.* Cambridge, Mass.: Harvard University Press, 2000.

Harkness, Bruce, and S. W. Reid. "The Texts: An Essay." In *The Secret Agent,* by Joseph Conrad. Cambridge, U.K.: Cambridge University Press, 1990.

Harms, Robert. "The End of Red Rubber: A Reassessment." *Journal of African History* 16, no. 1 (1975): 73–88.

——. *Games Against Nature: An Eco-Cultural History of the Nunu of Equatorial Africa.* Cambridge, U.K.: Cambridge University Press, 1987.

——. *River of Wealth, River of Sorrow: The Central Zaire Basin in the Era of the Slave and Ivory Trade, 1500–1891.* New Haven, Conn.: Yale University Press, 1981.

Harris, Wilson. "The Frontier on Which *Heart of Darkness* Stands." *Research on African Literatures* 12, no. 1 (Spring 1981): 86–93.

Hawkins, Hunt. "Conrad's Critique of Imperialism in *Heart of Darkness.*" *PMLA* 94, no. 2 (March 1979): 286–99.

Hawthorn, Jeremy. *Joseph Conrad: Language and Fictional Self-Consciousness.* London: Edward Arnold, 1979.

——. *Joseph Conrad: Narrative Technique and Ideological Commitment.* London: Edward Arnold, 1990.

——. *Sexuality and the Erotic in the Fiction of Joseph Conrad.* London: Continuum, 2007.

Hay, Louise Knapp. *The Political Novels of Joseph Conrad: A Critical Study.* Chicago: University of Chicago Press, 1963.

Hepburn, Allan. "Above Suspicion: Audience and Deception in *Under Western Eyes.*" *Studies in the Novel* 92, no. 4 (Fall 1992): 282–97.

Hervouet, Yves. *The French Face of Joseph Conrad.* Cambridge, U.K.: Cambridge University Press, 1990.

Hevia, James. "Looting and Its Discontents: Moral Discourse and the Plunder of Beijing, 1900–1901." *The Boxers, China, and the World.* Lanham, England: Rowman and Littlefield, 2007.

Hewitt, Douglas. *Conrad: A Reassessment.* Cambridge, U.K.: Bowes & Bowes, 1952.

Hochschild, Adam. *King Leopold's Ghost: A Story of Greed, Terror, and Heroism in Colonial Africa.* Boston: Houghton Mifflin, 1998.

Houen, Alex. *Terrorism and Modern Literature: From Joseph Conrad to Ciaran*

Carson. Oxford, U.K.: Oxford University Press, 2002.

——. "Order and Anarchy: The Political Novels Part I." *Kenyon Review* 15, no. 4 (Autumn 1953): 505–21.

——. "Order and Anarchy: The Political Novels Part II." *Kenyon Review* 16, no. 1 (Winter 1954): 1–19.

——. *Politics and the Novel*. New York: American New Library, 1987.

Huggan, Graham, and Helen Tiffin. *Postcolonial Ecocriticism: Literature, Animals, Environment*. London: Routledge, 2010.

Israel, Jonathan I. *Dutch Primacy in World Trade, 1585–1740*. Oxford, U.K.: Clarendon Press, 1990.

James, Henry. "The Younger Generation: Part II." *Times Literary Supplement* 637 (2 April 1914): 157–58.

Jameson, Fredric. *The Political Unconscious: Narrative as a Socially Symbolic Act*. Ithaca, N.Y.: Cornell University Press, 1981.

Jean-Aubry, G. *Joseph Conrad: Life and Letters*. 2 vols. Garden City, N.Y.: Doubleday, Page, 1927.

Jewsewiecki, Bogomil. "Rural Society and the Belgian Colonial Economy." In *History of Central Africa*, ed. David Birmingham and Phyllis Martin, vol. 2. London: Longman, 1983.

Johnson, Barbara, and Marjorie Garber. "Secret Sharing: Reading Conrad Psychoanalytically." *College English* 33 (October 1987): 628–40.

Johnson, Bruce. *Conrad's Models of Mind*. Minneapolis: University of Minnesota Press, 1971.

Jones, Susan. *Conrad and Women*. Oxford, U.K.: Clarendon Press, 1999.

Kaplan, Carola, Peter Lancelot Mallios, and Andrea White, eds. *Conrad in the Twenty-first Century: Contemporary Approaches and Perspectives*. New York: Routledge, 2005.

Karl, Frederick R. *Joseph Conrad: The Three Lives, A Biography*. New York: Farrar, Straus, and Giroux, 1979.

——. *A Reader's Guide to Joseph Conrad*. New York: Noonday Press, 1960.

——. *A Reader's Guide to Joseph Conrad*. Rev. ed. New York: Farrar, Straus, and Giroux, 1969.

Kettle, Arnold. "The Greatness of Joseph Conrad." *Modern Quarterly*, n.s. vol. 3, no. 3 (Summer 1948): 63–81.

Kirschner, Paul. *Conrad: The Psychologist as Artist*. Edinburgh, Scotland: Oliver & Boyd, 1968.

Knowles, Owen. *An Annotated Critical Bibliography of Joseph Conrad*. New York: St. Martin's Press, 1992.

——. *A Conrad Chronology*. Basingstoke: Macmillan Press Ltd., 1989.

——. "Conrad's Life." In *The Cambridge Companion to Joseph Conrad*. Cambridge, U.K.: Cambridge University Press, 1996.

——. *"My Dear Friend": Further Letters to and about Joseph Conrad*. Amsterdam: Rodopi, 2008.

Koropeckyj, Roman. "Adam Mickiewicz as a Polish National Icon." In *History of the Literary Cultures of East-Central Europe: Junctures and Disjunctures in the 19th and 20th Centuries*, ed. Marcel Cornel-Pope and John Neubauer, vol. 4: 19–20. Philadelphia: John Benjamins Publishing, 2010.

Kunz, George Frederick. *Ivory and the Elephant in Art, in Archaeology, and in Science*. Garden City, N.Y.: Doubleday, 1916.

Lackey, Michael. "The Moral Conditions for Genocide in Joseph Conrad's *Heart of Darkness*." *College Literature* 32, no. 1 (2005): 20–41.

Leavis, F. R. *The Great Tradition: George Eliot, Henry James, Joseph Conrad*. New York: George W. Stewart, 1950.

Lee, Robert F. *Conrad's Colonialism*. The Hague: Mouton, 1969.

Lester, John. *Conrad and Religion*. New York: St. Martin's Press, 1988.

Levine, George. *Darwin and the Novelists: Patterns of Science in Victorian Fiction*. Chicago: University of Chicago Press, 1988.

Lord, Ursula. *Solitude versus Solidarity in the Novels of Joseph Conrad.* Montreal: McGill Queen's University Press, 1998.

Lothe, Jakob. *Conrad's Narrative Method.* Oxford, U.K.: Clarendon Press, 1989.

Louis, William R., and Jean Stengers, eds. *E. D. Morel's History of the Congo Reform Movement.* Oxford, U.K.: Clarendon Press, 1968.

Lukowski, Jerzy, and Hubert Zawadzki. *A Concise History of Poland.* Cambridge, U.K.: Cambridge University Press, 2001.

Macy, John Albert. "Joseph Conrad." *Atlantic Monthly* 98, no. 5 (November 1906): 697–702.

Malia, Jennifer. "Media Sensationalism and Terrorism in *The Secret Agent.*" *The Conradian,* Autumn 2013: 53–71.

Mallios, Peter Lancelot. *Our Conrad: Constituting American Modernity.* Stanford, Calif.: Stanford University Press, 2010.

Marzec, Robert. *An Ecological and Postcolonial Study of Literature: From Daniel Defoe to Salman Rushdie.* New York: Palgrave, 2007.

McCarthy, Jeffrey Mathes. "'A Choice of Nightmares': The Ecology of *Heart of Darkness.*" *Modern Fiction Studies* 55, no. 3 (Fall 2009): 620–48.

McClure, John A. *Kipling & Conrad: The Colonial Fiction.* Cambridge, Mass.: Harvard University Press, 1981.

McDonald, Peter D. *British Literary Culture and Publishing Practice, 1880–1914.* Cambridge, U.K.: Cambridge University Press, 1997.

Mencken, H. L. *A Book of Prefaces.* New York: Alfred A. Knopf, 1917.

Meredith, Isabel. *A Girl Among the Anarchists.* London: Duckworth and Co., 1903.

Meredith, Martin. *Elephant Destiny: Biography of an Endangered Species in Africa.* New York: Public Affairs, 2003.

Meyer, Bernard C. *Joseph Conrad: A Psychoanalytic Biography.* Princeton, N.J.: Princeton University Press, 1967.

Middleton, Tim. *Joseph Conrad.* New York: Routledge, 2006.

Miller, C. Brook. "Holroyd's Man: Tradition, Fetishization, and the United States in *Nostromo.*" In *Nostromo: Centennial Essays,* ed. Allan H. Simmons and John Henry Stape, 14–30. Amsterdam: Editions Rodopi, 2004.

Miller, J. Hillis. *Poets of Reality: Six Twentieth-Century Writers.* Cambridge, Mass.: Harvard University Press, 1965.

Miller, Joseph B. *Way of Death: Merchant Capitalism and the Angolan Slave Trade 1730–1830.* Madison: University of Wisconsin Press, 1988.

Milosz, Czeslaw. "Apollo Nalecz Korzeniowski" *Kultura* (Paris), February 1956, 79.

——. "Joseph Conrad in Polish Eyes." *The Atlantic* 200, no. 5 (November 1957): 219–28.

Moffatt, Victoria. "Othering Through Gendering Discourses and Patriarchal Hegemonies in Joseph Conrad's *Heart of Darkness* and Barbara Kingsolver's *The Poisonwood Bible.*" *Legon Journal of the Humanities* 21 (2010): 163–78.

Mongia, Padmini. "Between Men: Conrad in the Fiction of Two Contemporary Indian Writers." In *Conrad in the Twenty-first Century,* ed. Kaplan, Mallios, and White, 85–100.

——. "Narrative Strategy and Imperialism in Conrad's *Lord Jim.*" *Studies in the Novel* 24, no. 2 (Summer 1992): 173–86.

Moore, Gene M., ed. *Conrad on Film.* Cambridge, U.K.: Cambridge University Press, 1997.

Morel, Edmund D. *The Congo Slave State: A Protest Against the New African Slavery.* London: John Richardson & Sons, 1903.

Morf, Gustav. *The Polish Heritage of Joseph Conrad.* London: Sampson Low, Marston, [1930].

——. *Polish Shades and Ghosts of Joseph Conrad.* New York: Astra Books, 1976.

Morrell, Lady Ottoline Violet Anne Cavendish-Bentinck. *The Early Memoirs of Lady Ottoline Morrell,* ed. Robert Gathorne-Hardy. London: Faber and Faber, 1963.

Moser, Thomas. *Joseph Conrad: Achievement and Decline.* Cambridge, Mass.: Harvard University Press, 1957.

Mulry, David. "Popular Accounts of the Greenwich Bombing and Conrad's *The Secret Agent.*" *Rocky Mountain Review,* Fall 2000: 43–64.

Murfin, Ross C., ed. *Conrad Revisited: Essays for the Eighties.* University: University of Alabama Press, 1985.

Myers, Jeffrey. "The Anxiety of Confluence: Evolution, Ecology, and Imperialism in Conrad's *Heart of Darkness.*" *ISLE (Interdisciplinary Studies in Literature and Environment),* vol. 8, no. 2 (Summer 2001): 97–108.

——. *Joseph Conrad: A Biography.* New York: Charles Scribner's Sons, 1991.

Nadelhaft, Ruth L. *Joseph Conrad.* Atlantic Highlands, N.J.: Humanities Press, 1991.

Naipaul, V. S. *A Bend in the River.* New York: Knopf, 1979.

——. "A New King for the Congo: Mobutu and the Nihilism of Africa." *Vintage Naipaul.* New York: Random House, 1975.

Najder, Zdzislaw. *Conrad Under Familiar Eyes.* Cambridge, U.K.: Cambridge University Press, 1983.

——. *Joseph Conrad: A Chronicle.* Trans. Halina Carroll-Najder. Cambridge, U.K.: Cambridge University Press, 1983.

——. *Joseph Conrad: A Life.* Rochester, N.Y.: Camden House, 2007.

——. ed. *Conrad's Polish Background: Letters to and from Polish Friends.* Trans. Halina Carroll. London: Oxford University Press, 1964.

Newton, Michael. "Four Notes on The Secret Agent: Sir William Harcourt, Ford and Helen Rossetti, Bourdin's Relations, and a Warning Against Δ." *The Conradian* (Amsterdam: Rodopi), vol. 32, no. 1 (Spring 2007): 129–48.

Ngũgĩ Wa Thiong'o. *Moving the Centre: The Struggle for Cultural Freedoms.* London: Heinemann, 1993.

Niland, Richard. *Conrad and History.* Oxford, U.K.: Oxford University Press, 2010.

Norris, Margot. "Modernism and Vietnam: Francis Ford Coppola'a *Apocalypse Now,*" *Modern Fiction Studies* 44.33 (1998): 730–66.

Nussbaum, Felicity. "One Part of Womankind: Prostitution and Sexual Geography in *Memoirs of a Woman of Pleasure.*" *Differences: A Journal of Feminist Cultural Studies* 7, no. 2 (1995): 16–40.

Orisabiyi, N. O. "*Heart of Darkness* as an Anatomy of Moral Failure," *Lagos Review of English Studies* 1 (1979): 94–103.

Ortner, Sherry. "Is female to male as nature is to culture?" In *Women, Culture and Society,* ed. Michelle Zimbalist Rosaldo and Louise Lamphere, 5–31. Stanford, Calif.: Stanford University Press, 1974.

Palmer, John A. *Joseph Conrad's Fiction: A Study in Literary Growth.* Ithaca, N.Y.: Cornell University Press, 1968.

Panichas, George A. *Joseph Conrad: His Moral Vision.* Rev. ed. Mercer, Ga.: Mercer University Press, 2007.

Parry, Benita. *Conrad and Imperialism: Ideological Boundaries and Visionary Frontiers.* London: Macmillan Press, 1983.

——. "The Moment and After-Life of *Heart of Darkness.*" In *Conrad in the Twenty-first Century,* ed. Kaplan, Mallios, and White, 39–54.

——. *Postcolonialism: A Materialist Critique.* London: Routledge, 2004.

Peters, John G. *The Cambridge Introduction to Joseph Conrad.* Cambridge, U.K.: Cambridge University Press, 2006.

——. *Conrad and Impressionism.* Cambridge, U.K.: Cambridge University Press, 2001.

——. *A Historical Guide to Joseph Conrad.* Oxford, U.K.: Oxford University Press, 2010.

——. *Joseph Conrad's Critical Reception.* Cambridge, U.K.: Cambridge University Press, 2013.

——. *Postcolonialism: A Materialist Critique.* London: Routledge, 2004.

Phelps, William Lyon. "The Advance of the

English Novel: VIII." *Bookman* 43, no. 3 (May 1916): 297–308.

Phillips, Gene D. *Conrad and Cinema: The Art of Adaptation.* New York: Peter Lang, 1995.

Pinsker, Sanford. *The Languages of Joseph Conrad.* Amsterdam: Rodopi, 1978.

Porter, Brian A. *When Nationalism Began to Hate: Imagining Modern Politics in Nineteenth-Century Poland.* New York: Oxford University Press, 2000.

Pound, Ezra. *ABC of Reading.* Norfolk, Va.: New Directions Press, 1960.

——. *The Spirit of Romance.* Norfolk, Va.: J. Laughlin Press, 1968.

Preston, Diana, *The Boxer Rebellion: The Dramatic Story of China's War on Foreigners that Shook the World in the Summer of 1900.* New York: Walker, 2000.

Pritchett. V. S. "The Exile," *The News Statesman,* 24 August 1957, 229.

Purdy, Dwight H. *Joseph Conrad's Bible.* Norman: University of Oklahoma Press, 1984.

Rabinbach, Anson. *In the Shadow of Catastrophe: German Intellectuals Between Apocalypse and Enlightenment.* Berkeley: University of California Press, 1997.

Rasula, Jed. "Make It New." *Modernism/Modernity* 17, no. 4 (2010): 713.

Raval, Suresh. *The Art of Failure: Conrad's Fiction.* Boston: Allen & Unwin, 1986.

Ravenstein, Ernest G. *The Strange Adventures of Andrew Battell of Leigh in Angola and Adjoining Regions.* London: Hakluyt Society, 1901.

Reilly, Joseph J. "The Short Stories of Joseph Conrad." *Catholic World* 650 (May 1919): 163–75.

Reveron, Derek S., and Jeffrey Stevenson Murer. *Flashpoints in the War on Terrorism.* New York: Routledge, 2006.

Reynolds, Stephen. "Joseph Conrad and Sea Fiction." *Quarterly Review* 432 (July 1912): 159–80.

Rice, Thomas Jackson. "*Typhoon*: Conrad's Christmas Story." *Cithara* 14, no. 2 (March 1975): 19–35.

Richardson, Brian. "Constructing Conrad's 'The Secret Sharer': Suppressed Narratives, Subaltern Reception, and the Act of Interpretation." *Studies in the Novel* 33, no. 3 (Fall 2001): 306–21.

Rieselbach, Helen Funk. *Conrad's Rebels: The Psychology of Revolution in the Novels from Nostromo to Victory.* Ann Arbor, Mich.: UMI Research Press, 1985.

Roberts, Andrew Michael. *Conrad and Masculinity.* New York: St. Martin's Press, 2000.

Roos, Bonnie, and Alex Hunt. *Postcolonial Green: Environmental Politics and World Narratives.* Charlottesville: University of Virginia Press, 2010.

Ross, Dora H. "Interleaf II: Elephant Hunters." In *Elephant,* ed. Ross, 60–62.

——. ed. *Elephant: The Animal and Its Ivory in African Culture.* Los Angeles: Fowler Museum of Cultural History, 1992.

Ross, Stephen. *Conrad and Empire.* Columbia: University of Missouri Press, 2004.

Rubery, Matthew. "The Foreign Correspondence: Joseph Conrad's 'Wild Story of a Journalist.'" *The Novelty of Newspapers: Victorian Fiction after the Invention of the News,* 141–58. Oxford, U.K.: Oxford University Press, 2009.

"A Russian Minister Assassinated." *The Guardian,* 29 July 1904.

Said, Edward. *Culture and Imperialism.* New York: Knopf, 1993.

——. *Joseph Conrad and the Fiction of Autobiography.* 1966. Rpt. New York: Columbia University Press, 2008.

Saveson, John E. *Conrad, the Later Moralist.* Amsterdam: Rodopi, 1974.

——. *Joseph Conrad: The Making of a Moralist.* Amsterdam: Rodopi, 1972.

Schwarz, Daniel R. *Conrad: The Later Fiction.* London: Macmillan, 1982.

——. *Rereading Conrad.* Columbia: University of Missouri Press, 2001.

Shayt, David H. "The Material Culture of Ivory Outside Africa." In *Elephant,* ed. Ross, 367–81.

Sheriff, Abdul. *Slaves, Spices, and Ivory in Zanzibar.* London: James Currey, 1987.

Sherry, Norman. *Conrad's Eastern World.* Cambridge, U.K.: Cambridge University Press, 1966.

——. *Conrad's Western World.* Cambridge, U.K.: Cambridge University Press, 1971.

——. *Joseph Conrad: The Critical Heritage.* London: Routledge and Kegan Paul, 1973.

Shoshani, Jeheskel. "The African Elephant and its Environment." In *Elephant,* ed. Ross, 43–61.

Simmons, Allan H., ed. *Joseph Conrad: Contemporary Reviews.* Vol. 1. Cambridge, U.K.: Cambridge University Press, 2012.

Singh, Francis B. "The Colonialistic Bias of *Heart of Darkness.*" *Conradiana* 10, no. 1 (Spring 1978): 41–54.

Slatter, John. "Bears in the Lion's Den: The Figure of the Russian Revolutionary Emigrant in English Fiction, 1880–1914." *Slavonic and East European Review* 77, no. 1 (Jan 1999): 30–55. www.jstor.org/stable/4212794.

Smith, Johanna. "'Too Beautiful Altogether': Ideologies of Gender and Empire in *Heart and Darkness.*" In *Heart of Darkness,* ed. Ross C. Murfin, 169–84. New York: Bedford/St. Martin's Press, 1996.

Smith, Kathryn Marie. "Revis(it)ing Joseph Conrad's 'Heart of Darkness': Women, Symbolism, and Resistance." MA diss., Faculty of Arts and Letters, Atlantic University, Boca Raton, Fla., 2009.

Soboleski, Paul. *Poets and Poetry of Poland: A Collection of Polish Verse.* Chicago: Knight & Leonard, 1881.

Soloman, Keith. "The Spectacle of War and the Specter of 'The Horror': *Apocalypse Now* and American Imperialism." *Journal of Popular Film and Television* 35, no. 1 (2007): 26–29.

Spivak, Gayatri. "Can the Subaltern Speak?" In *The Post-Colonial Studies Reader,* ed. Bill Ashcroft, Gareth Griffiths, and Helen Tiffin, 24–28. London: Routledge, 1995.

——. "Can the Subaltern Speak?" In *Marxism and the Interpretation of Culture,* ed. Cary Nelson and Lawrence Grossberg. London: Macmillan, 1988: 271–313.

Stanley, Henry Morton. *How I Found Livingstone: Travels, Adventures, and Discoveries in Central Africa.* London: Sampson Low, 1872.

——. *Through The Dark Continent.* 2 vols. New York: Harper Brothers, 1878.

Stape, J. H., and Owen Knowles, eds. *A Portrait in Letters: Correspondence to and about Joseph Conrad.* Amsterdam: Rodopi, 1996.

Stape, John. *The Several Lives of Joseph Conrad.* New York: Pantheon, 2007.

——. ed. *Notes on Life and Letters.* Cambridge, U.K.: Cambridge University Press, 2004.

Steiner, Joan. "'The Secret Sharer': Complexities of the Doubling Relationship." In *Joseph Conrad,* ed. Harold Bloom, 102–12. New York: Chelsea House Publishers, 1986.

Straus, Nina Pelikan. "The Exclusion of the Intended from Secret Sharing in Conrad's *Heart of Darkness.*" *Novel* 20, no. 2 (Winter 1987): 123–37.

Szczeszak-Brewer, Agata. *Empire and Pilgrimage in Conrad and Joyce.* Gainesville: University Press of Florida, 2011.

Szittya, Penn R. "Metafiction: Double Narration in *Under Western Eyes.*" *ELH* 48, no. 4 (Winter 1981): 817–40. www.jstor.org/stable/2872963.

Taylor, Jeffrey. *Facing the Congo: A Modern-Day Journey into the Heart of Darkness.* New York: Three Rivers Press, 2001.

Teets, Bruce E. *Joseph Conrad: An Annotated Bibliography.* New York: Garland, 1990.

——. and Helmut E. Gerber. *Joseph Conrad: An Annotated Bibliography of Writings about Him.* De Kalb: Northern Illinois University Press, 1971.

Tennant, Roger. *Joseph Conrad.* New York: Atheneum, 1981.

Tredell, Nicolas, ed. *Joseph Conrad's Heart of Darkness.* New York: Columbia University Press, 1998.

Twain, Mark. *King Leopold's Soliloquy: A Defense of His Congo Rule.* Boston: P. R. Warren, 1905.

Updike, John. *The Coup.* New York: Fawcett Crest, 1978.

Valentine, Marguerite. "'Death's Dream Kingdom': The Representation of the Unconscious in *Apocalypse Now.*" *British Journal of Psychotherapy* 26, no. 3 (2010): 357.

Van Couvering, John A. "Proboscideans, Hominids, and Prehistory." In *Elephant,* ed. Ross,

Vansina, Jan. *Paths in the Rainforest: Toward a History of Political Tradition in Equatorial Africa.* Madison: University of Wisconsin Press, 1990.

"Viatcheslav von Plehve." *The Literary Digest,* 27 June 1903. www.unz.org/Pub/LiteraryDigest-1903jun27-00932.

Vickers, Adrian. *A History of Modern Indonesia.* Cambridge, U.K.: Cambridge University Press, 2005.

Vlekke, Bernard H. M. *Nusantara: A History of Indonesia.* Rev. ed. Chicago: Quadrangle, 1960.

Walker, John Frederick. *Ivory's Ghosts: The White Gold of History and the Fate of Elephants.* New York: Atlantic Monthly Press, 2009.

Walonen, Michael. "Power, Patriarchy and Postcolonialism in the African Dictator Novel." *ALA Bulletin* 6, no. 1 (Summer–Fall 2011): 104–17.

Walpole, V. *Conrad's Method: Some Formal Aspects.* Cape Town, South Africa: Nasionale Pers Beperk, 1930.

Warren, Robert Penn. "*Nostromo.*" *Sewanee Review* 59, no. 3 (Summer 1951): 363–91.

Watt, Ian. *Conrad in the Nineteenth Century.* Berkeley: University of California Press, 1979.

——. *Essays on Conrad.* Cambridge, U.K.: Cambridge University Press, 2000.

Watts, Cedric. "'A Bloody Racist': About Achebe's View of Conrad." *Yearbook of English Studies* 13 (1983): 196–209.

——. *The Deceptive Text: An Introduction to Covert Plots.* Brighton, U.K.: Harvester Press, 1984.

——. *Joseph Conrad: A Literary Life.* New York: St. Martin's Press, 1989.

——. *A Preface to Conrad.* 2nd ed. London, Longman, 1993.

West, Rebecca. *1900.* New York: Viking, 1982.

Weubstein, Philip. *Unknowing: The Work of Modernist Fiction.* Ithaca, N.Y.: Cornell University Publishing, 2005.

White, Andrea. *Joseph Conrad and the Adventure Tradition: Constructing and Deconstructing the Imperial Subject.* Cambridge, U.K.: Cambridge University Press, 1993.

Whitehead, Lee. "The Tragic 'Idea.'" *Nineteenth-Century Fiction* 23, no. 4 (1969): 463–75.

Wiley, Paul L. *Conrad's Measure of Man.* Madison: University of Wisconsin Press, 1954.

Wilmott, Glenn. *Modernist Goods: Primitivism, the Market, and the Gift.* Toronto: University of Toronto Press, 2008.

Winternitz, Helen. *East Along the Equator: A Journey Up the Congo into Zaire.* New York: Atlantic Monthly Press, 1987.

Wisnicki, Adrian S. *Conspiracy, Revolution, and Terrorism from Victorian Fiction to the Modern Novel.* New York: Routledge, 2007.

Wittgenstein, Ludwig. *Philosophical Investigations.* Trans. G. E. M. Anscombe. Oxford, U.K.: Blackwell, 1978.

Wollaeger, Mark A. *Joseph Conrad and the Fictions of Skepticism.* Stanford, Calif.: Stanford University Press, 1990.

Woolf, Virginia. "A Disillusioned Romantic." *Times Literary Supplement* 963 (1 July 1920): 419.

——. "Joseph Conrad." In *The Common Reader I,* ed. Andrew McNeillie, 223–30. London: Hogarth Press, 1984.

——. "Mr. Conrad: A Conversation." *Nation and Atheneum* 33, no. 22 (1 September 1923): 681–82.

——. *The Voyage Out.* Ed. Lorna Sage. New York: Oxford University Press, 2001.

Wrong, Michaela. *In the Footsteps of Mr Kurtz.* London: Fourth Estate/Collins Publishers, 2000.

Yelton, Donald C. *Mimesis and Metaphor: An Inquiry into the Genesis and Scope of Conrad's Symbolic Imagery.* The Hague: Mouton, 1967.

Zabel, Morton Dauwen. "Editor's Introduction." *The Portable Conrad.* New York: Viking Press, 1947.

Zainu'ddin, Alisa G. *A Short History of Indonesia.* New York: Praeger, 1968.

Contributors

Mawuli Adjei is a British Chevening Fellow who has taught English in Nigeria, Libya, and Ghana. Currently, he is a senior lecturer at the Department of English, University of Ghana, Legon, where he teaches African literature, postcolonial literature, popular literature, practice in criticism, and creative writing. He is a creative writer with two novels to his credit, *The Jewel of Kabibi* (2011) and *Taboo* (2012). He is also a poet and a recipient of the Valco Trust Fund Literary Award for Poetry. His poetry has appeared in *The Mirror* and aired on Accra City radio.

William Atkinson is a professor in the English Department at Appalachian State University, where he teaches world and British literature. His publications include articles on Conrad, Synge, and Beckett.

Jonathan Elmore holds a PhD in English from the University of South Carolina. He has taught composition, literature, business communication, and philosophy at Wake Forest University; the Institute of Reading Development, Educational Testing Services, University of South Carolina; Beaufort College; and he presently teaches at Shepherd University. He has presented his writing at many conferences. His publications include: "The Life and Work of Vladimir Nabokov" in the *Encyclopedia of American Literature,* 6th ed. (2007); "'Other Forms Were Near': Nietzsche's Affirmative Revaluation in James Joyce's *Dubliners,*" *Working Papers* (2007); and "Hierarchy, Self, and Valuation in Iris Murdoch's The Black Prince," *The Criterion: An International Journal of English* (2012).

Andrew Glazzard is a postgraduate researcher at Royal Holloway, University of London, completing a PhD on Conrad and popular fiction. He is the author of "'Some Reader May Have Recognized': The Case of Edgar Wallace and The Secret Agent" (*The Conradian*, 2012).

Carola M. Kaplan is a former president of the Joseph Conrad Society of America; professor emerita of English at California State University, Pomona; and a member of the Institute of Contemporary Psychoanalysis, Los Angeles. She has published numerous articles in literary and psychoanalytic journals and has edited two collections of essays on modernist literature, including *Conrad in the Twenty-first Century* (with Peter Mallios and Andrea White, 2005). A research psychoanalyst, she is in private practice in Encino, California.

Anna Krauthammer teaches literature and composition at New York City College of Technology. She is the author of *The Representation of the Savage in James Fenimore Cooper and Herman Melville.* Her essay "Mardi: Melville's Search for Narrative" appears in the Critical Insights series of Salem Press. She has also reviewed books and critical essays for *Studies in the Novel, American Indian Culture,* and *Research Journal.* She currently resides in New York City.

Jennifer Malia has a PhD in English language and literature from the University of Southern California. She is currently an assistant professor of English at Norfolk State University. She has also taught at the American University of Sharjah in the United Arab Emirates. She is writing a book on satirical fiction on terrorism and sensational media responses to political violence in the late nineteenth and early twentieth centuries. She has published articles in *The Conradian, Extrapolation, Pacific Coast Philology,* and *Academic Exchange Quarterly.*

Nisha Manocha is a doctoral student at the University of Oxford, where she is completing a dissertation titled "Generic Insistence: Joseph Conrad and the Document in Selected British and American Modernist Fiction." She has published on Conrad in *Studies in the Novel,* and her book reviews have appeared in the *Journal of Postcolonial Writing, Modern Literature Review,* and *Modern Fiction Studies.*

Robert McParland, PhD, is an associate professor of English and chair of the English Department at Felician College in New Jersey. He is the author of *Charles Dickens's American Audience* (2010), *Bloom's How to Write About Joseph Conrad* (2011), *Music and Literary Modernism* (2008), and many journal articles and book chapters, including "Joseph Conrad and Ford Maddox Ford: A Bakhtinian Reading" in *Origins of English Literary Modernism* (2008), *"The Inversion of Home' in Robert Penn Warren's* All the King's Men (2011), "Sympathetic Participation: Charles Dickens and Human Rights" in *Literature and Ethics* (2010), and "Charles Dickens: Readers and the Material Circulation of the Text" in *Reading Audiences and Textual Materiality* (2009).

Barry Morton grew up in East and Southern Africa and obtained a PhD in African history at Indiana University in 1996. He has taught at University of Kwazulu–Natal and at Wabash College, and is currently a research fellow for the History Department, University of South Africa. He has published extensively on Botswana history and the growth of the Pentecostal movement in Africa.

Ruth Nadelhaft was born and educated in New York City. After graduating from Queens College she completed the PhD in English literature at the University of Wisconsin, where she worked with Paul L. Wiley. Her dissertation, "Character Doubles in the Works of Joseph Conrad," led to articles, a book, and an edition of *Nostromo* that has been widely praised. Professor Nadelhaft taught at the University of Maine for twenty-seven years and ended her career as the university honors director. With her husband, Jerome J.

Nadelhaft, retired professor of American history, she divides her time between Maine and New York City.

JOHN G. PETERS is a professor of English at the University of North Texas and former president of the Joseph Conrad Society of America. He is author of *Conrad and Impressionism* (2001) and *The Cambridge Introduction to Joseph Conrad* (2006) and is editor of *Conrad in the Public Eye* (2008), *A Historical Guide to Joseph Conrad* (2010), volume 2 of *Joseph Conrad: Contemporary Reviews* (2012), and the Broadview Press edition of Conrad's *Under Western Eyes* (2010). His *Joseph Conrad's Critical Reception* is forthcoming from Cambridge University Press.

CAMELIA RAGHINARU completed her BA in English literature from Transilvania University, Romania, her MA in English from the University of Central Arkansas, Conway, and her PhD in English from the University of Florida, Gainesville. Her doctoral dissertation addressed the influence of messianic theology in its secularized form on British modernist literature. She currently teaches literature at Concordia University, Irvine.

THOMAS JACKSON RICE is the author of nine books and over a hundred articles and papers, principally on nineteenth- and twentieth-century British, American, and world fiction. He is currently professor of English and director of graduate studies at the University of South Carolina.

AGATA SZCZESZAK-BREWER is associate professor of English at Wabash College. In 2007, she received the Joseph Conrad Society of America's Young Scholar Award, after which she served as trustee of the society (2011–13). She is the author of *Empire and Pilgrimage in Conrad and Joyce* (2010). Her other publications include essays on Joseph Conrad and James Joyce, as well as an interview with Derek Walcott.

GREG WINSTON is professor of English at Husson University, where his research explores historical and postcolonial contexts of modern Irish and British literatures. His essays have appeared in Études Irlandaises, James Joyce Quarterly, and *Blackwell's Companion to the British and Irish Short Story*. He is author of the book *Joyce and Militarism* (2012).

Index